Nature's Daily Guide to Success

The lunar cycle has an important influence on our lives, the effects are listed in the columns.
Easy to follow advice for every given day.

Discover more about the lunar cycle and it's effects in the reference book "Nature's Daily Guide". ISBN 978-0-9854637-8-6

Nature's Daily Guide
The Influence of the Lunar Cycle

• Considering the effect the moon has on certain body parts, you can maximize the results from medicines, supplements, and detox measures.

• If you incorporate the lunar cycle, you will improve and get the most benefit from body, nail and hair care.

• Get the best growth from your plants, optimize your harvest, and take advantage of sustainable gardening methods when you garden according to the moon's rhythm.

• Plan your business meetings on days when people are most open for negotiating, networking, and exchanging ideas. Learn about the days when it's advisable to focus on financial matters or routine work.

• Plan parties and activities when you and others enjoy them the most. Know in advance what will work best for family and social time, hobbies, exercises, and other leisure activities.

• Enjoy inspiring aphorisms on every page.

• The moon passes through a zodiac sign during the given days, activating the characteristics of the zodiac sign. The resulting influences are listed for easy use in the advice columns above.

• Qualities of the given zodiac sign.

• Space for your personal notes.

Success

The artistic instinct rules, but so, too, does indecisiveness. The forces swing back and forth until equilibrium is achieved.

It's easy to reach compromises with tactful sensitivity.

A sense of judgment will support legal matters.

Leisure

Pursuit for harmony and cooperativeness supports good times in romance, friendship, and partnership.

Enjoy cultural events. Relax and get pampered with a spa treatment.

Romance can be passionate yet sensitive.

Health

Sensitive body parts:
Hips, Kidneys, Bladder

All measures taken to flush out and detoxify the sensitive body parts are very effective.

Good for surgical operations except those on the sensitive body parts (see above), feet, and toes.

Scarring is less severe.

Teeth: Removal of tartar and amalgam. Best for fillings, crowns, and dentures! Avoid treatment of periodontitis and gums, avoid pulling teeth.

Blood-purifying, detoxifying herbal infusions and teas.

Sensitive glandular system.

Take special care to keep the area of the bladder and kidneys warm.

Apply special exercises for the hip region.

Sensitivity to light, so bring your sunglasses along.

Body Care

Aromas, scents:
Roses, Violets, Daffodils

Prepare home-made ointments and cosmetics.

Apply detoxing facial and body care.

Treatments of bumps and pimples on the skin, and exfoliating procedures.

Removing body hair.

Correction of the nail bed.

Massages that serve to relax, ease tension, and detoxify.

Reflexology massage.

Removal of callused skin.

Treating obstinate athlete's foot, nail fungus, and warts.

Garden/Nature

Plant part:
Flower

Sow plants and vegetables that grow below ground.

Dig over/plow to prepare soil for planting.

Trimming and cutting back plants.

Start a compost heap.

Weeding. Pest control.

Fertilize flowers that no longer bloom.

Transplanting.

Avoid watering plants.

Harvested produce should be consumed as soon as possible.

Gather herbs (roots) for kidneys, gall bladder and hip complaints.

Day off on 3/16.

Housework

Housework is dealt with much more successfully, efficiently, and effortlessly.

Problem stains are removed readily.

Best for doing laundry! Reduce on laundry detergent, support the environment.

Dry cleaning.

Clean and store seasonal clothing.

Thoroughly clean wooden and parquet floors, metals, china etc.

Cleaning windows and glass.

Cleaning, polishing, and waterproofing shoes.

Combating mold.

Ventilate rooms thoroughly.

Baking bread, cakes, and cookies (add more leavening agent).

Making preserves.

Painting.

Nutrition

Food quality:
Fat

Cauliflower, artichoke, broccoli, sunflower seeds, flax seeds, nuts, rose hip, elder.

Weight associated with overeating is less likely. If underweight, eat larger portions.

Cleansing and detox diets. Fruit and juice days.

Flush out poisons. Treatment for drug abuse.

Pay attention to any particularly tempting foods today: Most likely the "wrong" things taste best.

High cholesterol: eat a low fat diet.

• Doing housework in tune with nature and the lunar cycle will get you the best results for your efforts. Use the most favorable time for your work and visible results will be proof of your success.

• Discover simple ways to improve your diet. Know which fruits and vegetables benefit your body the most. Eat anything you like, but optimize the timing!

• Positive affirmations improve your well-being.

• Based on the declination of the moon all gardening work is unfavorable for the day.

• Benefit from the qualities of the waxing and the waning moon phases.

I think the next best thing to solving a problem is finding some humor in it. Frank Howard Clark

Color **Orange**
Day
Air/Light
Element

Libra — Air

15 Saturday
Holi, Purim
☾ Half Moon.

16 Sunday

2:43 PM PST
4:43 PM CST
5:43 PM EST
♎→♏

Positive affirmation:
"I trust in the beneficial rhythms of nature."

Planting Time
Descending forces!
Sap is drawn downward, enhancing root formation.
Best days for sowing, planting, and transplanting.

detox remove
be active

Waning Moon

M O N T H

• Half Moon marks the midpoint of waxing and waning moon phases.

• The exact times the moon moves in and out of a sign are shown in three different time zones: Eastern (EDT), Central(CDT) and Pacific Daylight Time (PDT) and respectively the daylight savings times.

• Ascending and descending forces reign in nature supporting planting and harvesting.

Easy to use!

How to best utilize the information in the advice columns:

Success

Considering the effect of the lunar cycle enables you to plan ahead to best utilize all opportunities, possibilities, and activities. You may have experienced a great many times that on some days work goes easier and more efficiently than on other days.

Knowing the subtle influence of the lunar cycle, any goal-oriented activity can be scheduled optimally to avoid any negative influences and achieve the most successful results while saving time, effort, and money.

Leisure

What is the best day for a successful party event? Have more fun! Plan parties and activities when you and others enjoy them the most. Know in advance what will work best for family and social time, hobbies, exercises, and other leisure activities in life.

Health

In the course of the lunar cycle every body part and organ gets affected, listed daily as 'sensitive body parts'. Knowing this you can plan ahead to improve your health: Whatever you do for the well-being of the sensitive body parts during that day is even more beneficial. Beware that everything that puts a special burden or strain on the 'sensitive body parts' is more harmful. If possible avoid any surgery on these parts.

During waxing moon all measures taken to supply nutrient materials and strengthen the body are more effective. When the moon is on the wane all measures taken to flush out and detoxify are more successful.

All this advice is based on century old knowledge to support and strengthen your health and well-being.

Body Care

You may have wondered why on some days your hair just doesn't retain its form, or why the same body treatments seem to yield different results on different days?

The lunar cycle has an effect on body, nail, and hair care. Massages are more effective during certain periods of the lunar cycle. Washing hair during the time the moon travels in Pisces may result in dandruff. Knowing all the details enables you to pick the best dates for your visit to the hair dresser. You will also save on hair restorers.

There is an old farmer's rule of cutting and filing fingernails and toenails any Friday after sunset. The result of that rule is healthy and strong nails.

Scents are assigned to each zodiac sign. Improve your well-being by surrounding yourself with these soothing scents.

Garden/Nature

For centuries gardeners and farmers all over the world used these powerful guidelines successfully.

The lunar cycle has an effect on each part of a plant: **roots, leaves, fruits or blossoms**. Pick the right timing for great results. For example, when planting leafy vegetables such as lettuce, spinach or cabbage, choose a leaf day for best results.

If you consider the lunar effect on plants, your plants will grow better, your harvest will be plentiful, and pests will be reduced or completely avoided. Weeding, fertilizing, and watering will be less frequent but more effective.

There are many opportunities to coordinate your agenda for the kind of work you want to do. Consider as well that on New Moon and Full Moon weather changes are more likely.

House Work

Doing housework in tune with nature and the lunar cycle will get you the best results for your efforts. It's like magic!

Housework is dealt with much more successfully, efficiently, and effortlessly during the waning moon. For example, problem stains are removed readily. Reduce your use of cleaners and save money. You will also be supporting the environment, since waste water is broken down much better. Get the best results with baking, cooking, and preserving foods.

Improve and refine your methods. Use the most favorable time for your work and visible results will be proof of your success, saving you time for the things you enjoy most.

Discover more in the reference book "Nature's Daily Guide. The Influence of the Lunar Cycle."

Nutrition

Discover simple ways to improve your diet. Know which fruits and vegetables benefit your body the most. Eat anything you like, but optimize the timing!

The food components of **protein, salt, fat, and carbohydrate** are linked to the elements of the zodiac signs on any given day. Healthy bodies absorb and digest the assigned food component the best, while sensitive or sick bodies may not fare well with the same food component. Observe how your body digests the assigned food components on any given day and factor this in for your choice of foods.

During waxing moon it's most beneficial to strengthen the body. Weight gain is easier than during waning moon, stimulants and vitamins are more effective as well. The waning moon phase is best for measures to detoxify the body.

Introduction

The moon governs the oceans on earth, it rules the tides. All of nature is affected by the lunar cycle. Since our human bodies consist to 80 per cent of water, the moon influences us as well. Powers activated by the moon affect us more than the powers activated by the sun.

Many of the ancient calendars followed the position of the moon. This knowledge has been used for centuries in all aspects of life. Generations of farmer's and people living close to nature observed these rules of nature, guided by the moon. You'll find plenty of valuable, easy to use information. You will know, what, when, and how to do the best. Plan your actions, revise your results, use your time, work, and money effectively. Improve and live a better, healthier, and more successful life.

Nature's Almanac 2026:
Nature's Daily Guide to Success.
Copyright © Edith Stadig, Raya Publishing LLC
service@rayapublishing.com
www.rayapublishing.com
ISBN 979-8-9864777-4-9
Author and Designer: Edith Stadig.
Originally published since 1997: "**Mein Leben mit dem Mondrhythmus**" by Clebitady Verlag in Rutesheim, Germany

Notice

This calendar book is intended as a reference volume only, not as a medical manual. The information given here is designed to help you make informed decisions about your health. It is not intended as a substitute for any treatment that may have been prescribed by your doctor. If you suspect that you have a medical problem, we urge you to seek competent medical help.

Reference list and further reading

Stadig, E.: Nature's Daily Guide: The Influence of the Lunar Cycle, 2018
Paungger, J./Poppe, T.: Guided by the Moon: Living in Harmony with the Lunar Cycles, 2002
The Power of Timing: Living in Harmony with Natural and Lunar Cycles, 2013
Thun, M.: The Biodynamic Year: Increasing Yield, Quality and Flavour: 100 Helpful Tips for the Gardener or Smallholder, 2010

How to use the calendar section on the bottom section of each page:

Zodiac Signs

Each pages depicts the position of the moon in the various zodiac signs.

Similar to the sun, the moon also travels through all of the zodiac signs. The moon only takes 28 days for all zodiac signs. This is called the lunar cycle.

Because it takes the moon 2 to 3 days to pass through a zodiac sign this calendar is divided in 1-3 days per page, considering the zodiac sign the moon is in, as well as the periods of waxing and waning moon.

Each zodiac sign represents certain characteristics which are activated while the moon passes through the sign. All characteristics and resulting influences are listed for easy use in the advice columns.

Beneath each picture of a zodiac sign, you find the matching astrological symbol.

Color

Colors apply to the lunar cycle and the position of the moon in each zodiac sign. Experiment with matching or complimentary colors in your daily outfit. Watch their effects on your well-being. The colors may also be applied to color therapy.

Day and Element

Each zodiac sign correlates with one of the **elements:** fire, earth, air, or water.

Linked to the elements of fire, earth, air, and water, every day reveals a different quality: Warm, Cool, Air/Light, or Wetness. As the moon travels through the signs these qualities are activated.

Summarized for a quick overview of the day, you find the effects listed in detail in the columns.

Calendar

The calendar is based on the waxing and waning moon phases as well as the moon passing through the zodiac signs. The moon takes 2 to 3 days to travel through a sign, and the same characteristics apply for these days. The exact times the moon moves in and out of a sign are shown in three different time zones: Eastern (EDT), Central (CDT), and Pacific Daylight Time (PDT), and respectively the daylight savings times EST, CST and PST. For all other US time zones please add hours accordingly.

Deviations occur on New Moon or Full Moon days and are listed accordingly. The highlighted tips for New Moon and Full Moon are effective only on the day of New Moon or Full Moon, with the exception of the advice on vaccinations (see below).

New Moon Day

On New Moon the body detoxifies most efficiently, but ingestion of food likely slows down. A day of fasting promotes health and can prevent illnesses. It's the best day to drop bad habits, change directions if necessary, confirm your resolutions, and finalize new decisions. Body and mind are more likely to stay calm and balanced in the face of changes, withdrawal, or loss.

Full Moon Day

A day of fasting promotes health and can prevent illnesses. Be cautious since the body utilizes nutrition most effectively during this time, it acts the same on any artificial flavors, additives, stimulants, drugs, as well as poisonous substances. Wounds might bleed more profusely than other times. Recovery after surgery is impeded. Vaccinations are unfavorable in the 3 days before or on Full Moon. The body is more likely to retain water. Healing herbs collected have greater curative power.

Ancient Rule: No meat on Wednesdays and Fridays.

Planting Time, Harvest Time, or Turning Points.

While the moon travels in Cancer, Leo, Virgo, Libra, and Scorpio, descending forces draw the sap downward in all plants, enhancing root formation. Hence these days are best for any sowing, planting, and transplanting of all plants, and harvesting of root plants.

When the moon travels in Capricorn, Aquarius, Pisces, Aries, and Taurus, ascending forces are raising the sap upward, enhancing plant growth above ground and resulting in the most juicy fruits and vegetables. This is a good time for harvesting any plant that grows above ground and for harvesting fruit and vegetables for storage.

Transitioning from ascending to descending forces and vice versa, both forces are at work, resulting in neutralizing effects on each other and preventing both harvesting and planting from yielding the best results.

Waxing Moon

The time of the waxing moon is best used to rest, recover, regroup, and gather strength. Since the body readily absorbs during this time, you are more likely to gain weight even with regular amount of food intake. Everything that is supplied to build up and strengthen the body is most effective. The closer it is to Full Moon the stronger the impact of the forces.

Waning Moon

Detoxify, remove, and be active. The body is ready to detoxify and cleanse, and weight gain associated with overeating is less likely. Housework yields better results. Dirt and spots are removed more easily. The closer to New Moon the stronger the impact of the forces.

You find the effects listed in detail in the columns.

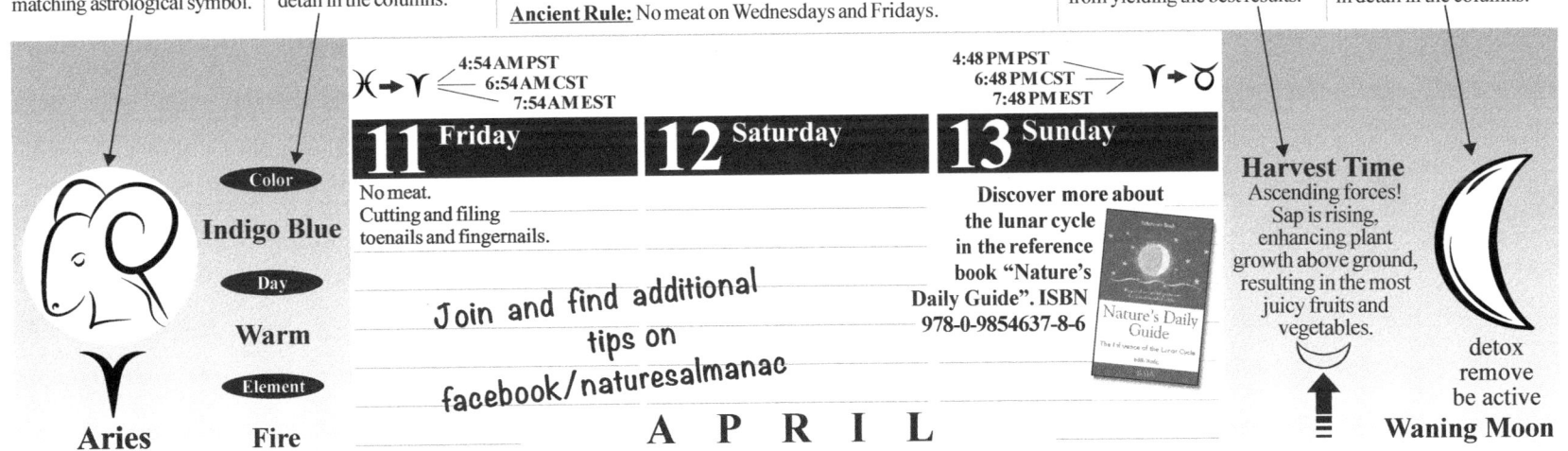

Color

Indigo Blue

Day

Warm

Element

Aries   **Fire**

H → Y
4:54 AM PST
6:54 AM CST
7:54 AM EST

11 Friday

No meat.
Cutting and filing toenails and fingernails.

Join and find additional tips on facebook/naturesalmanac

12 Saturday

4:48 PM PST
6:48 PM CST
7:48 PM EST
Y → ŏ

13 Sunday

Discover more about the lunar cycle in the reference book "Nature's Daily Guide". ISBN 978-0-9854637-8-6

Nature's Daily Guide

A P R I L

Harvest Time
Ascending forces! Sap is rising, enhancing plant growth above ground, resulting in the most juicy fruits and vegetables.

detox remove be active
Waning Moon

Overview 2026

Mercury is retrograde from 2/26 to 3/19/26, from 6/29 to 7/22/26, and from 10/24 to 11/12/26.

Ɣ-Aries ♉-Taurus ♊-Gemini ♋-Cancer ♌-Leo ♍-Virgo ♎-Libra ♏-Scorpio ♐-Sagittarius ♑-Capricorn ♒-Aquarius ♓-Pisces

Success

Open mindedness and curiosity. A changeable and hectic time.

Good time for talking, negotiating, networking, and exchanging ideas as well as for meetings of a nonbinding nature, conferences, and studies.

Leisure

Good time for family gatherings, parties, and short trips.

People enjoy stimulating their minds with reading and studying. Attending theater performances is a preferred enjoyment. Enhance friendships.

Stretching exercises.

Be prepared for sudden changes in weather or climate.

Health

Sensitive body parts:

Shoulders, Arms, Hands, Lungs

All measures taken to supply nutrient materials and strengthen the sensitive body parts are very effective.

Healing ointments are easily absorbed. Applying herbal ointments to the shoulders for rheumatic gout and alike.

Sensitive glandular system.

Make sure you are dressed warm enough in cool weather.

Exercises for shoulders. Breathing exercises.

Avoid having any teeth pulled.

Sensitivity to light, bring your sunglasses along.

Massages, lymphatic therapy, and chiropractic treatment to release blockages.

Body Care

Aromas, scents: Lavender, Lemon Balm, Magnolia, Verbena

Treatments with firming and moisturizing creams are more effective.

Massages that serve to regenerate, and strengthen, perhaps aided with beneficial massage oils.

Correcting and cutting ingrown nails.

Hair dyes applied now, will look more vibrant.

Garden/Nature

Plant part:

Flower

Sow plants, herbs, and vegetables that grow and flourish above ground.

Sowing and planting any creeping or climbing plants, flowers, and medicinal herbs.

Transplanting.

Avoid watering plants.

Gather herbs for tensions in the shoulder and lung complaints.

Changes in weather are more likely.

Housework

Light housework only.

Ventilate rooms thoroughly.

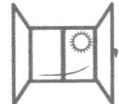

Making preserves.

Baking cakes and cookies. Dough rises faster. (Except on New Moon)

Nutrition

Food quality:

Fat

Cauliflower, artichoke, broccoli, sunflower seeds, flax seeds, nuts, rose hip, elder.

Weight gain: avoid indulging in rich foods. If overweight, eat smaller portions.

Supply nutrient materials to strengthen the body. Focus on foods that contain essential minerals and vitamins.

Stimulants and vitamins are more effective.

Pay attention to any particularly tempting foods today: Most likely the "wrong" things taste best.

High cholesterol: eat a low fat diet.

We wish all readers a Happy New Year!

Positive affirmation:
"I trust a life in harmony."

Turning Point

Transition of ascending to descending forces. Both forces are at work and neutralize each other.

gather strength
rest, recover
buildup

Waxing Moon

☿ → ♊
5:14 AM PST
7:14 AM CST
8:14 AM EST

31 Wednesday
New Year's Eve

No meat.

1 Thursday
New Year's Day

DECEMBER/JANUARY

Consistency requires you to be as ignorant today as you were a year ago.
Bernard Berenson

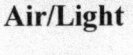
Color

Light Blue

Day

Air/Light

Element

Air   **Gemini**

Success

Feelings, sensitivity, and cooperativeness. Many are overly sensitive, so beware of treading on someone's toes.

Be cautious if you are easily influenced.

During negotiations make use of the cognitive ability of your senses.

Leisure

Relax within your close family.

Retreat to your safe haven and enjoy your fantasy while reading or listening to music. The inner world becomes more colorful than the outer.

Romance can be gentle. Deep feelings will prevail.

If you plan outdoor excursions, be prepared for a shower here and there.

Health

Sensitive body parts:
Chest, Lungs, Liver, Stomach, Gall Bladder

All measures taken to supply nutrient materials and strengthen the sensitive body parts are very effective.

Healing ointments are easily absorbed.

Sensitive nervous system.

Be cautious with alcohol since the liver is very sensitive.

Stomach could play up and cause gas and heartburn.

Rheumatism: Don't air bedding outside, damp will remain in the bedding.

Lymphatic therapy.

Body Care

Aromas, scents:
Lilac, Lilies of the Valley, Lilies, Violets

Treatments with firming and moisturizing creams are more effective.

Massages that serve to regenerate, and strengthen, perhaps aided with beneficial massage oils.

Correcting and cutting ingrown nails.

No haircuts, hair becomes shaggy and unmanageable. Avoid washing your hair.

Garden/Nature

Plant part:
Leaf

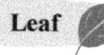

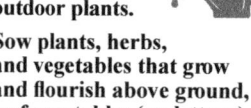

Watering all indoor and outdoor plants.

Sow plants, herbs, and vegetables that grow and flourish above ground, leaf vegetables (no lettuce).

Transplanting.

Trimming and cutting back plants. Avoid pruning fruit trees and bushes.

Cut trees, garlands, pick flowers to dry; they will last longer.

Sowing and mowing lawns.

Setting up a compost heap.

Gather herbs for bronchitis, stomach, liver, and gall bladder complaints.

Unfavorable for harvesting, storing, and preserving.

Housework

Light housework only.

Ventilate rooms briefly and rapidly. Don't air mattresses.

Any dirt and spots are easily removed in the laundry.

Avoid painting, as paint will take very long to dry.

Nutrition

Food quality:
Carbohydrate

Lettuce, spinach, lamb's lettuce, Endive, parsley, leek, cabbage (Brussels sprouts, kale, Chinese cabbage), all leafy herbs, asparagus, mushrooms, cress, Swiss chard, rhubarb.

Weight gain: avoid indulging in rich foods. If overweight, eat smaller portions and avoid carbohydrates. Moodiness may make you want to eat more than is healthy.

Supply nutrient materials to strengthen the body. Focus on foods that contain essential minerals and vitamins. Stimulants and vitamins are more effective.

If you get stomach troubles easily, avoid heavy meals.

Positive affirmation:
"I trust a life in harmony."

Planting Time
Descending forces!
Sap is drawn downward, enhancing root formation.
Best days for sowing, planting, and transplanting.

gather strength
rest, recover
buildup
Waxing Moon

♊ → ♋
5:10 AM PST
7:10 AM CST
8:10 AM EST

2 Friday

No meat. Cutting and filing toenails and fingernails.

J A N U A R Y

Systematise we must, but even in making and holding the system, we should always keep firm hold on this truth that all systems are in their nature transitory and incomplete.
Sri Aurobindo

Color
Green

Day
Wetness

Element
Water

Cancer

Success

Feelings, sensitivity, and cooperativeness. Many are overly sensitive, so beware of treading on someone's toes.

Be cautious if you are easily influenced.

During negotiations make use of the cognitive ability of your senses.

Leisure

Relax within your close family.

Retreat to your safe haven and enjoy your fantasy while reading or listening to music. The inner world becomes more colorful than the outer.

Romance can be gentle. Deep feelings will prevail.

If you plan outdoor excursions, be prepared for a shower here and there.

Health

Sensitive body parts:
Chest, Lungs, Liver, Stomach, Gall Bladder

All measures taken to flush out and detoxify the sensitive body parts are very effective.

Scarring is less severe.

Teeth: Removal of tartar and amalgam. Best for fillings, crowns, and dentures!

Blood-purifying, detoxifying herbal infusions and teas.

Sensitive nervous system.

Be cautious with alcohol since the liver is very sensitive.

Stomach could play up and cause gas and heartburn.

Rheumatism: Don't air bedding outside, damp will remain in the bedding.

Lymphatic therapy.

❍ *Full Moon: Avoid any surgery and vaccination if possible.*

Body Care

Aromas, scents:
Lilac, Lilies of the Valley, Lilies, Violets

Prepare home-made ointments and cosmetics.

Apply detoxing facial and body care.

Treatments of bumps and pimples on the skin, and exfoliating procedures.

Removing body hair.

Correction of the nail bed.

Massages that serve to relax, ease tension, and detoxify.

Reflexology massage.

Removal of callused skin.

Treating obstinate athlete's foot, nail fungus, and warts.

No haircuts, hair becomes shaggy and unmanageable. Avoid washing your hair.

Garden/Nature

Plant part:
Leaf

Water plants.

Fertilize flowers.

Sow plants and vegetables that grow below ground, leaf vegetables, and lettuce.

Dig over/plow to prepare soil for planting.

Trimming and cutting back plants. Transplanting. Weeding.

Combating pests above ground.

Start a compost heap.

Mowing lawns.

Gather herbs (roots) for bronchitis, stomach, liver, and gall bladder complaints.

Unfavorable for harvesting, storing, and preserving.

❍ *Full Moon: Weather and climate changes. Herbs are most powerful.*

Housework

Housework is dealt with much more successfully, efficiently, and effortlessly.

Problem stains are removed readily.

Dry cleaning.

Thoroughly clean wooden and parquet floors, metals, china etc.

Cleaning, polishing, and waterproofing shoes.

Combating mold.

Ventilate rooms briefly and rapidly.

❍ *Full Moon: Avoid doing laundry, cleaning windows, making preserves, painting.*

Nutrition

Food quality:
Carbohydrate

Lettuce, spinach, lamb's lettuce, Endive, parsley, leek, cabbage (Brussels sprouts, kale, Chinese cabbage), all leafy herbs, asparagus, mushrooms, cress, Swiss chard, rhubarb.

Weight associated with overeating is less likely. If underweight, eat larger portions.

Moodiness may make you want to eat more than is healthy. If overweight avoid carbohydrates.

Cleansing and detox diets. Fruit and juice days.

Flush out poisons. Treatment for drug abuse.

If you get stomach troubles easily, avoid heavy meals.

❍ *Full Moon: A day of fasting.*

The only way to get through life is to laugh your way through it. You either have to laugh or cry.
I prefer to laugh. Crying gives me a headache.
Marjorie Pay Hinckley

 Color
Green

Day
Wetness

Element
Cancer   Water

3 Saturday

❍ **Full Moon** 2:04 AM PST,
4:04 AM CST, 5:04 AM EST

J A N U A R Y

Positive affirmation:
"I trust a life in harmony."

Planting Time
Descending forces! Sap is drawn downward, enhancing root formation. Best days for sowing, planting, and transplanting.

detox
remove
be active
Waning Moon

Success

Determination reigns, and risks are taken more often. Master your tasks with more self-confidence and creativity.

Limits appear to be more easily surmountable.

Auspicious day for sales, advertising, and publicity.

Leisure

Zest for life is in the air. People want to have a fun time, enjoy parties, musical events, movies, etc.

Possessive feelings can harm a relationship. Romance can be very passionate.

Outings: even with cloudy skies the air still feels somewhat warm. Drying effect, get plenty to drink.

Danger of sudden storms, not only in the sky.

Health

Sensitive body parts:

Heart, Back, Diaphragm, Circulation, Arteries

All measures taken to flush out and detoxify the sensitive body parts are very effective.

Good for surgery, except on the sensitive body parts (see above), knees, bones, joints, and skin.
Scarring is less severe.

Teeth: Removal of tartar and amalgam. Best for fillings, crowns, and dentures!

Blood-purifying, detoxifying herbal infusions and teas.

Sensitive sense organs.

Back and heart problems are more likely to occur.

Avoid overstraining of the heart and circulation with unusual physical activities.

Expect sleepless nights.

Body Care

Aromas, scents:
Hibiscus, Oleander, Rose

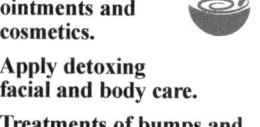

Prepare home-made ointments and cosmetics.

Apply detoxing facial and body care.

Treatments of bumps and pimples on the skin, and exfoliating procedures.

Removing body hair.

Correction of the nail bed.

Massages that serve to relax, ease tension, and detoxify.

Reflexology massage.

Removal of callused skin.

Treating obstinate athlete's foot, nail fungus, and warts.

Good days for haircuts, hair becomes stronger. But be aware that if you get a perm, curls will become quite frizzy. Baby's first haircut.

Garden/Nature

Plant part:
Fruit

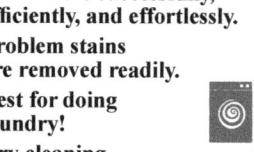

Sowing plants and vegetables that grow below ground.

Sowing and planting fruit. Also sow and plant vegetables that are highly perishable. Plant trees and bushes. Sow lawns.

Dig over/plow to prepare soil for planting.

Trimming and cutting back plants. Pruning of fruit trees and bushes.
Transplanting.
Not suitable for fertilizing. Weeding. Pest Control.

Harvested produce should be consumed as soon as possible.

Gather herbs (roots) for heart and circulation complaints.

Start compost heap.

Housework

Housework is dealt with much more successfully, efficiently, and effortlessly.

Problem stains are removed readily.

Best for doing laundry!

Dry cleaning.

Thoroughly clean wooden and parquet floors, metals, china, etc.

Cleaning windows and glass.

Cleaning, polishing, and waterproofing shoes.

Combating mold.

Ventilate rooms sufficiently.
Air beds.

Suitable for making cheese.

Preserving and freezing fruit and vegetables.

Baking bread, cakes, and cookies (use more leavening agent).

Avoid painting.

Nutrition

Food quality:
Protein

Beans, peas, corn, tomatoes, pumpkin, lentils, soybeans, cucumber, eggplant, zucchini, berries, fruit, chili, bell pepper, figs, avocado, melon, olives.

Weight associated with overeating is less likely. If underweight, eat larger portions.

Cleansing and detox diets. Fruit and juice days.

Flush out poisons. Treatment for drug abuse.

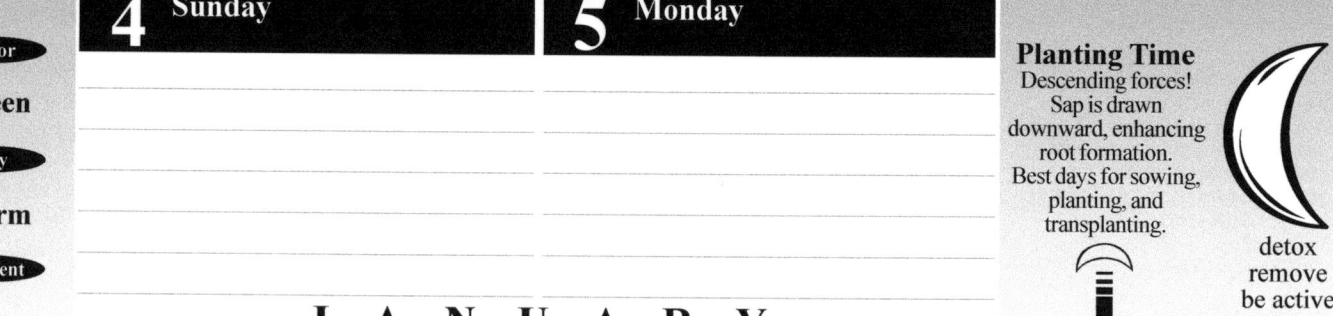

Color — **Green**
Day — **Warm**
Element — **Fire**

Leo

4 Sunday

♋ → ♌   5:45 AM PST
7:45 AM CST
8:45 AM EST

5 Monday

J A N U A R Y

Planting Time
Descending forces! Sap is drawn downward, enhancing root formation. Best days for sowing, planting, and transplanting.

detox remove be active
Waning Moon

Success

Good time for details, organization, routine, concentration, and duty.

Take care of financial and administrative tasks.

Prepare for future success now with realistic and critical assessment.

Leisure

Enjoy a nature walk.

Good time for health regimes. Improve your health with stretching exercises and yoga.

The earth feels cold to the touch, so take slightly warmer clothes.

Health

Sensitive body parts:
Digestive Organs, Nerves, Spleen, Pancreas

All measures taken to flush out and detoxify the sensitive body parts are very effective.

Good for surgery, except on the sensitive body parts (see above), knees, bones, joints, and skin.
Scarring is less severe.
Teeth: Removal of tartar and amalgam. Best for fillings, crowns, and dentures!
Avoiding treatment of periodontitis and gums.
Blood-purifying, detoxifying herbal infusions and teas.
Sensitive blood circulation.
For a sensitive digestive system, a wholesome diet is recommended.
Dress slightly warmer.
High blood pressure:
Avoid salty foods.
Massages, lymphatic therapy, and chiropractic treatment to release blockages.

Body Care

Aromas, scents:
Lavender, Spruce Needles, Sage, Meadow Flowers

Prepare home-made ointments and cosmetics.

Apply detoxing facial and body care.

Treatments of bumps and pimples on the skin, and exfoliating procedures.

Removing body hair.

Correction of the nail bed.

Massages that serve to relax, ease tension, and detoxify.

Reflexology massage.

Removal of callused skin.

Treating obstinate athlete's foot, nail fungus, and warts.

Best for haircuts because it retains its shape longer.
Perms turn out best.

Garden/Nature

Plant part:
Root

Best for sowing and planting, except lettuce.

Plant trees which are supposed to grow very tall.
Plant hedges and bushes that are meant to grow very fast.

Planting and re-potting balcony and indoor plants.

Dig over/plow to prepare soil for planting.

Trimming and cutting back plants. Planting cuttings.

Spread fertilizer and manure. Fertilize flowers with poorly formed roots.

Start a compost heap.

Transplanting. Mulching.

Weeding. Pest control (vermin in the soil).

Avoid harvesting and storing.

Gather herbs (roots) for digestive organs, pancreas, and nervous complaints.

Housework

Housework is dealt with much more successfully, efficiently, and effortlessly.

Problem stains are removed readily.

Best for doing laundry! Reduce on laundry detergent, support the environment.

Dry cleaning.

Thoroughly clean wooden and parquet floors, metals, china etc.

Cleaning, polishing, and waterproofing shoes.

Combating mold.

Air rooms only briefly.

Painting.

Making pickles, preserves, and cheese yields suboptimal results and should be avoided.

Nutrition

Food quality:
Salt

Garlic, carrots, red beets, reddish, rutabaga, sugar beet, celery, potatoes, onions, kohlrabi.

Weight associated with overeating is less likely. If underweight, eat larger portions.

Cleansing and detox diets. Fruit and juice days.

Flush out poisons. Treatment for drug abuse.

Avoid large quantities of salty foods like bacon, ham, salted herring, fatty cheese, and the like. Avoid heavy and greasy foods.

I'm not in this world to live up to your expectations and you're not in this world to live up to mine.
Bruce Lee

Color
Yellow

Day
Cool

Element

Virgo   **Earth**

♌ → ♍   8:58 AM PST
10:58 AM CST
11:58 AM EST

4:07 PM PST
6:07 PM CST   ♍ → ♎
7:07 PM EST

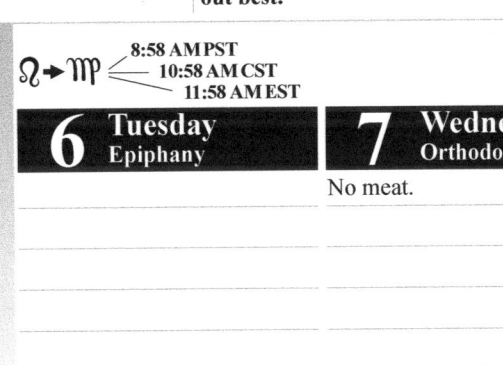

6 Tuesday Epiphany	**7** Wednesday Orthodox Christmas	**8** Thursday
	No meat.	

J A N U A R Y

Positive affirmation:
"I trust a life in harmony."

Planting Time
Descending forces! Sap is drawn downward, enhancing root formation. Best days for sowing, planting, and transplanting.

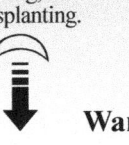

detox
remove
be active

Waning Moon

Success

The artistic instinct rules, but so, too, does indecisiveness. The forces swing back and forth until equilibrium is achieved.

It's easy to reach compromises with tactful sensitivity.

A sense of judgment will support legal matters.

Leisure

Pursuit for harmony and cooperativeness supports good times in romance, friendship, and partnership.

Enjoy cultural events. Relax and get pampered with a spa treatment.

Romance can be passionate yet sensitive.

Health

Sensitive body parts:

Hips, Kidneys, Bladder

All measures taken to flush out and detoxify the sensitive body parts are very effective.

Good for surgery, except on the sensitive body parts (see above), knees, bones, joints, and skin. Scarring is less severe.

Teeth: Removal of tartar and amalgam. Best for fillings, crowns, and dentures! Avoid treatment of periodontitis and gums, avoid pulling teeth.

Blood-purifying, detoxifying herbal infusions and teas.

Sensitive glandular system.

Take special care to keep the area of the bladder and kidneys warm.

Apply special exercises for the hip region.

Sensitivity to light, so bring your sunglasses along.

Body Care

Aromas, scents: Roses, Violets, Daffodils

Prepare home-made ointments and cosmetics.

Apply detoxing facial and body care.

Treatments of bumps and pimples on the skin, and exfoliating procedures.

Removing body hair.

Correction of the nail bed.

Massages that serve to relax, ease tension, and detoxify.

Reflexology massage.

Removal of callused skin.

Treating obstinate athlete's foot, nail fungus, and warts.

Garden/Nature

Plant part:

Flower

Sow plants and vegetables that grow below ground.

Dig over/plow to prepare soil for planting.

Trimming and cutting back plants.

Start a compost heap.

Weeding. Pest control.

Fertilize flowers that no longer bloom.

Transplanting.

Avoid watering plants.

Harvested produce should be consumed as soon as possible.

Gather herbs (roots) for kidneys, gall bladder and hip complaints.

Day off on 1/9.

Housework

Housework is dealt with much more successfully, efficiently, and effortlessly.

Problem stains are removed readily.

Best for doing laundry! Reduce on laundry detergent, support the environment.

Dry cleaning.

Clean and store seasonal clothing.

Thoroughly clean wooden and parquet floors, metals, china etc.

Cleaning windows and glass.

Cleaning, polishing, and waterproofing shoes.

Combating mold.

Ventilate rooms thoroughly.

Baking bread, cakes, and cookies (add more leavening agent).

Making preserves.

Painting.

Nutrition

Food quality:

Fat

Cauliflower, artichoke, broccoli, sunflower seeds, flax seeds, nuts, rose hip, elder.

Weight associated with overeating is less likely. If underweight, eat larger portions.

Cleansing and detox diets. Fruit and juice days.

Flush out poisons. Treatment for drug abuse.

Pay attention to any particularly tempting foods today: Most likely the "wrong" things taste best.

High cholesterol: eat a low fat diet.

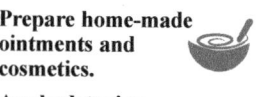

Discover more about the lunar cycle and it's effects in the reference book "Nature's Daily Guide". ISBN 978-0-9854637-8-6

Positive affirmation: *"I trust a life in harmony."*

Libra — Air

- Color: **Orange**
- Day: **Air/Light**
- Element: **Air**

9 Friday

No meat. Cutting and filing toenails and fingernails.

10 Saturday

☾ Half Moon.

Planting Time
Descending forces! Sap is drawn downward, enhancing root formation. Best days for sowing, planting, and transplanting.

detox
remove
be active

Waning Moon

JANUARY

Success

Critical and superstitious behavior emerges, especially pertaining to money.

A penetrating power will strengthen your capacity to act.

An increased perception opens our interest for the essentials and helps to discover hidden potentials.

Leisure

Relax within your close family, with meditation, and relaxation exercises.

A longing to feel safe will be nurtured if you focus on habits and rituals. An increased sensitivity will help to enjoy every moment.

Romance can be very passionate.

If you plan outdoor excursions, be prepared for a shower here and there.

Health

Sensitive body parts:

Sex organs, Ureter

All measures taken to flush out and detoxify the sensitive body parts are very effective.

Good for surgical operations except those on the sensitive body parts (see above), knees, bones, joints, and skin. Scarring is less severe.

Teeth: Removal of tartar and amalgam. Best for fillings, crowns, and dentures!

Blood-purifying, detoxifying herbal infusions and teas.

Sensitive nervous system.

Female disorders: As a preventative measure apply hip baths using yarrow.

Pregnancy: Avoid any exertion, miscarriages are more likely.

Keep region of the pelvis, kidneys, and feet warm to prevent infection of the bladder and kidneys.

Lymphatic therapy.

Body Care

Aromas, scents:
Anemone, Cornflower
Oregano, Thuja

Prepare home-made ointments and cosmetics.

Apply detoxing facial and body care.

Treatments of bumps and pimples on the skin, and exfoliating procedures.

Removing body hair.

Correction of the nail bed.

Massages that serve to relax, ease tension, and detoxify.

Reflexology massage.

Removal of callused skin.

Treating obstinate athlete's foot, nail fungus, and warts.

Garden/Nature

Plant part:
Leaf

Water plants.

Fertilize flowers and meadows, no vegetables.

Sow plants and vegetables that grow below ground, leaf vegetables, and lettuce.

Sowing, planting, harvesting, and drying every kind of medicinal herbs.

Dig over/plow to prepare soil for planting.

Trimming and cutting back plants. Transplanting. Weeding. Pest control. Start a compost heap.

Mowing lawns.

Harvested produce should be consumed as soon as possible.

Avoid cutting down trees, danger of bark beetles.

Housework

Housework is dealt with much more successfully, efficiently, and effortlessly.

Problem stains are removed readily.

Best for doing laundry! Reduce on laundry detergent, support the environment.

Dry cleaning.

Thoroughly clean wooden and parquet floors, metals, china etc.

Cleaning, polishing, and waterproofing shoes.

Combating mold.

Ventilate rooms briefly and rapidly.

Avoid painting.

Nutrition

Food quality:
Carbohydrate

Lettuce, spinach, lamb's lettuce, Endive, parsley, leek, cabbage (Brussels sprouts, kale, Chinese cabbage), all leafy herbs, asparagus, mushrooms, cress, Swiss chard, rhubarb.

Weight associated with overeating is less likely. If underweight, eat larger portions.

Cleansing and detox diets. Fruit and juice days.

Flush out poisons. Treatment for drug abuse.

All sacrifice and suffering is redemptive. It is used to either teach the individual or to help others. Nothing is by chance.
Arthur J. Russell

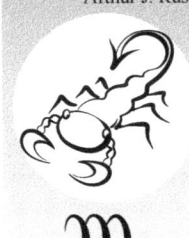

Color
Red

Day
Wetness

Element

Scorpio   **Water**

2:56 AM PST
4:56 AM CST
5:56 AM EST

11 Sunday

12 Monday

3:35 PM PST
5:35 PM CST
6:35 PM EST

13 Tuesday

J A N U A R Y

Planting Time
Descending forces! Sap is drawn downward, enhancing root formation. Best days for sowing, planting, and transplanting.

detox
remove
be active
Waning Moon

Success

Inquisitiveness and exuberant inspiration lead to new horizons. Insight and love for truth reign.

Bringing together is more important than splitting asunder.

Expansive forces will assist in legal matters, discussions, and debates.

Leisure

Expansion feels great, and travel, short trips, and outings are most welcome. A competitive spirit excites any sports event.

Talk things out when necessary.

Romance can be very passionate.

Good days for outings; even with cloudy skies the air still feels somewhat warm. Drying effect, get plenty to drink.

Health

Sensitive body parts:

Thighs and Veins

All measures taken to flush out and detoxify the sensitive body parts are very effective.

Good for surgical operations except those on the sensitive body parts (see above), knees, bones, joints, and skin.
Scarring is less severe.

Teeth: Removal of tartar and amalgam. Best for fillings, crowns, and dentures!

Blood-purifying, detoxifying herbal infusions and tea.

Sensitive sense organs.

Pains often arise in the sciatic nerve, veins, the small of the back, and thighs.

Avoid overstraining the body with unusual physical activities.

Body Care

Aromas, scents: Calendula (Marigold), Geranium, Rosemary

Prepare home-made ointments and cosmetics.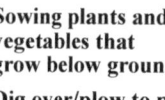

Apply detoxing facial and body care.

Treatments of bumps and pimples on the skin, and exfoliating procedures.

Removing body hair.

Correction of the nail bed.

Massages that serve to relax, ease tension, and detoxify.

Reflexology massage.

Removal of callused skin.

Treating obstinate athlete's foot, nail fungus, and warts.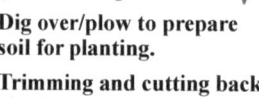

Garden/Nature

Plant part:

Fruit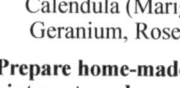

Sowing plants and vegetables that grow below ground.

Dig over/plow to prepare soil for planting.

Trimming and cutting back plants.

Pruning of fruit trees and bushes.

Cultivating grains, particularly corn.

Fertilize grains, vegetables, and fruit.

Combating pests above ground.

Weeding.

Gather herbs (roots) for vein diseases.

Avoid hoeing and harrowing.

Start a compost heap.

Housework

Housework is dealt with much more successfully, efficiently, and effortlessly.

Problem stains are removed readily.

Best for doing laundry!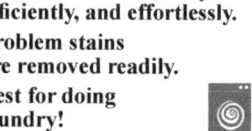

Dry cleaning.

Thoroughly clean wooden and parquet floors, metals, china, etc.

Cleaning windows and glass.

Cleaning, polishing, and waterproofing shoes.

Combating mold.

Ventilate rooms sufficiently. Air beds.

Suitable for making cheese.

Preserving and freezing fruit and vegetables.

Baking bread, cakes, and cookies (use more leavening agent).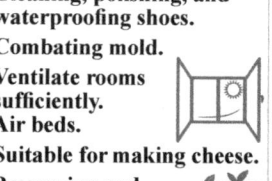

Painting.

Nutrition

Food quality:

Protein

Beans, peas, corn, tomatoes, pumpkin, lentils, soybeans, cucumber, eggplant, zucchini, berries, fruit, chili, bell pepper, figs, avocado, melon, olives.

Weight associated with overeating is less likely. If underweight, eat larger portions.

Cleansing and detox diets. Fruit and juice days.

Flush out poisons. Treatment for drug abuse.

Color
Orange/Yellow

Day
Warm

Element

Sagittarius   Fire

14 Wednesday
Orthodox New Year

No meat.

15 Thursday

Positive affirmation:
"I trust a life in harmony."

Turning Point

Transition of descending to ascending forces. Both forces are at work and neutralize each other.

detox remove be active
Waning Moon

J A N U A R Y

Success

Career and business are in the foreground now and thinking becomes clear and serious, but somewhat inflexible.

Perseverance and reasoning assist in financial matters, planning, and contracts.

The values of tradition, authority, and discipline impact our endeavors.

● *New Moon: Confirm your resolutions. Finalize new decisions. Drop bad habits.*

Leisure

Money is not likely to be wasted in a shopping spree.

Many are drawn to enjoy cultural events.

The earth feels cold to the touch, so take slightly warmer clothes.

Health

Sensitive body parts:
Knees, Joints, Bones, Skin

All measures taken to flush out and detoxify the sensitive body parts are very effective.

Scarring is less severe.

Teeth: Removal of tartar and amalgam. Best for fillings, crowns, and dentures!

Blood-purifying, detoxifying herbal infusions and teas.

Sensitive blood circulation.

Avoid overstraining bones and knees, and apply gentle stretching exercises only.

Problems with meniscus: Don't overstrain.

Dress slightly warmer.

High blood pressure: Avoid salty foods.

Massages, lymphatic therapy, and chiropractic treatment to release blockages.

● *New Moon: Avoid any surgery if possible.*

Body Care

Aromas, scents:
Cedar, Juniper

Prepare home-made ointments and cosmetics.

Apply detoxing facial and body care.

Treatments of bumps and pimples on the skin, and exfoliating procedures.

Remove body hair, it may not grow back.

Correction of the nail bed.

Massages that serve to relax, ease tension, and detoxify.

Reflexology massage.

Treating obstinate athlete's foot, nail fungus, and warts.

Cutting and filing toenails and fingernails will make the nails grow stronger over time.

Garden/Nature

Plant part:
Root

Sowing and planting root vegetables and winter vegetables

Weeding. Harrowing weeds. Dig over to prepare soil. Trimming and cutting back plants.
Clear and thin out plants, forest edges, and hedges.
Plant cuttings.
Spread fertilizer and manure.
Start a compost heap.
Combat vermin.

Fertilize flowers with poorly formed roots.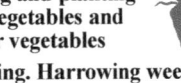

Mulching.

Harvest produce is suitable for storage. Harvest root vegetables.

Gather herbs (roots) for bone, joint, and skin diseases.

● *New Moon: Change of weather is likely. Care for sickly plants.*

Housework

Housework is dealt with much more successfully, efficiently, and effortlessly.
Problem stains are removed readily.

Best for doing laundry! Reduce on laundry detergent, support the environment.

Avoid dry cleaning, as the fabric may develop unwanted glossy blotches.

Thoroughly clean wooden and parquet floors, metals, china etc.

Cleaning, polishing, and waterproofing shoes.

Combating mold.

Air rooms only briefly.

Painting.

Preserving root vegetables. Slice cabbage now to ferment into sauerkraut.

Nutrition

Food quality:
Salt

Garlic, carrots, red beets, reddish, rutabaga, sugar beet, celery, potatoes, onions, kohlrabi.

Weight associated with overeating is less likely. If underweight, eat larger portions.

Cleansing and detox diets. Fruit and juice days.

Flush out poisons. Treatment for drug abuse.

Avoid large quantities of salty foods like bacon, ham, salted herring, fatty cheese, and the like. Avoid heavy and greasy foods.

● *New Moon: A day of fasting.*

Every man takes the limit of his own field of vision for the limits of the world.
Arthur Schopenhauer

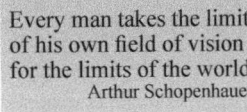

Capricorn

● Color
Yellow

● Day
Cool

● Element
Earth

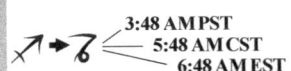

↗→♑ 3:48 AM PST
5:48 AM CST
6:48 AM EST

2:19 PM PST
4:19 PM CST ♑→♒
5:19 PM EST

16 Friday
Isra and Mi'raj
No meat. Cutting and filing toenails and fingernails.

17 Saturday

18 Sunday
● New Moon 11:53 AM PST, 1:53 PM CST, 2:53 PM EST

Harvest Time
Ascending forces! Sap is rising, enhancing plant growth above ground, resulting in the most juicy fruits and vegetables.

detox
remove
be active
Waning Moon

J A N U A R Y

Success

Inspiration, optimism, and impatience. Rational thinking, creativity and imagination spark new ideas and inspire planning for the future.

Shying away from routine tasks people will feel more drawn to anything new.

Instead of gridlocked structures choose new possibilities.

Leisure

Inspiration and optimism will boost friendship, social gatherings, and parties.

Express your creativity and imagination. Dwell in dreams and utopian ideas. It is easier now to perceive intuitive thoughts.

Health

Sensitive body parts:

Lower Legs, Veins

All measures taken to supply nutrient materials and strengthen the sensitive body parts are very effective.

Healing ointments are easily absorbed.

Sensitive glandular system.

Avoid inflammation of the veins. Apply ointments to lower legs, and rest legs in a raised position.

Varicose veins: Avoid long periods of standing.

While exercising go easy on the ankles.

Sensitivity to light, so bring your sunglasses along.

Body Care

Aromas, scents: Cyclamen, Peach, Wild Roses

Treatments with firming and moisturizing creams are more effective.

Massages that serve to regenerate, and strengthen, perhaps aided with beneficial massage oils.

Correcting and cutting ingrown nails.

Hair dyes applied now, will look more vibrant.

Garden/Nature

Plant part:

Flower

Avoid watering plants.

Harvested produce is well suitable for storage.

Gather herbs for vein diseases.

Housework

Light housework only.

Ventilate rooms thoroughly.

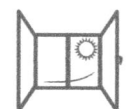

Baking cakes and cookies. Dough rises faster. (Except on New Moon)

Making preserves.

Nutrition

Food quality:

Fat

Cauliflower, artichoke, broccoli, sunflower seeds, flax seeds, nuts, rose hip, elder.

Weight gain: avoid indulging in rich foods. If overweight, eat smaller portions.

Supply nutrient materials to strengthen the body. Focus on foods that contain essential minerals and vitamins.

Stimulants and vitamins are more effective.

Pay attention to any particularly tempting foods today: Most likely the "wrong" things taste best.

High cholesterol: eat a low fat diet.

Positive affirmation:
"I nurture only good thoughts."

Harvest Time
Ascending forces! Sap is rising, enhancing plant growth above ground, resulting in the most juicy fruits and vegetables.

gather strength rest, recover buildup
Waxing Moon

19 Monday

20 Tuesday
Martin Luther King Day (US)

On the whole human beings want to be good, but not too good, and not quite all the time.
George Orwell

Color
Bright/ Dark Blue

Day
Air/Light

Element

Air   Aquarius

J A N U A R Y

Success

Sensibility, intuition, and helpfulness.

Where possible, retreating is more favorable than dealing with business matters.

Dissolve restrictions, be patient and wait. Be aware that people can be more easily influenced.

Leisure

Your helpfulness will boost friendships.

Enjoy dancing or swimming, or watch a movie that will inspire your fantasies and imagination.

Retreat, relax, and recover.

Romance can be gentle and coziness will prevail.

If you plan outdoor excursions, be prepared for a shower here and there.

Health

Sensitive body parts:

Feet and Toes

All measures taken to supply nutrient materials and strengthen the sensitive body parts are very effective.

Healing ointments are easily absorbed.

Sensitive nervous system.

Drugs have a much stronger effect on your body. Monitor closely what you put into your body.

Lymphatic therapy.

Sluggishness or fatigue may occur in the transition into the next Zodiac sign of Aries.

Body Care

Aromas, scents: Magnolia, Amaryllis, Clary Sage

Treatments with firming and moisturizing creams are more effective.

Massages that serve to regenerate, and strengthen, perhaps aided with beneficial massage oils. Reflexology massage. Carry out with special care, people are more sensitive.

Correcting and cutting ingrown nails.

Foot bath.

No haircuts, hair becomes shaggy and unmanageable. Avoid washing your hair. Dandruff could develop.

Garden/Nature

Plant part:

Leaf

Watering all indoor and outdoor plants.

Sow plants, herbs, and vegetables that grow and flourish above ground, and leaf vegetables.

Transplanting.

Mowing lawns.

Avoid pruning fruit trees and bushes.

Harvested produce should be consumed as soon as possible.

Gather herbs for foot complaints.

Housework

Light housework only.

Ventilate rooms briefly and rapidly. Don't air mattresses.

Any dirt and spots are easily removed in the laundry.

Avoid painting, as paint will take very long to dry.

Preserving and storing should be avoided.

Nutrition

Food quality:

Carbohydrate

Lettuce, spinach, lamb's lettuce, Endive, parsley, leek, cabbage (Brussels sprouts, kale, Chinese cabbage), all leafy herbs, asparagus, mushrooms, cress, Swiss chard, rhubarb.

Weight gain: avoid indulging in rich foods. If overweight, eat smaller portions and avoid carbohydrates.

Supply nutrient materials to strengthen the body. Focus on foods that contain essential minerals and vitamins.

Caffeine, alcohol, drugs, certain foods, and stimulants have a much stronger effect.

Positive affirmation:
"I nurture only good thoughts."

Harvest Time
Ascending forces! Sap is rising, enhancing plant growth above ground, resulting in the most juicy fruits and vegetables.

gather strength
rest, recover
buildup
Waxing Moon

10:51 PM PST Tuesday
12:51 AM CST
1:51 AM EST

21 Wednesday

No meat.

22 Thursday

J A N U A R Y

Two persons cannot long be friends if they cannot forgive each other's little failings.
Jean de La Bruyère

Color
Blueish White

Day

Wetness

Element

Water

Pisces

Success

Things get going and the way straight ahead seems the best.

People feel energetic, courageous, assertive, and at times anxious.

Good time for meetings and sales talks but impatience and selfishness do not favor teamwork.

Leisure

An enterprising spirit and spontaneity move people to enjoy outings, sports, competitions, cultural events, and travels.

Romance can be very passionate.

Good days for outings, even with cloudy skies the air still feels somewhat warm. Drying effect, get plenty to drink.

Health

Sensitive body parts:

Head, Brain, Eyes

All measures taken to supply nutrient materials and strengthen the sensitive body parts are very effective.

Healing ointments are easily absorbed.

Sensitive sense organs.

If you suffer from migraines drink plenty of water, and avoid coffee, chocolate, and sugar.

Body Care

Aromas, scents: Cloves, Peppermint, Thyme

Treatments with firming and moisturizing creams are more effective.

Massages that serve to regenerate, and strengthen, perhaps aided with beneficial massage oils.

Correcting and cutting ingrown nails.

Eye compresses for strained eyes.

Any kind of hair care. Hair dyes applied now, will look more vibrant.

Garden/Nature

Plant part:

Fruit 🍎

Sow plants and vegetables that grow and flourish above ground, especially fruit and tomatoes.

Sowing and planting anything that is supposed to grow fast and for immediate use.

Grafting onto fruit trees.

Cultivating grains.

Transplanting.

Harvesting and storing grains, vegetables, potatoes, fruit, and tomatoes.

Gather herbs for eye complaints and headaches.

Day off on 1/24.

Housework

Light housework only.

Ventilate sufficiently.

Preserving fruit.

Freezing fruit and vegetables.

Baking bread, cakes, and cookies. Dough rises faster. (Except on New Moon)

Suitable for making cheese.

Nutrition

Food quality:

Protein

Beans, peas, corn, tomatoes, pumpkin, lentils, soybeans, cucumber, eggplant, zucchini, berries, fruit, chili, bell pepper, figs, avocado, melon, olives.

Weight gain: avoid indulging in rich foods. If overweight, eat smaller portions.

Supply nutrient materials to strengthen the body. Focus on foods that contain essential minerals and vitamins.

Stimulants and vitamins are more effective.

Drink plenty of water.

Positive affirmation:
"I nurture only good thoughts."

Harvest Time
Ascending forces! Sap is rising, enhancing plant growth above ground, resulting in the most juicy fruits and vegetables.

gather strength
rest, recover
buildup
Waxing Moon

♓ ➔ ♈
5:27 AM PST
7:27 AM CST
8:27 AM EST

23 Friday
No meat. Cutting and filing toenails and fingernails.

24 Saturday

10:06 AM PST
12:06 PM CST
1:06 PM EST
♈ ➔ ♉

25 Sunday
☾ Half Moon.

The more credit you give away, the more will come back to you. The more you help others, the more they will want to help you.
Brian Tracy

Color
Indigo Blue

Day
Warm

Element
Fire

Aries ♈

J A N U A R Y

Success

Realism and material security are important. Persistence comes easy, thoughts and reactions are slower.

Assess financial areas.

Conservative tendencies may make people want to stay away from risk taking.

Leisure

Relax at a picnic/feast. Enjoy culinary pleasures and hobbies.

The earth feels cold to the touch, so take slightly warmer clothes.

Health

Sensitive body parts:

Head and Neck

All measures taken to supply nutrient materials and strengthen the sensitive body parts are very effective.

Healing ointments are easily absorbed.

Sensitive blood circulation.

Organs of speech, jaws, teeth, tonsils, thyroid gland, neck, and vocal chords get easily affected. Keep neck warm. On cold days ears should be protected. Sensitivity to noise.

High blood pressure: Avoid salty foods.

Massages, lymphatic therapy, and chiropractic treatment to release blockages.

Body Care

Aromas, scents: Geranium, Jasmine, Rose

Treatments with firming and moisturizing creams are more effective.

Massages that serve to regenerate, and strengthen, perhaps aided with beneficial massage oils.

Correcting and cutting ingrown nails.

Hair dyes applied now, will look more vibrant.

Garden/Nature

Plant part:

Root

Sow plants, herbs, and vegetables that grow and flourish above ground.

Sowing and planting trees, bushes, hedges, and root vegetables. Everything grows slowly and lasts well.

Transplanting.

Harvesting and storing root vegetables. Harvested produce is well suited for storage.

Gather herbs for sinus issues, sore throat, and ear complaints.

Housework

Light housework only.

Air rooms only briefly.

Preserving root vegetables.

Nutrition

Food quality:

Salt

Garlic, carrots, red beets, reddish, rutabaga, sugar beet, celery, potatoes, onions, kohlrabi.

Weight gain: avoid indulging in rich foods. If overweight, eat smaller portions.

Supply nutrient materials to strengthen the body. Focus on foods that contain essential minerals and vitamins.

Stimulants and vitamins are more effective.

Avoid large quantities of salty foods like bacon, ham, salted herring, fatty cheese, and the like.

Positive affirmation:
"I nurture only good thoughts."

Harvest Time
Ascending forces! Sap is rising, enhancing plant growth above ground, resulting in the most juicy fruits and vegetables.

gather strength rest, recover buildup
Waxing Moon

26 Monday

27 Tuesday

12:56 PM PST
2:56 PM CST
3:56 PM EST

If I love you, what business is it of yours?
Johann Wolfgang von Goethe

Color
Bright Blue

Day
Cool

Element
Earth

Taurus

J A N U A R Y

Success

Open mindedness and curiosity. A changeable and hectic time.

Good time for talking, negotiating, networking, and exchanging ideas as well as for meetings of a nonbinding nature, conferences, and studies.

Leisure

Good time for family gatherings, parties, and short trips.

People enjoy stimulating their minds with reading and studying. Attending theater performances is a preferred enjoyment. Enhance friendships.

Stretching exercises.

Be prepared for sudden changes in weather or climate.

Health

Sensitive body parts:
Shoulders, Arms, Hands, Lungs

All measures taken to supply nutrient materials and strengthen the sensitive body parts are very effective.

Healing ointments are easily absorbed. Applying herbal ointments to the shoulders for rheumatic gout and alike.

Sensitive glandular system.

Make sure you are dressed warm enough in cool weather.

Exercises for shoulders. Breathing exercises.

Avoid having any teeth pulled.

Sensitivity to light, bring your sunglasses along.

Massages, lymphatic therapy, and chiropractic treatment to release blockages.

Body Care

Aromas, scents:
Lavender, Lemon Balm, Magnolia, Verbena

Treatments with firming and moisturizing creams are more effective.

Massages that serve to regenerate, and strengthen, perhaps aided with beneficial massage oils.

Correcting and cutting ingrown nails.

Hair dyes applied now, will look more vibrant.

Garden/Nature

Plant part:
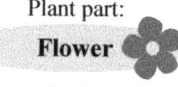
Flower

Sow plants, herbs, and vegetables that grow and flourish above ground.

Sowing and planting any creeping or climbing plants, flowers, and medicinal herbs.

Transplanting.

Avoid watering plants.

Gather herbs for tensions in the shoulder and lung complaints.

Changes in weather are more likely.

Housework

Light housework only.

Ventilate rooms thoroughly.

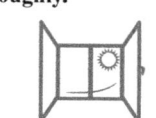

Making preserves.

Baking cakes and cookies. Dough rises faster. (Except on New Moon)

Nutrition

Food quality:
Fat

Cauliflower, artichoke, broccoli, sunflower seeds, flax seeds, nuts, rose hip, elder.

Weight gain: avoid indulging in rich foods. If overweight, eat smaller portions.

Supply nutrient materials to strengthen the body. Focus on foods that contain essential minerals and vitamins.

Stimulants and vitamins are more effective.

Pay attention to any particularly tempting foods today: Most likely the "wrong" things taste best.

High cholesterol: eat a low fat diet.

Positive affirmation:
"I nurture only good thoughts."

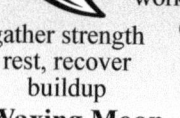

Turning Point
Transition of ascending to descending forces. Both forces are at work and neutralize each other.

gather strength rest, recover buildup
Waxing Moon

28 Wednesday
No meat.

2:33 PM PST
4:33 PM CST
5:33 PM EST

29 Thursday

We live, in fact, in a world starved for solitude, silence, and private: and therefore starved for meditation and true friendship.
C.S. Lewis

Color
Light Blue

Day
Air/Light

Element
Air

Gemini

J A N U A R Y

Success

Feelings, sensitivity, and cooperativeness. Many are overly sensitive, so beware of treading on someone's toes.

Be cautious if you are easily influenced.

During negotiations make use of the cognitive ability of your senses.

Leisure

Relax within your close family.

Retreat to your safe haven and enjoy your fantasy while reading or listening to music. The inner world becomes more colorful than the outer.

Romance can be gentle. Deep feelings will prevail.

If you plan outdoor excursions, be prepared for a shower here and there.

Health

Sensitive body parts:
Chest, Lungs, Liver, Stomach, Gall Bladder

All measures taken to supply nutrient materials and strengthen the sensitive body parts are very effective.

Healing ointments are easily absorbed.

Sensitive nervous system.

Be cautious with alcohol since the liver is very sensitive.

Stomach could play up and cause gas and heartburn.

Rheumatism: Don't air bedding outside, damp will remain in the bedding.

Lymphatic therapy.

Body Care

Aromas, scents:
Lilac, Lilies of the Valley, Lilies, Violets

Treatments with firming and moisturizing creams are more effective.

Massages that serve to regenerate, and strengthen, perhaps aided with beneficial massage oils.

Correcting and cutting ingrown nails.

No haircuts, hair becomes shaggy and unmanageable. Avoid washing your hair.

Garden/Nature

Plant part:
Leaf

Watering all indoor and outdoor plants.

Sow plants, herbs, and vegetables that grow and flourish above ground, leaf vegetables (no lettuce).

Transplanting.

Trimming and cutting back plants. Avoid pruning fruit trees and bushes.

Cut trees, garlands, pick flowers to dry; they will last longer.

Sowing and mowing lawns.

Setting up a compost heap.

Gather herbs for bronchitis, stomach, liver, and gall bladder complaints.

Unfavorable for harvesting, storing, and preserving.

Housework

Light housework only.

Ventilate rooms briefly and rapidly. Don't air mattresses.

Any dirt and spots are easily removed in the laundry.

Avoid painting, as paint will take very long to dry.

Nutrition

Food quality:
Carbohydrate

Lettuce, spinach, lamb's lettuce, Endive, parsley, leek, cabbage (Brussels sprouts, kale, Chinese cabbage), all leafy herbs, asparagus, mushrooms, cress, Swiss chard, rhubarb.

Weight gain: avoid indulging in rich foods. If overweight, eat smaller portions and avoid carbohydrates. Moodiness may make you want to eat more than is healthy.

Supply nutrient materials to strengthen the body. Focus on foods that contain essential minerals and vitamins. Stimulants and vitamins are more effective.

If you get stomach troubles easily, avoid heavy meals.

Positive affirmation:
"I nurture only good thoughts."

Planting Time
Descending forces! Sap is drawn downward, enhancing root formation. Best days for sowing, planting, and transplanting.

gather strength rest, recover buildup
Waxing Moon

4:10 PM PST
6:10 PM CST
7:10 PM EST

30 Friday

31 Saturday

No meat. Cutting and filing toenails and fingernails.

J A N U A R Y

The things you do for yourself are gone when you are gone, but the things you do for others remain as your legacy.
Kalu Ndukwe Kalu

Color
Green

Day
Wetness

Element
Water

Cancer

Success

Determination reigns, and risks are taken more often. Master your tasks with more self-confidence and creativity.

Limits appear to be more easily surmountable.

Auspicious day for sales, advertising, and publicity.

Leisure

Zest for life is in the air. People want to have a fun time, enjoy parties, musical events, movies, etc.

Possessive feelings can harm a relationship. Romance can be very passionate.

Outings: even with cloudy skies the air still feels somewhat warm. Drying effect, get plenty to drink.

Danger of sudden storms, not only in the sky.

Health

Sensitive body parts:

Heart, Back, Diaphragm, Circulation, Arteries

All measures taken to supply nutrient materials and strengthen the sensitive body parts are very effective.

Healing ointments are easily absorbed.

Sensitive sense organs.

Back and heart problems are more likely to occur.

Avoid over straining of the heart and circulation with unusual physical activities.

Expect sleepless nights.

○ *Full Moon: Avoid any surgery and vaccination if possible.*

Body Care

Aromas, scents: Hibiscus, Oleander, Rose

Treatments with firming and moisturizing creams are more effective.

Massages that serve to regenerate, and strengthen, perhaps aided with beneficial massage oils.

Correcting and cutting ingrown nails.

Good days for haircuts, hair becomes stronger. But be aware that if you get a perm, curls will become quite frizzy. Baby's first haircut.

Garden/Nature

Plant part:

Fruit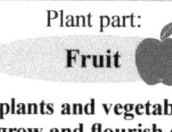

Sow plants and vegetables that grow and flourish above ground. Sowing and planting fruit. Also sow and plant vegetables that are highly perishable. Plant trees and bushes. Sow lawns.

Transplanting. Grafting onto fruit trees.

Trimming and cutting back plants.

Best for cultivating grains on wet fields.

Dig over/plow to prepare soil for planting.

Setting up a compost heap.

Not suitable for fertilizing.

Harvested produce should be consumed as soon as possible.

Gather herbs for heart and circulation complaints.

○ *Full Moon: Weather and climate changes. Herbs are most powerful.*

Housework

Light housework only.

Ventilate sufficiently.

Freezing fruit and vegetables.

Baking bread, cakes, and cookies. Dough rises faster. (Except on New Moon)

Suitable for making cheese.

Avoid painting.

○ *Full Moon: Avoid doing laundry, cleaning windows, making preserves, painting.*

Nutrition

Food quality:

Protein

Beans, peas, corn, tomatoes, pumpkin, lentils, soybeans, cucumber, eggplant, zucchini, berries, fruit, chili, bell pepper, figs, avocado, melon, olives.

Weight gain: avoid indulging in rich foods. If overweight, eat smaller portions.

Supply nutrient materials to strengthen the body. Focus on foods that contain essential minerals and vitamins.

Stimulants and vitamins are more effective.

○ *Full Moon: A day of fasting.*

Positive affirmation:
"I nurture only good thoughts."

Planting Time
Descending forces! Sap is drawn downward, enhancing root formation. Best days for sowing, planting, and transplanting.

gather strength rest, recover buildup
Waxing Moon

1 Sunday
National Freedom Day (US)

○ **Full Moon** 2:10 PM PST, 4:10 PM CST, 5:10 PM EST

Keep your best wishes, close to your heart and watch what happens.
Tony DeLiso

Color
Green

Day
Warm

Element
Fire

Leo

F E B R U A R Y

Success

Determination reigns, and risks are taken more often. Master your tasks with more self-confidence and creativity.

Limits appear to be more easily surmountable.

Auspicious day for sales, advertising, and publicity.

Leisure

Zest for life is in the air. People want to have a fun time, enjoy parties, musical events, movies, etc.

Possessive feelings can harm a relationship. Romance can be very passionate.

Outings: even with cloudy skies the air still feels somewhat warm. Drying effect, get plenty to drink.

Danger of sudden storms, not only in the sky.

Health

Sensitive body parts:
Heart, Back, Diaphragm, Circulation, Arteries

All measures taken to flush out and detoxify the sensitive body parts are very effective.

Scarring is less severe.

Teeth: Removal of tartar and amalgam. Best for fillings, crowns, and dentures!

Blood-purifying, detoxifying herbal infusions and teas.

Sensitive sense organs.

Back and heart problems are more likely to occur.

Avoid overstraining of the heart and circulation with unusual physical activities.

Expect sleepless nights.

Body Care

Aromas, scents:
Hibiscus,
Oleander, Rose

Prepare home-made ointments and cosmetics.

Apply detoxing facial and body care.

Treatments of bumps and pimples on the skin, and exfoliating procedures.

Removing body hair.

Correction of the nail bed.

Massages that serve to relax, ease tension, and detoxify.

Reflexology massage.

Removal of callused skin.

Treating obstinate athlete's foot, nail fungus, and warts.

Good days for haircuts, hair becomes stronger. But be aware that if you get a perm, curls will become quite frizzy. Baby's first haircut.

Garden/Nature

Plant part:
Fruit

Sowing plants and vegetables that grow below ground.

Sowing and planting fruit. Also sow and plant vegetables that are highly perishable. Plant trees and bushes. Sow lawns.

Dig over/plow to prepare soil for planting.

Trimming and cutting back plants. Pruning of fruit trees and bushes.
Transplanting.
Not suitable for fertilizing. Weeding. Pest Control.

Harvested produce should be consumed as soon as possible.

Gather herbs (roots) for heart and circulation complaints.

Start compost heap.

Housework

Housework is dealt with much more successfully, efficiently, and effortlessly.

Problem stains are removed readily.

Dry cleaning.

Thoroughly clean wooden and parquet floors, metals, china, etc.

Cleaning, polishing, and waterproofing shoes.

Combating mold.

Ventilate rooms sufficiently.
Air beds.

Suitable for making cheese.

Freezing fruit and vegetables.

Baking bread, cakes, and cookies (use more leavening agent).

Nutrition

Food quality:
Protein

Beans, peas, corn, tomatoes, pumpkin, lentils, soybeans, cucumber, eggplant, zucchini, berries, fruit, chili, bell pepper, figs, avocado, melon, olives.

Weight associated with overeating is less likely. If underweight, eat larger portions.

Cleansing and detox diets. Fruit and juice days.

Flush out poisons. Treatment for drug abuse.

There are moments when troubles enter our lives and we can do nothing to avoid them. But they are there for a reason. Only when we have overcome them will we understand why they were there.
Paulo Coelho

Color

Green

Day

Warm

Element

♌ Leo   **Fire**

7:22 PM PST
9:22 PM CST
10:22 PM EST ♌ → ♍

2 Monday
Groundhog Day (US), Tu B'shevat

F E B R U A R Y

Planting Time
Descending forces!
Sap is drawn downward, enhancing root formation.
Best days for sowing, planting, and transplanting.

detox
remove
be active

Waning Moon

Success

Good time for details, organization, routine, concentration, and duty.

Take care of financial and administrative tasks.

Prepare for future success now with realistic and critical assessment.

Leisure

Enjoy a nature walk.

Good time for health regimes. Improve your health with stretching exercises and yoga.

The earth feels cold to the touch, so take slightly warmer clothes.

Health

Sensitive body parts:
Digestive Organs, Nerves, Spleen, Pancreas

All measures taken to flush out and detoxify the sensitive body parts are very effective.

Good for surgery, except on the sensitive body parts (see above), lower legs, and veins. Scarring is less severe.

Teeth: Removal of tartar and amalgam. Best for fillings, crowns, and dentures! Avoiding treatment of periodontitis and gums.

Blood-purifying, detoxifying herbal infusions and teas.

Sensitive blood circulation.

For a sensitive digestive system, a wholesome diet is recommended.

Dress slightly warmer.

High blood pressure: Avoid salty foods.

Massages, lymphatic therapy, and chiropractic treatment to release blockages.

Body Care

Aromas, scents:
Lavender, Spruce Needles, Sage, Meadow Flowers

Prepare home-made ointments and cosmetics.

Apply detoxing facial and body care.

Treatments of bumps and pimples on the skin, and exfoliating procedures.

Removing body hair.

Correction of the nail bed.

Massages that serve to relax, ease tension, and detoxify.

Reflexology massage.

Removal of callused skin.

Treating obstinate athlete's foot, nail fungus, and warts.

Best for haircuts because it retains its shape longer. Perms turn out best.

Garden/Nature

Plant part:
Root

Best for sowing and planting, except lettuce.

Plant trees which are supposed to grow very tall. Plant hedges and bushes that are meant to grow very fast.

Planting and re-potting balcony and indoor plants.

Dig over/plow to prepare soil for planting.

Trimming and cutting back plants. Planting cuttings.

Spread fertilizer and manure. Fertilize flowers with poorly formed roots.

Start a compost heap.

Transplanting. Mulching.

Weeding. Pest control (vermin in the soil).

Avoid harvesting and storing.

Gather herbs (roots) for digestive organs, pancreas, and nervous complaints.

Housework

Housework is dealt with much more successfully, efficiently, and effortlessly.

Problem stains are removed readily.

Best for doing laundry! Reduce on laundry detergent, support the environment.

Dry cleaning.

Thoroughly clean wooden and parquet floors, metals, china etc.

Cleaning, polishing, and waterproofing shoes.

Combating mold.

Air rooms only briefly.

Painting.

Making pickles, preserves, and cheese yields suboptimal results and should be avoided.

Nutrition

Food quality:
Salt

Garlic, carrots, red beets, reddish, rutabaga, sugar beet, celery, potatoes, onions, kohlrabi.

Weight associated with overeating is less likely. If underweight, eat larger portions.

Cleansing and detox diets. Fruit and juice days.

Flush out poisons. Treatment for drug abuse.

Avoid large quantities of salty foods like bacon, ham, salted herring, fatty cheese, and the like. Avoid heavy and greasy foods.

It is unwise to be too sure of one's own wisdom. It is healthy to be reminded that the strongest might weaken and the wisest might err.
Mahatma Gandhi

Color — **Yellow**

Day — **Cool**

Element — **Earth**

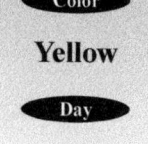
Virgo ♍

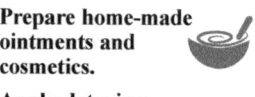

3 Tuesday

4 Wednesday
Rosa Parks Day (US)
No meat.

F E B R U A R Y

Positive affirmation:
"I nurture only good thoughts."

Planting Time
Descending forces! Sap is drawn downward, enhancing root formation. Best days for sowing, planting, and transplanting.

detox
remove
be active
Waning Moon

Success

The artistic instinct rules, but so, too, does indecisiveness. The forces swing back and forth until equilibrium is achieved.

It's easy to reach compromises with tactful sensitivity.

A sense of judgment will support legal matters.

Leisure

Pursuit for harmony and cooperativeness supports good times in romance, friendship, and partnership.

Enjoy cultural events. Relax and get pampered with a spa treatment.

Romance can be passionate yet sensitive.

Health

Sensitive body parts:

Hips, Kidneys, Bladder

All measures taken to flush out and detoxify the sensitive body parts are very effective.

Good for surgical operations except those on the sensitive body parts (see above), lower legs, and veins. Scarring is less severe.

Teeth: Removal of tartar and amalgam. Best for fillings, crowns, and dentures! Avoid treatment of periodontitis and gums, avoid pulling teeth.

Blood-purifying, detoxifying herbal infusions and teas.

Sensitive glandular system.

Take special care to keep the area of the bladder and kidneys warm.

Apply special exercises for the hip region.

Sensitivity to light, so bring your sunglasses along.

Body Care

Aromas, scents: Roses, Violets, Daffodils

Prepare home-made ointments and cosmetics.

Apply detoxing facial and body care.

Treatments of bumps and pimples on the skin, and exfoliating procedures.

Removing body hair.

Correction of the nail bed.

Massages that serve to relax, ease tension, and detoxify.

Reflexology massage.

Removal of callused skin.

Treating obstinate athlete's foot, nail fungus, and warts.

Garden/Nature

Plant part:

Flower

Sow plants and vegetables that grow below ground.

Dig over/plow to prepare soil for planting.

Trimming and cutting back plants.

Start a compost heap.

Weeding. Pest control.

Fertilize flowers that no longer bloom.

Transplanting.

Avoid watering plants.

Harvested produce should be consumed as soon as possible.

Gather herbs (roots) for kidneys, gall bladder and hip complaints.

Day off on 2/5.

Housework

Housework is dealt with much more successfully, efficiently, and effortlessly.

Problem stains are removed readily.

Best for doing laundry! Reduce on laundry detergent, support the environment.

Dry cleaning.

Clean and store seasonal clothing.

Thoroughly clean wooden and parquet floors, metals, china etc.

Cleaning windows and glass.

Cleaning, polishing, and waterproofing shoes.

Combating mold.

Ventilate rooms thoroughly.

Baking bread, cakes, and cookies (add more leavening agent).

Making preserves.

Painting.

Nutrition

Food quality:

Fat

Cauliflower, artichoke, broccoli, sunflower seeds, flax seeds, nuts, rose hip, elder.

Weight associated with overeating is less likely. If underweight, eat larger portions.

Cleansing and detox diets. Fruit and juice days.

Flush out poisons. Treatment for drug abuse.

Pay attention to any particularly tempting foods today: Most likely the "wrong" things taste best.

High cholesterol: eat a low fat diet.

It's not what you say out of your mouth that determines your life, it's what you whisper to yourself that has the most power!
Robert T. Kiyosaki

Color — **Orange**

Day — **Air/Light**

Element

Libra   **Air**

₩→♎ 1:34 AM PST / 3:34 AM CST / 4:34 AM EST

♎→♏ 11:14 AM PST / 1:14 PM CST / 2:14 PM EST

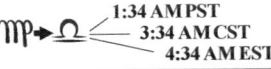
5 Thursday

6 Friday
Chinese New Year
No meat. Cutting and filing toenails and fingernails.

7 Saturday

Positive affirmation:
"I nurture only good thoughts."

Planting Time
Descending forces! Sap is drawn downward, enhancing root formation. Best days for sowing, planting, and transplanting.

detox
remove
be active

Waning Moon

F E B R U A R Y

Success

Critical and superstitious behavior emerges, especially pertaining to money.

A penetrating power will strengthen your capacity to act.

An increased perception opens our interest for the essentials and helps to discover hidden potentials.

Leisure

Relax within your close family, with meditation, and relaxation exercises.

A longing to feel safe will be nurtured if you focus on habits and rituals. An increased sensitivity will help to enjoy every moment.

Romance can be very passionate.

If you plan outdoor excursions, be prepared for a shower here and there.

Health

Sensitive body parts:

Sex organs, Ureter

All measures taken to flush out and detoxify the sensitive body parts are very effective.

Good for surgical operations except those on the sensitive body parts (see above), lower legs, and veins. Scarring is less severe.

Teeth: Removal of tartar and amalgam. Best for fillings, crowns, and dentures!

Blood-purifying, detoxifying herbal infusions and teas.

Sensitive nervous system.

Female disorders: As a preventative measure apply hip baths using yarrow.

Pregnancy: Avoid any exertion, miscarriages are more likely.

Keep region of the pelvis, kidneys, and feet warm to prevent infection of the bladder and kidneys.

Lymphatic therapy.

Body Care

Aromas, scents:
Anemone, Cornflower
Oregano, Thuja

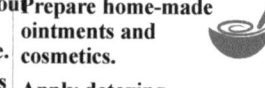

Prepare home-made ointments and cosmetics.

Apply detoxing facial and body care.

Treatments of bumps and pimples on the skin, and exfoliating procedures.

Removing body hair.

Correction of the nail bed.

Massages that serve to relax, ease tension, and detoxify.

Reflexology massage.

Removal of callused skin.

Treating obstinate athlete's foot, nail fungus, and warts.

Garden/Nature

Plant part:

Leaf

Water plants.

Fertilize flowers and meadows, no vegetables.

Sow plants and vegetables that grow below ground, leaf vegetables, and lettuce.

Sowing, planting, harvesting, and drying every kind of medicinal herbs.

Dig over/plow to prepare soil for planting.

Trimming and cutting back plants. Transplanting. Weeding. Pest control. Start a compost heap.

Mowing lawns.

Harvested produce should be consumed as soon as possible.

Avoid cutting down trees, danger of bark beetles.

Housework

Housework is dealt with much more successfully, efficiently, and effortlessly.

Problem stains are removed readily.

Best for doing laundry! Reduce on laundry detergent, support the environment.

Dry cleaning.

Thoroughly clean wooden and parquet floors, metals, china etc.

Cleaning, polishing, and waterproofing shoes.

Combating mold.

Ventilate rooms briefly and rapidly.

Avoid painting.

Nutrition

Food quality:

Carbohydrate

Lettuce, spinach, lamb's lettuce, Endive, parsley, leek, cabbage (Brussels sprouts, kale, Chinese cabbage), all leafy herbs, asparagus, mushrooms, cress, Swiss chard, rhubarb.

Weight associated with overeating is less likely. If underweight, eat larger portions.

Cleansing and detox diets. Fruit and juice days.

Flush out poisons. Treatment for drug abuse.

A little nonsense now and then, is cherished by the wisest men.
John August

Color
Red

Day
Wetness

Element
Water

♏ **Scorpio**

8 Sunday	**9** Monday
	☽ Half Moon.

F E B R U A R Y

Positive affirmation:
"I nurture only good thoughts."

Planting Time
Descending forces! Sap is drawn downward, enhancing root formation. Best days for sowing, planting, and transplanting.

detox
remove
be active
Waning Moon

Success

Inquisitiveness and exuberant inspiration lead to new horizons. Insight and love for truth reign.

Bringing together is more important than splitting asunder.

Expansive forces will assist in legal matters, discussions, and debates.

Leisure

Expansion feels great, and travel, short trips, and outings are most welcome. A competitive spirit excites any sports event.

Talk things out when necessary.

Romance can be very passionate.

Good days for outings; even with cloudy skies the air still feels somewhat warm. Drying effect, get plenty to drink.

Health

Sensitive body parts:

Thighs and Veins

All measures taken to flush out and detoxify the sensitive body parts are very effective.

Good for surgical operations except those on the sensitive body parts (see above), lower thighs. Scarring is less severe.

Teeth: Removal of tartar and amalgam. Best for fillings, crowns, and dentures!

Blood-purifying, detoxifying herbal infusions and tea.

Sensitive sense organs.

Pains often arise in the sciatic nerve, veins, the small of the back, and thighs.

Avoid overstraining the body with unusual physical activities.

Body Care

Aromas, scents: Calendula (Marigold), Geranium, Rosemary

Prepare home-made ointments and cosmetics.

Apply detoxing facial and body care.

Treatments of bumps and pimples on the skin, and exfoliating procedures.

Removing body hair.

Correction of the nail bed.

Massages that serve to relax, ease tension, and detoxify.

Reflexology massage.

Removal of callused skin.

Treating obstinate athlete's foot, nail fungus, and warts.

Garden/Nature

Plant part:

Fruit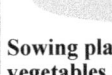

Sowing plants and vegetables that grow below ground.

Dig over/plow to prepare soil for planting.

Trimming and cutting back plants.

Pruning of fruit trees and bushes.

Cultivating grains, particularly corn.

Fertilize grains, vegetables, and fruit.

Combating pests above ground.

Weeding.

Gather herbs (roots) for vein diseases.

Avoid hoeing and harrowing.

Start a compost heap.

Housework

Housework is dealt with much more successfully, efficiently, and effortlessly.

Problem stains are removed readily.

Best for doing laundry!

Dry cleaning.

Thoroughly clean wooden and parquet floors, metals, china, etc.

Cleaning windows and glass.

Cleaning, polishing, and waterproofing shoes.

Combating mold.

Ventilate rooms sufficiently. Air beds.

Suitable for making cheese.

Preserving and freezing fruit and vegetables.

Baking bread, cakes, and cookies (use more leavening agent).

Painting.

Nutrition

Food quality:

Protein

Beans, peas, corn, tomatoes, pumpkin, lentils, soybeans, cucumber, eggplant, zucchini, berries, fruit, chili, bell pepper, figs, avocado, melon, olives.

Weight associated with overeating is less likely. If underweight, eat larger portions.

Cleansing and detox diets. Fruit and juice days.

Flush out poisons. Treatment for drug abuse.

Beauty is eternity gazing at itself in a mirror.
Khalil Gibran

Color
Orange/ Yellow

Day
Warm

Element

Sagittarius   Fire

11:23 PM PST Monday
1:23 AM CST
2:23 AM EST

10 Tuesday

11:46 AM PST
1:46 PM CST
2:46 PM EST

11 Wednesday

No meat.

12 Thursday
Lincoln's Birthday

F E B R U A R Y

Turning Point

Transition of descending to ascending forces. Both forces are at work and neutralize each other.

detox
remove
be active

Waning Moon

Success

Career and business are in the foreground now and thinking becomes clear and serious, but somewhat inflexible.

Perseverance and reasoning assist in financial matters, planning, and contracts.

The values of tradition, authority, and discipline impact our endeavors.

Leisure

Money is not likely to be wasted in a shopping spree.

Many are drawn to enjoy cultural events.

The earth feels cold to the touch, so take slightly warmer clothes.

Health

Sensitive body parts:

Knees, Joints, Bones, Skin

All measures taken to flush out and detoxify the sensitive body parts are very effective.

Good for surgical operations except those on the sensitive body parts (see above), lower legs, and veins. Scarring is less severe.

Teeth: Removal of tartar and amalgam. Best for fillings, crowns, and dentures!

Blood-purifying, detoxifying herbal infusions and teas.

Sensitive blood circulation.

Avoid overstraining bones and knees, and apply gentle stretching exercises only.

Problems with meniscus: Don't overstrain.

Dress slightly warmer.

High blood pressure: Avoid salty foods.

Massages, lymphatic therapy, and chiropractic treatment to release blockages.

Body Care

Aromas, scents:

Cedar, Juniper

Prepare home-made ointments and cosmetics.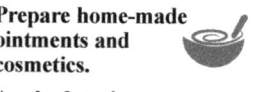

Apply detoxing facial and body care.

Treatments of bumps and pimples on the skin, and exfoliating procedures.

Remove body hair, it may not grow back.

Correction of the nail bed.

Massages that serve to relax, ease tension, and detoxify.

Reflexology massage.

Treating obstinate athlete's foot, nail fungus, and warts.

Cutting and filing toenails and fingernails will make the nails grow stronger over time.

Garden/Nature

Plant part:

Root

Sowing and planting root vegetables and winter vegetables

Weeding. Harrowing weeds. Dig over to prepare soil. Trimming and cutting back plants.
Clear and thin out plants, forest edges, and hedges. Plant cuttings.
Spread fertilizer and manure.
Start a compost heap.
Combat vermin.

Fertilize flowers with poorly formed roots.

Mulching.

Harvest produce is suitable for storage. Harvest root vegetables.

Gather herbs (roots) for bone, joint, and skin diseases.

Housework

Housework is dealt with much more successfully, efficiently, and effortlessly.

Problem stains are removed readily.

Best for doing laundry! Reduce on laundry detergent, support the environment.

Avoid dry cleaning, as the fabric may develop unwanted glossy blotches.

Thoroughly clean wooden and parquet floors, metals, china etc.

Cleaning, polishing, and waterproofing shoes.

Combating mold.

Air rooms only briefly.

Painting.

Preserving root vegetables. Slice cabbage now to ferment into sauerkraut.

Nutrition

Food quality:

Salt

Garlic, carrots, red beets, reddish, rutabaga, sugar beet, celery, potatoes, onions, kohlrabi.

Weight associated with overeating is less likely. If underweight, eat larger portions.

Cleansing and detox diets. Fruit and juice days.

Flush out poisons. Treatment for drug abuse.

Avoid large quantities of salty foods like bacon, ham, salted herring, fatty cheese, and the like. Avoid heavy and greasy foods.

You cannot teach a man anything, you can only help him find it within himself.
Galileo Galilei

Color
Yellow

Day

Cool

Element

Capricorn   **Earth**

13 Friday

No meat. Cutting and filing toenails and fingernails.

14 Saturday
Valentine's Day

Positive affirmation:
"I nurture only good thoughts."

Harvest Time
Ascending forces! Sap is rising, enhancing plant growth above ground, resulting in the most juicy fruits and vegetables.

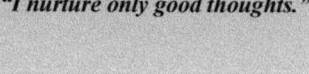
detox
remove
be active

Waning Moon

F E B R U A R Y

Success

Inspiration, optimism, and impatience. Rational thinking, creativity and imagination spark new ideas and inspire planning for the future.

Shying away from routine tasks people will feel more drawn to anything new.

Instead of gridlocked structures choose new possibilities.

Leisure

Inspiration and optimism will boost friendship, social gatherings, and parties.

Express your creativity and imagination. Dwell in dreams and utopian ideas. It is easier now to perceive intuitive thoughts.

Health

Sensitive body parts:

Lower Legs, Veins

All measures taken to flush out and detoxify the sensitive body parts are very effective.

Good for surgery, except on the sensitive body parts (see above).
Scarring is less severe.

Teeth: Removal of tartar and amalgam. Best for fillings, crowns, and dentures!

Blood-purifying, detoxifying herbal infusions and teas.

Sensitive glandular system.

Avoid inflammation of the veins. Apply ointments to lower legs, and rest legs in a raised position.

Varicose veins: Avoid long periods of standing.

While exercising go easy on the ankles.

Sensitivity to light, so bring your sunglasses along.

Body Care

Aromas, scents: Cyclamen, Peach, Wild Roses

Prepare home-made ointments and cosmetics.

Apply detoxing facial and body care.

Treatments of bumps and pimples on the skin, and exfoliating procedures.

Removing body hair.

Correction of the nail bed.

Massages that serve to relax, ease tension, and detoxify.

Reflexology massage.

Removal of callused skin.

Treating obstinate athlete's foot, nail fungus, and warts.

Garden/Nature

Plant part:

Flower

Fertilize flowers that no longer bloom.

Dig over/plow to prepare soil for planting.

Trimming and cutting back plants.

Hoeing and harrowing; weeds can be left to rot.

Pest control.

Start a compost heap.

Avoid watering plants.

Avoid transplanting sprouts.

Harvested produce is well suitable for storage.

Gather herbs (roots) for vein diseases.

Housework

Housework is dealt with much more successfully, efficiently, and effortlessly.

Problem stains are removed readily.

Best for doing laundry! Reduce on laundry detergent, support the environment.

Dry cleaning.

Clean and store seasonal clothing.

Best suited for a spring cleaning: Thoroughly clean wooden and parquet floors, metals, china etc.

Cleaning windows and glass.

Cleaning, polishing, and waterproofing shoes.

Combating mold.

Ventilate rooms thoroughly.

Baking bread, cakes, and cookies (add more leavening agent).

Making preserves.

Painting.

Nutrition

Food quality:

Fat

Cauliflower, artichoke, broccoli, sunflower seeds, flax seeds, nuts, rose hip, elder.

Weight associated with overeating is less likely. If underweight, eat larger portions.

Cleansing and detox diets. Fruit and juice days.

Flush out poisons. Treatment for drug abuse.

Pay attention to any particularly tempting foods today: Most likely the "wrong" things taste best.

High cholesterol: eat a low fat diet.

Sometimes you weren't supposed to share pain. Sometimes it was best just to deal with it alone.
Sarah Addison Allen

● Color
Bright/ Dark Blue
● Day
Air/Light
● Element

Aquarius   **Air**

10:18 PM PDT Saturday
12:18 AM CDT
1:18 AM EDT

15 Sunday
Maha Shivaratri

16 Monday
President's Day (US)

F E B R U A R Y

Harvest Time
Ascending forces! Sap is rising, enhancing plant growth above ground, resulting in the most juicy fruits and vegetables.

detox
remove
be active
Waning Moon

Success

Sensibility, intuition, and helpfulness.

Where possible, retreating is more favorable than dealing with business matters.

Dissolve restrictions, be patient and wait. Be aware that people can be more easily influenced.

● *New Moon: Confirm your resolutions. Finalize new decisions. Drop bad habits.*

Leisure

Your helpfulness will boost friendships.

Enjoy dancing or swimming, or watch a movie that will inspire your fantasies and imagination.

Retreat, relax, and recover.

Romance can be gentle and coziness will prevail.

If you plan outdoor excursions, be prepared for a shower here and there.

Health

Sensitive body parts:

Feet and Toes

All measures taken to supply nutrient materials and strengthen the sensitive body parts are very effective.

Healing ointments are easily absorbed.

Sensitive nervous system.

Drugs have a much stronger effect on your body. Monitor closely what you put into your body.

Lymphatic therapy.

Sluggishness or fatigue may occur in the transition into the next Zodiac sign of Aries.

● *New Moon: Avoid any surgery if possible.*

Body Care

Aromas, scents: Magnolia, Amaryllis, Clary Sage

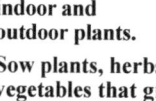

Treatments with firming and moisturizing creams are more effective.

Massages that serve to regenerate, and strengthen, perhaps aided with beneficial massage oils. Reflexology massage. Carry out with special care, people are more sensitive.

Correcting and cutting ingrown nails.

Foot bath.

No haircuts, hair becomes shaggy and unmanageable. Avoid washing your hair. Dandruff could develop.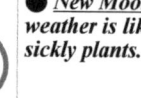

Garden/Nature

Plant part:

Leaf

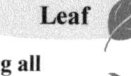

Watering all indoor and outdoor plants.

Sow plants, herbs, and vegetables that grow and flourish above ground, and leaf vegetables.

Transplanting.

Mowing lawns.

Avoid pruning fruit trees and bushes.

Harvested produce should be consumed as soon as possible.

Gather herbs for foot complaints.

● *New Moon: Change of weather is likely. Care for sickly plants.*

Housework

Light housework only.

Ventilate rooms briefly and rapidly. Don't air mattresses.

Any dirt and spots are easily removed in the laundry.

Avoid painting, as paint will take very long to dry.

Preserving and storing should be avoided.

Nutrition

Food quality:

Carbohydrate

Lettuce, spinach, lamb's lettuce, Endive, parsley, leek, cabbage (Brussels sprouts, kale, Chinese cabbage), all leafy herbs, asparagus, mushrooms, cress, Swiss chard, rhubarb.

Weight gain: avoid indulging in rich foods. If overweight, eat smaller portions and avoid carbohydrates.

Supply nutrient materials to strengthen the body. Focus on foods that contain essential minerals and vitamins.

Caffeine, alcohol, drugs, certain foods, and stimulants have a much stronger effect.

● *New Moon: A day of fasting.*

Positive affirmation:
"My loving heart succeeds."

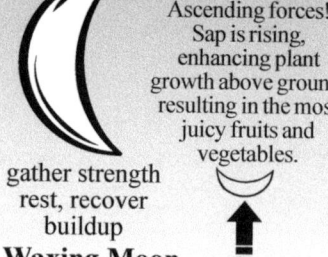

Harvest Time
Ascending forces! Sap is rising, enhancing plant growth above ground, resulting in the most juicy fruits and vegetables.

gather strength
rest, recover
buildup
Waxing Moon

♒ → ⓧ ← 8:10 AM PST
10:10 AM CST
11:10 AM EST

17 Tuesday Mardi Gras, Fat Tuesday
● **New Moon** 4:02 AM PST, 6:02 AM CST, 7:02 AM EST
Solar Eclipse 4:13 AM PST, 6:13 AM CST, 7:13 AM EST

18 Wednesday Ash Wednesday
Ramadan starts. No meat.

11:40 AM PST → ⓧ → ♈
1:40 PM CST
2:40 PM EST

19 Thursday

Challenges are gifts that force us to search for a new center of gravity. Don't fight them. Just find a new way to stand.
Oprah Winfrey

Color
Blueish White

Day
Wetness

Element
Water

Pisces

F E B R U A R Y

Success

Things get going and the way straight ahead seems the best.

People feel energetic, courageous, assertive, and at times anxious.

Good time for meetings and sales talks but impatience and selfishness do not favor teamwork.

Leisure

An enterprising spirit and spontaneity move people to enjoy outings, sports, competitions, cultural events, and travels.

Romance can be very passionate.

Good days for outings, even with cloudy skies the air still feels somewhat warm. Drying effect, get plenty to drink.

Health

Sensitive body parts:

Head, Brain, Eyes

All measures taken to supply nutrient materials and strengthen the sensitive body parts are very effective.

Healing ointments are easily absorbed.

Sensitive sense organs.

If you suffer from migraines drink plenty of water, and avoid coffee, chocolate, and sugar.

Body Care

Aromas, scents: Cloves, Peppermint, Thyme

Treatments with firming and moisturizing creams are more effective.

Massages that serve to regenerate, and strengthen, perhaps aided with beneficial massage oils.

Correcting and cutting ingrown nails.

Eye compresses for strained eyes.

Any kind of hair care. Hair dyes applied now, will look more vibrant.

Garden/Nature

Plant part:

Fruit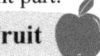

Sow plants and vegetables that grow and flourish above ground, especially fruit and tomatoes.

Sowing and planting anything that is supposed to grow fast and for immediate use.

Grafting onto fruit trees.

Cultivating grains.

Transplanting.

Harvesting and storing grains, vegetables, potatoes, fruit, and tomatoes.

Gather herbs for eye complaints and headaches.

Day off on 2/20.

Housework

Light housework only.

Ventilate sufficiently.

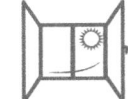

Preserving fruit.

Freezing fruit and vegetables.

Baking bread, cakes, and cookies. Dough rises faster. (Except on New Moon)

Suitable for making cheese.

Nutrition

Food quality:

Protein

Beans, peas, corn, tomatoes, pumpkin, lentils, soybeans, cucumber, eggplant, zucchini, berries, fruit, chili, bell pepper, figs, avocado, melon, olives.

Weight gain: avoid indulging in rich foods. If overweight, eat smaller portions.

Supply nutrient materials to strengthen the body. Focus on foods that contain essential minerals and vitamins.

Stimulants and vitamins are more effective.

Drink plenty of water.

Positive affirmation:
"My loving heart succeeds."

Harvest Time
Ascending forces! Sap is rising, enhancing plant growth above ground, resulting in the most juicy fruits and vegetables.

gather strength rest, recover buildup
Waxing Moon

3:32 PM PST
5:32 PM CST
6:32 PM EST
♈ ➤ ♉

20 Friday

No meat. Cutting and filing toenails and fingernails.

21 Saturday

F E B R U A R Y

Education is no substitute for intelligence.
Frank Herbert

Color
Indigo Blue

Day
Warm

Element
Fire

Aries

Success

Realism and material security are important. Persistence comes easy, thoughts and reactions are slower.

Assess financial areas.

Conservative tendencies may make people want to stay away from risk taking.

Leisure

Relax at a picnic/feast. Enjoy culinary pleasures and hobbies.

The earth feels cold to the touch, so take slightly warmer clothes.

Health

Sensitive body parts:

Head and Neck

All measures taken to supply nutrient materials and strengthen the sensitive body parts are very effective.

Healing ointments are easily absorbed.

Sensitive blood circulation.

Organs of speech, jaws, teeth, tonsils, thyroid gland, neck, and vocal chords get easily affected. Keep neck warm. On cold days ears should be protected. Sensitivity to noise.

High blood pressure: Avoid salty foods.

Massages, lymphatic therapy, and chiropractic treatment to release blockages.

Body Care

Aromas, scents: Geranium, Jasmine, Rose

Treatments with firming and moisturizing creams are more effective.

Massages that serve to regenerate, and strengthen, perhaps aided with beneficial massage oils.

Correcting and cutting ingrown nails.

Hair dyes applied now, will look more vibrant.

Garden/Nature

Plant part:

Root

Sow plants, herbs, and vegetables that grow and flourish above ground.

Sowing and planting trees, bushes, hedges, and root vegetables. Everything grows slowly and lasts well.

Transplanting.

Harvesting and storing root vegetables. Harvested produce is well suited for storage.

Gather herbs for sinus issues, sore throat, and ear complaints.

Housework

Light housework only.
Air rooms only briefly.
Preserving root vegetables.

Nutrition

Food quality:

Salt

Garlic, carrots, red beets, reddish, rutabaga, sugar beet, celery, potatoes, onions, kohlrabi.

Weight gain: avoid indulging in rich foods. If overweight, eat smaller portions.

Supply nutrient materials to strengthen the body. Focus on foods that contain essential minerals and vitamins.

Stimulants and vitamins are more effective.

Avoid large quantities of salty foods like bacon, ham, salted herring, fatty cheese, and the like.

Positive affirmation:
"My loving heart succeeds."

Harvest Time
Ascending forces! Sap is rising, enhancing plant growth above ground, resulting in the most juicy fruits and vegetables.

gather strength rest, recover buildup
Waxing Moon

22 Sunday

7:30 PM PST
9:30 PM CST
10:30 PM EST
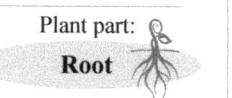

23 Monday

If more of us valued food and cheer and song above hoarded gold, it would be a merrier world.
J.R.R. Tolkien

Color
Bright Blue

Day
Cool

Element
Earth

Taurus

F E B R U A R Y

Success

Open mindedness and curiosity. A changeable and hectic time.

Good time for talking, negotiating, networking, and exchanging ideas as well as for meetings of a nonbinding nature, conferences, and studies.

Leisure

Good time for family gatherings, parties, and short trips.

People enjoy stimulating their minds with reading and studying. Attending theater performances is a preferred enjoyment. Enhance friendships.

Stretching exercises.

Be prepared for sudden changes in weather or climate.

Health

Sensitive body parts:

Shoulders, Arms, Hands, Lungs

All measures taken to supply nutrient materials and strengthen the sensitive body parts are very effective.

Healing ointments are easily absorbed. Applying herbal ointments to the shoulders for rheumatic gout and alike.

Sensitive glandular system.

Make sure you are dressed warm enough in cool weather.

Exercises for shoulders. Breathing exercises.

Avoid having any teeth pulled.

Sensitivity to light, bring your sunglasses along.

Massages, lymphatic therapy, and chiropractic treatment to release blockages.

Body Care

Aromas, scents: Lavender, Lemon Balm, Magnolia, Verbena

Treatments with firming and moisturizing creams are more effective.

Massages that serve to regenerate, and strengthen, perhaps aided with beneficial massage oils.

Correcting and cutting ingrown nails.

Hair dyes applied now, will look more vibrant.

Garden/Nature

Plant part:

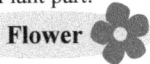

Flower

Sow plants, herbs, and vegetables that grow and flourish above ground.

Sowing and planting any creeping or climbing plants, flowers, and medicinal herbs.

Transplanting.

Avoid watering plants.

Gather herbs for tensions in the shoulder and lung complaints.

Changes in weather are more likely.

Housework

Light housework only.

Ventilate rooms thoroughly.

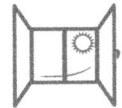

Making preserves.

Baking cakes and cookies. Dough rises faster. (Except on New Moon)

Nutrition

Food quality:

Fat

Cauliflower, artichoke, broccoli, sunflower seeds, flax seeds, nuts, rose hip, elder.

Weight gain: avoid indulging in rich foods. If overweight, eat smaller portions.

Supply nutrient materials to strengthen the body. Focus on foods that contain essential minerals and vitamins.

Stimulants and vitamins are more effective.

Pay attention to any particularly tempting foods today: Most likely the "wrong" things taste best.

High cholesterol: eat a low fat diet.

Discover more about the lunar cycle and it's effects in the reference book "Nature's Daily Guide". ISBN 978-0-9854637-8-6

Positive affirmation: *"My loving heart succeeds."*

Turning Point

Transition of ascending to descending forces. Both forces are at work and neutralize each other.

gather strength rest, recover buildup

Waxing Moon

9:12 PM PST
11:12 PM CST
Thursday 12:12 PM EST

24 Tuesday

☽ Half Moon.

25 Wednesday

No meat.

We know from daily life that we exist for other people first of all, for whose smiles and well-being our own happiness depends.
Albert Einstein

Color

Light Blue

Day

Air/Light

Element

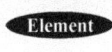

Air   **Gemini**

F E B R U A R Y

Success

Feelings, sensitivity, and cooperativeness. Many are overly sensitive, so beware of treading on someone's toes.

Be cautious if you are easily influenced.

During negotiations make use of the cognitive ability of your senses.

Leisure

Relax within your close family.

Retreat to your safe haven and enjoy your fantasy while reading or listening to music. The inner world becomes more colorful than the outer.

Romance can be gentle. Deep feelings will prevail.

If you plan outdoor excursions, be prepared for a shower here and there.

Health

Sensitive body parts:
Chest, Lungs, Liver, Stomach, Gall Bladder

All measures taken to supply nutrient materials and strengthen the sensitive body parts are very effective.

Healing ointments are easily absorbed.

Sensitive nervous system.

Be cautious with alcohol since the liver is very sensitive.

Stomach could play up and cause gas and heartburn.

Rheumatism: Don't air bedding outside, damp will remain in the bedding.

Lymphatic therapy.

Body Care

Aromas, scents:
Lilac, Lilies of the Valley, Lilies, Violets

Treatments with firming and moisturizing creams are more effective.

Massages that serve to regenerate, and strengthen, perhaps aided with beneficial massage oils.

Correcting and cutting ingrown nails.

No haircuts, hair becomes shaggy and unmanageable. Avoid washing your hair.

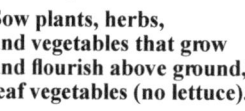

Garden/Nature

Plant part:
Leaf

Watering all indoor and outdoor plants.

Sow plants, herbs, and vegetables that grow and flourish above ground, leaf vegetables (no lettuce).

Transplanting.

Trimming and cutting back plants. Avoid pruning fruit trees and bushes.

Cut trees, garlands, pick flowers to dry; they will last longer.

Sowing and mowing lawns.

Setting up a compost heap.

Gather herbs for bronchitis, stomach, liver, and gall bladder complaints.

Unfavorable for harvesting, storing, and preserving.

Housework

Light housework only.

Ventilate rooms briefly and rapidly. Don't air mattresses.

Any dirt and spots are easily removed in the laundry.

Avoid painting, as paint will take very long to dry.

Nutrition

Food quality:
Carbohydrate

Lettuce, spinach, lamb's lettuce, Endive, parsley, leek, cabbage (Brussels sprouts, kale, Chinese cabbage), all leafy herbs, asparagus, mushrooms, cress, Swiss chard, rhubarb.

Weight gain: avoid indulging in rich foods. If overweight, eat smaller portions and avoid carbohydrates. Moodiness may make you want to eat more than is healthy.

Supply nutrient materials to strengthen the body. Focus on foods that contain essential minerals and vitamins. Stimulants and vitamins are more effective.

If you get stomach troubles easily, avoid heavy meals.

Positive affirmation:
"My loving heart succeeds."

Planting Time
Descending forces! Sap is drawn downward, enhancing root formation. Best days for sowing, planting, and transplanting.

gather strength
rest, recover
buildup
Waxing Moon

26 Thursday

27 Friday
No meat. Cutting and filing toenails and fingernails.

When it was dark, you always carried the sun in your hand for me.
Seán O'Casey

Color
Green

Day

Wetness

Element

Water

Cancer

F E B R U A R Y

Success

Determination reigns, and risks are taken more often. Master your tasks with more self-confidence and creativity.

Limits appear to be more easily surmountable.

Auspicious day for sales, advertising, and publicity.

Leisure

Zest for life is in the air. People want to have a fun time, enjoy parties, musical events, movies, etc.

Possessive feelings can harm a relationship. Romance can be very passionate.

Outings: even with cloudy skies the air still feels somewhat warm. Drying effect, get plenty to drink.

Danger of sudden storms, not only in the sky.

Health

Sensitive body parts:
Heart, Back, Diaphragm, Circulation, Arteries

All measures taken to supply nutrient materials and strengthen the sensitive body parts are very effective.

Healing ointments are easily absorbed.

Sensitive sense organs.

Back and heart problems are more likely to occur.

Avoid over straining of the heart and circulation with unusual physical activities.

Expect sleepless nights.

Body Care

Aromas, scents:
Hibiscus,
Oleander, Rose

Treatments with firming and moisturizing creams are more effective.

Massages that serve to regenerate, and strengthen, perhaps aided with beneficial massage oils.

Correcting and cutting ingrown nails.

Good days for haircuts, hair becomes stronger. But be aware that if you get a perm, curls will become quite frizzy. Baby's first haircut.

Garden/Nature

Plant part:
Fruit

Sow plants and vegetables that grow and flourish above ground. Sowing and planting fruit. Also sow and plant vegetables that are highly perishable. Plant trees and bushes. Sow lawns.

Transplanting. Grafting onto fruit trees.

Trimming and cutting back plants.

Best for cultivating grains on wet fields.

Dig over/plow to prepare soil for planting.

Setting up a compost heap.

Not suitable for fertilizing.

Harvested produce should be consumed as soon as possible.

Gather herbs for heart and circulation complaints.

Housework

Light housework only.

Ventilate sufficiently.

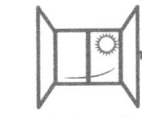

Freezing fruit and vegetables.

Baking bread, cakes, and cookies. Dough rises faster. (Except on New Moon)

Suitable for making cheese.

Avoid painting.

Nutrition

Food quality:
Protein

Beans, peas, corn, tomatoes, pumpkin, lentils, soybeans, cucumber, eggplant, zucchini, berries, fruit, chili, bell pepper, figs, avocado, melon, olives.

Weight gain: avoid indulging in rich foods. If overweight, eat smaller portions.

Supply nutrient materials to strengthen the body. Focus on foods that contain essential minerals and vitamins.

Stimulants and vitamins are more effective.

Planting Time
Descending forces! Sap is drawn downward, enhancing root formation. Best days for sowing, planting, and transplanting.

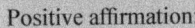

gather strength
rest, recover
buildup
Waxing Moon

12:18 AM PST
2:18 AM CST
3:18 PM EST

♋ → ♌

28 Saturday

1 Sunday

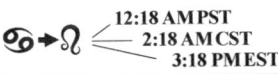

FEBRUARY/MARCH

Sometimes good things fall apart, so better things can fall together.
Jessica Howell

Color
Green

Day
Warm

Element
Fire

Leo ♌

Success

Good time for details, organization, routine, concentration, and duty.

Take care of financial and administrative tasks.

Prepare for future success now with realistic and critical assessment.

Leisure

Enjoy a nature walk.

Good time for health regimes. Improve your health with stretching exercises and yoga.

The earth feels cold to the touch, so take slightly warmer clothes.

Health

Sensitive body parts:
Digestive Organs, Nerves, Spleen, Pancreas

All measures taken to supply nutrient materials and strengthen the sensitive body parts are very effective.

Healing ointments are easily absorbed.

Sensitive blood circulation.

For a sensitive digestive system, a wholesome diet is recommended.

Dress slightly warmer.

High blood pressure: Avoid salty foods.

Massages, lymphatic therapy, and chiropractic treatment to release blockages.

Body Care

Aromas, scents:
Lavender, Spruce Needles, Sage, Meadow Flowers

Treatments with firming and moisturizing creams are more effective.

Massages that serve to regenerate, and strengthen, perhaps aided with beneficial massage oils.

Correcting and cutting ingrown nails.

Best for haircuts because it retains its shape longer. Perms turn out best. Hair dyes applied now, will look more vibrant.

Garden/Nature

Plant part:
Root

Best for sowing and planting, except lettuce.

Plant trees which are supposed to grow very tall. Plant hedges and bushes that are meant to grow very fast.

Sowing lawns.

Planting and re-potting balcony and indoor plants.

Transplanting.

Trimming and cutting back plants.

Planting cuttings.

Start a compost heap.

Avoid harvesting and storing.

Gather herbs (roots) for digestive organs, pancreas, and nervous complaints.

Housework

Light housework only.

Air rooms only briefly.

Making pickles, preserves, and cheese yields suboptimal results and should be avoided.

Nutrition

Food quality:
Salt

Garlic, carrots, red beets, reddish, rutabaga, sugar beet, celery, potatoes, onions, kohlrabi.

Weight gain: avoid indulging in rich foods. If overweight, eat smaller portions.

Supply nutrient materials to strengthen the body. Focus on foods that contain essential minerals and vitamins.

Stimulants and vitamins are more effective.

Avoid large quantities of salty foods like bacon, ham, salted herring, fatty cheese, and the like. Avoid heavy and greasy foods.

Positive affirmation:
"My loving heart succeeds."

Planting Time
Descending forces! No meat.
Sap is drawn downward, enhancing root formation.
Best days for sowing, planting, and transplanting.

gather strength rest, recover buildup
Waxing Moon

♌ ➤ ♍
4:35 AM PST
6:35 AM CST
7:35 AM EST

2 Monday

There is a saying in Tibetan, 'Tragedy should be utilized as a source of strength.' No matter what sort of difficulties, how painful experience is, if we lose our hope, that's our real disaster.
Dalai Lama XIV

Color
Yellow

Day
Cool

Element
Earth

♍
Virgo

M A R C H

Success

Good time for details, organization, routine, concentration, and duty.

Take care of financial and administrative tasks.

Prepare for future success now with realistic and critical assessment.

Leisure

Enjoy a nature walk.

Good time for health regimes. Improve your health with stretching exercises and yoga.

The earth feels cold to the touch, so take slightly warmer clothes.

Health

Sensitive body parts:
Digestive Organs, Nerves, Spleen, Pancreas

All measures taken to flush out and detoxify the sensitive body parts are very effective. Scarring is less severe.

Teeth: Removal of tartar and amalgam. Best for fillings, crowns, and dentures! Avoiding treatment of periodontitis and gums.

Blood-purifying, detoxifying herbal infusions and teas. Sensitive blood circulation.

For a sensitive digestive system, a wholesome diet is recommended.

Dress slightly warmer.

High blood pressure: Avoid salty foods.

Massages, lymphatic therapy, and chiropractic treatment to release blockages.

○ *Full Moon: Avoid any surgery and vaccination if possible.*

Body Care

Aromas, scents:
Lavender, Spruce Needles, Sage, Meadow Flowers

Prepare home-made ointments and cosmetics.

Apply detoxing facial and body care.

Treatments of bumps and pimples on the skin, and exfoliating procedures.

Removing body hair.

Correction of the nail bed.

Massages that serve to relax, ease tension, and detoxify.

Reflexology massage.

Removal of callused skin.

Treating obstinate athlete's foot, nail fungus, and warts.

Best for haircuts because it retains its shape longer. Perms turn out best.

Garden/Nature

Plant part:
Root

Best for sowing and planting, except lettuce.

Plant trees which are supposed to grow very tall. Plant hedges and bushes that are meant to grow very fast.

Planting and re-potting balcony and indoor plants.

Dig over/plow to prepare soil for planting.

Trimming and cutting back plants. Planting cuttings.

Spread fertilizer and manure. Fertilize flowers with poorly formed roots.

Start a compost heap.

Transplanting. Mulching.

Weeding. Pest control (vermin in the soil).

Avoid harvesting and storing.

Gather herbs (roots) for digestive organs, pancreas, and nervous complaints.

○ *Full Moon: Weather and climate changes. Herbs are most powerful.*

Housework

Housework is dealt with much more successfully, efficiently, and effortlessly.

Problem stains are removed readily.

Dry cleaning.

Thoroughly clean wooden and parquet floors, metals, china etc.

Cleaning, polishing, and waterproofing shoes.

Combating mold.

Air rooms only briefly.

Making pickles, and cheese yields suboptimal results and should be avoided.

○ *Full Moon: Avoid doing laundry, cleaning windows, making preserves, painting.*

Nutrition

Food quality:
Salt

Garlic, carrots, red beets, reddish, rutabaga, sugar beet, celery, potatoes, onions, kohlrabi.

Weight associated with overeating is less likely. If underweight, eat larger portions.

Cleansing and detox diets. Fruit and juice days.

Flush out poisons. Treatment for drug abuse.

Avoid large quantities of salty foods like bacon, ham, salted herring, fatty cheese, and the like. Avoid heavy and greasy foods.

○ *Full Moon: A day of fasting.*

Wonder is the beginning of wisdom.
Socrates

Color — **Yellow**
Day — **Cool**
Element — **Earth**

Virgo

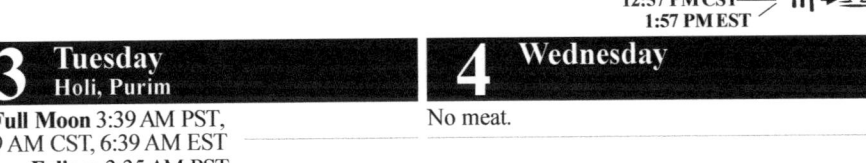

10:57 AM PST
12:57 PM CST
1:57 PM EST
♍ ➔ ♎

3 Tuesday
Holi, Purim

○ **Full Moon** 3:39 AM PST, 5:39 AM CST, 6:39 AM EST
Lunar Eclipse 3:35 AM PST, 5:35 AM CST, 6:35 AM EST

4 Wednesday

No meat.

Positive affirmation:
"My loving heart succeeds."

Planting Time
Descending forces! Sap is drawn downward, enhancing root formation. Best days for sowing, planting, and transplanting.

detox remove be active

Waning Moon

M A R C H

Success

The artistic instinct rules, but so, too, does indecisiveness. The forces swing back and forth until equilibrium is achieved.

It's easy to reach compromises with tactful sensitivity.

A sense of judgment will support legal matters.

Leisure

Pursuit for harmony and cooperativeness supports good times in romance, friendship, and partnership.

Enjoy cultural events. Relax and get pampered with a spa treatment.

Romance can be passionate yet sensitive.

Health

Sensitive body parts:

Hips, Kidneys, Bladder

All measures taken to flush out and detoxify the sensitive body parts are very effective.

Good for surgical operations except those on the sensitive body parts (see above), feet, and toes.
Scarring is less severe.

Teeth: Removal of tartar and amalgam. Best for fillings, crowns, and dentures! Avoid treatment of periodontitis and gums, avoid pulling teeth.

Blood-purifying, detoxifying herbal infusions and teas.

Sensitive glandular system.

Take special care to keep the area of the bladder and kidneys warm.

Apply special exercises for the hip region.

Sensitivity to light, so bring your sunglasses along.

Body Care

Aromas, scents: Roses, Violets, Daffodils

Prepare home-made ointments and cosmetics.

Apply detoxing facial and body care.

Treatments of bumps and pimples on the skin, and exfoliating procedures.

Removing body hair.

Correction of the nail bed.

Massages that serve to relax, ease tension, and detoxify.

Reflexology massage.

Removal of callused skin.

Treating obstinate athlete's foot, nail fungus, and warts.

Garden/Nature

Plant part:

Flower

Sow plants and vegetables that grow below ground.

Dig over/plow to prepare soil for planting.

Trimming and cutting back plants.

Start a compost heap.

Weeding. Pest control.

Fertilize flowers that no longer bloom.

Transplanting.

Avoid watering plants.

Harvested produce should be consumed as soon as possible.

Gather herbs (roots) for kidneys, gall bladder and hip complaints.

Day off on 3/5.

Housework

Housework is dealt with much more successfully, efficiently, and effortlessly.

Problem stains are removed readily.

Best for doing laundry! Reduce on laundry detergent, support the environment.

Dry cleaning.

Clean and store seasonal clothing.

Thoroughly clean wooden and parquet floors, metals, china etc.

Cleaning windows and glass.

Cleaning, polishing, and waterproofing shoes.

Combating mold.

Ventilate rooms thoroughly.

Baking bread, cakes, and cookies (add more leavening agent).

Making preserves.

Painting.

Nutrition

Food quality:

Fat

Cauliflower, artichoke, broccoli, sunflower seeds, flax seeds, nuts, rose hip, elder.

Weight associated with overeating is less likely. If underweight, eat larger portions.

Cleansing and detox diets. Fruit and juice days.

Flush out poisons. Treatment for drug abuse.

Pay attention to any particularly tempting foods today: Most likely the "wrong" things taste best.

High cholesterol: eat a low fat diet.

Your conscience is the measure of the honesty of your selfishness. Listen to it carefully.
Richard Bach

Color
Orange

Day
Air/Light

Element

Libra   **Air**

5 Thursday

8:03 PM PST
10:03 PM CST   ♎ ➔ ♏
11:03 PM EST

6 Friday

No meat. Cutting and filing toenails and fingernails.

Planting Time
Descending forces! Sap is drawn downward, enhancing root formation. Best days for sowing, planting, and transplanting.

detox
remove
be active
Waning Moon

M A R C H

Success

Critical and superstitious behavior emerges, especially pertaining to money.

A penetrating power will strengthen your capacity to act.

An increased perception opens our interest for the essentials and helps to discover hidden potentials.

Leisure

Relax within your close family, with meditation, and relaxation exercises.

A longing to feel safe will be nurtured if you focus on habits and rituals. An increased sensitivity will help to enjoy every moment.

Romance can be very passionate.

If you plan outdoor excursions, be prepared for a shower here and there.

Health

Sensitive body parts:
Sex organs, Ureter

All measures taken to flush out and detoxify the sensitive body parts are very effective.

Good for surgical operations except those on the sensitive body parts (see above), feet, and toes.
Scarring is less severe.

Teeth: Removal of tartar and amalgam. Best for fillings, crowns, and dentures!

Blood-purifying, detoxifying herbal infusions and teas.

Sensitive nervous system.

Female disorders: As a preventative measure apply hip baths using yarrow.

Pregnancy: Avoid any exertion, miscarriages are more likely.

Keep region of the pelvis, kidneys, and feet warm to prevent infection of the bladder and kidneys.

Lymphatic therapy.

Body Care

Aromas, scents:
Anemone, Cornflower
Oregano, Thuja

Prepare home-made ointments and cosmetics.

Apply detoxing facial and body care.

Treatments of bumps and pimples on the skin, and exfoliating procedures.

Removing body hair.

Correction of the nail bed.

Massages that serve to relax, ease tension, and detoxify.

Reflexology massage.

Removal of callused skin.

Treating obstinate athlete's foot, nail fungus, and warts.

Garden/Nature

Plant part:
Leaf

Water plants.

Fertilize flowers and meadows, no vegetables.

Sow plants and vegetables that grow below ground, leaf vegetables, and lettuce.

Sowing, planting, harvesting, and drying every kind of medicinal herbs.

Dig over/plow to prepare soil for planting.

Trimming and cutting back plants. Transplanting. Weeding. Pest control. Start a compost heap.

Mowing lawns.

Harvested produce should be consumed as soon as possible.

Avoid cutting down trees, danger of bark beetles.

Housework

Housework is dealt with much more successfully, efficiently, and effortlessly.

Problem stains are removed readily.

Best for doing laundry! Reduce on laundry detergent, support the environment.

Dry cleaning.

Thoroughly clean wooden and parquet floors, metals, china etc.

Cleaning, polishing, and waterproofing shoes.

Combating mold.

Ventilate rooms briefly and rapidly.

Avoid painting.

Nutrition

Food quality:
Carbohydrate

Lettuce, spinach, lamb's lettuce, Endive, parsley, leek, cabbage (Brussels sprouts, kale, Chinese cabbage), all leafy herbs, asparagus, mushrooms, cress, Swiss chard, rhubarb.

Weight associated with overeating is less likely. If underweight, eat larger portions.

Cleansing and detox diets. Fruit and juice days.

Flush out poisons. Treatment for drug abuse.

You do not write your life with words... You write it with actions. What you think is not important. It is only important what you do.
Patrick Ness

Color

Red

Day

Wetness

Element

Scorpio   **Water**

7 Saturday

8 Sunday
Daylight Saving Time starts.

M A R C H

Planting Time
Descending forces! Sap is drawn downward, enhancing root formation. Best days for sowing, planting, and transplanting.

detox
remove
be active

Waning Moon

Success

Inquisitiveness and exuberant inspiration lead to new horizons. Insight and love for truth reign.

Bringing together is more important than splitting asunder.

Expansive forces will assist in legal matters, discussions, and debates.

Leisure

Expansion feels great, and travel, short trips, and outings are most welcome. A competitive spirit excites any sports event.

Talk things out when necessary.

Romance can be very passionate.

Good days for outings; even with cloudy skies the air still feels somewhat warm. Drying effect, get plenty to drink.

Health

Sensitive body parts:

Thighs and Veins

All measures taken to flush out and detoxify the sensitive body parts are very effective.

Good for surgical operations except those on the sensitive body parts (see above), feet, and toes. Scarring is less severe.

Teeth: Removal of tartar and amalgam. Best for fillings, crowns, and dentures!

Blood-purifying, detoxifying herbal infusions and tea.

Sensitive sense organs.

Pains often arise in the sciatic nerve, veins, the small of the back, and thighs.

Avoid overstraining the body with unusual physical activities.

Body Care

Aromas, scents: Calendula (Marigold), Geranium, Rosemary

Prepare home-made ointments and cosmetics.

Apply detoxing facial and body care.

Treatments of bumps and pimples on the skin, and exfoliating procedures.

Removing body hair.

Correction of the nail bed.

Massages that serve to relax, ease tension, and detoxify.

Reflexology massage.

Removal of callused skin.

Treating obstinate athlete's foot, nail fungus, and warts.

Garden/Nature

Plant part:

Fruit

Sowing plants and vegetables that grow below ground.

Dig over/plow to prepare soil for planting.

Trimming and cutting back plants.

Pruning of fruit trees and bushes.

Cultivating grains, particularly corn.

Fertilize grains, vegetables, and fruit.

Combating pests above ground.

Weeding.

Gather herbs (roots) for vein diseases.

Avoid hoeing and harrowing.

Start a compost heap.

Housework

Housework is dealt with much more successfully, efficiently, and effortlessly.

Problem stains are removed readily.

Best for doing laundry!

Dry cleaning.

Thoroughly clean wooden and parquet floors, metals, china, etc.

Cleaning windows and glass.

Cleaning, polishing, and waterproofing shoes.

Combating mold.

Ventilate rooms sufficiently. Air beds.

Suitable for making cheese.

Preserving and freezing fruit and vegetables.

Baking bread, cakes, and cookies (use more leavening agent).

Painting.

Nutrition

Food quality:

Protein

Beans, peas, corn, tomatoes, pumpkin, lentils, soybeans, cucumber, eggplant, zucchini, berries, fruit, chili, bell pepper, figs, avocado, melon, olives.

Weight associated with overeating is less likely. If underweight, eat larger portions.

Cleansing and detox diets. Fruit and juice days.

Flush out poisons. Treatment for drug abuse.

Look for the good in every person and every situation. You'll almost always find it.
Brian Tracy

Color
Orange/ Yellow

Day
Warm

Element

Sagittarius   Fire

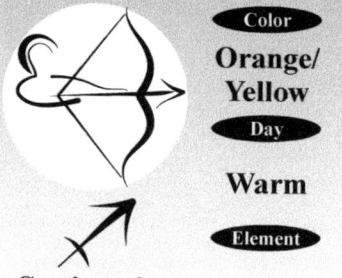

8:38 AM PDT
10:38 AM CDT
11:38 AM EDT

9 Monday

10 Tuesday

9:08 PM PDT
11:08 PM CDT
Thursday 12:08 AM EDT

11 Wednesday

☽ Half Moon. No meat.

M A R C H

Positive affirmation:
"My loving heart succeeds."

Turning Point
Transition of descending to ascending forces. Both forces are at work and neutralize each other.

detox remove be active
Waning Moon

Success

Career and business are in the foreground now and thinking becomes clear and serious, but somewhat inflexible.

Perseverance and reasoning assist in financial matters, planning, and contracts.

The values of tradition, authority, and discipline impact our endeavors.

Leisure

Money is not likely to be wasted in a shopping spree.

Many are drawn to enjoy cultural events.

The earth feels cold to the touch, so take slightly warmer clothes.

Health

Sensitive body parts:

Knees, Joints, Bones, Skin

All measures taken to flush out and detoxify the sensitive body parts are very effective.

Good for surgery, except on the sensitive body parts (see above), feet, and toes. Scarring is less severe.

Teeth: Removal of tartar and amalgam. Best for fillings, crowns, and dentures!

Blood-purifying, detoxifying herbal infusions and teas.

Sensitive blood circulation.

Avoid overstraining bones and knees, and apply gentle stretching exercises only.

Problems with meniscus: Don't overstrain.

Dress slightly warmer.

High blood pressure: Avoid salty foods.

Massages, lymphatic therapy, and chiropractic treatment to release blockages.

Body Care

Aromas, scents:

Cedar, Juniper

Prepare home-made ointments and cosmetics.

Apply detoxing facial and body care.

Treatments of bumps and pimples on the skin, and exfoliating procedures.

Remove body hair, it may not grow back.

Correction of the nail bed.

Massages that serve to relax, ease tension, and detoxify.

Reflexology massage.

Treating obstinate athlete's foot, nail fungus, and warts.

Cutting and filing toenails and fingernails will make the nails grow stronger over time.

Garden/Nature

Plant part:

Root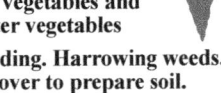

Sowing and planting root vegetables and winter vegetables

Weeding. Harrowing weeds. Dig over to prepare soil. Trimming and cutting back plants. Clear and thin out plants, forest edges, and hedges. Plant cuttings. Spread fertilizer and manure. Start a compost heap. Combat vermin.

Fertilize flowers with poorly formed roots.

Mulching.

Harvest produce is suitable for storage. Harvest root vegetables.

Gather herbs (roots) for bone, joint, and skin diseases.

Housework

Housework is dealt with much more successfully, efficiently, and effortlessly.

Problem stains are removed readily.

Best for doing laundry! Reduce on laundry detergent, support the environment.

Avoid dry cleaning, as the fabric may develop unwanted glossy blotches.

Thoroughly clean wooden and parquet floors, metals, china etc.

Cleaning, polishing, and waterproofing shoes.

Combating mold.

Air rooms only briefly.

Painting.

Preserving root vegetables. Slice cabbage now to ferment into sauerkraut.

Nutrition

Food quality:

Salt

Garlic, carrots, red beets, reddish, rutabaga, sugar beet, celery, potatoes, onions, kohlrabi.

Weight associated with overeating is less likely. If underweight, eat larger portions.

Cleansing and detox diets. Fruit and juice days.

Flush out poisons. Treatment for drug abuse.

Avoid large quantities of salty foods like bacon, ham, salted herring, fatty cheese, and the like. Avoid heavy and greasy foods.

Always forgive, but never forget, else you will be a prisoner of your own hatred, and doomed to repeat your mistakes forever.
Wil Zeus

Color
Yellow

Day
Cool

Element
Capricorn   Earth

12 Thursday

13 Friday

No meat. Cutting and filing toenails and fingernails.

M A R C H

Harvest Time
Ascending forces! Sap is rising, enhancing plant growth above ground, resulting in the most juicy fruits and vegetables.

detox
remove
be active
Waning Moon

Success

Inspiration, optimism, and impatience. Rational thinking, creativity and imagination spark new ideas and inspire planning for the future.

Shying away from routine tasks people will feel more drawn to anything new.

Instead of gridlocked structures choose new possibilities.

Leisure

Inspiration and optimism will boost friendship, social gatherings, and parties.

Express your creativity and imagination. Dwell in dreams and utopian ideas. It is easier now to perceive intuitive thoughts.

Health

Sensitive body parts:

Lower Legs, Veins

All measures taken to flush out and detoxify the sensitive body parts are very effective.

Good for surgery, except on the sensitive body parts (see above), feet, and toes. Scarring is less severe.

Teeth: Removal of tartar and amalgam. Best for fillings, crowns, and dentures!

Blood-purifying, detoxifying herbal infusions and teas.

Sensitive glandular system.

Avoid inflammation of the veins. Apply ointments to lower legs, and rest legs in a raised position.

Varicose veins: Avoid long periods of standing.

While exercising go easy on the ankles.

Sensitivity to light, so bring your sunglasses along.

Body Care

Aromas, scents: Cyclamen, Peach, Wild Roses

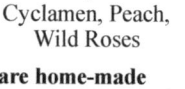

Prepare home-made ointments and cosmetics.

Apply detoxing facial and body care.

Treatments of bumps and pimples on the skin, and exfoliating procedures.

Removing body hair.

Correction of the nail bed.

Massages that serve to relax, ease tension, and detoxify.

Reflexology massage.

Removal of callused skin.

Treating obstinate athlete's foot, nail fungus, and warts.

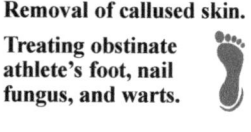

Garden/Nature

Plant part:

Flower

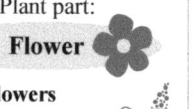

Fertilize flowers that no longer bloom.

Dig over/plow to prepare soil for planting.

Trimming and cutting back plants.

Hoeing and harrowing; weeds can be left to rot.

Pest control.

Start a compost heap.

Avoid watering plants.

Avoid transplanting sprouts.

Harvested produce is well suitable for storage.

Gather herbs (roots) for vein diseases.

Housework

Housework is dealt with much more successfully, efficiently, and effortlessly.

Problem stains are removed readily.

Best for doing laundry! Reduce on laundry detergent, support the environment.

Dry cleaning.

Clean and store seasonal clothing.

Best suited for a spring cleaning: Thoroughly clean wooden and parquet floors, metals, china etc.

Cleaning windows and glass.

Cleaning, polishing, and waterproofing shoes.

Combating mold.

Ventilate rooms thoroughly.

Baking bread, cakes, and cookies (add more leavening agent).

Making preserves.

Painting.

Nutrition

Food quality:

Fat

Cauliflower, artichoke, broccoli, sunflower seeds, flax seeds, nuts, rose hip, elder.

Weight associated with overeating is less likely. If underweight, eat larger portions.

Cleansing and detox diets. Fruit and juice days.

Flush out poisons. Treatment for drug abuse.

Pay attention to any particularly tempting foods today: Most likely the "wrong" things taste best.

High cholesterol: eat a low fat diet.

The rule of the universe is that others can do for us what we cannot do for ourselves, and one can paddle every canoe except one's own.
C.S. Lewis

Color
Bright/ Dark Blue

Day

Air/Light

Element

Aquarius   **Air**

8:15 AM PDT
10:15 AM CDT
11:15 AM EDT

14 Saturday

15 Sunday
Lailat al-Qadr

4:17 PM PDT
6:17 PM CDT
7:17 PM EDT

16 Monday

M A R C H

Positive affirmation:
"My loving heart succeeds."

Harvest Time
Ascending forces! Sap is rising, enhancing plant growth above ground, resulting in the most juicy fruits and vegetables.

detox remove be active

Waning Moon

Success

Sensibility, intuition, and helpfulness.

Where possible, retreating is more favorable than dealing with business matters.

Dissolve restrictions, be patient and wait. Be aware that people can be more easily influenced.

● *New Moon: Confirm your resolutions. Finalize new decisions. Drop bad habits.*

Leisure

Your helpfulness will boost friendships.

Enjoy dancing or swimming, or watch a movie that will inspire your fantasies and imagination.

Retreat, relax, and recover.

Romance can be gentle and coziness will prevail.

If you plan outdoor excursions, be prepared for a shower here and there.

Health

Sensitive body parts:
Feet and Toes

All measures taken to flush out and detoxify the sensitive body parts are very effective.

Scarring is less severe.

Teeth: Removal of tartar and amalgam. Best for fillings, crowns, and dentures!

Blood-purifying, detoxifying herbal infusions and teas.

Sensitive nervous system.

Drugs have a much stronger effect on your body. Monitor closely what you put into your body.

Lymphatic therapy.

Sluggishness or fatigue may occur in the transition into the next Zodiac sign of Aries.

● *New Moon: Avoid any surgery if possible.*

Body Care

Aromas, scents:
Magnolia, Amaryllis, Clary Sage

Prepare home-made ointments and cosmetics.

Apply detoxing facial and body care.

Treatments of bumps and pimples on the skin, and exfoliating procedures.

Removing body hair.

Correction of the nail bed.

Massages that serve to relax, ease tension, and detoxify. Reflexology massage. Carry out with special care, people are more sensitive.

Removal of callused skin.

Treating obstinate athlete's foot, nail fungus, and warts.

Foot bath.

No haircuts, hair becomes shaggy and unmanageable. Avoid washing your hair.

Garden/Nature

Plant part:
Leaf

Water plants.

Fertilize flowers.

Sow plants and vegetables that grow below ground, potatoes, leaf vegetables, and lettuce.

Dig over/plow to prepare soil for planting.
Trimming and cutting back plants.
Start a compost heap.

Mowing lawns.

Pest control. Weeding.

Harvested produce should be consumed as soon as possible.

Gather herbs for foot complaints.

● *New Moon: Change of weather is likely. Care for sickly plants.*

Housework

Housework is dealt with much more successfully, efficiently, and effortlessly.

Problem stains are removed readily.

Best for doing laundry! Reduce on laundry detergent, support the environment.

Dry cleaning.

Clean and store seasonal clothing.

Thoroughly clean wooden and parquet floors, metals, china etc.

Cleaning, polishing, and waterproofing shoes.

Combating mold.

Ventilate rooms briefly and rapidly.

Avoid painting.

Preserving and storing should be avoided.

Nutrition

Food quality:
Carbohydrate

Lettuce, spinach, lamb's lettuce, Endive, parsley, leek, cabbage (Brussels sprouts, kale, Chinese cabbage), all leafy herbs, asparagus, mushrooms, cress, Swiss chard, rhubarb.

Weight associated with overeating is less likely. If underweight, eat larger portions.

Cleansing and detox diets. Fruit and juice days.

Flush out poisons. Treatment for drug abuse.

Caffeine, alcohol, drugs, certain foods, and stimulants have a much stronger effect.

● *New Moon: A day of fasting.*

If people let the government decide what foods they eat and what medicines they take, their bodies will soon be in as sorry a state as the souls who live under tyranny.
Thomas Jefferson

Color
Blueish White
Day
Wetness
Element

Pisces   **Water**

9:04 PM PDT
11:04 PM CDT ⟶ ♓ ➜ ♈
Thursday 12:04 AM EDT

17 Tuesday
St. Patrick's Day

18 Wednesday

● **New Moon** 6:25 PM PDT, 8:25 PM CDT, 9:25 PM EDT
No meat.

M A R C H

Positive affirmation:
"My loving heart succeeds."

Harvest Time
Ascending forces! Sap is rising, enhancing plant growth above ground, resulting in the most juicy fruits and vegetables.

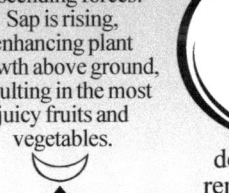

detox
remove
be active

Waning Moon

Success

Things get going and the way straight ahead seems the best.

People feel energetic, courageous, assertive, and at times anxious.

Good time for meetings and sales talks but impatience and selfishness do not favor teamwork.

Leisure

An enterprising spirit and spontaneity move people to enjoy outings, sports, competitions, cultural events, and travels.

Romance can be very passionate.

Good days for outings, even with cloudy skies the air still feels somewhat warm. Drying effect, get plenty to drink.

Health

Sensitive body parts:

Head, Brain, Eyes

All measures taken to supply nutrient materials and strengthen the sensitive body parts are very effective.

Healing ointments are easily absorbed.

Sensitive sense organs.

If you suffer from migraines drink plenty of water, and avoid coffee, chocolate, and sugar.

Body Care

Aromas, scents: Cloves, Peppermint, Thyme

Treatments with firming and moisturizing creams are more effective.

Massages that serve to regenerate, and strengthen, perhaps aided with beneficial massage oils.

Correcting and cutting ingrown nails.

Eye compresses for strained eyes.

Any kind of hair care. Hair dyes applied now, will look more vibrant.

Garden/Nature

Plant part:

Fruit

Sow plants and vegetables that grow and flourish above ground, especially fruit and tomatoes.

Sowing and planting anything that is supposed to grow fast and for immediate use.

Grafting onto fruit trees.

Cultivating grains.

Transplanting.

Harvesting and storing grains, vegetables, potatoes, fruit, and tomatoes.

Gather herbs for eye complaints and headaches.

Day off on 3/19.

Housework

Light housework only.

Ventilate sufficiently.

Preserving fruit.

Freezing fruit and vegetables.

Baking bread, cakes, and cookies. Dough rises faster. (Except on New Moon)

Suitable for making cheese.

Nutrition

Food quality:

Protein

Beans, peas, corn, tomatoes, pumpkin, lentils, soybeans, cucumber, eggplant, zucchini, berries, fruit, chili, bell pepper, figs, avocado, melon, olives.

Weight gain: avoid indulging in rich foods. If overweight, eat smaller portions.

Supply nutrient materials to strengthen the body. Focus on foods that contain essential minerals and vitamins.

Stimulants and vitamins are more effective.

Drink plenty of water.

Positive affirmation:
"This day is a golden opportunity."

Harvest Time
Ascending forces! Sap is rising, enhancing plant growth above ground, resulting in the most juicy fruits and vegetables.

gather strength rest, recover buildup
Waxing Moon

19 Thursday

20 Friday
Spring Equinox, Eid al-Fitr
No meat. Cutting and filing toenails and fingernails.

Don't cry because it's over, smile because it happened.
Dr. Seuss

Color
Indigo Blue

Day
Warm

Element
Fire

Aries

M A R C H

Success

Realism and material security are important. Persistence comes easy, thoughts and reactions are slower.

Assess financial areas.

Conservative tendencies may make people want to stay away from risk taking.

Leisure

Relax at a picnic/feast. Enjoy culinary pleasures and hobbies.

The earth feels cold to the touch, so take slightly warmer clothes.

Health

Sensitive body parts:

Head and Neck

All measures taken to supply nutrient materials and strengthen the sensitive body parts are very effective.

Healing ointments are easily absorbed.

Sensitive blood circulation.

Organs of speech, jaws, teeth, tonsils, thyroid gland, neck, and vocal chords get easily affected. Keep neck warm. On cold days ears should be protected. Sensitivity to noise.

High blood pressure: Avoid salty foods.

Massages, lymphatic therapy, and chiropractic treatment to release blockages.

Body Care

Aromas, scents: Geranium, Jasmine, Rose

Treatments with firming and moisturizing creams are more effective.

Massages that serve to regenerate, and strengthen, perhaps aided with beneficial massage oils.

Correcting and cutting ingrown nails.

Hair dyes applied now, will look more vibrant.

Garden/Nature

Plant part:

Root

Sow plants, herbs, and vegetables that grow and flourish above ground.

Sowing and planting trees, bushes, hedges, and root vegetables. Everything grows slowly and lasts well.

Transplanting.

Harvesting and storing root vegetables. Harvested produce is well suited for storage.

Gather herbs for sinus issues, sore throat, and ear complaints.

Housework

Light housework only.

Air rooms only briefly.

Preserving root vegetables.

Nutrition

Food quality:

Salt

Garlic, carrots, red beets, reddish, rutabaga, sugar beet, celery, potatoes, onions, kohlrabi.

Weight gain: avoid indulging in rich foods. If overweight, eat smaller portions.

Supply nutrient materials to strengthen the body. Focus on foods that contain essential minerals and vitamins.

Stimulants and vitamins are more effective.

Avoid large quantities of salty foods like bacon, ham, salted herring, fatty cheese, and the like.

Positive affirmation:
"This day is a golden opportunity."

Harvest Time
Ascending forces! Sap is rising, enhancing plant growth above ground, resulting in the most juicy fruits and vegetables.

gather strength rest, recover buildup
Waxing Moon

♈ → ♉ ← 11:36 PM PDT Friday
1:36 AM CDT
2:36 AM EDT

21 Saturday

22 Sunday

A thought is an arrow shot at the truth; it can hit a point, but not cover the whole target. But the archer is too well satisfied with his success to ask anything farther.
Sri Aurobindo

Color

Bright Blue

Day

Cool

Element

Earth

Taurus

M A R C H

Success

Open mindedness and curiosity. A changeable and hectic time.

Good time for talking, negotiating, networking, and exchanging ideas as well as for meetings of a nonbinding nature, conferences, and studies.

Leisure

Good time for family gatherings, parties, and short trips.

People enjoy stimulating their minds with reading and studying. Attending theater performances is a preferred enjoyment. Enhance friendships.

Stretching exercises.

Be prepared for sudden changes in weather or climate.

Health

Sensitive body parts:
Shoulders, Arms, Hands, Lungs

All measures taken to supply nutrient materials and strengthen the sensitive body parts are very effective.

Healing ointments are easily absorbed. Applying herbal ointments to the shoulders for rheumatic gout and alike.

Sensitive glandular system.

Make sure you are dressed warm enough in cool weather.

Exercises for shoulders. Breathing exercises.

Avoid having any teeth pulled.

Sensitivity to light, bring your sunglasses along.

Massages, lymphatic therapy, and chiropractic treatment to release blockages.

Body Care

Aromas, scents:
Lavender, Lemon Balm, Magnolia, Verbena

Treatments with firming and moisturizing creams are more effective.

Massages that serve to regenerate, and strengthen, perhaps aided with beneficial massage oils.

Correcting and cutting ingrown nails.

Hair dyes applied now, will look more vibrant.

Garden/Nature

Plant part:
Flower

Sow plants, herbs, and vegetables that grow and flourish above ground.

Sowing and planting any creeping or climbing plants, flowers, and medicinal herbs.

Transplanting.

Avoid watering plants.

Gather herbs for tensions in the shoulder and lung complaints.

Changes in weather are more likely.

Housework

Light housework only.

Ventilate rooms thoroughly.

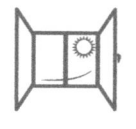

Making preserves.

Baking cakes and cookies. Dough rises faster. (Except on New Moon)

Nutrition

Food quality:
Fat

Cauliflower, artichoke, broccoli, sunflower seeds, flax seeds, nuts, rose hip, elder.

Weight gain: avoid indulging in rich foods. If overweight, eat smaller portions.

Supply nutrient materials to strengthen the body. Focus on foods that contain essential minerals and vitamins.

Stimulants and vitamins are more effective.

Pay attention to any particularly tempting foods today: Most likely the "wrong" things taste best.

High cholesterol: eat a low fat diet.

Positive affirmation:
"This day is a golden opportunity."

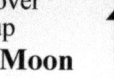

Turning Point
Transition of ascending to descending forces. Both forces are at work and neutralize each other.

gather strength rest, recover buildup
Waxing Moon

♂ → ♊
1:20 AM PDT
3:20 AM CDT
4:20 AM EDT

23 Monday

24 Tuesday

M A R C H

Some people come into our lives and quickly go. Some stay for a while, leave footprints on our hearts, and we are never, ever the same.
Adlai E. Stevenson II

Color
Light Blue

Day
Air/Light

Element
Air

Gemini

Success

Feelings, sensitivity, and cooperativeness. Many are overly sensitive, so beware of treading on someone's toes.

Be cautious if you are easily influenced.

During negotiations make use of the cognitive ability of your senses.

Leisure

Relax within your close family.

Retreat to your safe haven and enjoy your fantasy while reading or listening to music. The inner world becomes more colorful than the outer.

Romance can be gentle. Deep feelings will prevail.

If you plan outdoor excursions, be prepared for a shower here and there.

Health

Sensitive body parts:
Chest, Lungs, Liver, Stomach, Gall Bladder

All measures taken to supply nutrient materials and strengthen the sensitive body parts are very effective.

Healing ointments are easily absorbed.

Sensitive nervous system.

Be cautious with alcohol since the liver is very sensitive.

Stomach could play up and cause gas and heartburn.

Rheumatism: Don't air bedding outside, damp will remain in the bedding.

Lymphatic therapy.

Body Care

Aromas, scents:
Lilac, Lilies of the Valley, Lilies, Violets

Treatments with firming and moisturizing creams are more effective.

Massages that serve to regenerate, and strengthen, perhaps aided with beneficial massage oils.

Correcting and cutting ingrown nails.

No haircuts, hair becomes shaggy and unmanageable. Avoid washing your hair.

Garden/Nature

Plant part:
Leaf

Watering all indoor and outdoor plants.

Sow plants, herbs, and vegetables that grow and flourish above ground, leaf vegetables (no lettuce).

Transplanting.

Trimming and cutting back plants. Avoid pruning fruit trees and bushes.

Cut trees, garlands, pick flowers to dry; they will last longer.

Sowing and mowing lawns.

Setting up a compost heap.

Gather herbs for bronchitis, stomach, liver, and gall bladder complaints.

Unfavorable for harvesting, storing, and preserving.

Housework

Light housework only.

Ventilate rooms briefly and rapidly. Don't air mattresses.

Any dirt and spots are easily removed in the laundry.

Avoid painting, as paint will take very long to dry.

Nutrition

Food quality:
Carbohydrate

Lettuce, spinach, lamb's lettuce, Endive, parsley, leek, cabbage (Brussels sprouts, kale, Chinese cabbage), all leafy herbs, asparagus, mushrooms, cress, Swiss chard, rhubarb.

Weight gain: avoid indulging in rich foods. If overweight, eat smaller portions and avoid carbohydrates. Moodiness may make you want to eat more than is healthy.

Supply nutrient materials to strengthen the body. Focus on foods that contain essential minerals and vitamins. Stimulants and vitamins are more effective.

If you get stomach troubles easily, avoid heavy meals.

Positive affirmation:
"This day is a golden opportunity."

Planting Time
Descending forces! Sap is drawn downward, enhancing root formation. Best days for sowing, planting, and transplanting.

gather strength
rest, recover
buildup
Waxing Moon

♊ → ♋ 3:34 AM PDT
5:34 AM CDT
6:34 AM EDT

25 Wednesday

☾ **Half Moon.** No meat.

26 Thursday

M A R C H

Shoot for the moon, even if you fail, you'll land among the stars.
Cecelia Ahern

Color
Green

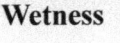
Day
Wetness

Element

Water   Cancer

Success

Determination reigns, and risks are taken more often. Master your tasks with more self-confidence and creativity.

Limits appear to be more easily surmountable.

Auspicious day for sales, advertising, and publicity.

Leisure

Zest for life is in the air. People want to have a fun time, enjoy parties, musical events, movies, etc.

Possessive feelings can harm a relationship. Romance can be very passionate.

Outings: even with cloudy skies the air still feels somewhat warm. Drying effect, get plenty to drink.

Danger of sudden storms, not only in the sky.

Health

Sensitive body parts:
Heart, Back, Diaphragm, Circulation, Arteries

All measures taken to supply nutrient materials and strengthen the sensitive body parts are very effective.

Healing ointments are easily absorbed.

Sensitive sense organs.

Back and heart problems are more likely to occur.

Avoid over straining of the heart and circulation with unusual physical activities.

Expect sleepless nights.

Body Care

Aromas, scents:
Hibiscus, Oleander, Rose

Treatments with firming and moisturizing creams are more effective.

Massages that serve to regenerate, and strengthen, perhaps aided with beneficial massage oils.

Correcting and cutting ingrown nails.

Good days for haircuts, hair becomes stronger. But be aware that if you get a perm, curls will become quite frizzy. Baby's first haircut.

Garden/Nature

Plant part:
Fruit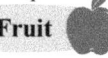

Sow plants and vegetables that grow and flourish above ground. Sowing and planting fruit. Also sow and plant vegetables that are highly perishable. Plant trees and bushes. Sow lawns.

Transplanting. Grafting onto fruit trees.

Trimming and cutting back plants.

Best for cultivating grains on wet fields.

Dig over/plow to prepare soil for planting.

Setting up a compost heap. Not suitable for fertilizing. Harvested produce should be consumed as soon as possible.

Gather herbs for heart and circulation complaints.

Housework

Light housework only.
Ventilate sufficiently.

Freezing fruit and vegetables.

Baking bread, cakes, and cookies. Dough rises faster. (Except on New Moon)

Suitable for making cheese.

Avoid painting.

Nutrition

Food quality:
Protein

Beans, peas, corn, tomatoes, pumpkin, lentils, soybeans, cucumber, eggplant, zucchini, berries, fruit, chili, bell pepper, figs, avocado, melon, olives.

Weight gain: avoid indulging in rich foods. If overweight, eat smaller portions.

Supply nutrient materials to strengthen the body. Focus on foods that contain essential minerals and vitamins.

Stimulants and vitamins are more effective.

Positive affirmation:
"This day is a golden opportunity."

Planting Time
Descending forces! Sap is drawn downward, enhancing root formation. Best days for sowing, planting, and transplanting.

gather strength rest, recover buildup
Waxing Moon

♋ ➙ ♌ 7:11 AM PDT
9:11 AM CDT
10:11 AM EDT

12:34 PM PDT
2:34 PM CDT   ♌ ➙ ♍
3:34 PM EDT

27 Friday
No meat. Cutting and filing toenails and fingernails.

28 Saturday

29 Sunday
Palm Sunday

What I want is so simple I almost can't say it: elementary kindness.
Barbara Kingsolver

Color — **Green**
Day — **Warm**
Element — Fire — **♌ Leo**

M A R C H

Success

Good time for details, organization, routine, concentration, and duty.

Take care of financial and administrative tasks.

Prepare for future success now with realistic and critical assessment.

Leisure

Enjoy a nature walk.

Good time for health regimes. Improve your health with stretching exercises and yoga.

The earth feels cold to the touch, so take slightly warmer clothes.

Health

Sensitive body parts:
Digestive Organs, Nerves, Spleen, Pancreas

All measures taken to supply nutrient materials and strengthen the sensitive body parts are very effective.

Healing ointments are easily absorbed.

Sensitive blood circulation.

For a sensitive digestive system, a wholesome diet is recommended.

Dress slightly warmer.

High blood pressure: Avoid salty foods.

Massages, lymphatic therapy, and chiropractic treatment to release blockages.

Body Care

Aromas, scents:
Lavender, Spruce Needles, Sage, Meadow Flowers

Treatments with firming and moisturizing creams are more effective.

Massages that serve to regenerate, and strengthen, perhaps aided with beneficial massage oils.

Correcting and cutting ingrown nails.

Best for haircuts because it retains its shape longer. Perms turn out best. Hair dyes applied now, will look more vibrant.

Garden/Nature

Plant part:
Root

Best for sowing and planting, except lettuce.

Plant trees which are supposed to grow very tall. Plant hedges and bushes that are meant to grow very fast.

Sowing lawns.

Planting and re-potting balcony and indoor plants.

Transplanting.

Trimming and cutting back plants.

Planting cuttings.

Start a compost heap.

Avoid harvesting and storing.

Gather herbs (roots) for digestive organs, pancreas, and nervous complaints.

Housework

Light housework only.

Air rooms only briefly.

Making pickles, preserves, and cheese yields suboptimal results and should be avoided.

Nutrition

Food quality:
Salt

Garlic, carrots, red beets, reddish, rutabaga, sugar beet, celery, potatoes, onions, kohlrabi.

Weight gain: avoid indulging in rich foods. If overweight, eat smaller portions.

Supply nutrient materials to strengthen the body. Focus on foods that contain essential minerals and vitamins.

Stimulants and vitamins are more effective.

Avoid large quantities of salty foods like bacon, ham, salted herring, fatty cheese, and the like. Avoid heavy and greasy foods.

Positive affirmation:
"This day is a golden opportunity."

Planting Time
Descending forces! Sap is drawn downward, enhancing root formation. Best days for sowing, planting, and transplanting.

gather strength rest, recover buildup
Waxing Moon

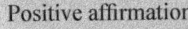

30 Monday

31 Tuesday

7:52 PM PDT
9:52 PM CDT
10:52 PM EDT
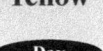

M A R C H

You don't have to burn books to destroy a culture. Just get people to stop reading them.
Ray Bradbury

Color
Yellow

Day
Cool

Element
Earth

Virgo

Success

The artistic instinct rules, but so, too, does indecisiveness. The forces swing back and forth until equilibrium is achieved.

It's easy to reach compromises with tactful sensitivity.

A sense of judgment will support legal matters.

Leisure

Pursuit for harmony and cooperativeness supports good times in romance, friendship, and partnership.

Enjoy cultural events. Relax and get pampered with a spa treatment.

Romance can be passionate yet sensitive.

Health

Sensitive body parts:

Hips, Kidneys, Bladder

All measures taken to supply nutrient materials and strengthen the sensitive body parts are very effective.

Healing ointments are easily absorbed.

Sensitive glandular system.

Take special care to keep the area of bladder and kidneys warm.

Apply special exercises for the hip region.

Avoid having any teeth pulled.

Sensitivity to light, bring your sunglasses along.

○ *Full Moon: Avoid any surgery and vaccination if possible.*

Body Care

Aromas, scents: Roses, Violets, Daffodils

Treatments with firming and moisturizing creams are more effective.

Massages that serve to regenerate, and strengthen, perhaps aided with beneficial massage oils.

Correcting and cutting ingrown nails.

Hair dyes applied now, will look more vibrant.

Garden/Nature

Plant part:

Flower

Sow plants and vegetables that grow and flourish above ground, specially flowers, and medicinal herbs.

Transplanting.

Trimming and cutting back plants.

Avoid watering plants.

Start a compost heap.

Harvested produce should be consumed as soon as possible.

Gather herbs for kidneys, gall bladder, and hip complaints.

Day off on 4/1.

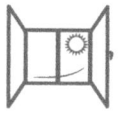

○ *Full Moon: Weather and climate changes. Herbs are most powerful.*

Housework

Light housework only.

Ventilate rooms thoroughly.

Baking cakes and cookies. Dough rises faster. (Except on New Moon)

○ *Full Moon: Avoid doing laundry, cleaning windows, making preserves, painting.*

Nutrition

Food quality:

Fat

Cauliflower, artichoke, broccoli, sunflower seeds, flax seeds, nuts, rose hip, elder.

Weight gain: avoid indulging in rich foods. If overweight, eat smaller portions.

Supply nutrient materials to strengthen the body. Focus on foods that contain essential minerals and vitamins.

Stimulants and vitamins are more effective.

Pay attention to any particularly tempting foods today: Most likely the "wrong" things taste best.

High cholesterol: eat a low fat diet.

○ *Full Moon: A day of fasting.*

Positive affirmation:
"This day is a golden opportunity."

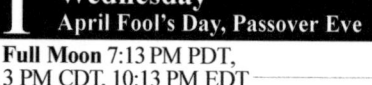

Planting Time
Descending forces! Sap is drawn downward, enhancing root formation. Best days for sowing, planting, and transplanting.

gather strength
rest, recover
buildup

Waxing Moon

1 Wednesday
April Fool's Day, Passover Eve

○ **Full Moon** 7:13 PM PDT, 9:13 PM CDT, 10:13 PM EDT
No meat.

A P R I L

You might think I lost all hope at that point. I did. And as a result I perked up and felt much better.
Yann Martel

Color
Orange

Day
Air/Light

Element
Air

Libra

Success

The artistic instinct rules, but so, too, does indecisiveness. The forces swing back and forth until equilibrium is achieved.

It's easy to reach compromises with tactful sensitivity.

A sense of judgment will support legal matters.

Leisure

Pursuit for harmony and cooperativeness supports good times in romance, friendship, and partnership.

Enjoy cultural events. Relax and get pampered with a spa treatment.

Romance can be passionate yet sensitive.

Health

Sensitive body parts:

Hips, Kidneys, Bladder

All measures taken to flush out and detoxify the sensitive body parts are very effective.

Scarring is less severe.

Teeth: Removal of tartar and amalgam. Best for fillings, crowns, and dentures! Avoid treatment of periodontitis and gums, avoid pulling teeth.

Blood-purifying, detoxifying herbal infusions and teas.

Sensitive glandular system.

Take special care to keep the area of the bladder and kidneys warm.

Apply special exercises for the hip region.

Sensitivity to light, so bring your sunglasses along.

Body Care

Aromas, scents: Roses, Violets, Daffodils

Prepare home-made ointments and cosmetics.

Apply detoxing facial and body care.

Treatments of bumps and pimples on the skin, and exfoliating procedures.

Removing body hair.

Correction of the nail bed.

Massages that serve to relax, ease tension, and detoxify.

Reflexology massage.

Removal of callused skin.

Treating obstinate athlete's foot, nail fungus, and warts.

Garden/Nature

Plant part:

Flower

Sow plants and vegetables that grow below ground.

Dig over/plow to prepare soil for planting.

Trimming and cutting back plants.

Start a compost heap.

Weeding. Pest control.

Fertilize flowers that no longer bloom.

Transplanting.

Avoid watering plants.

Harvested produce should be consumed as soon as possible.

Gather herbs (roots) for kidneys, gall bladder and hip complaints.

Housework

Housework is dealt with much more successfully, efficiently, and effortlessly.

Problem stains are removed readily.

Best for doing laundry! Reduce on laundry detergent, support the environment.

Dry cleaning.

Clean and store seasonal clothing.

Thoroughly clean wooden and parquet floors, metals, china etc.

Cleaning windows and glass.

Cleaning, polishing, and waterproofing shoes.

Combating mold.

Ventilate rooms thoroughly.

Baking bread, cakes, and cookies (add more leavening agent).

Making preserves.

Painting.

Nutrition

Food quality:

Fat

Cauliflower, artichoke, broccoli, sunflower seeds, flax seeds, nuts, rose hip, elder.

Weight associated with overeating is less likely. If underweight, eat larger portions.

Cleansing and detox diets. Fruit and juice days.

Flush out poisons. Treatment for drug abuse.

Pay attention to any particularly tempting foods today: Most likely the "wrong" things taste best.

High cholesterol: eat a low fat diet.

You cannot control what happens to you, but you can control your attitude toward what happens to you, and in that, you will be mastering change rather than allowing it to master you.
Brian Tracy

2 Thursday

Color

Orange

Day

Air/Light

Element

Libra   Air

A P R I L

Planting Time
Descending forces! Sap is drawn downward, enhancing root formation. Best days for sowing, planting, and transplanting.

detox
remove
be active

Waning Moon

Success

Critical and superstitious behavior emerges, especially pertaining to money.

A penetrating power will strengthen your capacity to act.

An increased perception opens our interest for the essentials and helps to discover hidden potentials.

Leisure

Relax within your close family, with meditation, and relaxation exercises.

A longing to feel safe will be nurtured if you focus on habits and rituals. An increased sensitivity will help to enjoy every moment.

Romance can be very passionate.

If you plan outdoor excursions, be prepared for a shower here and there.

Health

Sensitive body parts:

Sex organs, Ureter

All measures taken to flush out and detoxify the sensitive body parts are very effective.

Good for surgical operations except those on the sensitive body parts (see above), head, brain, and eyes. Scarring is less severe.

Teeth: Removal of tartar and amalgam. Best for fillings, crowns, and dentures!

Blood-purifying, detoxifying herbal infusions and teas.

Sensitive nervous system.

Female disorders: As a preventative measure apply hip baths using yarrow.

Pregnancy: Avoid any exertion, miscarriages are more likely.

Keep region of the pelvis, kidneys, and feet warm to prevent infection of the bladder and kidneys.

Lymphatic therapy.

Body Care

Aromas, scents: Anemone, Cornflower Oregano, Thuja

Prepare home-made ointments and cosmetics.

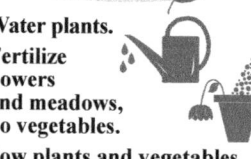

Apply detoxing facial and body care.

Treatments of bumps and pimples on the skin, and exfoliating procedures.

Removing body hair.

Correction of the nail bed.

Massages that serve to relax, ease tension, and detoxify.

Reflexology massage.

Removal of callused skin.

Treating obstinate athlete's foot, nail fungus, and warts.

Garden/Nature

Plant part:

Leaf

Water plants.

Fertilize flowers and meadows, no vegetables.

Sow plants and vegetables that grow below ground, leaf vegetables, and lettuce.

Sowing, planting, harvesting, and drying every kind of medicinal herbs.

Dig over/plow to prepare soil for planting.

Trimming and cutting back plants. Transplanting. Weeding. Pest control. Start a compost heap.

Mowing lawns.

Harvested produce should be consumed as soon as possible.

Avoid cutting down trees, danger of bark beetles.

Housework

Housework is dealt with much more successfully, efficiently, and effortlessly.

Problem stains are removed readily.

Best for doing laundry! Reduce on laundry detergent, support the environment.

Dry cleaning.

Thoroughly clean wooden and parquet floors, metals, china etc.

Cleaning, polishing, and waterproofing shoes.

Combating mold.

Ventilate rooms briefly and rapidly.

Avoid painting.

Nutrition

Food quality:

Carbohydrate

Lettuce, spinach, lamb's lettuce, Endive, parsley, leek, cabbage (Brussels sprouts, kale, Chinese cabbage), all leafy herbs, asparagus, mushrooms, cress, Swiss chard, rhubarb.

Weight associated with overeating is less likely. If underweight, eat larger portions.

Cleansing and detox diets. Fruit and juice days.

Flush out poisons. Treatment for drug abuse.

Can you look without the voice in your head commenting, drawing conclusions, comparing, or trying to figure something out?
Eckhart Tolle

Color

Red

Day

Wetness

Element

Scorpio   **Water**

♏

Ω→♏ 5:12 AM PDT
7:12 AM CDT
8:12 AM EDT

4:33 PM PDT
6:33 PM CDT → ♏→♐
7:33 PM EDT

3 Friday
Good Friday

No meat. Cutting and filing toenails and fingernails.

4 Saturday

5 Sunday
Easter Sunday

A P R I L

Positive affirmation:
"This day is a golden opportunity."

Planting Time
Descending forces! Sap is drawn downward, enhancing root formation. Best days for sowing, planting, and transplanting.

detox remove be active

Waning Moon

Success

Inquisitiveness and exuberant inspiration lead to new horizons. Insight and love for truth reign.

Bringing together is more important than splitting asunder.

Expansive forces will assist in legal matters, discussions, and debates.

Leisure

Expansion feels great, and travel, short trips, and outings are most welcome. A competitive spirit excites any sports event.

Talk things out when necessary.

Romance can be very passionate.

Good days for outings; even with cloudy skies the air still feels somewhat warm. Drying effect, get plenty to drink.

Health

Sensitive body parts:

Thighs and Veins

All measures taken to flush out and detoxify the sensitive body parts are very effective.

Good for surgical operations except those on the sensitive body parts (see above), head, brain, and eyes.
Scarring is less severe.

Teeth: Removal of tartar and amalgam. Best for fillings, crowns, and dentures!

Blood-purifying, detoxifying herbal infusions and tea.

Sensitive sense organs.

Pains often arise in the sciatic nerve, veins, the small of the back, and thighs.

Avoid overstraining the body with unusual physical activities.

Body Care

Aromas, scents:
Calendula (Marigold), Geranium, Rosemary

Prepare home-made ointments and cosmetics.

Apply detoxing facial and body care.

Treatments of bumps and pimples on the skin, and exfoliating procedures.

Removing body hair.

Correction of the nail bed.

Massages that serve to relax, ease tension, and detoxify.

Reflexology massage.

Removal of callused skin.

Treating obstinate athlete's foot, nail fungus, and warts.

Garden/Nature

Plant part:

Fruit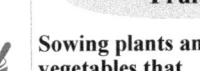

Sowing plants and vegetables that grow below ground.

Dig over/plow to prepare soil for planting.

Trimming and cutting back plants.

Pruning of fruit trees and bushes.

Cultivating grains, particularly corn.

Fertilize grains, vegetables, and fruit.

Combating pests above ground.

Weeding.

Gather herbs (roots) for vein diseases.

Avoid hoeing and harrowing.

Start a compost heap.

Housework

Housework is dealt with much more successfully, efficiently, and effortlessly.

Problem stains are removed readily.

Best for doing laundry!

Dry cleaning.

Thoroughly clean wooden and parquet floors, metals, china, etc.

Cleaning windows and glass.

Cleaning, polishing, and waterproofing shoes.

Combating mold.

Ventilate rooms sufficiently.
Air beds.

Suitable for making cheese.

Preserving and freezing fruit and vegetables.

Baking bread, cakes, and cookies (use more leavening agent).

Painting.

Nutrition

Food quality:

Protein

Beans, peas, corn, tomatoes, pumpkin, lentils, soybeans, cucumber, eggplant, zucchini, berries, fruit, chili, bell pepper, figs, avocado, melon, olives.

Weight associated with overeating is less likely. If underweight, eat larger portions.

Cleansing and detox diets. Fruit and juice days.

Flush out poisons. Treatment for drug abuse.

It is easier to be wise for others than for ourselves.
François de La Rochefoucauld

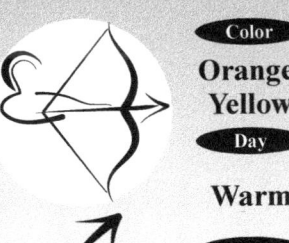

Color
Orange/ Yellow

Day

Warm

Element

Sagittarius — Fire

6 Monday
Easter Monday (CAN)

7 Tuesday

A P R I L

Positive affirmation:
"This day is a golden opportunity."

Turning Point
Transition of descending to ascending forces. Both forces are at work and neutralize each other.

detox
remove
be active

Waning Moon

Success

Career and business are in the foreground now and thinking becomes clear and serious, but somewhat inflexible.

Perseverance and reasoning assist in financial matters, planning, and contracts.

The values of tradition, authority, and discipline impact our endeavors.

Leisure

Money is not likely to be wasted in a shopping spree.

Many are drawn to enjoy cultural events.

The earth feels cold to the touch, so take slightly warmer clothes.

Health

Sensitive body parts:

Knees, Joints, Bones, Skin

All measures taken to flush out and detoxify the sensitive body parts are very effective.

Good for surgery, except on the sensitive body parts (see above), head, brain, and eyes. Scarring is less severe.

Teeth: Removal of tartar and amalgam. Best for fillings, crowns, and dentures!

Blood-purifying, detoxifying herbal infusions and teas.

Sensitive blood circulation.

Avoid overstraining bones and knees, and apply gentle stretching exercises only.

Problems with meniscus: Don't overstrain.

Dress slightly warmer.

High blood pressure: Avoid salty foods.

Massages, lymphatic therapy, and chiropractic treatment to release blockages.

Body Care

Aromas, scents:

Cedar, Juniper

Prepare home-made ointments and cosmetics.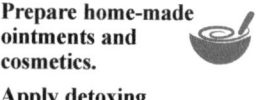

Apply detoxing facial and body care.

Treatments of bumps and pimples on the skin, and exfoliating procedures.

Remove body hair, it may not grow back.

Correction of the nail bed.

Massages that serve to relax, ease tension, and detoxify.

Reflexology massage.

Treating obstinate athlete's foot, nail fungus, and warts.

Cutting and filing toenails and fingernails will make the nails grow stronger over time.

Garden/Nature

Plant part:

Root

Sowing and planting root vegetables and winter vegetables

Weeding. Harrowing weeds. Dig over to prepare soil. Trimming and cutting back plants.
Clear and thin out plants, forest edges, and hedges. Plant cuttings.
Spread fertilizer and manure.
Start a compost heap.
Combat vermin.

Fertilize flowers with poorly formed roots.

Mulching.

Harvest produce is suitable for storage. Harvest root vegetables.

Gather herbs (roots) for bone, joint, and skin diseases.

Housework

Housework is dealt with much more successfully, efficiently, and effortlessly.

Problem stains are removed readily.

Best for doing laundry! Reduce on laundry detergent, support the environment.

Avoid dry cleaning, as the fabric may develop unwanted glossy blotches.

Thoroughly clean wooden and parquet floors, metals, china etc.

Cleaning, polishing, and waterproofing shoes.

Combating mold.

Air rooms only briefly.

Painting.

Preserving root vegetables. Slice cabbage now to ferment into sauerkraut.

Nutrition

Food quality:

Salt

Garlic, carrots, red beets, reddish, rutabaga, sugar beet, celery, potatoes, onions, kohlrabi.

Weight associated with overeating is less likely. If underweight, eat larger portions.

Cleansing and detox diets. Fruit and juice days.

Flush out poisons. Treatment for drug abuse.

Avoid large quantities of salty foods like bacon, ham, salted herring, fatty cheese, and the like. Avoid heavy and greasy foods.

Is there a difference between happiness and inner peace? Yes. Happiness depends on conditions being perceived as positive; inner peace does not.
Eckhart Tolle

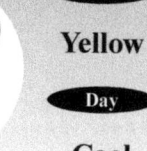

Color

Yellow

Day

Cool

Element

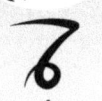

Capricorn   **Earth**

	5:05 AM PDT
↗→♑ ←	7:05 AM CDT
	8:05 AM EDT

8 Wednesday

No meat.

9 Thursday

☽ Half Moon.

4:57 PM PDT	
6:57 PM CDT →	♑→♒
7:57 PM EDT	

10 Friday Orthodox Good Friday

No meat. Cutting and filing toenails and fingernails.

A P R I L

Positive affirmation:
"This day is a golden opportunity."

Harvest Time
Ascending forces! Sap is rising, enhancing plant growth above ground, resulting in the most juicy fruits and vegetables.

detox
remove
be active
Waning Moon

Success

Inspiration, optimism, and impatience. Rational thinking, creativity and imagination spark new ideas and inspire planning for the future.

Shying away from routine tasks people will feel more drawn to anything new.

Instead of gridlocked structures choose new possibilities.

Leisure

Inspiration and optimism will boost friendship, social gatherings, and parties.

Express your creativity and imagination. Dwell in dreams and utopian ideas. It is easier now to perceive intuitive thoughts.

Health

Sensitive body parts:

Lower Legs, Veins

All measures taken to flush out and detoxify the sensitive body parts are very effective.

Good for surgery, except on the sensitive body parts (see above), head, brain, and eyes. Scarring is less severe.

Teeth: Removal of tartar and amalgam. Best for fillings, crowns, and dentures!

Blood-purifying, detoxifying herbal infusions and teas.

Sensitive glandular system.

Avoid inflammation of the veins. Apply ointments to lower legs, and rest legs in a raised position.

Varicose veins: Avoid long periods of standing.

While exercising go easy on the ankles.

Sensitivity to light, so bring your sunglasses along.

Body Care

Aromas, scents: Cyclamen, Peach, Wild Roses

Prepare home-made ointments and cosmetics.

Apply detoxing facial and body care.

Treatments of bumps and pimples on the skin, and exfoliating procedures.

Removing body hair.

Correction of the nail bed.

Massages that serve to relax, ease tension, and detoxify.

Reflexology massage.

Removal of callused skin.

Treating obstinate athlete's foot, nail fungus, and warts.

Garden/Nature

Plant part:

Flower

Fertilize flowers that no longer bloom.

Dig over/plow to prepare soil for planting.

Trimming and cutting back plants.

Hoeing and harrowing; weeds can be left to rot.

Pest control.

Start a compost heap.

Avoid watering plants.

Avoid transplanting sprouts.

Harvested produce is well suitable for storage.

Gather herbs (roots) for vein diseases.

Housework

Housework is dealt with much more successfully, efficiently, and effortlessly.

Problem stains are removed readily.

Best for doing laundry! Reduce on laundry detergent, support the environment.

Dry cleaning.

Clean and store seasonal clothing.

Best suited for a spring cleaning: Thoroughly clean wooden and parquet floors, metals, china etc.

Cleaning windows and glass.

Cleaning, polishing, and waterproofing shoes.

Combating mold.

Ventilate rooms thoroughly.

Baking bread, cakes, and cookies (add more leavening agent).

Making preserves.

Painting.

Nutrition

Food quality:

Fat

Cauliflower, artichoke, broccoli, sunflower seeds, flax seeds, nuts, rose hip, elder.

Weight associated with overeating is less likely. If underweight, eat larger portions.

Cleansing and detox diets. Fruit and juice days.

Flush out poisons. Treatment for drug abuse.

Pay attention to any particularly tempting foods today: Most likely the "wrong" things taste best.

High cholesterol: eat a low fat diet.

Everybody gets so much information all day long that they lose their common sense.
Gertrude Stein

Color
Bright/ Dark Blue

Day
Air/Light

Element

Aquarius   Air

11 Saturday

12 Sunday
Orthodox Easter

A P R I L

Positive affirmation:
"This day is a golden opportunity."

Harvest Time
Ascending forces! Sap is rising, enhancing plant growth above ground, resulting in the most juicy fruits and vegetables.

detox remove be active

Waning Moon

Success

Sensibility, intuition, and helpfulness.

Where possible, retreating is more favorable than dealing with business matters.

Dissolve restrictions, be patient and wait. Be aware that people can be more easily influenced.

Leisure

Your helpfulness will boost friendships.

Enjoy dancing or swimming, or watch a movie that will inspire your fantasies and imagination.

Retreat, relax, and recover.

Romance can be gentle and coziness will prevail.

If you plan outdoor excursions, be prepared for a shower here and there.

Health

Sensitive body parts:
Feet and Toes

All measures taken to flush out and detoxify the sensitive body parts are very effective.

Good for surgical operations except those on the sensitive body parts (see above), head, brain, and eyes.
Scarring is less severe.

Teeth: Removal of tartar and amalgam. Best for fillings, crowns, and dentures!

Blood-purifying, detoxifying herbal infusions and teas.

Sensitive nervous system.

Drugs have a much stronger effect on your body. Monitor closely what you put into your body.

Lymphatic therapy.

Sluggishness or fatigue may occur in the transition into the next Zodiac sign of Aries.

Body Care

Aromas, scents:
Magnolia, Amaryllis, Clary Sage

Prepare home-made ointments and cosmetics.

Apply detoxing facial and body care.

Treatments of bumps and pimples on the skin, and exfoliating procedures.

Removing body hair.

Correction of the nail bed.

Massages that serve to relax, ease tension, and detoxify. Reflexology massage. Carry out with special care, people are more sensitive.

Removal of callused skin.

Treating obstinate athlete's foot, nail fungus, and warts.

Foot bath.

No haircuts, hair becomes shaggy and unmanageable.
Avoid washing your hair.

Garden/Nature

Plant part:
Leaf

Water plants.

Fertilize flowers.

Sow plants and vegetables that grow below ground, potatoes, leaf vegetables, and lettuce.

Dig over/plow to prepare soil for planting.
Trimming and cutting back plants.
Start a compost heap.

Mowing lawns.

Pest control. Weeding.

Harvested produce should be consumed as soon as possible.

Gather herbs for foot complaints.

Housework

Housework is dealt with much more successfully, efficiently, and effortlessly.

Problem stains are removed readily.

Best for doing laundry! Reduce on laundry detergent, support the environment.

Dry cleaning.

Clean and store seasonal clothing.

Thoroughly clean wooden and parquet floors, metals, china etc.

Cleaning, polishing, and waterproofing shoes.

Combating mold.

Ventilate rooms briefly and rapidly.

Avoid painting.

Preserving and storing should be avoided.

Nutrition

Food quality:
Carbohydrate

Lettuce, spinach, lamb's lettuce, Endive, parsley, leek, cabbage (Brussels sprouts, kale, Chinese cabbage), all leafy herbs, asparagus, mushrooms, cress, Swiss chard, rhubarb.

Weight associated with overeating is less likely. If underweight, eat larger portions.

Cleansing and detox diets. Fruit and juice days.

Flush out poisons. Treatment for drug abuse.

Caffeine, alcohol, drugs, certain foods, and stimulants have a much stronger effect.

We do learn and develop when we are exposed to those who are greater than we are. Perhaps this is the chief way we mature.
Madeleine L'Engle

Pisces

Color
Blueish White

Day

Wetness

Element

Water

♒ ➤ ♓
1:57 AM PDT
3:57 AM CDT
4:57 AM EDT

13 Monday
Orthodox Easter Monday

14 Tuesday
Yom HaShoah

A P R I L

Harvest Time
Ascending forces! Sap is rising, enhancing plant growth above ground, resulting in the most juicy fruits and vegetables.

detox
remove
be active

Waning Moon

Success

Things get going and the way straight ahead seems the best.

People feel energetic, courageous, assertive, and at times anxious.

Good time for meetings and sales talks but impatience and selfishness do not favor teamwork.

Leisure

An enterprising spirit and spontaneity move people to enjoy outings, sports, competitions, cultural events, and travels.

Romance can be very passionate.

Good days for outings, even with cloudy skies the air still feels somewhat warm. Drying effect, get plenty to drink.

Health

Sensitive body parts:

Head, Brain, Eyes

All measures taken to flush out and detoxify the sensitive body parts are very effective.

Good for surgery, except on the sensitive body parts (see above).

Scarring is less severe.

Teeth: Removal of tartar and amalgam. Best for fillings, crowns, and dentures! Avoiding treatment of periodontitis and gums.

Blood-purifying, detoxifying herbal infusions and teas.

Sensitive sense organs.

If you suffer from migraines drink plenty of water, and avoid coffee, chocolate, and sugar.

Body Care

Aromas, scents:
Cloves, Peppermint, Thyme

Prepare home-made ointments and cosmetics.

Apply detoxing facial and body care.

Treatments of bumps and pimples on the skin, and exfoliating procedures.

Removing body hair.

Correction of the nail bed.

Massages that serve to relax, ease tension, and detoxify.

Reflexology massage.

Removal of callused skin.

Treating obstinate athlete's foot, nail fungus, and warts.

Eye compresses to relieve strained eyes.

Any kind of hair care.

Garden/Nature

Plant part:

Fruit

Sowing plants and vegetables that grow below ground. Sowing and planting anything that is supposed to grow fast. Sowing and planting fruit and tomatoes. Dig over/plow the soil to prepare for planting. Spreading manure. Fertilizing grains, vegetables, and fruit. Weeding. Pest control. Pruning of fruit trees and bushes. Harvesting and storing grains, vegetables, potatoes, fruits, and tomatoes. Start a compost heap. Gather herbs (roots) for eye complaints and headaches. Day off on 4/16.

Housework

Housework is dealt with much more successfully, efficiently, and effortlessly.

Problem stains are removed readily.
Best for doing laundry!
Dry cleaning.
Clean and store seasonal clothing.
Thoroughly clean wooden and parquet floors, metals, china, etc.
Cleaning windows and glass.
Cleaning, polishing, and waterproofing shoes.
Combating mold.
Ventilate rooms sufficiently.
Air beds.
Suitable for making cheese.
Preserving and freezing fruit and vegetables.
Baking bread, cakes, and cookies (use more leavening agent).
Painting.

Nutrition

Food quality:

Protein

Beans, peas, corn, tomatoes, pumpkin, lentils, soybeans, cucumber, eggplant, zucchini, berries, fruit, chili, bell pepper, figs, avocado, melon, olives.

Weight associated with overeating is less likely. If underweight, eat larger portions.

Cleansing and detox diets. Fruit and juice days.

Flush out poisons. Treatment for drug abuse.

Drink plenty of water.

Imitation is sometimes a good training-ship; but it will never fly the flags of the admiral.
Sri Aurobindo

Color
Indigo Blue

Day
Warm

Element

Aries   Fire

7:05 AM PDT
9:05 AM CDT
10:05 AM EDT

15 Wednesday
No meat.

16 Thursday

A P R I L

Positive affirmation:
"This day is a golden opportunity."

Harvest Time
Ascending forces! Sap is rising, enhancing plant growth above ground, resulting in the most juicy fruits and vegetables.

detox
remove
be active

Waning Moon

Success

Realism and material security are important. Persistence comes easy, thoughts and reactions are slower.

Assess financial areas.

Conservative tendencies may make people want to stay away from risk taking.

● *New Moon: Confirm your resolutions. Finalize new decisions. Drop bad habits.*

Leisure

Relax at a picnic/feast. Enjoy culinary pleasures and hobbies.

The earth feels cold to the touch, so take slightly warmer clothes.

Health

Sensitive body parts:

Head and Neck

All measures taken to supply nutrient materials and strengthen the sensitive body parts are very effective.

Healing ointments are easily absorbed.

Sensitive blood circulation.

Organs of speech, jaws, teeth, tonsils, thyroid gland, neck, and vocal chords get easily affected. Keep neck warm. On cold days ears should be protected. Sensitivity to noise.

High blood pressure: Avoid salty foods.

Massages, lymphatic therapy, and chiropractic treatment to release blockages.

● *New Moon: Avoid any surgery if possible.*

Body Care

Aromas, scents: Geranium, Jasmine, Rose

Treatments with firming and moisturizing creams are more effective.

Massages that serve to regenerate, and strengthen, perhaps aided with beneficial massage oils.

Correcting and cutting ingrown nails.

Hair dyes applied now, will look more vibrant.

Garden/Nature

Plant part:

Root

Sow plants, herbs, and vegetables that grow and flourish above ground.

Sowing and planting trees, bushes, hedges, and root vegetables. Everything grows slowly and lasts well.

Transplanting.

Harvesting and storing root vegetables. Harvested produce is well suited for storage.

Gather herbs for sinus issues, sore throat, and ear complaints.

● *New Moon: Change of weather is likely. Care for sickly plants.*

Housework

Light housework only.

Air rooms only briefly.

Preserving root vegetables.

Nutrition

Food quality:

Salt

Garlic, carrots, red beets, reddish, rutabaga, sugar beet, celery, potatoes, onions, kohlrabi.

Weight gain: avoid indulging in rich foods. If overweight, eat smaller portions.

Supply nutrient materials to strengthen the body. Focus on foods that contain essential minerals and vitamins.

Stimulants and vitamins are more effective.

Avoid large quantities of salty foods like bacon, ham, salted herring, fatty cheese, and the like.

● *New Moon: A day of fasting.*

Positive affirmation:
"I trust in the power of my inner joy."

Harvest Time
Ascending forces! Sap is rising, enhancing plant growth above ground, resulting in the most juicy fruits and vegetables.

gather strength
rest, recover
buildup
Waxing Moon

♈ → ♉   8:59 AM PDT
10:59 AM CDT
11:59 AM EDT

17 Friday

● **New Moon** 4:53 AM PDT
6:53 AM CDT, 7:53 AM EDT
No meat. Cutting and filing
toenails and fingernails.

18 Saturday

Never trust anyone who has not brought a book with them.
Lemony Snicket

Color
Bright Blue

Day
Cool

Element
Earth

Taurus

A P R I L

Success

Open mindedness and curiosity. A changeable and hectic time.

Good time for talking, negotiating, networking, and exchanging ideas as well as for meetings of a nonbinding nature, conferences, and studies.

Leisure

Good time for family gatherings, parties, and short trips.

People enjoy stimulating their minds with reading and studying. Attending theater performances is a preferred enjoyment. Enhance friendships.

Stretching exercises.

Be prepared for sudden changes in weather or climate.

Health

Sensitive body parts:
Shoulders, Arms, Hands, Lungs

All measures taken to supply nutrient materials and strengthen the sensitive body parts are very effective.

Healing ointments are easily absorbed. Applying herbal ointments to the shoulders for rheumatic gout and alike.

Sensitive glandular system.

Make sure you are dressed warm enough in cool weather.

Exercises for shoulders. Breathing exercises.

Avoid having any teeth pulled.

Sensitivity to light, bring your sunglasses along.

Massages, lymphatic therapy, and chiropractic treatment to release blockages.

Body Care

Aromas, scents:
Lavender, Lemon Balm, Magnolia, Verbena

Treatments with firming and moisturizing creams are more effective.

Massages that serve to regenerate, and strengthen, perhaps aided with beneficial massage oils.

Correcting and cutting ingrown nails.

Hair dyes applied now, will look more vibrant.

Garden/Nature

Plant part:
Flower

Sow plants, herbs, and vegetables that grow and flourish above ground.

Sowing and planting any creeping or climbing plants, flowers, and medicinal herbs.

Transplanting.

Avoid watering plants.

Gather herbs for tensions in the shoulder and lung complaints.

Changes in weather are more likely.

Housework

Light housework only.

Ventilate rooms thoroughly.

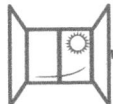

Making preserves.

Baking cakes and cookies. Dough rises faster. (Except on New Moon)

Nutrition

Food quality:
Fat

Cauliflower, artichoke, broccoli, sunflower seeds, flax seeds, nuts, rose hip, elder.

Weight gain: avoid indulging in rich foods. If overweight, eat smaller portions.

Supply nutrient materials to strengthen the body. Focus on foods that contain essential minerals and vitamins.

Stimulants and vitamins are more effective.

Pay attention to any particularly tempting foods today: Most likely the "wrong" things taste best.

High cholesterol: eat a low fat diet.

Positive affirmation:
"I trust in the power of my inner joy."

Turning Point
Transition of ascending to descending forces. Both forces are at work and neutralize each other.

gather strength rest, recover buildup
Waxing Moon

♂→Ⅱ   9:19 AM PDT
11:19 AM CDT
12:19 PM EDT

10:01 AM PDT
12:01 PM CDT
1:01 PM EDT   Ⅱ→♋

19 Sunday

20 Monday

21 Tuesday

A P R I L

Life's under no obligation to give us what we expect.
Margaret Mitchell

Color
Light Blue

Day
Air/Light

Element

Air

Gemini

Success

Feelings, sensitivity, and cooperativeness. Many are overly sensitive, so beware of treading on someone's toes.

Be cautious if you are easily influenced.

During negotiations make use of the cognitive ability of your senses.

Leisure

Relax within your close family.

Retreat to your safe haven and enjoy your fantasy while reading or listening to music. The inner world becomes more colorful than the outer.

Romance can be gentle. Deep feelings will prevail.

If you plan outdoor excursions, be prepared for a shower here and there.

Health

Sensitive body parts:
Chest, Lungs, Liver, Stomach, Gall Bladder

All measures taken to supply nutrient materials and strengthen the sensitive body parts are very effective.

Healing ointments are easily absorbed.

Sensitive nervous system.

Be cautious with alcohol since the liver is very sensitive.

Stomach could play up and cause gas and heartburn.

Rheumatism: Don't air bedding outside, damp will remain in the bedding.

Lymphatic therapy.

Body Care

Aromas, scents:
Lilac, Lilies of the Valley, Lilies, Violets

Treatments with firming and moisturizing creams are more effective.

Massages that serve to regenerate, and strengthen, perhaps aided with beneficial massage oils.

Correcting and cutting ingrown nails.

No haircuts, hair becomes shaggy and unmanageable. Avoid washing your hair.

Garden/Nature

Plant part:
Leaf

Watering all indoor and outdoor plants.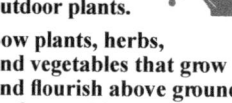

Sow plants, herbs, and vegetables that grow and flourish above ground, leaf vegetables (no lettuce).

Transplanting.

Trimming and cutting back plants. Avoid pruning fruit trees and bushes.

Cut trees, garlands, pick flowers to dry; they will last longer.

Sowing and mowing lawns.

Setting up a compost heap.

Gather herbs for bronchitis, stomach, liver, and gall bladder complaints.

Unfavorable for harvesting, storing, and preserving.

Housework

Light housework only.

Ventilate rooms briefly and rapidly. Don't air mattresses.

Any dirt and spots are easily removed in the laundry.

Avoid painting, as paint will take very long to dry.

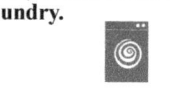

Nutrition

Food quality:
Carbohydrate

Lettuce, spinach, lamb's lettuce, Endive, parsley, leek, cabbage (Brussels sprouts, kale, Chinese cabbage), all leafy herbs, asparagus, mushrooms, cress, Swiss chard, rhubarb.

Weight gain: avoid indulging in rich foods. If overweight, eat smaller portions and avoid carbohydrates. Moodiness may make you want to eat more than is healthy.

Supply nutrient materials to strengthen the body. Focus on foods that contain essential minerals and vitamins. Stimulants and vitamins are more effective.

If you get stomach troubles easily, avoid heavy meals.

Positive affirmation:
"I trust in the power of my inner joy."

Planting Time
Descending forces! Sap is drawn downward, enhancing root formation. Best days for sowing, planting, and transplanting.

gather strength rest, recover buildup
Waxing Moon

22 **Wednesday**
Yom Ha'atzmaut
No meat.

12:42 PM PDT
2:42 PM CDT
3:42 PM EDT
 ➔ ♌

23 **Thursday**
☽ Half Moon.

Walk on with hope in your heart, and you'll never walk alone.
Shah Rukh Khan

Color
Green

Day
Wetness

Element
Water

Cancer

A P R I L

Success

Determination reigns, and risks are taken more often. Master your tasks with more self-confidence and creativity.

Limits appear to be more easily surmountable.

Auspicious day for sales, advertising, and publicity.

Leisure

Zest for life is in the air. People want to have a fun time, enjoy parties, musical events, movies, etc.

Possessive feelings can harm a relationship. Romance can be very passionate.

Outings: even with cloudy skies the air still feels somewhat warm. Drying effect, get plenty to drink.

Danger of sudden storms, not only in the sky.

Health

Sensitive body parts:
Heart, Back, Diaphragm, Circulation, Arteries

All measures taken to supply nutrient materials and strengthen the sensitive body parts are very effective.

Healing ointments are easily absorbed.

Sensitive sense organs.

Back and heart problems are more likely to occur.

Avoid over straining of the heart and circulation with unusual physical activities.

Expect sleepless nights.

Body Care

Aromas, scents:
Hibiscus,
Oleander, Rose

Treatments with firming and moisturizing creams are more effective.

Massages that serve to regenerate, and strengthen, perhaps aided with beneficial massage oils.

Correcting and cutting ingrown nails.

Good days for haircuts, hair becomes stronger. But be aware that if you get a perm, curls will become quite frizzy. Baby's first haircut.

Garden/Nature

Plant part:
Fruit

Sow plants and vegetables that grow and flourish above ground. Sowing and planting fruit. Also sow and plant vegetables that are highly perishable. Plant trees and bushes. Sow lawns.

Transplanting. Grafting onto fruit trees.

Trimming and cutting back plants.

Best for cultivating grains on wet fields.

Dig over/plow to prepare soil for planting.

Setting up a compost heap.

Not suitable for fertilizing.

Harvested produce should be consumed as soon as possible.

Gather herbs for heart and circulation complaints.

Housework

Light housework only.

Ventilate sufficiently.

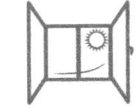

Freezing fruit and vegetables.

Baking bread, cakes, and cookies. Dough rises faster. (Except on New Moon)

Suitable for making cheese.

Avoid painting.

Nutrition

Food quality:
Protein

Beans, peas, corn, tomatoes, pumpkin, lentils, soybeans, cucumber, eggplant, zucchini, berries, fruit, chili, bell pepper, figs, avocado, melon, olives.

Weight gain: avoid indulging in rich foods. If overweight, eat smaller portions.

Supply nutrient materials to strengthen the body. Focus on foods that contain essential minerals and vitamins.

Stimulants and vitamins are more effective.

Positive affirmation:
"I trust in the power of my inner joy."

Planting Time
Descending forces!
Sap is drawn downward, enhancing root formation.
Best days for sowing, planting, and transplanting.

gather strength
rest, recover
buildup
Waxing Moon

24 **Friday**
Arbor Day

No meat. Cutting and filing toenails and fingernails.

6:06 PM PDT
8:06 PM CDT
9:06 PM EDT
♌ → ♍

25 **Saturday**

A P R I L

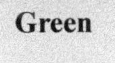
Color
Green

Day
Warm

Element
Fire

Leo
♌

Success

Good time for details, organization, routine, concentration, and duty.

Take care of financial and administrative tasks.

Prepare for future success now with realistic and critical assessment.

Leisure

Enjoy a nature walk.

Good time for health regimes. Improve your health with stretching exercises and yoga.

The earth feels cold to the touch, so take slightly warmer clothes.

Health

Sensitive body parts:
Digestive Organs, Nerves, Spleen, Pancreas

All measures taken to supply nutrient materials and strengthen the sensitive body parts are very effective.

Healing ointments are easily absorbed.

Sensitive blood circulation.

For a sensitive digestive system, a wholesome diet is recommended.

Dress slightly warmer.

High blood pressure: Avoid salty foods.

Massages, lymphatic therapy, and chiropractic treatment to release blockages.

Body Care

Aromas, scents:
Lavender, Spruce Needles, Sage, Meadow Flowers

Treatments with firming and moisturizing creams are more effective.

Massages that serve to regenerate, and strengthen, perhaps aided with beneficial massage oils.

Correcting and cutting ingrown nails.

Best for haircuts because it retains its shape longer. Perms turn out best. Hair dyes applied now, will look more vibrant.

Garden/Nature

Plant part:
Root

Best for sowing and planting, except lettuce.

Plant trees which are supposed to grow very tall. Plant hedges and bushes that are meant to grow very fast.

Sowing lawns.

Planting and re-potting balcony and indoor plants.

Transplanting.

Trimming and cutting back plants.

Planting cuttings.

Start a compost heap.

Avoid harvesting and storing.

Gather herbs (roots) for digestive organs, pancreas, and nervous complaints.

Housework

Light housework only.

Air rooms only briefly.

Making pickles, preserves, and cheese yields suboptimal results and should be avoided.

Nutrition

Food quality:
Salt

Garlic, carrots, red beets, reddish, rutabaga, sugar beet, celery, potatoes, onions, kohlrabi.

Weight gain: avoid indulging in rich foods. If overweight, eat smaller portions.

Supply nutrient materials to strengthen the body. Focus on foods that contain essential minerals and vitamins.

Stimulants and vitamins are more effective.

Avoid large quantities of salty foods like bacon, ham, salted herring, fatty cheese, and the like. Avoid heavy and greasy foods.

Positive affirmation:
"I trust in the power of my inner joy."

Planting Time
Descending forces!
Sap is drawn downward, enhancing root formation.
Best days for sowing, planting, and transplanting.

gather strength
rest, recover
buildup
Waxing Moon

26 Sunday

27 Monday

Never doubt that a small group of thoughtful, committed, citizens can change the world. Indeed, it is the only thing that ever has.
Margaret Mead

Color
Yellow

Day
Cool

Element
Earth

Virgo

A P R I L

Success

The artistic instinct rules, but so, too, does indecisiveness. The forces swing back and forth until equilibrium is achieved.

It's easy to reach compromises with tactful sensitivity.

A sense of judgment will support legal matters.

Leisure

Pursuit for harmony and cooperativeness supports good times in romance, friendship, and partnership.

Enjoy cultural events. Relax and get pampered with a spa treatment.

Romance can be passionate yet sensitive.

Health

Sensitive body parts:

Hips, Kidneys, Bladder

All measures taken to supply nutrient materials and strengthen the sensitive body parts are very effective.

Healing ointments are easily absorbed.

Sensitive glandular system.

Take special care to keep the area of bladder and kidneys warm.

Apply special exercises for the hip region.

Avoid having any teeth pulled.

Sensitivity to light, bring your sunglasses along.

Body Care

Aromas, scents: Roses, Violets, Daffodils

Treatments with firming and moisturizing creams are more effective.

Massages that serve to regenerate, and strengthen, perhaps aided with beneficial massage oils.

Correcting and cutting ingrown nails.

Hair dyes applied now, will look more vibrant.

Garden/Nature

Plant part:

Flower

Sow plants and vegetables that grow and flourish above ground, specially flowers, and medicinal herbs.

Transplanting.

Trimming and cutting back plants.

Avoid watering plants.

Start a compost heap.

Harvested produce should be consumed as soon as possible.

Gather herbs for kidneys, gall bladder, and hip complaints.

Day off on 4/28.

Housework

Light housework only.

Ventilate rooms thoroughly.

Baking cakes and cookies. Dough rises faster. (Except on New Moon)

Nutrition

Food quality:

Fat

Cauliflower, artichoke, broccoli, sunflower seeds, flax seeds, nuts, rose hip, elder.

Weight gain: avoid indulging in rich foods. If overweight, eat smaller portions.

Supply nutrient materials to strengthen the body. Focus on foods that contain essential minerals and vitamins.

Stimulants and vitamins are more effective.

Pay attention to any particularly tempting foods today: Most likely the "wrong" things taste best.

High cholesterol: eat a low fat diet.

Positive affirmation:
"I trust in the power of my inner joy."

Planting Time
Descending forces! Sap is drawn downward, enhancing root formation. Best days for sowing, planting, and transplanting.

gather strength rest, recover buildup

Waxing Moon

2:04 AM PDT
♍→♎ 4:04 AM CDT
5:04 AM EDT

12:03 PM PDT
2:03 PM CDT ♎→♏
3:03 PM EDT

28 Tuesday

29 Wednesday
No meat.

30 Thursday

A P R I L

There may be times when we are powerless to prevent injustice, but there must never be a time when we fail to protest.
Elie Wiesel

Color

Orange

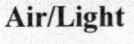
Day

Air/Light

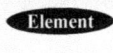
Element

Air

Libra

Success

Critical and superstitious behavior emerges, especially pertaining to money.

A penetrating power will strengthen your capacity to act.

An increased perception opens our interest for the essentials and helps to discover hidden potentials.

Leisure

Relax within your close family, with meditation, and relaxation exercises.

A longing to feel safe will be nurtured if you focus on habits and rituals. An increased sensitivity will help to enjoy every moment.

Romance can be very passionate.

If you plan outdoor excursions, be prepared for a shower here and there.

Health

Sensitive body parts:

Sex organs, Ureter

All measures taken to supply nutrient materials and strengthen the sensitive body parts are very effective.

Healing ointments are easily absorbed. Applying herbal ointments to the shoulders for rheumatic gout and alike.

Sensitive nervous system.

Female disorders: As a preventative measure apply hip baths using yarrow.

Pregnancy: Avoid any exertion, miscarriages are more likely.

Keep region of the pelvis, kidneys, and feet warm to prevent infection of the bladder and kidneys.

Lymphatic therapy.

○ *Full Moon: Avoid any surgery and vaccination if possible.*

Body Care

Aromas, scents:
Anemone, Cornflower
Oregano, Thuja

Treatments with firming and moisturizing creams are more effective.

Massages that serve to regenerate, and strengthen, perhaps aided with beneficial massage oils.

Correcting and cutting ingrown nails.

Hair dyes applied now, will look more vibrant.

Garden/Nature

Plant part:
Leaf

Watering all indoor and outdoor plants.

Sow plants, herbs, and vegetables that grow and flourish above ground, leaf vegetables (no lettuce).

Sowing, planting, harvesting, and drying every kind of medicinal herbs.

Transplanting.

Trimming and cutting back plants.

Combating slugs and snails. Mowing lawns.

Start a compost heap.

Avoid pruning fruit trees and bushes. Avoid cutting down any trees.

Harvested produce should be consumed as soon as possible.

○ *Full Moon: Weather and climate changes. Herbs are most powerful.*

Housework

Light housework only.

Ventilate rooms briefly and rapidly. Don't air mattresses.

○ *Full Moon: Avoid doing laundry, cleaning windows, making preserves, painting.*

Nutrition

Food quality:
Carbohydrate

Lettuce, spinach, lamb's lettuce, Endive, parsley, leek, cabbage (Brussels sprouts, kale, Chinese cabbage), all leafy herbs, asparagus, mushrooms, cress, Swiss chard, rhubarb.

Weight gain: avoid indulging in rich foods. If overweight, eat smaller portions and avoid carbohydrates.

Supply nutrient materials to strengthen the body. Focus on foods that contain essential minerals and vitamins. Stimulants and vitamins are more effective.

○ *Full Moon: A day of fasting.*

Positive affirmation:
"I trust in the power of my inner joy."

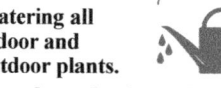

Planting Time
Descending forces!
Sap is drawn downward, enhancing root formation.
Best days for sowing, planting, and transplanting.

gather strength
rest, recover
buildup
Waxing Moon

1 Friday
May Day

○ **Full Moon** 10:24 AM PDT, 12:24 PM CDT, 1:24 PM EDT
No meat. Cutting and filing toenails and fingernails.

Grown-ups never understand anything by themselves, and it is tiresome for children to be always and forever explaining things to them.
Antoine de Saint-Exupéry

Color
Red

Day
Wetness

Element
Water

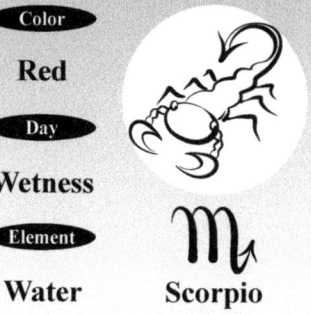

Scorpio

M A Y

Success

Critical and superstitious behavior emerges, especially pertaining to money.

A penetrating power will strengthen your capacity to act.

An increased perception opens our interest for the essentials and helps to discover hidden potentials.

Leisure

Relax within your close family, with meditation, and relaxation exercises.

A longing to feel safe will be nurtured if you focus on habits and rituals. An increased sensitivity will help to enjoy every moment.

Romance can be very passionate.

If you plan outdoor excursions, be prepared for a shower here and there.

Health

Sensitive body parts:
Sex organs, Ureter

All measures taken to flush out and detoxify the sensitive body parts are very effective.

Scarring is less severe.

Teeth: Removal of tartar and amalgam. Best for fillings, crowns, and dentures!

Blood-purifying, detoxifying herbal infusions and teas.

Sensitive nervous system.

Female disorders: As a preventative measure apply hip baths using yarrow.

Pregnancy: Avoid any exertion, miscarriages are more likely.

Keep region of the pelvis, kidneys, and feet warm to prevent infection of the bladder and kidneys.

Lymphatic therapy.

Body Care

Aromas, scents:
Anemone, Cornflower
Oregano, Thuja

Prepare home-made ointments and cosmetics.

Apply detoxing facial and body care.

Treatments of bumps and pimples on the skin, and exfoliating procedures.

Removing body hair.

Correction of the nail bed.

Massages that serve to relax, ease tension, and detoxify.

Reflexology massage.

Removal of callused skin.

Treating obstinate athlete's foot, nail fungus, and warts.

Garden/Nature

Plant part:
Leaf

Water plants.

Fertilize flowers and meadows, no vegetables.

Sow plants and vegetables that grow below ground, leaf vegetables, and lettuce.

Sowing, planting, harvesting, and drying every kind of medicinal herbs.

Dig over/plow to prepare soil for planting.

Trimming and cutting back plants. Transplanting. Weeding. Pest control. Start a compost heap.

Mowing lawns.

Harvested produce should be consumed as soon as possible.

Avoid cutting down trees, danger of bark beetles.

Housework

Housework is dealt with much more successfully, efficiently, and effortlessly.

Problem stains are removed readily.

Best for doing laundry! Reduce on laundry detergent, support the environment.

Dry cleaning.

Thoroughly clean wooden and parquet floors, metals, china etc.

Cleaning, polishing, and waterproofing shoes.

Combating mold.

Ventilate rooms briefly and rapidly.

Avoid painting.

Nutrition

Food quality:
Carbohydrate

Lettuce, spinach, lamb's lettuce, Endive, parsley, leek, cabbage (Brussels sprouts, kale, Chinese cabbage), all leafy herbs, asparagus, mushrooms, cress, Swiss chard, rhubarb.

Weight associated with overeating is less likely. If underweight, eat larger portions.

Cleansing and detox diets. Fruit and juice days.

Flush out poisons. Treatment for drug abuse.

Develop an attitude of gratitude, and give thanks for everything that happens to you, knowing that every step forward is a step toward achieving something bigger and better than your current situation.
Brian Tracy

Color — **Red**

Day — **Wetness**

Element — **Water**

Scorpio

2 Saturday

M A Y

Planting Time
Descending forces!
Sap is drawn downward, enhancing root formation.
Best days for sowing, planting, and transplanting.

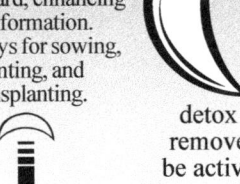

detox
remove
be active

Waning Moon

Success

Inquisitiveness and exuberant inspiration lead to new horizons. Insight and love for truth reign.

Bringing together is more important than splitting asunder.

Expansive forces will assist in legal matters, discussions, and debates.

Leisure

Expansion feels great, and travel, short trips, and outings are most welcome. A competitive spirit excites any sports event.

Talk things out when necessary.

Romance can be very passionate.

Good days for outings; even with cloudy skies the air still feels somewhat warm. Drying effect, get plenty to drink.

Health

Sensitive body parts:

Thighs and Veins

All measures taken to flush out and detoxify the sensitive body parts are very effective.

Good for surgical operations except those on the sensitive body parts (see above), head, and neck. Scarring is less severe.

Teeth: Removal of tartar and amalgam. Best for fillings, crowns, and dentures!

Blood-purifying, detoxifying herbal infusions and tea.

Sensitive sense organs.

Pains often arise in the sciatic nerve, veins, the small of the back, and thighs.

Avoid overstraining the body with unusual physical activities.

Body Care

Aromas, scents: Calendula (Marigold), Geranium, Rosemary

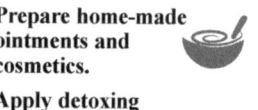

Prepare home-made ointments and cosmetics.

Apply detoxing facial and body care.

Treatments of bumps and pimples on the skin, and exfoliating procedures.

Removing body hair.

Correction of the nail bed.

Massages that serve to relax, ease tension, and detoxify.

Reflexology massage.

Removal of callused skin.

Treating obstinate athlete's foot, nail fungus, and warts.

Garden/Nature

Plant part:

Fruit

Sowing plants and vegetables that grow below ground.

Dig over/plow to prepare soil for planting.

Trimming and cutting back plants.

Pruning of fruit trees and bushes.

Cultivating grains, particularly corn.

Fertilize grains, vegetables, and fruit.

Combating pests above ground.

Weeding.

Gather herbs (roots) for vein diseases.

Avoid hoeing and harrowing.

Start a compost heap.

Housework

Housework is dealt with much more successfully, efficiently, and effortlessly.

Problem stains are removed readily.

Best for doing laundry!

Dry cleaning.

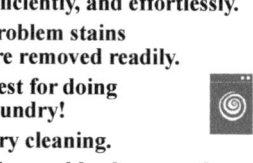

Thoroughly clean wooden and parquet floors, metals, china, etc.

Cleaning windows and glass.

Cleaning, polishing, and waterproofing shoes.

Combating mold.

Ventilate rooms sufficiently. Air beds.

Suitable for making cheese.

Preserving and freezing fruit and vegetables.

Baking bread, cakes, and cookies (use more leavening agent).

Painting.

Nutrition

Food quality:

Protein

Beans, peas, corn, tomatoes, pumpkin, lentils, soybeans, cucumber, eggplant, zucchini, berries, fruit, chili, bell pepper, figs, avocado, melon, olives.

Weight associated with overeating is less likely. If underweight, eat larger portions.

Cleansing and detox diets. Fruit and juice days.

Flush out poisons. Treatment for drug abuse.

A man is not called wise because he talks and talks again; but if he is peaceful, loving and fearless then he is in truth called wise.
Gautama Buddha

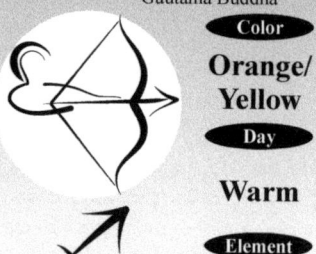

Color

Orange/ Yellow

Day

Warm

Element

Sagittarius   **Fire**

♏ ➔ ♐ 11:35 PM PDT Saturday
1:35 AM CDT
2:35 AM EDT

3 Sunday	**4** Monday	**5** Tuesday — Cinco de Mayo (US)

12:07 PM PDT
2:07 PM CDT ➔ ♐ ➔ ♑
3:07 PM EDT

M A Y

Positive affirmation:
"I trust in the power of my inner joy."

Turning Point

Transition of descending to ascending forces. Both forces are at work and neutralize each other.

⬆⬇

detox remove be active

Waning Moon

Success

Career and business are in the foreground now and thinking becomes clear and serious, but somewhat inflexible.

Perseverance and reasoning assist in financial matters, planning, and contracts.

The values of tradition, authority, and discipline impact our endeavors.

Leisure

Money is not likely to be wasted in a shopping spree.

Many are drawn to enjoy cultural events.

The earth feels cold to the touch, so take slightly warmer clothes.

Health

Sensitive body parts:
Knees, Joints, Bones, Skin

All measures taken to flush out and detoxify the sensitive body parts are very effective.

Good for surgery, except on the sensitive body parts (see above), head, and neck. Scarring is less severe.

Teeth: Removal of tartar and amalgam. Best for fillings, crowns, and dentures!

Blood-purifying, detoxifying herbal infusions and teas.

Sensitive blood circulation.

Avoid overstraining bones and knees, and apply gentle stretching exercises only.

Problems with meniscus: Don't overstrain.

Dress slightly warmer.

High blood pressure: Avoid salty foods.

Massages, lymphatic therapy, and chiropractic treatment to release blockages.

Body Care

Aromas, scents:
Cedar, Juniper

Prepare home-made ointments and cosmetics.

Apply detoxing facial and body care.

Treatments of bumps and pimples on the skin, and exfoliating procedures.

Remove body hair, it may not grow back.

Correction of the nail bed.

Massages that serve to relax, ease tension, and detoxify.

Reflexology massage.

Treating obstinate athlete's foot, nail fungus, and warts.

Cutting and filing toenails and fingernails will make the nails grow stronger over time.

Garden/Nature

Plant part:
Root

Sowing and planting root vegetables and winter vegetables

Weeding. Harrowing weeds. Dig over to prepare soil. Trimming and cutting back plants.
Clear and thin out plants, forest edges, and hedges.
Plant cuttings.
Spread fertilizer and manure.
Start a compost heap.
Combat vermin.

Fertilize flowers with poorly formed roots.

Mulching.

Harvest produce is suitable for storage. Harvest root vegetables.

Gather herbs (roots) for bone, joint, and skin diseases.

Housework

Housework is dealt with much more successfully, efficiently, and effortlessly.
Problem stains are removed readily.

Best for doing laundry! Reduce on laundry detergent, support the environment.

Avoid dry cleaning, as the fabric may develop unwanted glossy blotches.

Thoroughly clean wooden and parquet floors, metals, china etc.

Cleaning, polishing, and waterproofing shoes.

Combating mold.

Air rooms only briefly.

Painting.

Preserving root vegetables. Slice cabbage now to ferment into sauerkraut.

Nutrition

Food quality:
Salt

Garlic, carrots, red beets, reddish, rutabaga, sugar beet, celery, potatoes, onions, kohlrabi.

Weight associated with overeating is less likely. If underweight, eat larger portions.

Cleansing and detox diets. Fruit and juice days.

Flush out poisons. Treatment for drug abuse.

Avoid large quantities of salty foods like bacon, ham, salted herring, fatty cheese, and the like. Avoid heavy and greasy foods.

Healthy citizens are the greatest asset any country can have.
Winston Churchill

- Color
Yellow

- Day

Cool

- Element

Capricorn　　**Earth**

6 Wednesday

No meat.

7 Thursday
National Day of Prayer (US)

M A Y

Harvest Time
Ascending forces! Sap is rising, enhancing plant growth above ground, resulting in the most juicy fruits and vegetables.

detox
remove
be active

Waning Moon

Success

Inspiration, optimism, and impatience. Rational thinking, creativity and imagination spark new ideas and inspire planning for the future.

Shying away from routine tasks people will feel more drawn to anything new.

Instead of gridlocked structures choose new possibilities.

Leisure

Inspiration and optimism will boost friendship, social gatherings, and parties.

Express your creativity and imagination. Dwell in dreams and utopian ideas. It is easier now to perceive intuitive thoughts.

Health

Sensitive body parts:

Lower Legs, Veins

All measures taken to flush out and detoxify the sensitive body parts are very effective.

Good for surgery, except on the sensitive body parts (see above), head, and neck. Scarring is less severe.

Teeth: Removal of tartar and amalgam. Best for fillings, crowns, and dentures!

Blood-purifying, detoxifying herbal infusions and teas.

Sensitive glandular system.

Avoid inflammation of the veins. Apply ointments to lower legs, and rest legs in a raised position.

Varicose veins: Avoid long periods of standing.

While exercising go easy on the ankles.

Sensitivity to light, so bring your sunglasses along.

Body Care

Aromas, scents: Cyclamen, Peach, Wild Roses

Prepare home-made ointments and cosmetics.

Apply detoxing facial and body care.

Treatments of bumps and pimples on the skin, and exfoliating procedures.

Removing body hair.

Correction of the nail bed.

Massages that serve to relax, ease tension, and detoxify.

Reflexology massage.

Removal of callused skin.

Treating obstinate athlete's foot, nail fungus, and warts.

Garden/Nature

Plant part:

Flower

Fertilize flowers that no longer bloom.

Dig over/plow to prepare soil for planting.

Trimming and cutting back plants.

Hoeing and harrowing; weeds can be left to rot.

Pest control.

Start a compost heap.

Avoid watering plants.

Avoid transplanting sprouts.

Harvested produce is well suitable for storage.

Gather herbs (roots) for vein diseases.

Housework

Housework is dealt with much more successfully, efficiently, and effortlessly.

Problem stains are removed readily.

Best for doing laundry! Reduce on laundry detergent, support the environment.

Dry cleaning.

Clean and store seasonal clothing.

Best suited for a spring cleaning: Thoroughly clean wooden and parquet floors, metals, china etc.

Cleaning windows and glass.

Cleaning, polishing, and waterproofing shoes.

Combating mold.

Ventilate rooms thoroughly.

Baking bread, cakes, and cookies (add more leavening agent).

Making preserves.

Painting.

Nutrition

Food quality:

Fat

Cauliflower, artichoke, broccoli, sunflower seeds, flax seeds, nuts, rose hip, elder.

Weight associated with overeating is less likely. If underweight, eat larger portions.

Cleansing and detox diets. Fruit and juice days.

Flush out poisons. Treatment for drug abuse.

Pay attention to any particularly tempting foods today: Most likely the "wrong" things taste best.

High cholesterol: eat a low fat diet.

Wisdom is knowing I am nothing, love is knowing I am everything, and between the two my life moves.
Sri Nisargadatta Maharaj

Color
Bright/ Dark Blue

Day
Air/Light

Element

Aquarius   **Air**

12:29 AM PDT
2:29 AM CDT
3:29 AM EDT

10:41 AM PDT
12:41 PM CDT
1:41 PM EDT

8 Friday

No meat. Cutting and filing toenails and fingernails.

9 Saturday

☽ Half Moon.

10 Sunday
Mother's Day

M A Y

Positive affirmation:
"I trust in the power of my inner joy."

Harvest Time
Ascending forces! Sap is rising, enhancing plant growth above ground, resulting in the most juicy fruits and vegetables.

detox
remove
be active

Waning Moon

Success

Sensibility, intuition, and helpfulness.

Where possible, retreating is more favorable than dealing with business matters.

Dissolve restrictions, be patient and wait. Be aware that people can be more easily influenced.

Leisure

Your helpfulness will boost friendships.

Enjoy dancing or swimming, or watch a movie that will inspire your fantasies and imagination.

Retreat, relax, and recover.

Romance can be gentle and coziness will prevail.

If you plan outdoor excursions, be prepared for a shower here and there.

Health

Sensitive body parts:

Feet and Toes

All measures taken to flush out and detoxify the sensitive body parts are very effective.

Good for surgical operations except those on the sensitive body parts (see above), head, and neck.
Scarring is less severe.

Teeth: Removal of tartar and amalgam. Best for fillings, crowns, and dentures!

Blood-purifying, detoxifying herbal infusions and teas.

Sensitive nervous system.

Drugs have a much stronger effect on your body.
Monitor closely what you put into your body.

Lymphatic therapy.

Sluggishness or fatigue may occur in the transition into the next Zodiac sign of Aries.

Body Care

Aromas, scents:
Magnolia, Amaryllis, Clary Sage

Prepare home-made ointments and cosmetics.

Apply detoxing facial and body care.

Treatments of bumps and pimples on the skin, and exfoliating procedures.

Removing body hair.

Correction of the nail bed.

Massages that serve to relax, ease tension, and detoxify. Reflexology massage. Carry out with special care, people are more sensitive.

Removal of callused skin.

Treating obstinate athlete's foot, nail fungus, and warts.

Foot bath.

No haircuts, hair becomes shaggy and unmanageable.
Avoid washing your hair.

Garden/Nature

Plant part:

Leaf

Water plants.

Fertilize flowers.

Sow plants and vegetables that grow below ground, potatoes, leaf vegetables, and lettuce.

Dig over/plow to prepare soil for planting.
Trimming and cutting back plants.
Start a compost heap.

Mowing lawns.

Pest control. Weeding.

Harvested produce should be consumed as soon as possible.

Gather herbs for foot complaints.

Housework

Housework is dealt with much more successfully, efficiently, and effortlessly.

Problem stains are removed readily.

Best for doing laundry! Reduce on laundry detergent, support the environment.

Dry cleaning.

Clean and store seasonal clothing.

Thoroughly clean wooden and parquet floors, metals, china etc.

Cleaning, polishing, and waterproofing shoes.

Combating mold.

Ventilate rooms briefly and rapidly.

Avoid painting.

Preserving and storing should be avoided.

Nutrition

Food quality:

Carbohydrate

Lettuce, spinach, lamb's lettuce, Endive, parsley, leek, cabbage (Brussels sprouts, kale, Chinese cabbage), all leafy herbs, asparagus, mushrooms, cress, Swiss chard, rhubarb.

Weight associated with overeating is less likely. If underweight, eat larger portions.

Cleansing and detox diets. Fruit and juice days.

Flush out poisons. Treatment for drug abuse.

Caffeine, alcohol, drugs, certain foods, and stimulants have a much stronger effect.

Examine thyself without pity, then thou wilt be more charitable and pitiful to others.
Sri Aurobindo

Pisces

- Color: **Blueish White**
- Day: **Wetness**
- Element: **Water**

5:05 PM PDT
7:05 PM CDT
8:05 PM EDT
♓ → ♈

11 Monday

12 Tuesday

M A Y

Positive affirmation:
"I trust in the power of my inner joy."

Harvest Time
Ascending forces! Sap is rising, enhancing plant growth above ground, resulting in the most juicy fruits and vegetables.

detox
remove
be active

Waning Moon

Success

Things get going and the way straight ahead seems the best.

People feel energetic, courageous, assertive, and at times anxious.

Good time for meetings and sales talks but impatience and selfishness do not favor teamwork.

Leisure

An enterprising spirit and spontaneity move people to enjoy outings, sports, competitions, cultural events, and travels.

Romance can be very passionate.

Good days for outings, even with cloudy skies the air still feels somewhat warm. Drying effect, get plenty to drink.

Health

Sensitive body parts:

Head, Brain, Eyes

All measures taken to flush out and detoxify the sensitive body parts are very effective.

Good for surgery, except on the sensitive body parts (see above), and neck.

Scarring is less severe.

Teeth: Removal of tartar and amalgam. Best for fillings, crowns, and dentures! Avoiding treatment of periodontitis and gums.

Blood-purifying, detoxifying herbal infusions and teas.

Sensitive sense organs.

If you suffer from migraines drink plenty of water, and avoid coffee, chocolate, and sugar.

Body Care

Aromas, scents: Cloves, Peppermint, Thyme

Prepare home-made ointments and cosmetics.

Apply detoxing facial and body care.

Treatments of bumps and pimples on the skin, and exfoliating procedures.

Removing body hair.

Correction of the nail bed.

Massages that serve to relax, ease tension, and detoxify.

Reflexology massage.

Removal of callused skin.

Treating obstinate athlete's foot, nail fungus, and warts.

Eye compresses to relieve strained eyes.

Any kind of hair care.

Garden/Nature

Plant part:

Fruit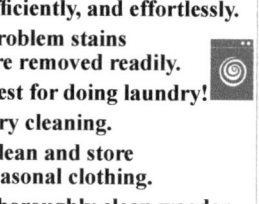

Sowing plants and vegetables that grow below ground.

Sowing and planting anything that is supposed to grow fast. Sowing and planting fruit and tomatoes.

Dig over/plow the soil to prepare for planting.

Spreading manure. Fertilizing grains, vegetables, and fruit.

Weeding. Pest control.

Pruning of fruit trees and bushes.

Harvesting and storing grains, vegetables, potatoes, fruits, and tomatoes.

Start a compost heap.

Gather herbs (roots) for eye complaints and headaches.

Day off on 5/13.

Housework

Housework is dealt with much more successfully, efficiently, and effortlessly.

Problem stains are removed readily.

Best for doing laundry!

Dry cleaning.

Clean and store seasonal clothing.

Thoroughly clean wooden and parquet floors, metals, china, etc.

Cleaning windows and glass.

Cleaning, polishing, and waterproofing shoes.

Combating mold.

Ventilate rooms sufficiently. Air beds.

Suitable for making cheese.

Preserving and freezing fruit and vegetables.

Baking bread, cakes, and cookies (use more leavening agent).

Painting.

Nutrition

Food quality:

Protein

Beans, peas, corn, tomatoes, pumpkin, lentils, soybeans, cucumber, eggplant, zucchini, berries, fruit, chili, bell pepper, figs, avocado, melon, olives.

Weight associated with overeating is less likely. If underweight, eat larger portions.

Cleansing and detox diets. Fruit and juice days.

Flush out poisons. Treatment for drug abuse.

Drink plenty of water.

Whether you live to be 50 or 100 makes no difference, if you made no difference in the world.
Jarod Kintz

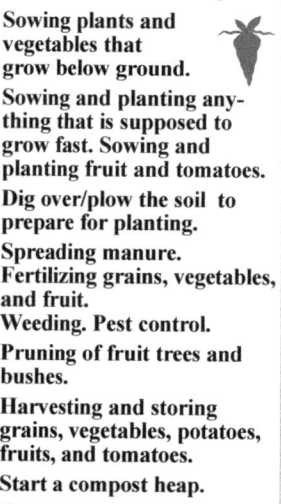

Indigo Blue — Color

Warm — Day

Fire — Element

Aries

7:32 PM PDT
9:32 PM CDT
10:32 PM EDT
♈ ➤ ♉

13 Wednesday
No meat.

14 Thursday
Ascension Day

Harvest Time
Ascending forces! Sap is rising, enhancing plant growth above ground, resulting in the most juicy fruits and vegetables.

detox remove be active

Waning Moon

M A Y

Success

Realism and material security are important. Persistence comes easy, thoughts and reactions are slower.

Assess financial areas.

Conservative tendencies may make people want to stay away from risk taking.

● ***New Moon:* *Confirm your resolutions. Finalize new decisions. Drop bad habits.***

Leisure

Relax at a picnic/feast. Enjoy culinary pleasures and hobbies.

The earth feels cold to the touch, so take slightly warmer clothes.

Health

Sensitive body parts:

Head and Neck

All measures taken to flush out and detoxify the sensitive body parts are very effective.

Scarring is less severe.

Teeth: Removal of tartar and amalgam. Best for fillings, crowns, and dentures! Avoiding treatment of periodontitis and gums.

Blood-purifying, detoxifying herbal infusions and teas.

Sensitive blood circulation.

Organs of speech, jaws, teeth, tonsils, thyroid gland, neck, and vocal chords get easily affected. Keep neck warm. On cold days ears should be protected. Sensitivity to noise.

High blood pressure: Avoid salty foods.

Massages, lymphatic therapy, and chiropractic treatment to release blockages.

● ***New Moon:* *Avoid any surgery if possible.***

Body Care

Aromas, scents: Geranium, Jasmine, Rose

Prepare home-made ointments and cosmetics.

Apply detoxing facial and body care.

Treatments of bumps and pimples on the skin, and exfoliating procedures.

Removing body hair.

Correction of the nail bed.

Massages that serve to relax, ease tension, and detoxify.

Reflexology massage.

Removal of callused skin.

Treating obstinate athlete's foot, nail fungus, and warts.

Garden/Nature

Plant part:

Root

Sow plants and vegetables that grow below ground.

Everything grows slowly and lasts well.

Dig over to prepare soil.

Trimming/cutting back plants. Weeding. Mulching.

Start a compost heap.

Combat vermin found in the soil.

Spread fertilizer and liquid manure.

Fertilize flowers with poorly formed roots.

Harvested produce is well suited for storage. Harvesting root vegetables.

Gather herbs (roots) for sinus issues, sore throat, and ear complaints.

● ***New Moon:* *Change of weather is likely. Care for sickly plants.***

Housework

Housework is dealt with much more successfully, efficiently, and effortlessly.

Problem stains are removed readily.

Best for doing laundry! Reduce on laundry detergent, support the environment.

Dry cleaning.

Clean and store seasonal clothing.

Thoroughly clean wooden and parquet floors, metals, china etc.

Cleaning, polishing, and waterproofing shoes.

Combating mold.

Air rooms only briefly.

Painting.

Preserving root vegetables.

Nutrition

Food quality:

Salt

Garlic, carrots, red beets, reddish, rutabaga, sugar beet, celery, potatoes, onions, kohlrabi.

Weight associated with overeating is less likely. If underweight, eat larger portions.

Cleansing and detox diets. Fruit and juice days.

Flush out poisons. Treatment for drug abuse.

Avoid large quantities of salty foods like bacon, ham, salted herring, fatty cheese, and the like.

● ***New Moon:* *A day of fasting.***

The slope contains many wonders not found at the summit.
Marty Rubin

♉ **Taurus**

Color: **Bright Blue**

Day: **Cool**

Element: **Earth**

7:24 PM PDT
9:24 PM CDT
10:24 PM EDT
♉ → ♊

15 Friday

No meat. Cutting and filing toenails and fingernails.

16 Saturday
Armed Forces Day (US)

● **New Moon** 1:02 PM PDT
3:02 PM CDT, 4:02 PM EDT

M A Y

Positive affirmation:
"I trust in the power of my inner joy."

Harvest Time
Ascending forces! Sap is rising, enhancing plant growth above ground, resulting in the most juicy fruits and vegetables.

detox
remove
be active

Waning Moon

Success

Open mindedness and curiosity. A changeable and hectic time.

Good time for talking, negotiating, networking, and exchanging ideas as well as for meetings of a nonbinding nature, conferences, and studies.

Leisure

Good time for family gatherings, parties, and short trips.

People enjoy stimulating their minds with reading and studying. Attending theater performances is a preferred enjoyment. Enhance friendships.

Stretching exercises.

Be prepared for sudden changes in weather or climate.

Health

Sensitive body parts:
Shoulders, Arms, Hands, Lungs

All measures taken to supply nutrient materials and strengthen the sensitive body parts are very effective.

Healing ointments are easily absorbed. Applying herbal ointments to the shoulders for rheumatic gout and alike.

Sensitive glandular system.

Make sure you are dressed warm enough in cool weather.

Exercises for shoulders. Breathing exercises.

Avoid having any teeth pulled.

Sensitivity to light, bring your sunglasses along.

Massages, lymphatic therapy, and chiropractic treatment to release blockages.

Body Care

Aromas, scents: Lavender, Lemon Balm, Magnolia, Verbena

Treatments with firming and moisturizing creams are more effective.

Massages that serve to regenerate, and strengthen, perhaps aided with beneficial massage oils.

Correcting and cutting ingrown nails.

Hair dyes applied now, will look more vibrant.

Garden/Nature

Plant part:
Flower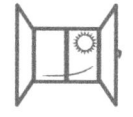

Sow plants, herbs, and vegetables that grow and flourish above ground.

Sowing and planting any creeping or climbing plants, flowers, and medicinal herbs.

Transplanting.

Avoid watering plants.

Gather herbs for tensions in the shoulder and lung complaints.

Changes in weather are more likely.

Housework

Light housework only.

Ventilate rooms thoroughly.

Making preserves.

Baking cakes and cookies. Dough rises faster. (Except on New Moon)

Nutrition

Food quality:
Fat

Cauliflower, artichoke, broccoli, sunflower seeds, flax seeds, nuts, rose hip, elder.

Weight gain: avoid indulging in rich foods. If overweight, eat smaller portions.

Supply nutrient materials to strengthen the body. Focus on foods that contain essential minerals and vitamins.

Stimulants and vitamins are more effective.

Pay attention to any particularly tempting foods today: Most likely the "wrong" things taste best.

High cholesterol: eat a low fat diet.

Positive affirmation:
"I never give up."

Turning Point
Transition of ascending to descending forces. Both forces are at work and neutralize each other.

gather strength rest, recover buildup
Waxing Moon

17 Sunday

18 Monday
Victoria Day (CAN)

6:47 PM PDT
8:47 PM CDT
9:47 PM EDT

Books are the quietest and most constant of friends; they are the most accessible and wisest of counselors, and the most patient of teachers.
Charles William Eliot

Color
Light Blue

Day
Air/Light

Element
Air

Gemini

M A Y

Success

Feelings, sensitivity, and cooperativeness. Many are overly sensitive, so beware of treading on someone's toes.

Be cautious if you are easily influenced.

During negotiations make use of the cognitive ability of your senses.

Leisure

Relax within your close family.

Retreat to your safe haven and enjoy your fantasy while reading or listening to music. The inner world becomes more colorful than the outer.

Romance can be gentle. Deep feelings will prevail.

If you plan outdoor excursions, be prepared for a shower here and there.

Health

Sensitive body parts:
Chest, Lungs, Liver, Stomach, Gall Bladder

All measures taken to supply nutrient materials and strengthen the sensitive body parts are very effective.

Healing ointments are easily absorbed.

Sensitive nervous system.

Be cautious with alcohol since the liver is very sensitive.

Stomach could play up and cause gas and heartburn.

Rheumatism: Don't air bedding outside, damp will remain in the bedding.

Lymphatic therapy.

Body Care

Aromas, scents:
Lilac, Lilies of the Valley, Lilies, Violets

Treatments with firming and moisturizing creams are more effective.

Massages that serve to regenerate, and strengthen, perhaps aided with beneficial massage oils.

Correcting and cutting ingrown nails.

No haircuts, hair becomes shaggy and unmanageable. Avoid washing your hair.

Garden/Nature

Plant part:
Leaf

Watering all indoor and outdoor plants.

Sow plants, herbs, and vegetables that grow and flourish above ground, leaf vegetables (no lettuce).

Transplanting.

Trimming and cutting back plants. Avoid pruning fruit trees and bushes.

Cut trees, garlands, pick flowers to dry; they will last longer.

Sowing and mowing lawns.

Setting up a compost heap.

Gather herbs for bronchitis, stomach, liver, and gall bladder complaints.

Unfavorable for harvesting, storing, and preserving.

Housework

Light housework only.

Ventilate rooms briefly and rapidly. Don't air mattresses.

Any dirt and spots are easily removed in the laundry.

Avoid painting, as paint will take very long to dry.

Nutrition

Food quality:
Carbohydrate

Lettuce, spinach, lamb's lettuce, Endive, parsley, leek, cabbage (Brussels sprouts, kale, Chinese cabbage), all leafy herbs, asparagus, mushrooms, cress, Swiss chard, rhubarb.

Weight gain: avoid indulging in rich foods. If overweight, eat smaller portions and avoid carbohydrates. Moodiness may make you want to eat more than is healthy.

Supply nutrient materials to strengthen the body. Focus on foods that contain essential minerals and vitamins. Stimulants and vitamins are more effective.

If you get stomach troubles easily, avoid heavy meals.

Positive affirmation:
"I never give up."

Planting Time
Descending forces!
Sap is drawn downward, enhancing root formation.
Best days for sowing, planting, and transplanting.

gather strength rest, recover buildup
Waxing Moon

19 Tuesday

20 Wednesday
No meat. .

7:49 PM PDT
9:49 PM CDT
10:49 PM EDT

M A Y

One resolution I have made, and try always to keep, is this: 'To rise above little things'.
John Burroughs

 Color
Green

 Day
Wetness

 Element
Water

Cancer

Success

Determination reigns, and risks are taken more often. Master your tasks with more self-confidence and creativity.

Limits appear to be more easily surmountable.

Auspicious day for sales, advertising, and publicity.

Leisure

Zest for life is in the air. People want to have a fun time, enjoy parties, musical events, movies, etc.

Possessive feelings can harm a relationship. Romance can be very passionate.

Outings: even with cloudy skies the air still feels somewhat warm. Drying effect, get plenty to drink.

Danger of sudden storms, not only in the sky.

Health

Sensitive body parts:
Heart, Back, Diaphragm, Circulation, Arteries

All measures taken to supply nutrient materials and strengthen the sensitive body parts are very effective.

Healing ointments are easily absorbed.

Sensitive sense organs.

Back and heart problems are more likely to occur.

Avoid over straining of the heart and circulation with unusual physical activities.

Expect sleepless nights.

Body Care

Aromas, scents:
Hibiscus, Oleander, Rose

Treatments with firming and moisturizing creams are more effective.

Massages that serve to regenerate, and strengthen, perhaps aided with beneficial massage oils.

Correcting and cutting ingrown nails.

Good days for haircuts, hair becomes stronger. But be aware that if you get a perm, curls will become quite frizzy. Baby's first haircut.

Garden/Nature

Plant part:
Fruit

Sow plants and vegetables that grow and flourish above ground. Sowing and planting fruit. Also sow and plant vegetables that are highly perishable. Plant trees and bushes. Sow lawns.

Transplanting. Grafting onto fruit trees.

Trimming and cutting back plants.

Best for cultivating grains on wet fields.

Dig over/plow to prepare soil for planting.

Setting up a compost heap.

Not suitable for fertilizing.

Harvested produce should be consumed as soon as possible.

Gather herbs for heart and circulation complaints.

Housework

Light housework only.

Ventilate sufficiently.

Freezing fruit and vegetables.

Baking bread, cakes, and cookies. Dough rises faster. (Except on New Moon)

Suitable for making cheese.

Avoid painting.

Nutrition

Food quality:
Protein

Beans, peas, corn, tomatoes, pumpkin, lentils, soybeans, cucumber, eggplant, zucchini, berries, fruit, chili, bell pepper, figs, avocado, melon, olives.

Weight gain: avoid indulging in rich foods. If overweight, eat smaller portions.

Supply nutrient materials to strengthen the body. Focus on foods that contain essential minerals and vitamins.

Stimulants and vitamins are more effective.

Positive affirmation:
"I never give up."

Planting Time
Descending forces!
Sap is drawn downward, enhancing root formation.
Best days for sowing, planting, and transplanting.

gather strength
rest, recover
buildup
Waxing Moon

21 Thursday

22 Friday
Shavuot
No meat. Cutting and filing toenails and fingernails.

We promise according to our hopes and perform according to our fears.
François de La Rochefoucauld

Color
Green

Day
Warm

Element
Fire

Leo

M A Y

Success

Good time for details, organization, routine, concentration, and duty.

Take care of financial and administrative tasks.

Prepare for future success now with realistic and critical assessment.

Leisure

Enjoy a nature walk.

Good time for health regimes. Improve your health with stretching exercises and yoga.

The earth feels cold to the touch, so take slightly warmer clothes.

Health

Sensitive body parts:
Digestive Organs, Nerves, Spleen, Pancreas

All measures taken to supply nutrient materials and strengthen the sensitive body parts are very effective.

Healing ointments are easily absorbed.

Sensitive blood circulation.

For a sensitive digestive system, a wholesome diet is recommended.

Dress slightly warmer.

High blood pressure: Avoid salty foods.

Massages, lymphatic therapy, and chiropractic treatment to release blockages.

Body Care

Aromas, scents:
Lavender, Spruce Needles, Sage, Meadow Flowers

Treatments with firming and moisturizing creams are more effective.

Massages that serve to regenerate, and strengthen, perhaps aided with beneficial massage oils.

Correcting and cutting ingrown nails.

Best for haircuts because it retains its shape longer. Perms turn out best. Hair dyes applied now, will look more vibrant.

Garden/Nature

Plant part:
Root

Best for sowing and planting, except lettuce.

Plant trees which are supposed to grow very tall. Plant hedges and bushes that are meant to grow very fast.

Sowing lawns.

Planting and re-potting balcony and indoor plants.

Transplanting.

Trimming and cutting back plants.

Planting cuttings.

Start a compost heap.

Avoid harvesting and storing.

Gather herbs (roots) for digestive organs, pancreas, and nervous complaints.

Housework

Light housework only.

Air rooms only briefly.

Making pickles, preserves, and cheese yields suboptimal results and should be avoided.

Nutrition

Food quality:
Salt

Garlic, carrots, red beets, reddish, rutabaga, sugar beet, celery, potatoes, onions, kohlrabi.

Weight gain: avoid indulging in rich foods. If overweight, eat smaller portions.

Supply nutrient materials to strengthen the body. Focus on foods that contain essential minerals and vitamins.

Stimulants and vitamins are more effective.

Avoid large quantities of salty foods like bacon, ham, salted herring, fatty cheese, and the like. Avoid heavy and greasy foods.

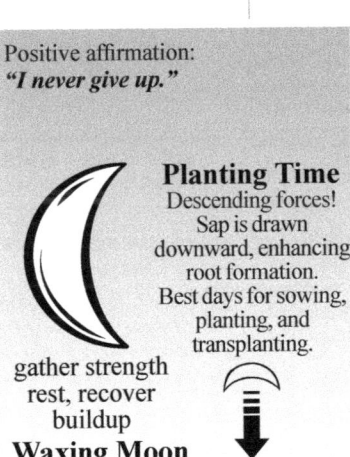

Positive affirmation:
"I never give up."

Planting Time
Descending forces! Sap is drawn downward, enhancing root formation. Best days for sowing, planting, and transplanting.

gather strength
rest, recover
buildup
Waxing Moon

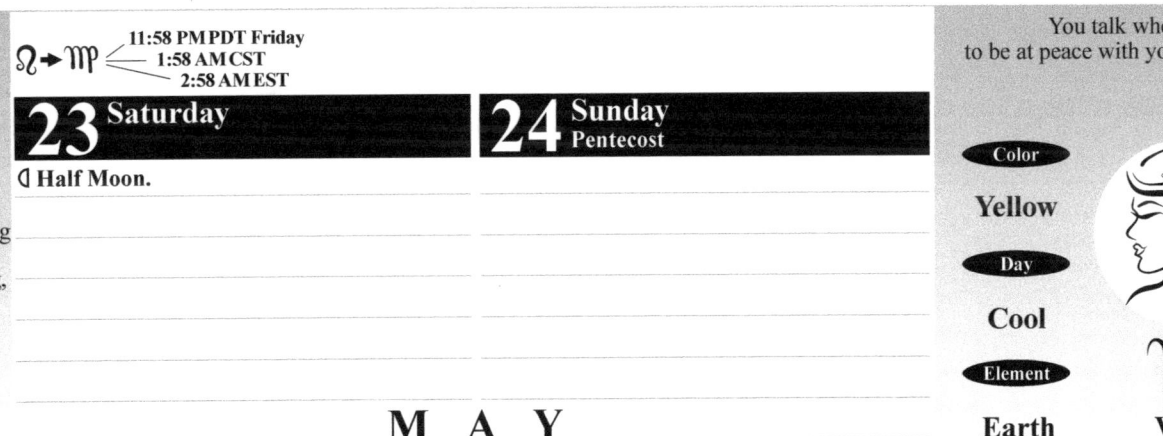

11:58 PM PDT Friday
♌ → ♍ ← 1:58 AM CST
2:58 AM EST

23 Saturday
☽ Half Moon.

24 Sunday
Pentecost

M A Y

You talk when you cease to be at peace with your thoughts.
Kahlil Gibran

Color
Yellow

Day
Cool

Element
Earth

♍ **Virgo**

Success

The artistic instinct rules, but so, too, does indecisiveness. The forces swing back and forth until equilibrium is achieved.

It's easy to reach compromises with tactful sensitivity.

A sense of judgment will support legal matters.

Leisure

Pursuit for harmony and cooperativeness supports good times in romance, friendship, and partner-ship.

Enjoy cultural events. Relax and get pampered with a spa treatment.

Romance can be passionate yet sensitive.

Health

Sensitive body parts:

Hips, Kidneys, Bladder

All measures taken to supply nutrient materials and strengthen the sensitive body parts are very effective.

Healing ointments are easily absorbed.

Sensitive glandular system.

Take special care to keep the area of bladder and kidneys warm.

Apply special exercises for the hip region.

Avoid having any teeth pulled.

Sensitivity to light, bring your sunglasses along.

Body Care

Aromas, scents: Roses, Violets, Daffodils

Treatments with firming and moisturizing creams are more effective.

Massages that serve to regenerate, and strengthen, perhaps aided with beneficial massage oils.

Correcting and cutting ingrown nails.

Hair dyes applied now, will look more vibrant.

Garden/Nature

Plant part:

Flower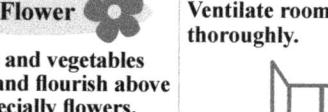

Sow plants and vegetables that grow and flourish above ground, specially flowers, and medicinal herbs.

Transplanting.

Trimming and cutting back plants.

Avoid watering plants.

Start a compost heap.

Harvested produce should be consumed as soon as possible.

Gather herbs for kidneys, gall bladder, and hip complaints.

Day off on 5/26.

Housework

Light housework only.

Ventilate rooms thoroughly.

Baking cakes and cookies. Dough rises faster. (Except on New Moon)

Nutrition

Food quality:

Fat

Cauliflower, artichoke, broccoli, sunflower seeds, flax seeds, nuts, rose hip, elder.

Weight gain: avoid indulging in rich foods. If overweight, eat smaller portions.

Supply nutrient materials to strengthen the body. Focus on foods that contain essential minerals and vitamins.

Stimulants and vitamins are more effective.

Pay attention to any particularly tempting foods today: Most likely the "wrong" things taste best.

High cholesterol: eat a low fat diet.

Positive affirmation:
"I never give up."

Planting Time
Descending forces! Sap is drawn downward, enhancing root formation. Best days for sowing, planting, and transplanting.

gather strength rest, recover buildup
Waxing Moon

♍→♎ 7:35 AM PDT
9:35 AM CDT
10:35 AM EDT

25 Monday
Memorial Day (US)

26 Tuesday

5:54 PM PDT
7:54 PM CDT ♎→♏
8:54 PM EDT

27 Wednesday
Eid al-Adha

No meat.

M A Y

Without deviation from the norm, progress is not possible.
Frank Zappa

Color
Orange

Day
Air/Light

Element
♎

Air   **Libra**

Success

Critical and superstitious behavior emerges, especially pertaining to money.

A penetrating power will strengthen your capacity to act.

An increased perception opens our interest for the essentials and helps to discover hidden potentials.

Leisure

Relax within your close family, with meditation, and relaxation exercises.

A longing to feel safe will be nurtured if you focus on habits and rituals. An increased sensitivity will help to enjoy every moment.

Romance can be very passionate.

If you plan outdoor excursions, be prepared for a shower here and there.

Health

Sensitive body parts:

Sex organs, Ureter

All measures taken to supply nutrient materials and strengthen the sensitive body parts are very effective.

Healing ointments are easily absorbed. Applying herbal ointments to the shoulders for rheumatic gout and alike.

Sensitive nervous system.

Female disorders: As a preventative measure apply hip baths using yarrow.

Pregnancy: Avoid any exertion, miscarriages are more likely.

Keep region of the pelvis, kidneys, and feet warm to prevent infection of the bladder and kidneys.

Lymphatic therapy.

Body Care

Aromas, scents: Anemone, Cornflower Oregano, Thuja

Treatments with firming and moisturizing creams are more effective.

Massages that serve to regenerate, and strengthen, perhaps aided with beneficial massage oils.

Correcting and cutting ingrown nails.

Hair dyes applied now, will look more vibrant.

Garden/Nature

Plant part:

Leaf

Watering all indoor and outdoor plants.

Sow plants, herbs, and vegetables that grow and flourish above ground, leaf vegetables (no lettuce).

Sowing, planting, harvesting, and drying every kind of medicinal herbs.

Transplanting.

Trimming and cutting back plants.
Combating slugs and snails.
Mowing lawns.

Start a compost heap.

Avoid pruning fruit trees and bushes. Avoid cutting down any trees.

Harvested produce should be consumed as soon as possible.

Housework

Light housework only.

Ventilate rooms briefly and rapidly. Don't air mattresses.

Any dirt and spots are easily removed in the laundry.

Avoid painting, as paint will take very long to dry.

Nutrition

Food quality:

Carbohydrate

Lettuce, spinach, lamb's lettuce, Endive, parsley, leek, cabbage (Brussels sprouts, kale, Chinese cabbage), all leafy herbs, asparagus, mushrooms, cress, Swiss chard, rhubarb.

Weight gain: avoid indulging in rich foods. If overweight, eat smaller portions and avoid carbohydrates.

Supply nutrient materials to strengthen the body. Focus on foods that contain essential minerals and vitamins. Stimulants and vitamins are more effective.

Positive affirmation:
"I never give up."

Planting Time
Descending forces!
Sap is drawn downward, enhancing root formation.
Best days for sowing, planting, and transplanting.

gather strength rest, recover buildup

Waxing Moon

28 Thursday

29 Friday

No meat. Cutting and filing toenails and fingernails.

To be beyond good and evil is not to act sin or virtue indifferently, but to arrive at a high and universal good.
Sri Aurobindo

Color
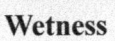
Red

Day

Wetness

Element
Water

Scorpio ♏

M A Y

Success

Inquisitiveness and exuberant inspiration lead to new horizons. Insight and love for truth reign.

Bringing together is more important than splitting asunder.

Expansive forces will assist in legal matters, discussions, and debates.

Leisure

Expansion feels great, and travel, short trips, and outings are most welcome. A competitive spirit excites any sports event.

Talk things out when necessary.

Romance can be very passionate.

Good days for outings; even with cloudy skies the air still feels somewhat warm. Drying effect, get plenty to drink.

Health

Sensitive body parts:

Thighs and Veins

All measures taken to supply nutrient materials and strengthen the sensitive body parts are very effective.

Healing ointments are easily absorbed.

Sensitive sense organs.

Pains often arise in the sciatic nerve, veins, the small of the back, and thighs.

Avoid overstraining the body with unusual physical activities.

Body Care

Aromas, scents: Calendula (Marigold), Geranium, Rosemary

Treatments with firming and moisturizing creams are more effective.

Massages that serve to regenerate, and strengthen, perhaps aided with beneficial massage oils.

Correcting and cutting ingrown nails.

Hair dyes applied now, will look more vibrant.

Garden/Nature

Plant part:

Fruit

Sow plants and vegetables that grow and flourish above ground.

Sowing and planting fruit and vegetables that grow tall, and tomatoes, but no lettuce.

Transplanting.

Grafting onto fruit trees.

Cultivating grains, particularly corn.

Gather herbs for vein diseases.

Housework

Light housework only.

Ventilate sufficiently.

Freezing fruit and vegetables.

Baking bread, cakes, and cookies. Dough rises faster. (Except on New Moon)

Suitable for making cheese.

Making preserves.

Nutrition

Food quality:

Protein

Beans, peas, corn, tomatoes, pumpkin, lentils, soybeans, cucumber, eggplant, zucchini, berries, fruit, chili, bell pepper, figs, avocado, melon, olives.

Weight gain: avoid indulging in rich foods. If overweight, eat smaller portions.

Supply nutrient materials to strengthen the body. Focus on foods that contain essential minerals and vitamins.

Stimulants and vitamins are more effective.

Positive affirmation:
"I never give up."

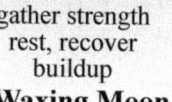

Turning Point
Transition of descending to ascending forces. Both forces are at work and neutralize each other.

gather strength rest, recover buildup
Waxing Moon

♏ → ↗ ⟵ 5:46 AM PDT
7:46 AM CDT
8:46 AM EDT

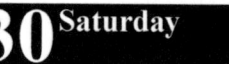

30 Saturday

M A Y

Think left and think right and think low and think high. Oh, the thinks you can think up if only you try!
Dr. Seuss

Color
Orange/ Yellow

Day
Warm

Element
Fire   **Sagittarius**

Success

Inquisitiveness and exuberant inspiration lead to new horizons. Insight and love for truth reign.

Bringing together is more important than splitting asunder.

Expansive forces will assist in legal matters, discussions, and debates.

Leisure

Expansion feels great, and travel, short trips, and outings are most welcome. A competitive spirit excites any sports event.

Talk things out when necessary.

Romance can be very passionate.

Good days for outings; even with cloudy skies the air still feels somewhat warm. Drying effect, get plenty to drink.

Health

Sensitive body parts:

Thighs and Veins

All measures taken to flush out and detoxify the sensitive body parts are very effective.

Scarring is less severe.

Teeth: Removal of tartar and amalgam. Best for fillings, crowns, and dentures!

Blood-purifying, detoxifying herbal infusions and tea.

Sensitive sense organs.

Pains often arise in the sciatic nerve, veins, the small of the back, and thighs.

Avoid overstraining the body with unusual physical activities.

○ *Full Moon: Avoid any surgery and vaccination if possible.*

Body Care

Aromas, scents: Calendula (Marigold), Geranium, Rosemary

Prepare home-made ointments and cosmetics.

Apply detoxing facial and body care.

Treatments of bumps and pimples on the skin, and exfoliating procedures.

Removing body hair.

Correction of the nail bed.

Massages that serve to relax, ease tension, and detoxify.

Reflexology massage.

Removal of callused skin.

Treating obstinate athlete's foot, nail fungus, and warts.

Garden/Nature

Plant part:

Fruit

Sowing plants and vegetables that grow below ground.

Dig over/plow to prepare soil for planting.

Trimming and cutting back plants.

Pruning of fruit trees and bushes.

Cultivating grains, particularly corn.

Fertilize grains, vegetables, and fruit.

Combating pests above ground.

Weeding.

Gather herbs (roots) for vein diseases.

Avoid hoeing and harrowing.

Start a compost heap.

○ *Full Moon: Weather and climate changes. Herbs are most powerful.*

Housework

Housework is dealt with much more successfully, efficiently, and effortlessly.

Problem stains are removed readily.

Dry cleaning.

Thoroughly clean wooden and parquet floors, metals, china, etc.

Cleaning, polishing, and waterproofing shoes.

Combating mold.

Ventilate rooms sufficiently. Air beds.

Suitable for making cheese.

Freezing fruit and vegetables.

Baking bread, cakes, and cookies (use more leavening agent).

○ *Full Moon: Avoid doing laundry, cleaning windows, making preserves, painting.*

Nutrition

Food quality:

Protein

Beans, peas, corn, tomatoes, pumpkin, lentils, soybeans, cucumber, eggplant, zucchini, berries, fruit, chili, bell pepper, figs, avocado, melon, olives.

Weight associated with overeating is less likely. If underweight, eat larger portions.

Cleansing and detox diets. Fruit and juice days.

Flush out poisons. Treatment for drug abuse.

○ *Full Moon: A day of fasting.*

The worst thing: to give yourself away in exchange for not enough love.
Joyce Carol Oates

Sagittarius

Color
Orange/ Yellow

Day
Warm

Element

Fire

6:20 PM PDT
8:20 PM CDT
9:20 PM EDT

31 Sunday

○ **Full Moon** 1:46 AM PDT, 3:46 AM CDT, 4:46 AM EDT

1 Monday

M A Y / J U N E

Positive affirmation:
"I never give up."

Turning Point
Transition of descending to ascending forces. Both forces are at work and neutralize each other.

detox
remove
be active

Waning Moon

Success

Career and business are in the foreground now and thinking becomes clear and serious, but somewhat inflexible.

Perseverance and reasoning assist in financial matters, planning, and contracts.

The values of tradition, authority, and discipline impact our endeavors.

Leisure

Money is not likely to be wasted in a shopping spree.

Many are drawn to enjoy cultural events.

The earth feels cold to the touch, so take slightly warmer clothes.

Health

Sensitive body parts:

Knees, Joints, Bones, Skin

All measures taken to flush out and detoxify the sensitive body parts are very effective.

Good for surgery, except on the sensitive body parts (see above), shoulders, arms, hands, and lungs. Scarring is less severe.

Teeth: Removal of tartar and amalgam. Best for fillings, crowns, and dentures!

Blood-purifying, detoxifying herbal infusions and teas.

Sensitive blood circulation.

Avoid overstraining bones and knees, and apply gentle stretching exercises only.

Problems with meniscus: Don't overstrain.

Dress slightly warmer.

High blood pressure: Avoid salty foods.

Massages, lymphatic therapy, and chiropractic treatment to release blockages.

Body Care

Aromas, scents:

Cedar, Juniper

Prepare home-made ointments and cosmetics.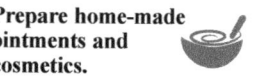

Apply detoxing facial and body care.

Treatments of bumps and pimples on the skin, and exfoliating procedures.

Remove body hair, it may not grow back.

Correction of the nail bed.

Massages that serve to relax, ease tension, and detoxify.

Reflexology massage.

Treating obstinate athlete's foot, nail fungus, and warts.

Cutting and filing toenails and fingernails will make the nails grow stronger over time.

Garden/Nature

Plant part: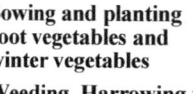

Root

Sowing and planting root vegetables and winter vegetables

Weeding. Harrowing weeds. Dig over to prepare soil. Trimming and cutting back plants. Clear and thin out plants, forest edges, and hedges. Plant cuttings. Spread fertilizer and manure. Start a compost heap. Combat vermin.

Fertilize flowers with poorly formed roots.

Mulching.

Harvest produce is suitable for storage. Harvest root vegetables.

Gather herbs (roots) for bone, joint, and skin diseases.

Housework

Housework is dealt with much more successfully, efficiently, and effortlessly.

Problem stains are removed readily.

Best for doing laundry! Reduce on laundry detergent, support the environment.

Avoid dry cleaning, as the fabric may develop unwanted glossy blotches.

Thoroughly clean wooden and parquet floors, metals, china etc.

Cleaning, polishing, and waterproofing shoes.

Combating mold.

Air rooms only briefly.

Painting.

Preserving root vegetables. Slice cabbage now to ferment into sauerkraut.

Nutrition

Food quality:

Salt

Garlic, carrots, red beets, reddish, rutabaga, sugar beet, celery, potatoes, onions, kohlrabi.

Weight associated with overeating is less likely. If underweight, eat larger portions.

Cleansing and detox diets. Fruit and juice days.

Flush out poisons. Treatment for drug abuse.

Avoid large quantities of salty foods like bacon, ham, salted herring, fatty cheese, and the like. Avoid heavy and greasy foods.

This is a miracle that men can love God, yet fail to love humanity. With whom are they in love then?
Sri Aurobindo

Capricorn

- Color: **Yellow**
- Day: **Cool**
- Element: **Earth**

2 Tuesday

3 Wednesday

No meat.

J U N E

Harvest Time
Ascending forces! Sap is rising, enhancing plant growth above ground, resulting in the most juicy fruits and vegetables.

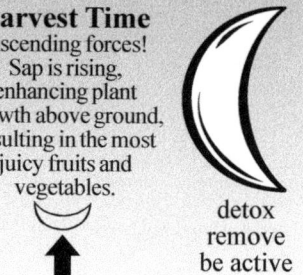

detox
remove
be active

Waning Moon

Success

Inspiration, optimism, and impatience. Rational thinking, creativity and imagination spark new ideas and inspire planning for the future.

Shying away from routine tasks people will feel more drawn to anything new.

Instead of gridlocked structures choose new possibilities.

Leisure

Inspiration and optimism will boost friendship, social gatherings, and parties.

Express your creativity and imagination. Dwell in dreams and utopian ideas. It is easier now to perceive intuitive thoughts.

Health

Sensitive body parts:
Lower Legs, Veins

All measures taken to flush out and detoxify the sensitive body parts are very effective.

Good for surgery, except on the sensitive body parts (see above), shoulders, arms, hands, and lungs. Scarring is less severe.

Teeth: Removal of tartar and amalgam. Best for fillings, crowns, and dentures!

Blood-purifying, detoxifying herbal infusions and teas.

Sensitive glandular system.

Avoid inflammation of the veins. Apply ointments to lower legs, and rest legs in a raised position.

Varicose veins: Avoid long periods of standing.

While exercising go easy on the ankles.

Sensitivity to light, so bring your sunglasses along.

Body Care

Aromas, scents: Cyclamen, Peach, Wild Roses

Prepare home-made ointments and cosmetics.

Apply detoxing facial and body care.

Treatments of bumps and pimples on the skin, and exfoliating procedures.

Removing body hair.

Correction of the nail bed.

Massages that serve to relax, ease tension, and detoxify.

Reflexology massage.

Removal of callused skin.

Treating obstinate athlete's foot, nail fungus, and warts.

Garden/Nature

Plant part:
Flower

Fertilize flowers that no longer bloom.

Dig over/plow to prepare soil for planting.

Trimming and cutting back plants.

Hoeing and harrowing; weeds can be left to rot.

Pest control.

Start a compost heap.

Avoid watering plants.

Avoid transplanting sprouts.

Harvested produce is well suitable for storage.

Gather herbs (roots) for vein diseases.

Housework

Housework is dealt with much more successfully, efficiently, and effortlessly.

Problem stains are removed readily.

Best for doing laundry! Reduce on laundry detergent, support the environment.

Dry cleaning.

Clean and store seasonal clothing.

Best suited for a spring cleaning: Thoroughly clean wooden and parquet floors, metals, china etc.

Cleaning windows and glass.

Cleaning, polishing, and waterproofing shoes.

Combating mold.

Ventilate rooms thoroughly.

Baking bread, cakes, and cookies (add more leavening agent).

Making preserves.

Painting.

Nutrition

Food quality:
Fat

Cauliflower, artichoke, broccoli, sunflower seeds, flax seeds, nuts, rose hip, elder.

Weight associated with overeating is less likely. If underweight, eat larger portions.

Cleansing and detox diets. Fruit and juice days.

Flush out poisons. Treatment for drug abuse.

Pay attention to any particularly tempting foods today: Most likely the "wrong" things taste best.

High cholesterol: eat a low fat diet.

Keep me away from the wisdom which does not cry, the philosophy which does not laugh and the greatness which does not bow before children.
Kahlil Gibran

Color
Bright/ Dark Blue

Day

Air/Light

Element

Aquarius   **Air**

6:47 AM PDT
8:47 AM CDT
9:47 AM EDT

4	**Thursday** Corpus Christi

5	**Friday**

No meat. Cutting and filing toenails and fingernails.

5:44 PM PDT
7:44 PM CDT
8:44 PM EDT

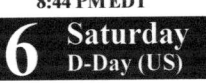

6	**Saturday** D-Day (US)

J U N E

Positive affirmation:
"I never give up."

Harvest Time
Ascending forces! Sap is rising, enhancing plant growth above ground, resulting in the most juicy fruits and vegetables.

detox remove be active

Waning Moon

Success

Sensibility, intuition, and helpfulness.

Where possible, retreating is more favorable than dealing with business matters.

Dissolve restrictions, be patient and wait. Be aware that people can be more easily influenced.

Leisure

Your helpfulness will boost friendships.

Enjoy dancing or swimming, or watch a movie that will inspire your fantasies and imagination.

Retreat, relax, and recover.

Romance can be gentle and coziness will prevail.

If you plan outdoor excursions, be prepared for a shower here and there.

Health

Sensitive body parts:

Feet and Toes

All measures taken to flush out and detoxify the sensitive body parts are very effective.

Good for surgical operations except those on the sensitive body parts (see above), shoulders, arms, hands, and lungs.
Scarring is less severe.

Teeth: Removal of tartar and amalgam. Best for fillings, crowns, and dentures!

Blood-purifying, detoxifying herbal infusions and teas.

Sensitive nervous system.

Drugs have a much stronger effect on your body.
Monitor closely what you put into your body.

Lymphatic therapy.

Sluggishness or fatigue may occur in the transition into the next Zodiac sign of Aries.

Body Care

Aromas, scents:
Magnolia, Amaryllis, Clary Sage

Prepare home-made ointments and cosmetics.

Apply detoxing facial and body care.

Treatments of bumps and pimples on the skin, and exfoliating procedures.

Removing body hair.

Correction of the nail bed.

Massages that serve to relax, ease tension, and detoxify. Reflexology massage. Carry out with special care, people are more sensitive.

Removal of callused skin.

Treating obstinate athlete's foot, nail fungus, and warts.

Foot bath.

No haircuts, hair becomes shaggy and unmanageable.
Avoid washing your hair.

Garden/Nature

Plant part:

Leaf

Water plants.

Fertilize flowers.

Sow plants and vegetables that grow below ground, potatoes, leaf vegetables, and lettuce.

Dig over/plow to prepare soil for planting.
Trimming and cutting back plants.
Start a compost heap.

Mowing lawns.

Pest control. Weeding.

Harvested produce should be consumed as soon as possible.

Gather herbs for foot complaints.

Housework

Housework is dealt with much more successfully, efficiently, and effortlessly.

Problem stains are removed readily.

Best for doing laundry! Reduce on laundry detergent, support the environment.

Dry cleaning.

Clean and store seasonal clothing.

Thoroughly clean wooden and parquet floors, metals, china etc.

Cleaning, polishing, and waterproofing shoes.

Combating mold.

Ventilate rooms briefly and rapidly.

Avoid painting.

Preserving and storing should be avoided.

Nutrition

Food quality:

Carbohydrate

Lettuce, spinach, lamb's lettuce, Endive, parsley, leek, cabbage (Brussels sprouts, kale, Chinese cabbage), all leafy herbs, asparagus, mushrooms, cress, Swiss chard, rhubarb.

Weight associated with overeating is less likely. If underweight, eat larger portions.

Cleansing and detox diets. Fruit and juice days.

Flush out poisons. Treatment for drug abuse.

Caffeine, alcohol, drugs, certain foods, and stimulants have a much stronger effect.

There are some experiences in life they haven't invented the right words for.
Lisa Kleypas

Color
Blueish White

Day
Wetness

Element
Water

Pisces

7 Sunday

8 Monday

☾ Half Moon.

J U N E

Positive affirmation:
"I never give up."

Harvest Time
Ascending forces! Sap is rising, enhancing plant growth above ground, resulting in the most juicy fruits and vegetables.

detox
remove
be active
Waning Moon

Success

Things get going and the way straight ahead seems the best.

People feel energetic, courageous, assertive, and at times anxious.

Good time for meetings and sales talks but impatience and selfishness do not favor teamwork.

Leisure

An enterprising spirit and spontaneity move people to enjoy outings, sports, competitions, cultural events, and travels.

Romance can be very passionate.

Good days for outings, even with cloudy skies the air still feels somewhat warm. Drying effect, get plenty to drink.

Health

Sensitive body parts:

Head, Brain, Eyes

All measures taken to flush out and detoxify the sensitive body parts are very effective.

Good for surgery, except on the sensitive body parts (see above), shoulders, arms, hands, and lungs.

Scarring is less severe.

Teeth: Removal of tartar and amalgam. Best for fillings, crowns, and dentures! Avoiding treatment of periodontitis and gums.

Blood-purifying, detoxifying herbal infusions and teas.

Sensitive sense organs.

If you suffer from migraines drink plenty of water, and avoid coffee, chocolate, and sugar.

Body Care

Aromas, scents:
Cloves, Peppermint, Thyme

Prepare home-made ointments and cosmetics.

Apply detoxing facial and body care.

Treatments of bumps and pimples on the skin, and exfoliating procedures.

Removing body hair.

Correction of the nail bed.

Massages that serve to relax, ease tension, and detoxify.

Reflexology massage.

Removal of callused skin.

Treating obstinate athlete's foot, nail fungus, and warts.

Eye compresses to relieve strained eyes.

Any kind of hair care.

Garden/Nature

Plant part:
Fruit

Sowing plants and vegetables that grow below ground.

Sowing and planting anything that is supposed to grow fast. Sowing and planting fruit and tomatoes.

Dig over/plow the soil to prepare for planting.

Spreading manure. Fertilizing grains, vegetables, and fruit.
Weeding. Pest control.

Pruning of fruit trees and bushes.

Harvesting and storing grains, vegetables, potatoes, fruits, and tomatoes.

Start a compost heap.

Gather herbs (roots) for eye complaints and headaches.

Day off on 6/9.

Housework

Housework is dealt with much more successfully, efficiently, and effortlessly.

Problem stains are removed readily.

Best for doing laundry!

Dry cleaning.

Clean and store seasonal clothing.

Thoroughly clean wooden and parquet floors, metals, china, etc.

Cleaning windows and glass.

Cleaning, polishing, and waterproofing shoes.

Combating mold.

Ventilate rooms sufficiently.
Air beds.

Suitable for making cheese.

Preserving and freezing fruit and vegetables.

Baking bread, cakes, and cookies (use more leavening agent).

Painting.

Nutrition

Food quality:
Protein

Beans, peas, corn, tomatoes, pumpkin, lentils, soybeans, cucumber, eggplant, zucchini, berries, fruit, chili, bell pepper, figs, avocado, melon, olives.

Weight associated with overeating is less likely. If underweight, eat larger portions.

Cleansing and detox diets. Fruit and juice days.

Flush out poisons. Treatment for drug abuse.

Drink plenty of water.

That which yields is not always weak.
Jacqueline Carey

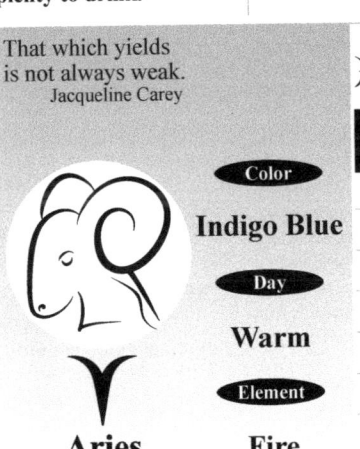

Color
Indigo Blue

Day
Warm

Element

Aries Fire

♓ → ♈ ← 1:35 AM PDT
3:35 AM CDT
4:35 AM EDT

9 Tuesday

10 Wednesday
No meat.

J U N E

Positive affirmation:
"I never give up."

Harvest Time
Ascending forces! Sap is rising, enhancing plant growth above ground, resulting in the most juicy fruits and vegetables.

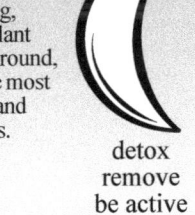

detox
remove
be active

Waning Moon

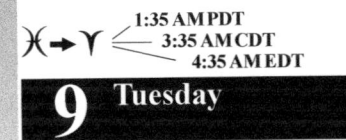

Success

Realism and material security are important. Persistence comes easy, thoughts and reactions are slower.

Assess financial areas.

Conservative tendencies may make people want to stay away from risk taking.

Leisure

Relax at a picnic/feast. Enjoy culinary pleasures and hobbies.

The earth feels cold to the touch, so take slightly warmer clothes.

Health

Sensitive body parts:
Head and Neck

All measures taken to flush out and detoxify the sensitive body parts are very effective.
Good for surgery, except on the sensitive body parts (see above), shoulders, arms, hands, and lungs.
Scarring is less severe.
Teeth: Removal of tartar and amalgam. Best for fillings, crowns, and dentures!
Avoiding treatment of periodontitis and gums.
Blood-purifying, detoxifying herbal infusions and teas.
Sensitive blood circulation.
Organs of speech, jaws, teeth, tonsils, thyroid gland, neck, and vocal chords get easily affected. Keep neck warm. On cold days ears should be protected. Sensitivity to noise.
High blood pressure: Avoid salty foods.
Massages, lymphatic therapy, and chiropractic treatment to release blockages.

Body Care

Aromas, scents: Geranium, Jasmine, Rose

Prepare home-made ointments and cosmetics.

Apply detoxing facial and body care.

Treatments of bumps and pimples on the skin, and exfoliating procedures.

Removing body hair.

Correction of the nail bed.

Massages that serve to relax, ease tension, and detoxify.

Reflexology massage.

Removal of callused skin.

Treating obstinate athlete's foot, nail fungus, and warts.

Garden/Nature

Plant part:
Root

Sow plants and vegetables that grow below ground.

Everything grows slowly and lasts well.

Dig over to prepare soil.

Trimming/cutting back plants. Weeding. Mulching.

Start a compost heap.

Combat vermin found in the soil.

Spread fertilizer and liquid manure.

Fertilize flowers with poorly formed roots.

Harvested produce is well suited for storage.
Harvesting root vegetables.

Gather herbs (roots) for sinus issues, sore throat, and ear complaints.

Housework

Housework is dealt with much more successfully, efficiently, and effortlessly.

Problem stains are removed readily.

Best for doing laundry! Reduce on laundry detergent, support the environment.

Dry cleaning.

Clean and store seasonal clothing.

Thoroughly clean wooden and parquet floors, metals, china etc.

Cleaning, polishing, and waterproofing shoes.

Combating mold.

Air rooms only briefly.

Painting.

Preserving root vegetables.

Nutrition

Food quality:
Salt

Garlic, carrots, red beets, reddish, rutabaga, sugar beet, celery, potatoes, onions, kohlrabi.

Weight associated with overeating is less likely. If underweight, eat larger portions.

Cleansing and detox diets. Fruit and juice days.

Flush out poisons. Treatment for drug abuse.

Avoid large quantities of salty foods like bacon, ham, salted herring, fatty cheese, and the like.

I did not attend his funeral, but I sent a nice letter saying I approved of it.
Mark Twain

Color
Bright Blue

Day
Cool

Element
Earth

Taurus

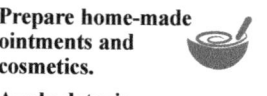
♈ → ♉
5:29 AM PDT
7:29 AM CDT
8:29 AM EDT

11 Thursday

12 Friday
No meat. Cutting and filing toenails and fingernails.

J U N E

Positive affirmation:
"I never give up."

Harvest Time
Ascending forces! Sap is rising, enhancing plant growth above ground, resulting in the most juicy fruits and vegetables.

detox
remove
be active

Waning Moon

Success

Open mindedness and curiosity. A changeable and hectic time.

Good time for talking, negotiating, networking, and exchanging ideas as well as for meetings of a nonbinding nature, conferences, and studies.

● *New Moon: Confirm your resolutions. Finalize new decisions. Drop bad habits.*

Leisure

Good time for family gatherings, parties, and short trips.

People enjoy stimulating their minds with reading and studying. Attending theater performances is a preferred enjoyment. Enhance friendships.

Stretching exercises.

Be prepared for sudden changes in weather or climate.

Health

Sensitive body parts:
Shoulders, Arms, Hands, Lungs

All measures taken to flush out and detoxify the sensitive body parts are very effective.

Scarring is less severe.

Teeth: Removal of tartar and amalgam. Best for fillings, crowns, and dentures! Avoid having any teeth pulled.

Blood-purifying, detoxifying herbal infusions and teas.

Sensitive glandular system.

Make sure you are dressed warm enough in cool weather.

Exercises for shoulders. Breathing exercises.

Sensitivity to light, bring your sunglasses along.

Massages, lymphatic therapy, and chiropractic treatment to release blockages.

● *New Moon: Avoid any surgery if possible.*

Body Care

Aromas, scents:
Lavender, Lemon Balm, Magnolia, Verbena

Prepare home-made ointments and cosmetics.

Apply detoxing facial and body care.

Treatments of bumps and pimples on the skin, and exfoliating procedures.

Removing body hair.

Correction of the nail bed.

Massages that serve to relax, ease tension, and detoxify.

Reflexology massage.

Removal of callused skin.

Treating obstinate athlete's foot, nail fungus, and warts.

Garden/Nature

Plant part:
Flower

Sow plants and vegetables that grow below ground.

Trimming and cutting back plants.

Start a compost heap.

Weeding. Pest control.

Fertilize flowers that no longer bloom.

Avoid watering plants.

Changes in weather are more likely.

Gather herbs (roots) for tensions in the shoulder and lung complaints.

● *New Moon: Change of weather is likely. Care for sickly plants.*

Housework

Housework is dealt with much more successfully, efficiently, and effortlessly.

Problem stains are removed readily.

Best for doing laundry! Reduce on laundry detergent, support the environment.

Dry cleaning.

Clean and store seasonal clothing.

Thoroughly clean wooden and parquet floors, metals, china etc.

Cleaning windows and glass.

Cleaning, polishing, and waterproofing shoes.

Combating mold.

Ventilate rooms thoroughly.

Baking bread, cakes, and cookies (add more leavening agent).

Making preserves.

Painting.

Nutrition

Food quality:
Fat

Cauliflower, artichoke, broccoli, sunflower seeds, flax seeds, nuts, rose hip, elder.

Weight associated with overeating is less likely. If underweight, eat larger portions.

Cleansing and detox diets. Fruit and juice days.

Flush out poisons. Treatment for drug abuse.

Pay attention to any particularly tempting foods today: Most likely the "wrong" things taste best.

High cholesterol: eat a low fat diet.

● *New Moon: A day of fasting.*

If you can't do anything about it, laugh like hell.
David Cook

Color
Light Blue

Day
Air/Light

Element

Gemini **Air**

♂ → ♊ ← 6:07 AM PDT
8:07 AM CDT
9:07 AM EDT

13 Saturday

14 Sunday
Flag Day (US)
● New Moon 7:55 PM PDT, 9:55 PM CDT, 10:55 PM EDT

J U N E

Positive affirmation:
"I never give up."

Turning Point
Transition of ascending to descending forces. Both forces are at work and neutralize each other.

detox
remove
be active
Waning Moon

Success

Feelings, sensitivity, and cooperativeness. Many are overly sensitive, so beware of treading on someone's toes.

Be cautious if you are easily influenced.

During negotiations make use of the cognitive ability of your senses.

Leisure

Relax within your close family.

Retreat to your safe haven and enjoy your fantasy while reading or listening to music. The inner world becomes more colorful than the outer.

Romance can be gentle. Deep feelings will prevail.

If you plan outdoor excursions, be prepared for a shower here and there.

Health

Sensitive body parts:

Chest, Lungs, Liver, Stomach, Gall Bladder

All measures taken to supply nutrient materials and strengthen the sensitive body parts are very effective.

Healing ointments are easily absorbed.

Sensitive nervous system.

Be cautious with alcohol since the liver is very sensitive.

Stomach could play up and cause gas and heartburn.

Rheumatism: Don't air bedding outside, damp will remain in the bedding.

Lymphatic therapy.

Body Care

Aromas, scents:
Lilac, Lilies of the Valley, Lilies, Violets

Treatments with firming and moisturizing creams are more effective.

Massages that serve to regenerate, and strengthen, perhaps aided with beneficial massage oils.

Correcting and cutting ingrown nails.

No haircuts, hair becomes shaggy and unmanageable. Avoid washing your hair.

Garden/Nature

Plant part:

Leaf

Watering all indoor and outdoor plants.

Sow plants, herbs, and vegetables that grow and flourish above ground, leaf vegetables (no lettuce).

Transplanting.

Trimming and cutting back plants. Avoid pruning fruit trees and bushes.

Cut trees, garlands, pick flowers to dry; they will last longer.

Sowing and mowing lawns.

Setting up a compost heap.

Gather herbs for bronchitis, stomach, liver, and gall bladder complaints.

Unfavorable for harvesting, storing, and preserving.

Housework

Light housework only.

Ventilate rooms briefly and rapidly. Don't air mattresses.

Any dirt and spots are easily removed in the laundry.

Avoid painting, as paint will take very long to dry.

Nutrition

Food quality:

Carbohydrate

Lettuce, spinach, lamb's lettuce, Endive, parsley, leek, cabbage (Brussels sprouts, kale, Chinese cabbage), all leafy herbs, asparagus, mushrooms, cress, Swiss chard, rhubarb.

Weight gain: avoid indulging in rich foods. If overweight, eat smaller portions and avoid carbohydrates. Moodiness may make you want to eat more than is healthy.

Supply nutrient materials to strengthen the body. Focus on foods that contain essential minerals and vitamins. Stimulants and vitamins are more effective.

If you get stomach troubles easily, avoid heavy meals.

Positive affirmation:
"My love is universal."

Planting Time
Descending forces!
Sap is drawn downward, enhancing root formation. Best days for sowing, planting, and transplanting.

gather strength
rest, recover
buildup
Waxing Moon

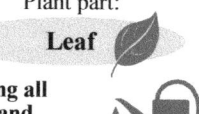

5:15 AM PDT
7:15 AM CDT
8:15 AM EDT

15 Monday

16 Tuesday

J U N E

If we will be quiet and ready enough, we shall find compensation in every disapointment.
Henry David Thoreau

Color
Green

Day
Wetness

Element
Water

Cancer

Success

Determination reigns, and risks are taken more often. Master your tasks with more self-confidence and creativity.

Limits appear to be more easily surmountable.

Auspicious day for sales, advertising, and publicity.

Leisure

Zest for life is in the air. People want to have a fun time, enjoy parties, musical events, movies, etc.

Possessive feelings can harm a relationship. Romance can be very passionate.

Outings: even with cloudy skies the air still feels somewhat warm. Drying effect, get plenty to drink.

Danger of sudden storms, not only in the sky.

Health

Sensitive body parts:
Heart, Back, Diaphragm, Circulation, Arteries

All measures taken to supply nutrient materials and strengthen the sensitive body parts are very effective.

Healing ointments are easily absorbed.

Sensitive sense organs.

Back and heart problems are more likely to occur.

Avoid over straining of the heart and circulation with unusual physical activities.

Expect sleepless nights.

Body Care

Aromas, scents:
Hibiscus,
Oleander, Rose

Treatments with firming and moisturizing creams are more effective.

Massages that serve to regenerate, and strengthen, perhaps aided with beneficial massage oils.

Correcting and cutting ingrown nails.

Good days for haircuts, hair becomes stronger. But be aware that if you get a perm, curls will become quite frizzy.
Baby's first haircut.

Garden/Nature

Plant part:
Fruit

Sow plants and vegetables that grow and flourish above ground. Sowing and planting fruit. Also sow and plant vegetables that are highly perishable. Plant trees and bushes. Sow lawns.

Transplanting. Grafting onto fruit trees.

Trimming and cutting back plants.

Best for cultivating grains on wet fields.

Dig over/plow to prepare soil for planting.

Setting up a compost heap.

Not suitable for fertilizing.

Harvested produce should be consumed as soon as possible.

Gather herbs for heart and circulation complaints.

Weeding on 6/18 before noon will help prevent weeds from growing back.

Housework

Light housework only.

Ventilate sufficiently.

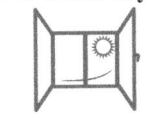

Freezing fruit and vegetables.

Baking bread, cakes, and cookies. Dough rises faster. (Except on New Moon)

Suitable for making cheese.

Avoid painting.

Nutrition

Food quality:
Protein

Beans, peas, corn, tomatoes, pumpkin, lentils, soybeans, cucumber, eggplant, zucchini, berries, fruit, chili, bell pepper, figs, avocado, melon, olives.

Weight gain: avoid indulging in rich foods. If overweight, eat smaller portions.

Supply nutrient materials to strengthen the body. Focus on foods that contain essential minerals and vitamins.

Stimulants and vitamins are more effective.

Positive affirmation:
"My love is universal."

Planting Time
Descending forces! Sap is drawn downward, enhancing root formation. Best days for sowing, planting, and transplanting.

gather strength rest, recover buildup
Waxing Moon

♋ → ♌ 5:06 PM PDT
7:06 AM CDT
8:06 AM EDT

17 Wednesday
Muharram

No meat.

18 Thursday

J U N E

Everything is relative in this world, where change alone endures.
Leon Trotsky

Color
Green

Day
Warm

Element
Fire

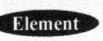

♌
Leo

Success

Good time for details, organization, routine, concentration, and duty.

Take care of financial and administrative tasks.

Prepare for future success now with realistic and critical assessment.

Leisure

Enjoy a nature walk.

Good time for health regimes. Improve your health with stretching exercises and yoga.

The earth feels cold to the touch, so take slightly warmer clothes.

Health

Sensitive body parts:
Digestive Organs, Nerves, Spleen, Pancreas

All measures taken to supply nutrient materials and strengthen the sensitive body parts are very effective.

Healing ointments are easily absorbed.

Sensitive blood circulation.

For a sensitive digestive system, a wholesome diet is recommended.

Dress slightly warmer.

High blood pressure: Avoid salty foods.

Massages, lymphatic therapy, and chiropractic treatment to release blockages.

Body Care

Aromas, scents: Lavender, Spruce Needles, Sage, Meadow Flowers

Treatments with firming and moisturizing creams are more effective.

Massages that serve to regenerate, and strengthen, perhaps aided with beneficial massage oils.

Correcting and cutting ingrown nails.

Best for haircuts because it retains its shape longer. Perms turn out best. Hair dyes applied now, will look more vibrant.

Garden/Nature

Plant part:
Root

Best for sowing and planting, except lettuce.

Plant trees which are supposed to grow very tall. Plant hedges and bushes that are meant to grow very fast.

Sowing lawns.

Planting and re-potting balcony and indoor plants.

Transplanting.

Trimming and cutting back plants.

Planting cuttings.

Start a compost heap.

Avoid harvesting and storing.

Gather herbs (roots) for digestive organs, pancreas, and nervous complaints.

Housework

Light housework only.

Air rooms only briefly.

Making pickles, preserves, and cheese yields suboptimal results and should be avoided.

Nutrition

Food quality:
Salt

Garlic, carrots, red beets, reddish, rutabaga, sugar beet, celery, potatoes, onions, kohlrabi.

Weight gain: avoid indulging in rich foods. If overweight, eat smaller portions.

Supply nutrient materials to strengthen the body. Focus on foods that contain essential minerals and vitamins.

Stimulants and vitamins are more effective.

Avoid large quantities of salty foods like bacon, ham, salted herring, fatty cheese, and the like. Avoid heavy and greasy foods.

Positive affirmation:
"My love is universal."

Planting Time
Descending forces! Sap is drawn downward, enhancing root formation. Best days for sowing, planting, and transplanting.

gather strength
rest, recover
buildup
Waxing Moon

Ω → ♍ 7:38 AM PDT
9:38 AM CDT
10:38 AM EDT

1:56 PM PDT
3:56 PM CDT   ♍ → Ω
4:56 PM EDT

19 Friday
Juneteenth (US)
No meat. Cutting and filing toenails and fingernails.

20 Saturday

21 Sunday Father's Day, Summer Solstice
National Indigenous Peoples Day
☽ Half Moon.

We all give up great expectations along the way.
Carlos Ruiz Zafón

Color
Yellow

Day
Cool

Element
Earth

♍
Virgo

J U N E

Success

The artistic instinct rules, but so, too, does indecisiveness. The forces swing back and forth until equilibrium is achieved.

It's easy to reach compromises with tactful sensitivity.

A sense of judgment will support legal matters.

Leisure

Pursuit for harmony and cooperativeness supports good times in romance, friendship, and partnership.

Enjoy cultural events. Relax and get pampered with a spa treatment.

Romance can be passionate yet sensitive.

Health

Sensitive body parts:

Hips, Kidneys, Bladder

All measures taken to supply nutrient materials and strengthen the sensitive body parts are very effective.

Healing ointments are easily absorbed.

Sensitive glandular system.

Take special care to keep the area of bladder and kidneys warm.

Apply special exercises for the hip region.

Avoid having any teeth pulled.

Sensitivity to light, bring your sunglasses along.

Body Care

Aromas, scents: Roses, Violets, Daffodils

Treatments with firming and moisturizing creams are more effective.

Massages that serve to regenerate, and strengthen, perhaps aided with beneficial massage oils.

Correcting and cutting ingrown nails.

Hair dyes applied now, will look more vibrant.

Garden/Nature

Plant part:

Flower

Sow plants and vegetables that grow and flourish above ground, specially flowers, and medicinal herbs.

Transplanting.

Trimming and cutting back plants.

Avoid watering plants.

Start a compost heap.

Harvested produce should be consumed as soon as possible.

Gather herbs for kidneys, gall bladder, and hip complaints.

Day off on 6/22.

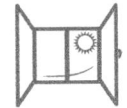

Housework

Light housework only.

Ventilate rooms thoroughly.

Baking cakes and cookies. Dough rises faster. (Except on New Moon)

Nutrition

Food quality:

Fat

Cauliflower, artichoke, broccoli, sunflower seeds, flax seeds, nuts, rose hip, elder.

Weight gain: avoid indulging in rich foods. If overweight, eat smaller portions.

Supply nutrient materials to strengthen the body. Focus on foods that contain essential minerals and vitamins.

Stimulants and vitamins are more effective.

Pay attention to any particularly tempting foods today: Most likely the "wrong" things taste best.

High cholesterol: eat a low fat diet.

Positive affirmation:
"My love is universal."

Planting Time
Descending forces! Sap is drawn downward, enhancing root formation. Best days for sowing, planting, and transplanting.

gather strength rest, recover buildup
Waxing Moon

22 Monday

23 Tuesday

J U N E

The easy confidence with which I know another man's religion is folly teaches me to suspect that my own is also.
Mark Twain

Color
Orange

Day
Air/Light

Element
Air

Libra

Success

Critical and superstitious behavior emerges, especially pertaining to money.

A penetrating power will strengthen your capacity to act.

An increased perception opens our interest for the essentials and helps to discover hidden potentials.

Leisure

Relax within your close family, with meditation, and relaxation exercises.

A longing to feel safe will be nurtured if you focus on habits and rituals. An increased sensitivity will help to enjoy every moment.

Romance can be very passionate.

If you plan outdoor excursions, be prepared for a shower here and there.

Health

Sensitive body parts:

Sex organs, Ureter

All measures taken to supply nutrient materials and strengthen the sensitive body parts are very effective.

Healing ointments are easily absorbed. Applying herbal ointments to the shoulders for rheumatic gout and alike.

Sensitive nervous system.

Female disorders: As a preventative measure apply hip baths using yarrow.

Pregnancy: Avoid any exertion, miscarriages are more likely.

Keep region of the pelvis, kidneys, and feet warm to prevent infection of the bladder and kidneys.

Lymphatic therapy.

Body Care

Aromas, scents:
Anemone, Cornflower
Oregano, Thuja

Treatments with firming and moisturizing creams are more effective.

Massages that serve to regenerate, and strengthen, perhaps aided with beneficial massage oils.

Correcting and cutting ingrown nails.

Hair dyes applied now, will look more vibrant.

Garden/Nature

Plant part:

Leaf

Watering all indoor and outdoor plants.

Sow plants, herbs, and vegetables that grow and flourish above ground, leaf vegetables (no lettuce).

Sowing, planting, harvesting, and drying every kind of medicinal herbs.

Transplanting.

Trimming and cutting back plants.
Combating slugs and snails.
Mowing lawns.

Start a compost heap.

Avoid pruning fruit trees and bushes. Avoid cutting down any trees.

Harvested produce should be consumed as soon as possible.

Housework

Light housework only.

Ventilate rooms briefly and rapidly. Don't air mattresses.

Any dirt and spots are easily removed in the laundry.

Avoid painting, as paint will take very long to dry.

Nutrition

Food quality:

Carbohydrate

Lettuce, spinach, lamb's lettuce, Endive, parsley, leek, cabbage (Brussels sprouts, kale, Chinese cabbage), all leafy herbs, asparagus, mushrooms, cress, Swiss chard, rhubarb.

Weight gain: avoid indulging in rich foods. If overweight, eat smaller portions and avoid carbohydrates.

Supply nutrient materials to strengthen the body. Focus on foods that contain essential minerals and vitamins. Stimulants and vitamins are more effective.

Positive affirmation:
"My love is universal."

Planting Time
Descending forces!
Sap is drawn downward, enhancing root formation.
Best days for sowing, planting, and transplanting.

gather strength
rest, recover
buildup
Waxing Moon

♎ → ♏ 11:44 PM PDT Tuesday
1:44 AM CDT
2:44 AM EDT

24 Wednesday
No meat.

25 Thursday

11:42 AM PDT
1:42 PM CDT ♏ → ♐
2:42 PM EDT

26 Friday
Ashura
No meat. Cutting and filing toenails and fingernails.

J U N E

Color
Red

Day

Wetness

Element

Water

♏ Scorpio

Success

Inquisitiveness and exuberant inspiration lead to new horizons. Insight and love for truth reign.

Bringing together is more important than splitting asunder.

Expansive forces will assist in legal matters, discussions, and debates.

Leisure

Expansion feels great, and travel, short trips, and outings are most welcome. A competitive spirit excites any sports event.

Talk things out when necessary.

Romance can be very passionate.

Good days for outings; even with cloudy skies the air still feels somewhat warm. Drying effect, get plenty to drink.

Health

Sensitive body parts:

Thighs and Veins

All measures taken to supply nutrient materials and strengthen the sensitive body parts are very effective.

Healing ointments are easily absorbed.

Sensitive sense organs.

Pains often arise in the sciatic nerve, veins, the small of the back, and thighs.

Avoid overstraining the body with unusual physical activities.

Body Care

Aromas, scents: Calendula (Marigold), Geranium, Rosemary

Treatments with firming and moisturizing creams are more effective.

Massages that serve to regenerate, and strengthen, perhaps aided with beneficial massage oils.

Correcting and cutting ingrown nails.

Hair dyes applied now, will look more vibrant.

Garden/Nature

Plant part:

Fruit

Sow plants and vegetables that grow and flourish above ground.

Sowing and planting fruit and vegetables that grow tall, and tomatoes, but no lettuce.

Transplanting.

Grafting onto fruit trees.

Cultivating grains, particularly corn.

Gather herbs for vein diseases.

Housework

Light housework only.

Ventilate sufficiently.

Freezing fruit and vegetables.

Baking bread, cakes, and cookies. Dough rises faster. (Except on New Moon)

Suitable for making cheese.

Making preserves.

Nutrition

Food quality:

Protein

Beans, peas, corn, tomatoes, pumpkin, lentils, soybeans, cucumber, eggplant, zucchini, berries, fruit, chili, bell pepper, figs, avocado, melon, olives.

Weight gain: avoid indulging in rich foods. If overweight, eat smaller portions.

Supply nutrient materials to strengthen the body. Focus on foods that contain essential minerals and vitamins.

Stimulants and vitamins are more effective.

Positive affirmation:
"My love is universal."

Turning Point

Transition of descending to ascending forces. Both forces are at work and neutralize each other.

gather strength rest, recover buildup

Waxing Moon

27 Saturday

28 Sunday

J U N E

I count him braver who overcomes his desires than him who overcomes his enemies.
Aristotle

Color
Orange/ Yellow

Day
Warm

Element
Fire

Sagittarius

Success

Career and business are in the foreground now and thinking becomes clear and serious, but somewhat inflexible.

Perseverance and reasoning assist in financial matters, planning, and contracts.

The values of tradition, authority, and discipline impact our endeavors.

Leisure

Money is not likely to be wasted in a shopping spree.

Many are drawn to enjoy cultural events.

The earth feels cold to the touch, so take slightly warmer clothes.

Health

Sensitive body parts:

Knees, Joints, Bones, Skin

All measures taken to supply nutrient materials and strengthen the sensitive body parts are very effective.

Healing ointments are easily absorbed.

Sensitive blood circulation.

Avoid overstraining bones and knees, and apply gentle stretching exercises only.

Problems with meniscus: Don't overstrain.

Dress slightly warmer.

High blood pressure: Avoid salty foods.

Massages, lymphatic therapy, and chiropractic treatment to release blockages.

○ *Full Moon: Avoid any surgery and vaccination if possible.*

Body Care

Aromas, scents:

Cedar, Juniper

Treatments with firming and moisturizing creams are more effective.

Massages that serve to regenerate, and strengthen, perhaps aided with beneficial massage oils.

Correcting and cutting ingrown nails.

Every kind of skin care is beneficial.

Cutting and filing toenails and fingernails will make the nails grow stronger over time.

Hair dyes applied now, will look more vibrant.

Garden/Nature

Plant part: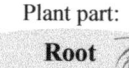

Root

Sow plants, herbs, and vegetables that grow and flourish above ground.

Transplanting.

Harvest produce is suitable for storage. Harvest root vegetables.

Gather herbs for bone, joint, and skin diseases.

○ *Full Moon: Weather and climate changes. Herbs are most powerful.*

Discover more about the lunar cycle and it's effects in the reference book "Nature's Daily Guide". ISBN 978-0-9854637-8-6

Housework

Light housework only.

Air rooms only briefly.

Preserving root vegetables.

Avoid dry cleaning, as the fabric may develop unwanted glossy blotches.

○ *Full Moon: Avoid doing laundry, cleaning windows, making preserves, painting.*

Nutrition

Food quality:

Salt

Garlic, carrots, red beets, reddish, rutabaga, sugar beet, celery, potatoes, onions, kohlrabi.

Weight gain: avoid indulging in rich foods. If overweight, eat smaller portions.

Supply nutrient materials to strengthen the body. Focus on foods that contain essential minerals and vitamins.

Stimulants and vitamins are more effective.

Avoid large quantities of salty foods like bacon, ham, salted herring, fatty cheese, and the like. Avoid heavy and greasy foods.

○ *Full Moon: A day of fasting.*

Positive affirmation:
"My love is universal."

Harvest Time
Ascending forces! Sap is rising, enhancing plant growth above ground, resulting in the most juicy fruits and vegetables.

No meat.

gather strength rest, recover buildup
Waxing Moon

12:20 AM PDT
2:20 AM CDT
3:20 AM EDT

29 Monday

○ **Full Moon** 4:58 PM PDT, 6:58 PM CDT, 7:58 PM EDT

J U N E

We are addicted to our thoughts. We cannot change anything if we cannot change our thinking.
Santosh Kalwar

Color
Yellow

Day
Cool

Element
Earth   **Capricorn**

Success

Career and business are in the foreground now and thinking becomes clear and serious, but somewhat inflexible.

Perseverance and reasoning assist in financial matters, planning, and contracts.

The values of tradition, authority, and discipline impact our endeavors.

Leisure

Money is not likely to be wasted in a shopping spree.

Many are drawn to enjoy cultural events.

The earth feels cold to the touch, so take slightly warmer clothes.

Health

Sensitive body parts:
Knees, Joints, Bones, Skin

All measures taken to flush out and detoxify the sensitive body parts are very effective.

Good for surgery, except on the sensitive body parts (see above), chest, stomach, liver, and gallbladder. Scarring is less severe.

Teeth: Removal of tartar and amalgam. Best for fillings, crowns, and dentures!

Blood-purifying, detoxifying herbal infusions and teas.

Sensitive blood circulation.

Avoid overstraining bones and knees, and apply gentle stretching exercises only.

Problems with meniscus: Don't overstrain.

Dress slightly warmer.

High blood pressure: Avoid salty foods.

Massages, lymphatic therapy, and chiropractic treatment to release blockages.

Body Care

Aromas, scents:
Cedar, Juniper

Prepare home-made ointments and cosmetics.

Apply detoxing facial and body care.

Treatments of bumps and pimples on the skin, and exfoliating procedures.

Remove body hair, it may not grow back.

Correction of the nail bed.

Massages that serve to relax, ease tension, and detoxify.

Reflexology massage.

Treating obstinate athlete's foot, nail fungus, and warts.

Cutting and filing toenails and fingernails will make the nails grow stronger over time.

Garden/Nature

Plant part:
Root

Sowing and planting root vegetables and winter vegetables

Weeding. Harrowing weeds. Dig over to prepare soil. Trimming and cutting back plants. Clear and thin out plants, forest edges, and hedges. Plant cuttings. Spread fertilizer and manure. Start a compost heap. Combat vermin.

Fertilize flowers with poorly formed roots.

Mulching.

Harvest produce is suitable for storage. Harvest root vegetables.

Gather herbs (roots) for bone, joint, and skin diseases.

Housework

Housework is dealt with much more successfully, efficiently, and effortlessly.

Problem stains are removed readily.

Best for doing laundry! Reduce on laundry detergent, support the environment.

Avoid dry cleaning, as the fabric may develop unwanted glossy blotches.

Thoroughly clean wooden and parquet floors, metals, china etc.

Cleaning, polishing, and waterproofing shoes.

Combating mold.

Air rooms only briefly.

Painting.

Preserving root vegetables. Slice cabbage now to ferment into sauerkraut.

Nutrition

Food quality:
Salt

Garlic, carrots, red beets, reddish, rutabaga, sugar beet, celery, potatoes, onions, kohlrabi.

Weight associated with overeating is less likely. If underweight, eat larger portions.

Cleansing and detox diets. Fruit and juice days.

Flush out poisons. Treatment for drug abuse.

Avoid large quantities of salty foods like bacon, ham, salted herring, fatty cheese, and the like. Avoid heavy and greasy foods.

What great thing would you attempt if you knew you could not fail?
Robert H. Schuller

Color

Yellow

Day

Cool

Element

Capricorn   **Earth**

30 Tuesday

1 Wednesday
Canada Day (CAN)

No meat.

10:34 AM PST
12:34 PM CST
1:34 PM EST

J U N E / J U L Y

Harvest Time
Ascending forces! Sap is rising, enhancing plant growth above ground, resulting in the most juicy fruits and vegetables.

detox
remove
be active

Waning Moon

Success

Inspiration, optimism, and impatience. Rational thinking, creativity and imagination spark new ideas and inspire planning for the future.

Shying away from routine tasks people will feel more drawn to anything new.

Instead of gridlocked structures choose new possibilities.

Leisure

Inspiration and optimism will boost friendship, social gatherings, and parties.

Express your creativity and imagination. Dwell in dreams and utopian ideas. It is easier now to perceive intuitive thoughts.

Health

Sensitive body parts:
Lower Legs, Veins

All measures taken to flush out and detoxify the sensitive body parts are very effective.

Good for surgery, except on the sensitive body parts (see above), chest, lungs, stomach, liver, and gallbladder. Scarring is less severe.

Teeth: Removal of tartar and amalgam. Best for fillings, crowns, and dentures!

Blood-purifying, detoxifying herbal infusions and teas.

Sensitive glandular system.

Avoid inflammation of the veins. Apply ointments to lower legs, and rest legs in a raised position.

Varicose veins: Avoid long periods of standing.

While exercising go easy on the ankles.

Sensitivity to light, so bring your sunglasses along.

Body Care

Aromas, scents:
Cyclamen, Peach, Wild Roses

Prepare home-made ointments and cosmetics.

Apply detoxing facial and body care.

Treatments of bumps and pimples on the skin, and exfoliating procedures.

Removing body hair.

Correction of the nail bed.

Massages that serve to relax, ease tension, and detoxify.

Reflexology massage.

Removal of callused skin.

Treating obstinate athlete's foot, nail fungus, and warts.

Garden/Nature

Plant part:
Flower

Fertilize flowers that no longer bloom.

Dig over/plow to prepare soil for planting.

Trimming and cutting back plants.

Hoeing and harrowing; weeds can be left to rot.

Pest control.

Start a compost heap.

Avoid watering plants.

Avoid transplanting sprouts.

Harvested produce is well suitable for storage.

Gather herbs (roots) for vein diseases.

Housework

Housework is dealt with much more successfully, efficiently, and effortlessly.

Problem stains are removed readily.

Best for doing laundry! Reduce on laundry detergent, support the environment.

Dry cleaning.

Clean and store seasonal clothing.

Best suited for a spring cleaning: Thoroughly clean wooden and parquet floors, metals, china etc.

Cleaning windows and glass.

Cleaning, polishing, and waterproofing shoes.

Combating mold.

Ventilate rooms thoroughly.

Baking bread, cakes, and cookies (add more leavening agent).

Making preserves.

Painting.

Nutrition

Food quality:
Fat

Cauliflower, artichoke, broccoli, sunflower seeds, flax seeds, nuts, rose hip, elder.

Weight associated with overeating is less likely. If underweight, eat larger portions.

Cleansing and detox diets. Fruit and juice days.

Flush out poisons. Treatment for drug abuse.

Pay attention to any particularly tempting foods today: Most likely the "wrong" things taste best.

High cholesterol: eat a low fat diet.

Even as a solid rock is unshaken by the wind, so are the wise unshaken by praise or blame.
Gautama Buddha

Color
Bright/Dark Blue

Day

Air/Light

Element

Aquarius   **Air**

2 Thursday

3 Friday

No meat. Cutting and filing toenails and fingernails.

Positive affirmation:
"My love is universal."

Harvest Time
Ascending forces! Sap is rising, enhancing plant growth above ground, resulting in the most juicy fruits and vegetables.

detox remove be active

Waning Moon

J U L Y

Success

Sensibility, intuition, and helpfulness.

Where possible, retreating is more favorable than dealing with business matters.

Dissolve restrictions, be patient and wait. Be aware that people can be more easily influenced.

Leisure

Your helpfulness will boost friendships.

Enjoy dancing or swimming, or watch a movie that will inspire your fantasies and imagination.

Retreat, relax, and recover.

Romance can be gentle and coziness will prevail.

If you plan outdoor excursions, be prepared for a shower here and there.

Health

Sensitive body parts:

Feet and Toes

All measures taken to flush out and detoxify the sensitive body parts are very effective.

Good for surgical operations except those on the sensitive body parts (see above), chest, lungs, stomach, liver, and gallbladder.
Scarring is less severe.

Teeth: Removal of tartar and amalgam. Best for fillings, crowns, and dentures!

Blood-purifying, detoxifying herbal infusions and teas.

Sensitive nervous system.

Drugs have a much stronger effect on your body.
Monitor closely what you put into your body.

Lymphatic therapy.

Sluggishness or fatigue may occur in the transition into the next Zodiac sign of Aries.

Body Care

Aromas, scents:
Magnolia, Amaryllis, Clary Sage

Prepare home-made ointments and cosmetics.

Apply detoxing facial and body care.

Treatments of bumps and pimples on the skin, and exfoliating procedures.

Removing body hair.

Correction of the nail bed.

Massages that serve to relax, ease tension, and detoxify. Reflexology massage. Carry out with special care, people are more sensitive.

Removal of callused skin.

Treating obstinate athlete's foot, nail fungus, and warts.

Foot bath.

No haircuts, hair becomes shaggy and unmanageable.
Avoid washing your hair.

Garden/Nature

Plant part:

Leaf

Water plants.

Fertilize flowers.

Sow plants and vegetables that grow below ground, potatoes, leaf vegetables, and lettuce.

Dig over/plow to prepare soil for planting.
Trimming and cutting back plants.
Start a compost heap.

Mowing lawns.

Pest control. Weeding.

Harvested produce should be consumed as soon as possible.

Gather herbs for foot complaints.

Housework

Housework is dealt with much more successfully, efficiently, and effortlessly.

Problem stains are removed readily.

Best for doing laundry! Reduce on laundry detergent, support the environment.

Dry cleaning.

Clean and store seasonal clothing.

Thoroughly clean wooden and parquet floors, metals, china etc.

Cleaning, polishing, and waterproofing shoes.

Combating mold.

Ventilate rooms briefly and rapidly.

Avoid painting.

Preserving and storing should be avoided.

Nutrition

Food quality:

Carbohydrate

Lettuce, spinach, lamb's lettuce, Endive, parsley, leek, cabbage (Brussels sprouts, kale, Chinese cabbage), all leafy herbs, asparagus, mushrooms, cress, Swiss chard, rhubarb.

Weight associated with overeating is less likely. If underweight, eat larger portions.

Cleansing and detox diets. Fruit and juice days.

Flush out poisons. Treatment for drug abuse.

Caffeine, alcohol, drugs, certain foods, and stimulants have a much stronger effect.

If opportunity doesn't knock, build a door.
Milton Berle

Color

Blueish White

Day

Wetness

Element

Pisces   Water

11:31 PM PDT Friday

1:31 AM CDT
2:31 AM EDT

4 Saturday
Independence Day

5 Sunday

J U L Y

Positive affirmation:
"My love is universal."

Harvest Time
Ascending forces! Sap is rising, enhancing plant growth above ground, resulting in the most juicy fruits and vegetables.

detox
remove
be active

Waning Moon

Success

Things get going and the way straight ahead seems the best.

People feel energetic, courageous, assertive, and at times anxious.

Good time for meetings and sales talks but impatience and selfishness do not favor teamwork.

Leisure

An enterprising spirit and spontaneity move people to enjoy outings, sports, competitions, cultural events, and travels.

Romance can be very passionate.

Good days for outings, even with cloudy skies the air still feels somewhat warm. Drying effect, get plenty to drink.

Health

Sensitive body parts:

Head, Brain, Eyes

All measures taken to flush out and detoxify the sensitive body parts are very effective.

Good for surgery, except on the sensitive body parts (see above), chest, lungs, stomach, liver, and gallbladder.

Scarring is less severe.

Teeth: Removal of tartar and amalgam. Best for fillings, crowns, and dentures! Avoiding treatment of periodontitis and gums.

Blood-purifying, detoxifying herbal infusions and teas.

Sensitive sense organs.

If you suffer from migraines drink plenty of water, and avoid coffee, chocolate, and sugar.

Body Care

Aromas, scents: Cloves, Peppermint, Thyme

Prepare home-made ointments and cosmetics.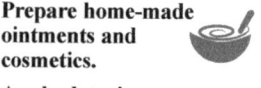

Apply detoxing facial and body care.

Treatments of bumps and pimples on the skin, and exfoliating procedures.

Removing body hair.

Correction of the nail bed.

Massages that serve to relax, ease tension, and detoxify.

Reflexology massage.

Removal of callused skin.

Treating obstinate athlete's foot, nail fungus, and warts.

Eye compresses to relieve strained eyes.

Any kind of hair care.

Garden/Nature

Plant part:

Fruit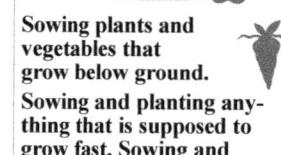

Sowing plants and vegetables that grow below ground.

Sowing and planting anything that is supposed to grow fast. Sowing and planting fruit and tomatoes.

Dig over/plow the soil to prepare for planting.

Spreading manure. Fertilizing grains, vegetables, and fruit.

Weeding. Pest control.

Pruning of fruit trees and bushes.

Harvesting and storing grains, vegetables, potatoes, fruits, and tomatoes.

Start a compost heap.

Gather herbs (roots) for eye complaints and headaches.

Day off on 7/7.

Housework

Housework is dealt with much more successfully, efficiently, and effortlessly.

Problem stains are removed readily.

Best for doing laundry!

Dry cleaning.

Clean and store seasonal clothing.

Thoroughly clean wooden and parquet floors, metals, china, etc.

Cleaning windows and glass.

Cleaning, polishing, and waterproofing shoes.

Combating mold.

Ventilate rooms sufficiently. Air beds.

Suitable for making cheese.

Preserving and freezing fruit and vegetables.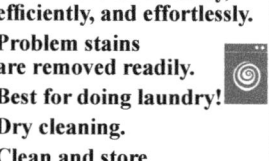

Baking bread, cakes, and cookies (use more leavening agent).

Painting.

Nutrition

Food quality:

Protein

Beans, peas, corn, tomatoes, pumpkin, lentils, soybeans, cucumber, eggplant, zucchini, berries, fruit, chili, bell pepper, figs, avocado, melon, olives.

Weight associated with overeating is less likely. If underweight, eat larger portions.

Cleansing and detox diets. Fruit and juice days.

Flush out poisons. Treatment for drug abuse.

Drink plenty of water.

All human beings should try to learn before they die what they are running from, and to, and why.
James Thurber

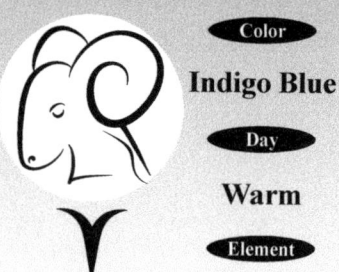

Color — **Indigo Blue**

Day — **Warm**

Element — **Fire**

Aries

$\math333{H} \to \Upsilon$ ← 8:08 AM PDT / 10:08 AM CDT / 11:08 AM EDT

1:32 PM PDT / 3:32 PM CDT / 4:32 PM EDT → $\Upsilon \to \bigcirc$

6 Monday

☽ Half Moon.

7 Tuesday

No meat.

8 Wednesday

J U L Y

Harvest Time
Ascending forces! Sap is rising, enhancing plant growth above ground, resulting in the most juicy fruits and vegetables.

detox remove be active

Waning Moon

Success

Realism and material security are important. Persistence comes easy, thoughts and reactions are slower.

Assess financial areas.

Conservative tendencies may make people want to stay away from risk taking.

Leisure

Relax at a picnic/feast. Enjoy culinary pleasures and hobbies.

The earth feels cold to the touch, so take slightly warmer clothes.

Health

Sensitive body parts:

Head and Neck

All measures taken to flush out and detoxify the sensitive body parts are very effective.

Good for surgery, except on the sensitive body parts (see above), chest, lungs, stomach, liver, and gallbladder. Scarring is less severe.

Teeth: Removal of tartar and amalgam. Best for fillings, crowns, and dentures! Avoiding treatment of periodontitis and gums.

Blood-purifying, detoxifying herbal infusions and teas.

Sensitive blood circulation.

Organs of speech, jaws, teeth, tonsils, thyroid gland, neck, and vocal chords get easily affected. Keep neck warm. On cold days ears should be protected. Sensitivity to noise.

High blood pressure: Avoid salty foods.

Massages, lymphatic therapy, and chiropractic treatment to release blockages.

Body Care

Aromas, scents: Geranium, Jasmine, Rose

Prepare home-made ointments and cosmetics.

Apply detoxing facial and body care.

Treatments of bumps and pimples on the skin, and exfoliating procedures.

Removing body hair.

Correction of the nail bed.

Massages that serve to relax, ease tension, and detoxify.

Reflexology massage.

Removal of callused skin.

Treating obstinate athlete's foot, nail fungus, and warts.

Garden/Nature

Plant part:

Root

Sow plants and vegetables that grow below ground.

Everything grows slowly and lasts well.

Dig over to prepare soil.

Trimming/cutting back plants. Weeding. Mulching.

Start a compost heap.

Combat vermin found in the soil.

Spread fertilizer and liquid manure.

Fertilize flowers with poorly formed roots.

Harvested produce is well suited for storage. Harvesting root vegetables.

Gather herbs (roots) for sinus issues, sore throat, and ear complaints.

Housework

Housework is dealt with much more successfully, efficiently, and effortlessly.

Problem stains are removed readily.

Best for doing laundry! Reduce on laundry detergent, support the environment.

Dry cleaning.

Clean and store seasonal clothing.

Thoroughly clean wooden and parquet floors, metals, china etc.

Cleaning, polishing, and waterproofing shoes.

Combating mold.

Air rooms only briefly.

Painting.

Preserving root vegetables.

Nutrition

Food quality:

Salt

Garlic, carrots, red beets, reddish, rutabaga, sugar beet, celery, potatoes, onions, kohlrabi.

Weight associated with overeating is less likely. If underweight, eat larger portions.

Cleansing and detox diets. Fruit and juice days.

Flush out poisons. Treatment for drug abuse.

Avoid large quantities of salty foods like bacon, ham, salted herring, fatty cheese, and the like.

A lie gets halfway around the world before the truth has a chance to get its pants on.
Winston Churchill

Color

Bright Blue

Day

Cool

Element

Taurus   **Earth**

9 Thursday

3:43 PM PDT
5:43 PM CDT ♉ ➔ ♊
6:43 PM EDT

10 Friday

No meat. Cutting and filing toenails and fingernails.

J U L Y

Positive affirmation:
"My love is universal."

Harvest Time
Ascending forces! Sap is rising, enhancing plant growth above ground, resulting in the most juicy fruits and vegetables.

detox
remove
be active

Waning Moon

Success

Open mindedness and curiosity. A changeable and hectic time.

Good time for talking, negotiating, networking, and exchanging ideas as well as for meetings of a nonbinding nature, conferences, and studies.

Leisure

Good time for family gatherings, parties, and short trips.

People enjoy stimulating their minds with reading and studying. Attending theater performances is a preferred enjoyment. Enhance friendships.

Stretching exercises.

Be prepared for sudden changes in weather or climate.

Health

Sensitive body parts:

Shoulders, Arms, Hands, Lungs

All measures taken to flush out and detoxify the sensitive body parts are very effective.

Good for surgery, except on the sensitive body parts (see above), chest, stomach, liver, and gallbladder. Scarring is less severe.

Teeth: Removal of tartar and amalgam. Best for fillings, crowns, and dentures! Avoid having any teeth pulled.

Blood-purifying, detoxifying herbal infusions and teas.

Sensitive glandular system.

Make sure you are dressed warm enough in cool weather.

Exercises for shoulders. Breathing exercises.

Sensitivity to light, bring your sunglasses along.

Massages, lymphatic therapy, and chiropractic treatment to release blockages.

Body Care

Aromas, scents: Lavender, Lemon Balm, Magnolia, Verbena

Prepare home-made ointments and cosmetics.

Apply detoxing facial and body care.

Treatments of bumps and pimples on the skin, and exfoliating procedures.

Removing body hair.

Correction of the nail bed.

Massages that serve to relax, ease tension, and detoxify.

Reflexology massage.

Removal of callused skin.

Treating obstinate athlete's foot, nail fungus, and warts.

Garden/Nature

Plant part:

Flower

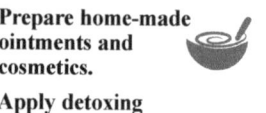

Sow plants and vegetables that grow below ground.

Trimming and cutting back plants.

Start a compost heap.

Weeding. Pest control.

Fertilize flowers that no longer bloom.

Avoid watering plants.

Changes in weather are more likely.

Gather herbs (roots) for tensions in the shoulder and lung complaints.

Housework

Housework is dealt with much more successfully, efficiently, and effortlessly.

Problem stains are removed readily.

Best for doing laundry! Reduce on laundry detergent, support the environment.

Dry cleaning.

Clean and store seasonal clothing.

Thoroughly clean wooden and parquet floors, metals, china etc.

Cleaning windows and glass.

Cleaning, polishing, and waterproofing shoes.

Combating mold.

Ventilate rooms thoroughly.

Baking bread, cakes, and cookies (add more leavening agent).

Making preserves.

Painting.

Nutrition

Food quality:

Fat

Cauliflower, artichoke, broccoli, sunflower seeds, flax seeds, nuts, rose hip, elder.

Weight associated with overeating is less likely. If underweight, eat larger portions.

Cleansing and detox diets. Fruit and juice days.

Flush out poisons. Treatment for drug abuse.

Pay attention to any particularly tempting foods today: Most likely the "wrong" things taste best.

High cholesterol: eat a low fat diet.

No one can make you feel inferior without your consent.
Eleanor Roosevelt

Color
Light Blue

Day
Air/Light

Element

Gemini   **Air**

3:48 PM PDT
5:48 PM CDT ⟶ Ⅱ➔♋
6:48 PM EDT

11 Saturday

12 Sunday

Positive affirmation:
"My love is universal."

Turning Point
Transition of ascending to descending forces. Both forces are at work and neutralize each other.

detox
remove
be active
Waning Moon

J U L Y

Success

Feelings, sensitivity, and cooperativeness. Many are overly sensitive, so beware of treading on someone's toes.

Be cautious if you are easily influenced.

During negotiations make use of the cognitive ability of your senses.

Leisure

Relax within your close family.

Retreat to your safe haven and enjoy your fantasy while reading or listening to music. The inner world becomes more colorful than the outer.

Romance can be gentle. Deep feelings will prevail.

If you plan outdoor excursions, be prepared for a shower here and there.

Health

Sensitive body parts:
Chest, Lungs, Liver, Stomach, Gall Bladder

All measures taken to flush out and detoxify the sensitive body parts are very effective.

Scarring is less severe.

Teeth: Removal of tartar and amalgam. Best for fillings, crowns, and dentures!

Blood-purifying, detoxifying herbal infusions and teas.

Sensitive nervous system.

Be cautious with alcohol since the liver is very sensitive.

Stomach could play up and cause gas and heartburn.

Rheumatism: Don't air bedding outside, damp will remain in the bedding.

Lymphatic therapy.

Body Care

Aromas, scents:
Lilac, Lilies of the Valley, Lilies, Violets

Prepare home-made ointments and cosmetics.

Apply detoxing facial and body care.

Treatments of bumps and pimples on the skin, and exfoliating procedures.

Removing body hair.

Correction of the nail bed.

Massages that serve to relax, ease tension, and detoxify.

Reflexology massage.

Removal of callused skin.

Treating obstinate athlete's foot, nail fungus, and warts.

No haircuts, hair becomes shaggy and unmanageable. Avoid washing your hair.

Garden/Nature

Plant part:
Leaf

Water plants.

Fertilize flowers.

Sow plants and vegetables that grow below ground, leaf vegetables, and lettuce.

Dig over/plow to prepare soil for planting.

Trimming and cutting back plants. Transplanting. Weeding.

Combating pests above ground.

Start a compost heap.

Mowing lawns.

Gather herbs (roots) for bronchitis, stomach, liver, and gall bladder complaints.

Unfavorable for harvesting, storing, and preserving.

Housework

Housework is dealt with much more successfully, efficiently, and effortlessly.

Problem stains are removed readily.

Best for doing laundry! Reduce on laundry detergent, support the environment.

Dry cleaning.

Thoroughly clean wooden and parquet floors, metals, china etc.

Cleaning, polishing, and waterproofing shoes.

Combating mold.

Ventilate rooms briefly and rapidly.

Avoid painting.

Nutrition

Food quality:
Carbohydrate

Lettuce, spinach, lamb's lettuce, Endive, parsley, leek, cabbage (Brussels sprouts, kale, Chinese cabbage), all leafy herbs, asparagus, mushrooms, cress, Swiss chard, rhubarb.

Weight associated with overeating is less likely. If underweight, eat larger portions.

Moodiness may make you want to eat more than is healthy. If overweight avoid carbohydrates.

Cleansing and detox diets. Fruit and juice days.

Flush out poisons. Treatment for drug abuse.

If you get stomach troubles easily, avoid heavy meals.

The best index to a person's character is how he treats people who can't do him any good, and how he treats people who can't fight back.
Abigail Van Buren

 Color

Green

Day

Wetness

  Element

Cancer **Water**

13 Monday

J U L Y

Planting Time
Descending forces! Sap is drawn downward, enhancing root formation. Best days for sowing, planting, and transplanting.

detox
remove
be active

Waning Moon

Success

Feelings, sensitivity, and cooperativeness. Many are overly sensitive, so beware of treading on someone's toes.

Be cautious if you are easily influenced.

During negotiations make use of the cognitive ability of your senses.

● *New Moon: Confirm your resolutions. Finalize new decisions. Drop bad habits.*

Leisure

Relax within your close family.

Retreat to your safe haven and enjoy your fantasy while reading or listening to music. The inner world becomes more colorful than the outer.

Romance can be gentle. Deep feelings will prevail.

If you plan outdoor excursions, be prepared for a shower here and there.

Health

Sensitive body parts:
Chest, Lungs, Liver, Stomach, Gall Bladder

All measures taken to supply nutrient materials and strengthen the sensitive body parts are very effective.

Healing ointments are easily absorbed.

Sensitive nervous system.

Be cautious with alcohol since the liver is very sensitive.

Stomach could play up and cause gas and heartburn.

Rheumatism: Don't air bedding outside, damp will remain in the bedding.

Lymphatic therapy.

● *New Moon: Avoid any surgery if possible.*

Body Care

Aromas, scents:
Lilac, Lilies of the Valley, Lilies, Violets

Treatments with firming and moisturizing creams are more effective.

Massages that serve to regenerate, and strengthen, perhaps aided with beneficial massage oils.

Correcting and cutting ingrown nails.

No haircuts, hair becomes shaggy and unmanageable. Avoid washing your hair.

Garden/Nature

Plant part:
Leaf

Watering all indoor and outdoor plants.

Sow plants, herbs, and vegetables that grow and flourish above ground, leaf vegetables (no lettuce).

Transplanting.

Trimming and cutting back plants. Avoid pruning fruit trees and bushes.

Cut trees, garlands, pick flowers to dry; they will last longer.

Sowing and mowing lawns.

Setting up a compost heap.

Gather herbs for bronchitis, stomach, liver, and gall bladder complaints.

Unfavorable for harvesting, storing, and preserving.

● *New Moon: Change of weather is likely. Care for sickly plants.*

Housework

Light housework only.

Ventilate rooms briefly and rapidly. Don't air mattresses.

Any dirt and spots are easily removed in the laundry.

Avoid painting, as paint will take very long to dry.

Nutrition

Food quality:
Carbohydrate

Lettuce, spinach, lamb's lettuce, Endive, parsley, leek, cabbage (Brussels sprouts, kale, Chinese cabbage), all leafy herbs, asparagus, mushrooms, cress, Swiss chard, rhubarb.

Weight gain: avoid indulging in rich foods. If overweight, eat smaller portions and avoid carbohydrates. Moodiness may make you want to eat more than is healthy.

Supply nutrient materials to strengthen the body. Focus on foods that contain essential minerals and vitamins. Stimulants and vitamins are more effective.

If you get stomach troubles easily, avoid heavy meals.

● *New Moon: A day of fasting.*

Positive affirmation:
"My courage grows each day."

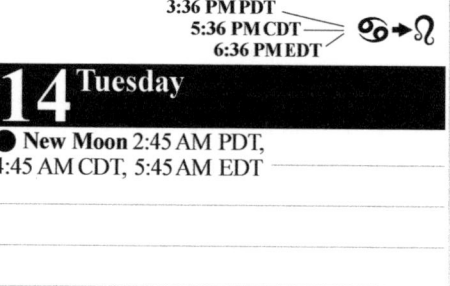

Planting Time
Descending forces!
Sap is drawn downward, enhancing root formation.
Best days for sowing, planting, and transplanting.

gather strength
rest, recover
buildup
Waxing Moon

3:36 PM PDT
5:36 PM CDT
6:36 PM EDT

14 Tuesday

● **New Moon** 2:45 AM PDT, 4:45 AM CDT, 5:45 AM EDT

J U L Y

Science talks and behaves as if it had conquered all knowledge: Wisdom, as she walks, hears her solitary tread echoing on the margin of immeasurable oceans.
Sri Aurobindo

Color
Green

Day
Wetness

Element
Water

Cancer

Success

Determination reigns, and risks are taken more often. Master your tasks with more self-confidence and creativity.

Limits appear to be more easily surmountable.

Auspicious day for sales, advertising, and publicity.

Leisure

Zest for life is in the air. People want to have a fun time, enjoy parties, musical events, movies, etc.

Possessive feelings can harm a relationship. Romance can be very passionate.

Outings: even with cloudy skies the air still feels somewhat warm. Drying effect, get plenty to drink.

Danger of sudden storms, not only in the sky.

Health

Sensitive body parts:
Heart, Back, Diaphragm, Circulation, Arteries

All measures taken to supply nutrient materials and strengthen the sensitive body parts are very effective.

Healing ointments are easily absorbed.

Sensitive sense organs.

Back and heart problems are more likely to occur.

Avoid over straining of the heart and circulation with unusual physical activities.

Expect sleepless nights.

Body Care

Aromas, scents:
Hibiscus,
Oleander, Rose

Treatments with firming and moisturizing creams are more effective.

Massages that serve to regenerate, and strengthen, perhaps aided with beneficial massage oils.

Correcting and cutting ingrown nails.

Good days for haircuts, hair becomes stronger. But be aware that if you get a perm, curls will become quite frizzy. Baby's first haircut.

Garden/Nature

Plant part:
Fruit

Sow plants and vegetables that grow and flourish above ground. Sowing and planting fruit. Also sow and plant vegetables that are highly perishable. Plant trees and bushes. Sow lawns.

Transplanting. Grafting onto fruit trees.

Trimming and cutting back plants.

Best for cultivating grains on wet fields.

Dig over/plow to prepare soil for planting.

Setting up a compost heap.

Not suitable for fertilizing.

Harvested produce should be consumed as soon as possible.

Gather herbs for heart and circulation complaints.

Housework

Light housework only.

Ventilate sufficiently.

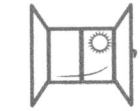

Freezing fruit and vegetables.

Baking bread, cakes, and cookies. Dough rises faster. (Except on New Moon)

Suitable for making cheese.

Avoid painting.

Nutrition

Food quality:
Protein

Beans, peas, corn, tomatoes, pumpkin, lentils, soybeans, cucumber, eggplant, zucchini, berries, fruit, chili, bell pepper, figs, avocado, melon, olives.

Weight gain: avoid indulging in rich foods. If overweight, eat smaller portions.

Supply nutrient materials to strengthen the body. Focus on foods that contain essential minerals and vitamins.

Stimulants and vitamins are more effective.

Positive affirmation:
"My courage grows each day."

Planting Time
Descending forces!
Sap is drawn downward, enhancing root formation.
Best days for sowing, planting, and transplanting.

gather strength
rest, recover
buildup
Waxing Moon

15 Wednesday
No meat.

5:08 PM PDT
7:08 PM CDT   ♌ ➔ ♍
8:08 PM EDT

16 Thursday

J U L Y

Sadness is but a wall between two gardens.
Kahlil Gibran

 Color
Green

 Day
Warm

 Element
Fire

Leo ♌

Success

Good time for details, organization, routine, concentration, and duty.

Take care of financial and administrative tasks.

Prepare for future success now with realistic and critical assessment.

Leisure

Enjoy a nature walk.

Good time for health regimes. Improve your health with stretching exercises and yoga.

The earth feels cold to the touch, so take slightly warmer clothes.

Health

Sensitive body parts:
Digestive Organs, Nerves, Spleen, Pancreas

All measures taken to supply nutrient materials and strengthen the sensitive body parts are very effective.

Healing ointments are easily absorbed.

Sensitive blood circulation.

For a sensitive digestive system, a wholesome diet is recommended.

Dress slightly warmer.

High blood pressure: Avoid salty foods.

Massages, lymphatic therapy, and chiropractic treatment to release blockages.

Body Care

Aromas, scents:
Lavender, Spruce Needles, Sage, Meadow Flowers

Treatments with firming and moisturizing creams are more effective.

Massages that serve to regenerate, and strengthen, perhaps aided with beneficial massage oils.

Correcting and cutting ingrown nails.

Best for haircuts because it retains its shape longer. Perms turn out best. Hair dyes applied now, will look more vibrant.

Garden/Nature

Plant part:
Root

Best for sowing and planting, except lettuce.

Plant trees which are supposed to grow very tall. Plant hedges and bushes that are meant to grow very fast.

Sowing lawns.

Planting and re-potting balcony and indoor plants.

Transplanting.

Trimming and cutting back plants.

Planting cuttings.

Start a compost heap.

Avoid harvesting and storing.

Gather herbs (roots) for digestive organs, pancreas, and nervous complaints.

Housework

Light housework only.

Air rooms only briefly.

Making pickles, preserves, and cheese yields suboptimal results and should be avoided.

Nutrition

Food quality:
Salt

Garlic, carrots, red beets, reddish, rutabaga, sugar beet, celery, potatoes, onions, kohlrabi.

Weight gain: avoid indulging in rich foods. If overweight, eat smaller portions.

Supply nutrient materials to strengthen the body. Focus on foods that contain essential minerals and vitamins.

Stimulants and vitamins are more effective.

Avoid large quantities of salty foods like bacon, ham, salted herring, fatty cheese, and the like. Avoid heavy and greasy foods.

Positive affirmation:
"My courage grows each day."

Planting Time
Descending forces! Sap is drawn downward, enhancing root formation. Best days for sowing, planting, and transplanting.

gather strength
rest, recover
buildup
Waxing Moon

9:58 PM PDT
11:58 PM CDT
Sunday 12:58 AM EDT   ♍➔♎

17 Friday

No meat. Cutting and filing toenails and fingernails.

18 Saturday

It is hard enough to remember my opinions, without also remembering my reasons for them!
Friedrich Nietzsche

Color
Yellow

Day
Cool

Element
Earth

♍
Virgo

J U L Y

Success

The artistic instinct rules, but so, too, does indecisiveness. The forces swing back and forth until equilibrium is achieved.

It's easy to reach compromises with tactful sensitivity.

A sense of judgment will support legal matters.

Leisure

Pursuit for harmony and cooperativeness supports good times in romance, friendship, and partnership.

Enjoy cultural events. Relax and get pampered with a spa treatment.

Romance can be passionate yet sensitive.

Health

Sensitive body parts:
Hips, Kidneys, Bladder

All measures taken to supply nutrient materials and strengthen the sensitive body parts are very effective.

Healing ointments are easily absorbed.

Sensitive glandular system.

Take special care to keep the area of bladder and kidneys warm.

Apply special exercises for the hip region.

Avoid having any teeth pulled.

Sensitivity to light, bring your sunglasses along.

Body Care

Aromas, scents:
Roses, Violets, Daffodils

Treatments with firming and moisturizing creams are more effective.

Massages that serve to regenerate, and strengthen, perhaps aided with beneficial massage oils.

Correcting and cutting ingrown nails.

Hair dyes applied now, will look more vibrant.

Garden/Nature

Plant part:
Flower

Sow plants and vegetables that grow and flourish above ground, specially flowers, and medicinal herbs.

Transplanting.

Trimming and cutting back plants.

Avoid watering plants.

Start a compost heap.

Harvested produce should be consumed as soon as possible.

Gather herbs for kidneys, gall bladder, and hip complaints.

Day off on 7/19.

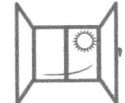

Housework

Light housework only.

Ventilate rooms thoroughly.

Baking cakes and cookies. Dough rises faster. (Except on New Moon)

Nutrition

Food quality:
Fat

Cauliflower, artichoke, broccoli, sunflower seeds, flax seeds, nuts, rose hip, elder.

Weight gain: avoid indulging in rich foods. If overweight, eat smaller portions.

Supply nutrient materials to strengthen the body. Focus on foods that contain essential minerals and vitamins.

Stimulants and vitamins are more effective.

Pay attention to any particularly tempting foods today: Most likely the "wrong" things taste best.

High cholesterol: eat a low fat diet.

Positive affirmation:
"My courage grows each day."

Planting Time
Descending forces! Sap is drawn downward, enhancing root formation. Best days for sowing, planting, and transplanting.

gather strength rest, recover buildup
Waxing Moon

19 Sunday

20 Monday

J U L Y

Color
Orange

Day
Air/Light

Element
Air

Libra

Success

Critical and superstitious behavior emerges, especially pertaining to money.

A penetrating power will strengthen your capacity to act.

An increased perception opens our interest for the essentials and helps to discover hidden potentials.

Leisure

Relax within your close family, with meditation, and relaxation exercises.

A longing to feel safe will be nurtured if you focus on habits and rituals. An increased sensitivity will help to enjoy every moment.

Romance can be very passionate.

If you plan outdoor excursions, be prepared for a shower here and there.

Health

Sensitive body parts:

Sex organs, Ureter

All measures taken to supply nutrient materials and strengthen the sensitive body parts are very effective.

Healing ointments are easily absorbed. Applying herbal ointments to the shoulders for rheumatic gout and alike.

Sensitive nervous system.

Female disorders: As a preventative measure apply hip baths using yarrow.

Pregnancy: Avoid any exertion, miscarriages are more likely.

Keep region of the pelvis, kidneys, and feet warm to prevent infection of the bladder and kidneys.

Lymphatic therapy.

Body Care

Aromas, scents:
Anemone, Cornflower
Oregano, Thuja

Treatments with firming and moisturizing creams are more effective.

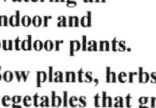

Massages that serve to regenerate, and strengthen, perhaps aided with beneficial massage oils.

Correcting and cutting ingrown nails.

Hair dyes applied now, will look more vibrant.

Garden/Nature

Plant part:

Leaf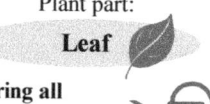

Watering all indoor and outdoor plants.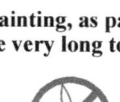

Sow plants, herbs, and vegetables that grow and flourish above ground, leaf vegetables (no lettuce).

Sowing, planting, harvesting, and drying every kind of medicinal herbs.

Transplanting.

Trimming and cutting back plants.
Combating slugs and snails.
Mowing lawns.

Start a compost heap.

Avoid pruning fruit trees and bushes. Avoid cutting down any trees.

Harvested produce should be consumed as soon as possible.

Housework

Light housework only.

Ventilate rooms briefly and rapidly. Don't air mattresses.

Any dirt and spots are easily removed in the laundry.

Avoid painting, as paint will take very long to dry.

Nutrition

Food quality:

Carbohydrate

Lettuce, spinach, lamb's lettuce, Endive, parsley, leek, cabbage (Brussels sprouts, kale, Chinese cabbage), all leafy herbs, asparagus, mushrooms, cress, Swiss chard, rhubarb.

Weight gain: avoid indulging in rich foods. If overweight, eat smaller portions and avoid carbohydrates.

Supply nutrient materials to strengthen the body. Focus on foods that contain essential minerals and vitamins. Stimulants and vitamins are more effective.

Planting Time
Descending forces!
Sap is drawn downward, enhancing root formation.
Best days for sowing, planting, and transplanting.

gather strength rest, recover buildup
Waxing Moon

♎ → ♏ 6:36 AM PDT
8:36 AM CDT
9:36 AM EDT

6:08 PM PDT
8:08 PM CDT   ♏ → ♐
9:08 PM EDT

21 Tuesday
☽ Half Moon.

22 Wednesday
No meat.

23 Thursday
Tisha B'Av

J U L Y

Color
Red

Day

Wetness

Element

Water   **Scorpio** ♏

Success

Inquisitiveness and exuberant inspiration lead to new horizons. Insight and love for truth reign.

Bringing together is more important than splitting asunder.

Expansive forces will assist in legal matters, discussions, and debates.

Leisure

Expansion feels great, and travel, short trips, and outings are most welcome. A competitive spirit excites any sports event.

Talk things out when necessary.

Romance can be very passionate.

Good days for outings; even with cloudy skies the air still feels somewhat warm. Drying effect, get plenty to drink.

Health

Sensitive body parts:

Thighs and Veins

All measures taken to supply nutrient materials and strengthen the sensitive body parts are very effective.

Healing ointments are easily absorbed.

Sensitive sense organs.

Pains often arise in the sciatic nerve, veins, the small of the back, and thighs.

Avoid overstraining the body with unusual physical activities.

Body Care

Aromas, scents:
Calendula (Marigold), Geranium, Rosemary

Treatments with firming and moisturizing creams are more effective.

Massages that serve to regenerate, and strengthen, perhaps aided with beneficial massage oils.

Correcting and cutting ingrown nails.

Hair dyes applied now, will look more vibrant.

Garden/Nature

Plant part:

Fruit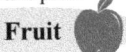

Sow plants and vegetables that grow and flourish above ground.

Sowing and planting fruit and vegetables that grow tall, and tomatoes, but no lettuce.

Transplanting.

Grafting onto fruit trees.

Cultivating grains, particularly corn.

Gather herbs for vein diseases.

Housework

Light housework only.

Ventilate sufficiently.

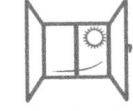

Freezing fruit and vegetables.

Baking bread, cakes, and cookies. Dough rises faster. (Except on New Moon)

Suitable for making cheese.

Making preserves.

Nutrition

Food quality:

Protein

Beans, peas, corn, tomatoes, pumpkin, lentils, soybeans, cucumber, eggplant, zucchini, berries, fruit, chili, bell pepper, figs, avocado, melon, olives.

Weight gain: avoid indulging in rich foods. If overweight, eat smaller portions.

Supply nutrient materials to strengthen the body. Focus on foods that contain essential minerals and vitamins.

Stimulants and vitamins are more effective.

Positive affirmation:
"My courage grows each day."

Turning Point

Transition of descending to ascending forces. Both forces are at work and neutralize each other.

gather strength rest, recover buildup

Waxing Moon

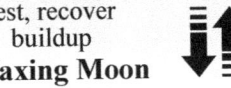

24 Friday

No meat. Cutting and filing toenails and fingernails.

25 Saturday

J U L Y

The seed of suffering in you may be strong, but don't wait until you have no more suffering before allowing yourself to be happy.
Thich Nhat Hanh

Color
Orange/Yellow

Day
Warm

Element

Fire   **Sagittarius**

Success

Career and business are in the foreground now and thinking becomes clear and serious, but somewhat inflexible.

Perseverance and reasoning assist in financial matters, planning, and contracts.

The values of tradition, authority, and discipline impact our endeavors.

Leisure

Money is not likely to be wasted in a shopping spree.

Many are drawn to enjoy cultural events.

The earth feels cold to the touch, so take slightly warmer clothes.

Health

Sensitive body parts:

Knees, Joints, Bones, Skin

All measures taken to supply nutrient materials and strengthen the sensitive body parts are very effective.

Healing ointments are easily absorbed.

Sensitive blood circulation.

Avoid overstraining bones and knees, and apply gentle stretching exercises only.

Problems with meniscus: Don't overstrain.

Dress slightly warmer.

High blood pressure: Avoid salty foods.

Massages, lymphatic therapy, and chiropractic treatment to release blockages.

Body Care

Aromas, scents:

Cedar, Juniper

Treatments with firming and moisturizing creams are more effective.

Massages that serve to regenerate, and strengthen, perhaps aided with beneficial massage oils.

Correcting and cutting ingrown nails.

Every kind of skin care is beneficial.

Cutting and filing toenails and fingernails will make the nails grow stronger over time.

Hair dyes applied now, will look more vibrant.

Garden/Nature

Plant part:

Root

Sow plants, herbs, and vegetables that grow and flourish above ground.

Transplanting.

Harvest produce is suitable for storage. Harvest root vegetables.

Gather herbs for bone, joint, and skin diseases.

Housework

Light housework only.

Air rooms only briefly.

Preserving root vegetables.

Avoid dry cleaning, as the fabric may develop unwanted glossy blotches.

Nutrition

Food quality:

Salt

Garlic, carrots, red beets, reddish, rutabaga, sugar beet, celery, potatoes, onions, kohlrabi.

Weight gain: avoid indulging in rich foods. If overweight, eat smaller portions.

Supply nutrient materials to strengthen the body. Focus on foods that contain essential minerals and vitamins.

Stimulants and vitamins are more effective.

Avoid large quantities of salty foods like bacon, ham, salted herring, fatty cheese, and the like. Avoid heavy and greasy foods.

Positive affirmation:
"My courage grows each day."

Harvest Time
Ascending forces! Sap is rising, enhancing plant growth above ground, resulting in the most juicy fruits and vegetables.

gather strength
rest, recover
buildup
Waxing Moon

6:45 AM PDT
8:45 AM CDT
9:45 AM EDT
♐ → ♑

6:47 PM PST
8:47 PM CST
9:47 PM EST
♑ → ♒

26 Sunday
Parent's Day (US)

27 Monday

28 Tuesday

J U L Y

The important thing is not to stop questioning. Curiosity has its own reason for existing.
Albert Einstein

Color
Yellow

Day
Cool

Element
Earth

♑
Capricorn

Success

Inspiration, optimism, and impatience. Rational thinking, creativity and imagination spark new ideas and inspire planning for the future.

Shying away from routine tasks people will feel more drawn to anything new.

Instead of gridlocked structures choose new possibilities.

Leisure

Inspiration and optimism will boost friendship, social gatherings, and parties.

Express your creativity and imagination. Dwell in dreams and utopian ideas. It is easier now to perceive intuitive thoughts.

Health

Sensitive body parts:

Lower Legs, Veins

All measures taken to flush out and detoxify the sensitive body parts are very effective.

Scarring is less severe.

Teeth: Removal of tartar and amalgam. Best for fillings, crowns, and dentures!

Blood-purifying, detoxifying herbal infusions and teas.

Sensitive glandular system.

Avoid inflammation of the veins. Apply ointments to lower legs, and rest legs in a raised position.

Varicose veins: Avoid long periods of standing.

While exercising go easy on the ankles.

Sensitivity to light, so bring your sunglasses along.

○ _**Full Moon:** Avoid any surgery and vaccination if possible._

Body Care

Aromas, scents: Cyclamen, Peach, Wild Roses

Prepare home-made ointments and cosmetics.

Apply detoxing facial and body care.

Treatments of bumps and pimples on the skin, and exfoliating procedures.

Removing body hair.

Correction of the nail bed.

Massages that serve to relax, ease tension, and detoxify.

Reflexology massage.

Removal of callused skin.

Treating obstinate athlete's foot, nail fungus, and warts.

Garden/Nature

Plant part:

Flower

Fertilize flowers that no longer bloom.

Dig over/plow to prepare soil for planting.

Trimming and cutting back plants.

Hoeing and harrowing; weeds can be left to rot.

Pest control.

Start a compost heap.

Avoid watering plants.

Avoid transplanting sprouts.

Harvested produce is well suitable for storage.

Gather herbs (roots) for vein diseases.

○ _**Full Moon:** Weather and climate changes. Herbs are most powerful._

Housework

Housework is dealt with much more successfully, efficiently, and effortlessly.

Problem stains are removed readily.

Dry cleaning.

Clean and store seasonal clothing.

Best suited for a spring cleaning: Thoroughly clean wooden and parquet floors, metals, china etc.

Cleaning, polishing, and waterproofing shoes.

Combating mold.

Ventilate rooms thoroughly.

Baking bread, cakes, and cookies (add more leavening agent).

○ _**Full Moon:** Avoid doing laundry, cleaning windows, making preserves, painting._

Nutrition

Food quality:

Fat

Cauliflower, artichoke, broccoli, sunflower seeds, flax seeds, nuts, rose hip, elder.

Weight associated with overeating is less likely. If underweight, eat larger portions.

Cleansing and detox diets. Fruit and juice days.

Flush out poisons. Treatment for drug abuse.

Pay attention to any particularly tempting foods today: Most likely the "wrong" things taste best.

High cholesterol: eat a low fat diet.

○ _**Full Moon:** A day of fasting._

The ability to discipline yourself to delay gratification in the short term in order to enjoy greater rewards in the long term, is the indispensable prerequisite for success.
Brian Tracy

Color
Bright/Dark Blue

Day
Air/Light

Element

Aquarius   **Air**

29 Wednesday

○ **Full Moon** 7:37 AM PDT, 9:37 AM CDT, 10:37 AM EDT
No meat.

30 Thursday

J U L Y

Harvest Time
Ascending forces! Sap is rising, enhancing plant growth above ground, resulting in the most juicy fruits and vegetables.

detox
remove
be active

Waning Moon

Success

Sensibility, intuition, and helpfulness.

Where possible, retreating is more favorable than dealing with business matters.

Dissolve restrictions, be patient and wait. Be aware that people can be more easily influenced.

Leisure

Your helpfulness will boost friendships.

Enjoy dancing or swimming, or watch a movie that will inspire your fantasies and imagination.

Retreat, relax, and recover.

Romance can be gentle and coziness will prevail.

If you plan outdoor excursions, be prepared for a shower here and there.

Health

Sensitive body parts:
Feet and Toes

All measures taken to flush out and detoxify the sensitive body parts are very effective.

Good for surgical operations except those on the sensitive body parts (see above), heart, back, diaphragm, circulation, and arteries.
Scarring is less severe.

Teeth: Removal of tartar and amalgam. Best for fillings, crowns, and dentures!

Blood-purifying, detoxifying herbal infusions and teas.

Sensitive nervous system.

Drugs have a much stronger effect on your body. Monitor closely what you put into your body.

Lymphatic therapy.

Sluggishness or fatigue may occur in the transition into the next Zodiac sign of Aries.

Body Care

Aromas, scents:
Magnolia, Amaryllis, Clary Sage

Prepare home-made ointments and cosmetics.

Apply detoxing facial and body care.

Treatments of bumps and pimples on the skin, and exfoliating procedures.

Removing body hair.

Correction of the nail bed.

Massages that serve to relax, ease tension, and detoxify. Reflexology massage. Carry out with special care, people are more sensitive.

Removal of callused skin.

Treating obstinate athlete's foot, nail fungus, and warts.

Foot bath.

No haircuts, hair becomes shaggy and unmanageable.
Avoid washing your hair.

Garden/Nature

Plant part:
Leaf

Water plants.

Fertilize flowers.

Sow plants and vegetables that grow below ground, potatoes, leaf vegetables, and lettuce.

Dig over/plow to prepare soil for planting.
Trimming and cutting back plants.
Start a compost heap.

Mowing lawns.

Pest control. Weeding.

Harvested produce should be consumed as soon as possible.

Gather herbs for foot complaints.

Housework

Housework is dealt with much more successfully, efficiently, and effortlessly.

Problem stains are removed readily.

Best for doing laundry! Reduce on laundry detergent, support the environment.

Dry cleaning.

Clean and store seasonal clothing.

Thoroughly clean wooden and parquet floors, metals, china etc.

Cleaning, polishing, and waterproofing shoes.

Combating mold.

Ventilate rooms briefly and rapidly.

Avoid painting.

Preserving and storing should be avoided.

Nutrition

Food quality:
Carbohydrate

Lettuce, spinach, lamb's lettuce, Endive, parsley, leek, cabbage (Brussels sprouts, kale, Chinese cabbage), all leafy herbs, asparagus, mushrooms, cress, Swiss chard, rhubarb.

Weight associated with overeating is less likely. If underweight, eat larger portions.

Cleansing and detox diets. Fruit and juice days.

Flush out poisons. Treatment for drug abuse.

Caffeine, alcohol, drugs, certain foods, and stimulants have a much stronger effect.

More people would learn from their mistakes if they weren't so busy denying them.
Harold J. Smith

Color
Blueish White

Day

Wetness

Element

Pisces   Water

5:15 AM PDT
7:15 AM CDT
8:15 AM EDT

1:38 PM PDT
3:38 PM CDT
4:38 PM EDT

31 Friday	**1** Saturday	**2** Sunday
No meat. Cutting and filing toenails and fingernails.		

JULY / AUGUST

Harvest Time
Ascending forces! Sap is rising, enhancing plant growth above ground, resulting in the most juicy fruits and vegetables.

detox
remove
be active
Waning Moon

Success

Things get going and the way straight ahead seems the best.

People feel energetic, courageous, assertive, and at times anxious.

Good time for meetings and sales talks but impatience and selfishness do not favor teamwork.

Leisure

An enterprising spirit and spontaneity move people to enjoy outings, sports, competitions, cultural events, and travels.

Romance can be very passionate.

Good days for outings, even with cloudy skies the air still feels somewhat warm. Drying effect, get plenty to drink.

Health

Sensitive body parts:
Head, Brain, Eyes

All measures taken to flush out and detoxify the sensitive body parts are very effective.

Good for surgery, except on the sensitive body parts (see above), heart, diaphragm, back, circulation, and arteries.

Scarring is less severe.

Teeth: Removal of tartar and amalgam. Best for fillings, crowns, and dentures! Avoiding treatment of periodontitis and gums.

Blood-purifying, detoxifying herbal infusions and teas.

Sensitive sense organs.

If you suffer from migraines drink plenty of water, and avoid coffee, chocolate, and sugar.

Body Care

Aromas, scents:
Cloves, Peppermint, Thyme

Prepare home-made ointments and cosmetics.

Apply detoxing facial and body care.

Treatments of bumps and pimples on the skin, and exfoliating procedures.

Removing body hair.

Correction of the nail bed.

Massages that serve to relax, ease tension, and detoxify.

Reflexology massage.

Removal of callused skin.

Treating obstinate athlete's foot, nail fungus, and warts.

Eye compresses to relieve strained eyes.

Any kind of hair care.

Garden/Nature

Plant part:
Fruit

Sowing plants and vegetables that grow below ground.

Sowing and planting anything that is supposed to grow fast. Sowing and planting fruit and tomatoes.

Dig over/plow the soil to prepare for planting.

Spreading manure. Fertilizing grains, vegetables, and fruit.
Weeding. Pest control.

Pruning of fruit trees and bushes.

Harvesting and storing grains, vegetables, potatoes, fruits, and tomatoes.

Start a compost heap.

Gather herbs (roots) for eye complaints and headaches.

Day off on 8/3.

Housework

Housework is dealt with much more successfully, efficiently, and effortlessly.

Problem stains are removed readily.

Best for doing laundry!

Dry cleaning.

Clean and store seasonal clothing.

Thoroughly clean wooden and parquet floors, metals, china, etc.

Cleaning windows and glass.

Cleaning, polishing, and waterproofing shoes.

Combating mold.

Ventilate rooms sufficiently.
Air beds.

Suitable for making cheese.

Preserving and freezing fruit and vegetables.

Baking bread, cakes, and cookies (use more leavening agent).

Painting.

Nutrition

Food quality:
Protein

Beans, peas, corn, tomatoes, pumpkin, lentils, soybeans, cucumber, eggplant, zucchini, berries, fruit, chili, bell pepper, figs, avocado, melon, olives.

Weight associated with overeating is less likely. If underweight, eat larger portions.

Cleansing and detox diets. Fruit and juice days.

Flush out poisons. Treatment for drug abuse.

Drink plenty of water.

It's only words... unless they're true.
David Mamet

7:37 PM PDT
9:37 PM CDT
10:37 PM EDT
♈ ➜ ♉

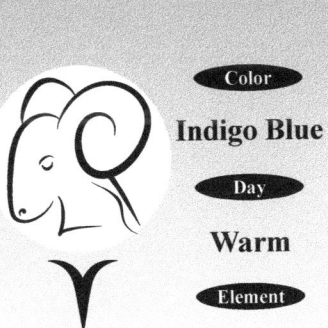

Color
Indigo Blue

Day
Warm

Element
♈
Aries   **Fire**

3 Monday
Civic Holiday (CAN)

4 Tuesday

A U G U S T

Harvest Time
Ascending forces! Sap is rising, enhancing plant growth above ground, resulting in the most juicy fruits and vegetables.

detox
remove
be active
Waning Moon

Success

Realism and material security are important. Persistence comes easy, thoughts and reactions are slower.

Assess financial areas.

Conservative tendencies may make people want to stay away from risk taking.

Leisure

Relax at a picnic/feast. Enjoy culinary pleasures and hobbies.

The earth feels cold to the touch, so take slightly warmer clothes.

Health

Sensitive body parts:
Head and Neck

All measures taken to flush out and detoxify the sensitive body parts are very effective.

Good for surgery, except on the sensitive body parts (see above), heart, back, diaphragm circulation, and arteries. Scarring is less severe.

Teeth: Removal of tartar and amalgam. Best for fillings, crowns, and dentures! Avoiding treatment of periodontitis and gums.

Blood-purifying, detoxifying herbal infusions and teas. Sensitive blood circulation.

Organs of speech, jaws, teeth, tonsils, thyroid gland, neck, and vocal chords get easily affected. Keep neck warm. On cold days ears should be protected. Sensitivity to noise.

High blood pressure: Avoid salty foods.

Massages, lymphatic therapy, and chiropractic treatment to release blockages.

Body Care

Aromas, scents: Geranium, Jasmine, Rose

Prepare home-made ointments and cosmetics.

Apply detoxing facial and body care.

Treatments of bumps and pimples on the skin, and exfoliating procedures.

Removing body hair.

Correction of the nail bed.

Massages that serve to relax, ease tension, and detoxify.

Reflexology massage.

Removal of callused skin.

Treating obstinate athlete's foot, nail fungus, and warts.

Garden/Nature

Plant part:
Root

Sow plants and vegetables that grow below ground.

Everything grows slowly and lasts well.

Dig over to prepare soil.

Trimming/cutting back plants. Weeding. Mulching.

Start a compost heap.

Combat vermin found in the soil.

Spread fertilizer and liquid manure.

Fertilize flowers with poorly formed roots.

Harvested produce is well suited for storage. Harvesting root vegetables.

Gather herbs (roots) for sinus issues, sore throat, and ear complaints.

Housework

Housework is dealt with much more successfully, efficiently, and effortlessly.

Problem stains are removed readily.

Best for doing laundry! Reduce on laundry detergent, support the environment.

Dry cleaning.

Clean and store seasonal clothing.

Thoroughly clean wooden and parquet floors, metals, china etc.

Cleaning, polishing, and waterproofing shoes.

Combating mold.

Air rooms only briefly.

Painting.

Preserving root vegetables.

Nutrition

Food quality:
Salt

Garlic, carrots, red beets, reddish, rutabaga, sugar beet, celery, potatoes, onions, kohlrabi.

Weight associated with overeating is less likely. If underweight, eat larger portions.

Cleansing and detox diets. Fruit and juice days.

Flush out poisons. Treatment for drug abuse.

Avoid large quantities of salty foods like bacon, ham, salted herring, fatty cheese, and the like.

By three methods we may learn wisdom: First, by reflection, which is noblest; Second, by imitation, which is easiest; and third by experience, which is the bitterest.
Confucius

Color
Bright Blue

Day
Cool

Element
Earth

Taurus

---

5 Wednesday

☾ **Half Moon.** No meat.

6 Thursday

A U G U S T

Positive affirmation:
"My courage grows each day."

Harvest Time
Ascending forces! Sap is rising, enhancing plant growth above ground, resulting in the most juicy fruits and vegetables.

detox
remove
be active

Waning Moon

Success

Open mindedness and curiosity. A changeable and hectic time.

Good time for talking, negotiating, networking, and exchanging ideas as well as for meetings of a nonbinding nature, conferences, and studies.

Leisure

Good time for family gatherings, parties, and short trips.

People enjoy stimulating their minds with reading and studying. Attending theater performances is a preferred enjoyment. Enhance friendships.

Stretching exercises.

Be prepared for sudden changes in weather or climate.

Health

Sensitive body parts:
Shoulders, Arms, Hands, Lungs

All measures taken to flush out and detoxify the sensitive body parts are very effective.

Good for surgery, except on the sensitive body parts (see above), heart, back, diaphragm, circulation, arteries. Scarring is less severe.

Teeth: Removal of tartar and amalgam. Best for fillings, crowns, and dentures! Avoid having any teeth pulled.

Blood-purifying, detoxifying herbal infusions and teas.

Sensitive glandular system.

Make sure you are dressed warm enough in cool weather.

Exercises for shoulders. Breathing exercises.

Sensitivity to light, bring your sunglasses along.

Massages, lymphatic therapy, and chiropractic treatment to release blockages.

Body Care

Aromas, scents:
Lavender, Lemon Balm, Magnolia, Verbena

Prepare home-made ointments and cosmetics.

Apply detoxing facial and body care.

Treatments of bumps and pimples on the skin, and exfoliating procedures.

Removing body hair.

Correction of the nail bed.

Massages that serve to relax, ease tension, and detoxify.

Reflexology massage.

Removal of callused skin.

Treating obstinate athlete's foot, nail fungus, and warts.

Garden/Nature

Plant part:
Flower

Sow plants and vegetables that grow below ground.

Trimming and cutting back plants.

Start a compost heap.

Weeding. Pest control.

Fertilize flowers that no longer bloom.

Avoid watering plants.

Changes in weather are more likely.

Gather herbs (roots) for tensions in the shoulder and lung complaints.

Housework

Housework is dealt with much more successfully, efficiently, and effortlessly.

Problem stains are removed readily.

Best for doing laundry! Reduce on laundry detergent, support the environment.

Dry cleaning.

Clean and store seasonal clothing.

Thoroughly clean wooden and parquet floors, metals, china etc.

Cleaning windows and glass.

Cleaning, polishing, and waterproofing shoes.

Combating mold.

Ventilate rooms thoroughly.

Baking bread, cakes, and cookies (add more leavening agent).

Making preserves.

Painting.

Nutrition

Food quality:
Fat

Cauliflower, artichoke, broccoli, sunflower seeds, flax seeds, nuts, rose hip, elder.

Weight associated with overeating is less likely. If underweight, eat larger portions.

Cleansing and detox diets. Fruit and juice days.

Flush out poisons. Treatment for drug abuse.

Pay attention to any particularly tempting foods today: Most likely the "wrong" things taste best.

High cholesterol: eat a low fat diet.

Those who educate children well are more to be honored than they who produce them; for these only gave them life, those the art of living well.
Aristotle

Color

Light Blue

Day

Air/Light

Element

Gemini   **Air**

♂→♊   11:09 PM PDT Thursday
1:09 AM CDT
2:09 AM EDT

7 Friday

No meat. Cutting and filing toenails and fingernails.

8 Saturday

A U G U S T

Turning Point
Transition of ascending to descending forces. Both forces are at work and neutralize each other.

detox
remove
be active
Waning Moon

Success

Feelings, sensitivity, and cooperativeness. Many are overly sensitive, so beware of treading on someone's toes.

Be cautious if you are easily influenced.

During negotiations make use of the cognitive ability of your senses.

Leisure

Relax within your close family.

Retreat to your safe haven and enjoy your fantasy while reading or listening to music. The inner world becomes more colorful than the outer.

Romance can be gentle. Deep feelings will prevail.

If you plan outdoor excursions, be prepared for a shower here and there.

Health

Sensitive body parts:
Chest, Lungs, Liver, Stomach, Gall Bladder

All measures taken to flush out and detoxify the sensitive body parts are very effective.

Good for surgical operations except those on the sensitive body parts (see above), heart, diaphragm, back, circulation, and arteries. Scarring is less severe.

Teeth: Removal of tartar and amalgam. Best for fillings, crowns, and dentures!

Blood-purifying, detoxifying herbal infusions and teas.

Sensitive nervous system.

Be cautious with alcohol since the liver is very sensitive.

Stomach could play up and cause gas and heartburn.

Rheumatism: Don't air bedding outside, damp will remain in the bedding.

Lymphatic therapy.

Body Care

Aromas, scents:
Lilac, Lilies of the Valley, Lilies, Violets

Prepare home-made ointments and cosmetics.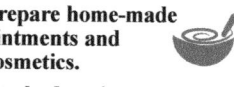

Apply detoxing facial and body care.

Treatments of bumps and pimples on the skin, and exfoliating procedures.

Removing body hair.

Correction of the nail bed.

Massages that serve to relax, ease tension, and detoxify.

Reflexology massage.

Removal of callused skin.

Treating obstinate athlete's foot, nail fungus, and warts.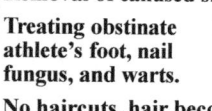

No haircuts, hair becomes shaggy and unmanageable. Avoid washing your hair.

Garden/Nature

Plant part:
Leaf

Water plants.

Fertilize flowers.

Sow plants and vegetables that grow below ground, leaf vegetables, and lettuce.

Dig over/plow to prepare soil for planting.

Trimming and cutting back plants. Transplanting. Weeding.

Combating pests above ground.

Start a compost heap.

Mowing lawns.

Gather herbs (roots) for bronchitis, stomach, liver, and gall bladder complaints.

Unfavorable for harvesting, storing, and preserving.

Housework

Housework is dealt with much more successfully, efficiently, and effortlessly.

Problem stains are removed readily.

Best for doing laundry! Reduce on laundry detergent, support the environment.

Dry cleaning.

Thoroughly clean wooden and parquet floors, metals, china etc.

Cleaning, polishing, and waterproofing shoes.

Combating mold.

Ventilate rooms briefly and rapidly.

Avoid painting.

Nutrition

Food quality:
Carbohydrate

Lettuce, spinach, lamb's lettuce, Endive, parsley, leek, cabbage (Brussels sprouts, kale, Chinese cabbage), all leafy herbs, asparagus, mushrooms, cress, Swiss chard, rhubarb.

Weight associated with overeating is less likely. If underweight, eat larger portions.

Moodiness may make you want to eat more than is healthy. If overweight avoid carbohydrates.

Cleansing and detox diets. Fruit and juice days.

Flush out poisons. Treatment for drug abuse.

If you get stomach troubles easily, avoid heavy meals.

Don't be so humble –
you are not that great.
Golda Meir

Color
Green

Day
Wetness

Element
Water

Cancer

Ⅱ ➔ ♋ 12:47 AM PDT
2:47 AM CDT
3:47 AM EDT

9 Sunday

10 Monday

Positive affirmation:
"My courage grows each day."

Planting Time
Descending forces!
Sap is drawn
downward, enhancing
root formation.
Best days for sowing,
planting, and
transplanting.

detox
remove
be active

Waning Moon

A U G U S T

Success

Determination reigns, and risks are taken more often. Master your tasks with more self-confidence and creativity.

Limits appear to be more easily surmountable.

Auspicious day for sales, advertising, and publicity.

● *New Moon: Confirm your resolutions. Finalize new decisions. Drop bad habits.*

Leisure

Zest for life is in the air. People want to have a fun time, enjoy parties, musical events, movies, etc.

Possessive feelings can harm a relationship. Romance can be very passionate.

Outings: even with cloudy skies the air still feels somewhat warm. Drying effect, get plenty to drink.

Danger of sudden storms, not only in the sky.

Health

Sensitive body parts:
Heart, Back, Diaphragm, Circulation, Arteries

All measures taken to flush out and detoxify the sensitive body parts are very effective.

Scarring is less severe.

Teeth: Removal of tartar and amalgam. Best for fillings, crowns, and dentures!

Blood-purifying, detoxifying herbal infusions and teas.

Sensitive sense organs.

Back and heart problems are more likely to occur.

Avoid overstraining of the heart and circulation with unusual physical activities.

Expect sleepless nights.

● *New Moon: Avoid any surgery if possible.*

Body Care

Aromas, scents:
Hibiscus,
Oleander, Rose

Prepare home-made ointments and cosmetics.

Apply detoxing facial and body care.

Treatments of bumps and pimples on the skin, and exfoliating procedures.

Removing body hair.

Correction of the nail bed.

Massages that serve to relax, ease tension, and detoxify.

Reflexology massage.

Removal of callused skin.

Treating obstinate athlete's foot, nail fungus, and warts.

Good days for haircuts, hair becomes stronger. But be aware that if you get a perm, curls will become quite frizzy. Baby's first haircut.

Garden/Nature

Plant part:
Fruit

Sowing plants and vegetables that grow below ground.

Sowing and planting fruit. Also sow and plant vegetables that are highly perishable. Plant trees and bushes. Sow lawns.

Dig over/plow to prepare soil for planting.

Trimming and cutting back plants. Pruning of fruit trees and bushes.

Transplanting.

Not suitable for fertilizing.

Weeding. Pest Control.

Harvested produce should be consumed as soon as possible.

Gather herbs (roots) for heart and circulation complaints.

Start compost heap.

● *New Moon: Change of weather is likely. Care for sickly plants.*

Housework

Housework is dealt with much more successfully, efficiently, and effortlessly.

Problem stains are removed readily.

Best for doing laundry!

Dry cleaning.

Thoroughly clean wooden and parquet floors, metals, china, etc.

Cleaning windows and glass.

Cleaning, polishing, and waterproofing shoes.

Combating mold.

Ventilate rooms sufficiently. Air beds.

Suitable for making cheese.

Preserving and freezing fruit and vegetables.

Baking bread, cakes, and cookies (use more leavening agent).

Avoid painting.

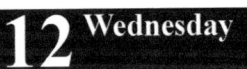

Nutrition

Food quality:
Protein

Beans, peas, corn, tomatoes, pumpkin, lentils, soybeans, cucumber, eggplant, zucchini, berries, fruit, chili, bell pepper, figs, avocado, melon, olives.

Weight associated with overeating is less likely. If underweight, eat larger portions.

Cleansing and detox diets. Fruit and juice days.

Flush out poisons. Treatment for drug abuse.

● *New Moon: A day of fasting.*

Never, never, never give in!
Winston Churchill

Color **Green**

Day **Warm**

Element

Leo Fire

♋ → ♌ ← 1:39 AM PDT
3:39 AM CDT
4:39 AM EDT

11 Tuesday

12 Wednesday

● **New Moon** 10:38 AM PDT
12:38 PM CDT, 1:38 PM EDT
Solar Eclipse 10:47 AM PDT
12:47 PM CDT, 1:47 PM EDT
No meat.

A U G U S T

Positive affirmation:
"My courage grows each day."

Planting Time
Descending forces!
Sap is drawn downward, enhancing root formation.
Best days for sowing, planting, and transplanting.

detox
remove
be active

Waning Moon

Success

Good time for details, organization, routine, concentration, and duty.

Take care of financial and administrative tasks.

Prepare for future success now with realistic and critical assessment.

Leisure

Enjoy a nature walk.

Good time for health regimes. Improve your health with stretching exercises and yoga.

The earth feels cold to the touch, so take slightly warmer clothes.

Health

Sensitive body parts:
Digestive Organs, Nerves, Spleen, Pancreas

All measures taken to supply nutrient materials and strengthen the sensitive body parts are very effective.

Healing ointments are easily absorbed.

Sensitive blood circulation.

For a sensitive digestive system, a wholesome diet is recommended.

Dress slightly warmer.

High blood pressure: Avoid salty foods.

Massages, lymphatic therapy, and chiropractic treatment to release blockages.

Body Care

Aromas, scents:
Lavender, Spruce Needles, Sage, Meadow Flowers

Treatments with firming and moisturizing creams are more effective.

Massages that serve to regenerate, and strengthen, perhaps aided with beneficial massage oils.

Correcting and cutting ingrown nails.

Best for haircuts because it retains its shape longer. Perms turn out best. Hair dyes applied now, will look more vibrant.

Garden/Nature

Plant part:
Root

Best for sowing and planting, except lettuce.

Plant trees which are supposed to grow very tall. Plant hedges and bushes that are meant to grow very fast.

Sowing lawns.

Planting and re-potting balcony and indoor plants.

Transplanting.

Trimming and cutting back plants.

Planting cuttings.

Start a compost heap.

Avoid harvesting and storing.

Gather herbs (roots) for digestive organs, pancreas, and nervous complaints.

Housework

Light housework only.

Air rooms only briefly.

Making pickles, preserves, and cheese yields suboptimal results and should be avoided.

Nutrition

Food quality:
Salt

Garlic, carrots, red beets, reddish, rutabaga, sugar beet, celery, potatoes, onions, kohlrabi.

Weight gain: avoid indulging in rich foods. If overweight, eat smaller portions.

Supply nutrient materials to strengthen the body. Focus on foods that contain essential minerals and vitamins.

Stimulants and vitamins are more effective.

Avoid large quantities of salty foods like bacon, ham, salted herring, fatty cheese, and the like. Avoid heavy and greasy foods.

Positive affirmation:
"My heart is at peace."

Planting Time
Descending forces!
Sap is drawn downward, enhancing root formation.
Best days for sowing, planting, and transplanting.

gather strength
rest, recover
buildup
Waxing Moon

♌ → ♍
3:19 AM PDT
5:19 AM CDT
6:19 AM EDT

13 Thursday

14 Friday

No meat. Cutting and filing toenails and fingernails.

A U G U S T

If a cluttered desk is a sign of a cluttered mind, of what, then, is an empty desk a sign?
Albert Einstein

Color
Yellow

Day
Cool

Element
Earth

♍
Virgo

Success

The artistic instinct rules, but so, too, does indecisiveness. The forces swing back and forth until equilibrium is achieved.

It's easy to reach compromises with tactful sensitivity.

A sense of judgment will support legal matters.

Leisure

Pursuit for harmony and cooperativeness supports good times in romance, friendship, and partnership.

Enjoy cultural events. Relax and get pampered with a spa treatment.

Romance can be passionate yet sensitive.

Health

Sensitive body parts:

Hips, Kidneys, Bladder

All measures taken to supply nutrient materials and strengthen the sensitive body parts are very effective.

Healing ointments are easily absorbed.

Sensitive glandular system.

Take special care to keep the area of bladder and kidneys warm.

Apply special exercises for the hip region.

Avoid having any teeth pulled.

Sensitivity to light, bring your sunglasses along.

Body Care

Aromas, scents: Roses, Violets, Daffodils

Treatments with firming and moisturizing creams are more effective.

Massages that serve to regenerate, and strengthen, perhaps aided with beneficial massage oils.

Correcting and cutting ingrown nails.

Hair dyes applied now, will look more vibrant.

Garden/Nature

Plant part:

Flower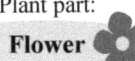

Sow plants and vegetables that grow and flourish above ground, specially flowers, and medicinal herbs.

Transplanting.

Trimming and cutting back plants.

Avoid watering plants.

Start a compost heap.

Harvested produce should be consumed as soon as possible.

Gather herbs for kidneys, gall bladder, and hip complaints.

Day off on 8/16.

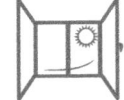

Housework

Light housework only.

Ventilate rooms thoroughly.

Baking cakes and cookies. Dough rises faster. (Except on New Moon)

Nutrition

Food quality:

Fat

Cauliflower, artichoke, broccoli, sunflower seeds, flax seeds, nuts, rose hip, elder.

Weight gain: avoid indulging in rich foods. If overweight, eat smaller portions.

Supply nutrient materials to strengthen the body. Focus on foods that contain essential minerals and vitamins.

Stimulants and vitamins are more effective.

Pay attention to any particularly tempting foods today: Most likely the "wrong" things taste best.

High cholesterol: eat a low fat diet.

Positive affirmation:
"My heart is at peace."

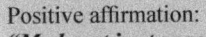

Planting Time
Descending forces! Sap is drawn downward, enhancing root formation. Best days for sowing, planting, and transplanting.

gather strength rest, recover buildup

Waxing Moon

	7:21 AM PDT		
♍→♎	9:21 AM CDT		
	10:21 AM EDT		

2:47 PM PDT	
4:47 PM CDT	♎→♏
5:47 PM EDT	

15 Saturday Assumption of Mary

16 Sunday National Senior Citizens Day (US)

17 Monday

A U G U S T

Morality is simply the attitude we adopt towards people we personally dislike.
Oscar Wilde

Color **Orange**

Day **Air/Light**

Element **Air**

Libra ♎

Success

Critical and superstitious behavior emerges, especially pertaining to money.

A penetrating power will strengthen your capacity to act.

An increased perception opens our interest for the essentials and helps to discover hidden potentials.

Leisure

Relax within your close family, with meditation, and relaxation exercises.

A longing to feel safe will be nurtured if you focus on habits and rituals. An increased sensitivity will help to enjoy every moment.

Romance can be very passionate.

If you plan outdoor excursions, be prepared for a shower here and there.

Health

Sensitive body parts:

Sex organs, Ureter

All measures taken to supply nutrient materials and strengthen the sensitive body parts are very effective.

Healing ointments are easily absorbed. Applying herbal ointments to the shoulders for rheumatic gout and alike.

Sensitive nervous system.

Female disorders: As a preventative measure apply hip baths using yarrow.

Pregnancy: Avoid any exertion, miscarriages are more likely.

Keep region of the pelvis, kidneys, and feet warm to prevent infection of the bladder and kidneys.

Lymphatic therapy.

Body Care

Aromas, scents:
Anemone, Cornflower
Oregano, Thuja

Treatments with firming and moisturizing creams are more effective.

Massages that serve to regenerate, and strengthen, perhaps aided with beneficial massage oils.

Correcting and cutting ingrown nails.

Hair dyes applied now, will look more vibrant.

Garden/Nature

Plant part:

Leaf

Watering all indoor and outdoor plants.

Sow plants, herbs, and vegetables that grow and flourish above ground, leaf vegetables (no lettuce).

Sowing, planting, harvesting, and drying every kind of medicinal herbs.

Transplanting.

Trimming and cutting back plants.
Combating slugs and snails.
Mowing lawns.

Start a compost heap.

Avoid pruning fruit trees and bushes. Avoid cutting down any trees.

Harvested produce should be consumed as soon as possible.

Housework

Light housework only.

Ventilate rooms briefly and rapidly. Don't air mattresses.

Any dirt and spots are easily removed in the laundry.

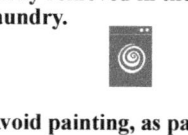

Avoid painting, as paint will take very long to dry.

Nutrition

Food quality:

Carbohydrate

Lettuce, spinach, lamb's lettuce, Endive, parsley, leek, cabbage (Brussels sprouts, kale, Chinese cabbage), all leafy herbs, asparagus, mushrooms, cress, Swiss chard, rhubarb.

Weight gain: avoid indulging in rich foods. If overweight, eat smaller portions and avoid carbohydrates.

Supply nutrient materials to strengthen the body. Focus on foods that contain essential minerals and vitamins. Stimulants and vitamins are more effective.

Positive affirmation:
"My heart is at peace."

Planting Time
Descending forces!
Sap is drawn downward, enhancing root formation.
Best days for sowing, planting, and transplanting.

gather strength
rest, recover
buildup
Waxing Moon

18 Tuesday

19 Wednesday

☾ Half Moon. No meat.

Music is a form of mathematics you can sense.
Negar Knowles

Color
Red

Day
Wetness

Element
Water

A U G U S T

♏

Scorpio

Success

Inquisitiveness and exuberant inspiration lead to new horizons. Insight and love for truth reign.

Bringing together is more important than splitting asunder.

Expansive forces will assist in legal matters, discussions, and debates.

Leisure

Expansion feels great, and travel, short trips, and outings are most welcome. A competitive spirit excites any sports event.

Talk things out when necessary.

Romance can be very passionate.

Good days for outings; even with cloudy skies the air still feels somewhat warm. Drying effect, get plenty to drink.

Health

Sensitive body parts:

Thighs and Veins

All measures taken to supply nutrient materials and strengthen the sensitive body parts are very effective.

Healing ointments are easily absorbed.

Sensitive sense organs.

Pains often arise in the sciatic nerve, veins, the small of the back, and thighs.

Avoid overstraining the body with unusual physical activities.

Body Care

Aromas, scents: Calendula (Marigold), Geranium, Rosemary

Treatments with firming and moisturizing creams are more effective.

Massages that serve to regenerate, and strengthen, perhaps aided with beneficial massage oils.

Correcting and cutting ingrown nails.

Hair dyes applied now, will look more vibrant.

Garden/Nature

Plant part:

Fruit

Sow plants and vegetables that grow and flourish above ground.

Sowing and planting fruit and vegetables that grow tall, and tomatoes, but no lettuce.

Transplanting.

Grafting onto fruit trees.

Cultivating grains, particularly corn.

Gather herbs for vein diseases.

Housework

Light housework only.

Ventilate sufficiently.

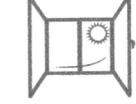

Freezing fruit and vegetables.

Baking bread, cakes, and cookies. Dough rises faster. (Except on New Moon)

Suitable for making cheese.

Making preserves.

Nutrition

Food quality:

Protein

Beans, peas, corn, tomatoes, pumpkin, lentils, soybeans, cucumber, eggplant, zucchini, berries, fruit, chili, bell pepper, figs, avocado, melon, olives.

Weight gain: avoid indulging in rich foods. If overweight, eat smaller portions.

Supply nutrient materials to strengthen the body. Focus on foods that contain essential minerals and vitamins.

Stimulants and vitamins are more effective.

Positive affirmation:
"My heart is at peace."

Turning Point

Transition of descending to ascending forces. Both forces are at work and neutralize each other.

gather strength rest, recover buildup

Waxing Moon

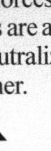

♏ ➔ ♐
1:31 AM PDT
3:31 AM CDT
4:31 AM EDT

20 Thursday

21 Friday

No meat. Cutting and filing toenails and fingernails.

22 Saturday

2:00 PM PDT
4:00 PM CDT
5:00 PM EDT
♐ ➔ ♑

A U G U S T

What you are is God's gift to you, what you become is your gift to God.
Hans Urs von Balthasar

Color
Orange/Yellow

Day
Warm

Element
Fire

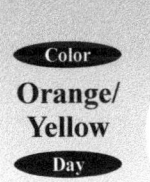

Sagittarius

Success

Career and business are in the foreground now and thinking becomes clear and serious, but somewhat inflexible.

Perseverance and reasoning assist in financial matters, planning, and contracts.

The values of tradition, authority, and discipline impact our endeavors.

Leisure

Money is not likely to be wasted in a shopping spree.

Many are drawn to enjoy cultural events.

The earth feels cold to the touch, so take slightly warmer clothes.

Health

Sensitive body parts:

Knees, Joints, Bones, Skin

All measures taken to supply nutrient materials and strengthen the sensitive body parts are very effective.

Healing ointments are easily absorbed.

Sensitive blood circulation.

Avoid overstraining bones and knees, and apply gentle stretching exercises only.

Problems with meniscus: Don't overstrain.

Dress slightly warmer.

High blood pressure: Avoid salty foods.

Massages, lymphatic therapy, and chiropractic treatment to release blockages.

Body Care

Aromas, scents:

Cedar, Juniper

Treatments with firming and moisturizing creams are more effective.

Massages that serve to regenerate, and strengthen, perhaps aided with beneficial massage oils.

Correcting and cutting ingrown nails.

Every kind of skin care is beneficial.

Cutting and filing toenails and fingernails will make the nails grow stronger over time.

Hair dyes applied now, will look more vibrant.

Garden/Nature

Plant part:

Root

Sow plants, herbs, and vegetables that grow and flourish above ground.

Transplanting.

Harvest produce is suitable for storage. Harvest root vegetables.

Gather herbs for bone, joint, and skin diseases.

Housework

Light housework only.

Air rooms only briefly.

Preserving root vegetables.

Avoid dry cleaning, as the fabric may develop unwanted glossy blotches.

Nutrition

Food quality:

Salt

Garlic, carrots, red beets, reddish, rutabaga, sugar beet, celery, potatoes, onions, kohlrabi.

Weight gain: avoid indulging in rich foods. If overweight, eat smaller portions.

Supply nutrient materials to strengthen the body. Focus on foods that contain essential minerals and vitamins.

Stimulants and vitamins are more effective.

Avoid large quantities of salty foods like bacon, ham, salted herring, fatty cheese, and the like. Avoid heavy and greasy foods.

Positive affirmation:
"My heart is at peace."

Harvest Time
Ascending forces! Sap is rising, enhancing plant growth above ground, resulting in the most juicy fruits and vegetables.

gather strength rest, recover buildup
Waxing Moon

23 Sunday

24 Monday

Trust yourself. You know more than you think you do.
Benjamin Spock

Color
Yellow

Day

Cool

Element

Earth

Capricorn

A U G U S T

Success

Inspiration, optimism, and impatience. Rational thinking, creativity and imagination spark new ideas and inspire planning for the future.

Shying away from routine tasks people will feel more drawn to anything new.

Instead of gridlocked structures choose new possibilities.

Leisure

Inspiration and optimism will boost friendship, social gatherings, and parties.

Express your creativity and imagination. Dwell in dreams and utopian ideas. It is easier now to perceive intuitive thoughts.

Health

Sensitive body parts:
Lower Legs, Veins

All measures taken to supply nutrient materials and strengthen the sensitive body parts are very effective.

Healing ointments are easily absorbed.

Sensitive glandular system.

Avoid inflammation of the veins. Apply ointments to lower legs, and rest legs in a raised position.

Varicose veins: Avoid long periods of standing.

While exercising go easy on the ankles.

Sensitivity to light, so bring your sunglasses along.

○ *Full Moon: Avoid any surgery and vaccination if possible.*

Body Care

Aromas, scents: Cyclamen, Peach, Wild Roses

Treatments with firming and moisturizing creams are more effective.

Massages that serve to regenerate, and strengthen, perhaps aided with beneficial massage oils.

Correcting and cutting ingrown nails.

Hair dyes applied now, will look more vibrant.

Garden/Nature

Plant part:
Flower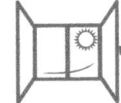

Avoid watering plants.

Harvested produce is well suitable for storage.

Gather herbs for vein diseases.

○ *Full Moon: Weather and climate changes. Herbs are most powerful.*

Housework

Light housework only.

Ventilate rooms thoroughly.

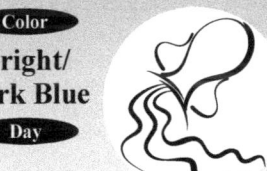

Baking cakes and cookies. Dough rises faster. (Except on New Moon)

○ *Full Moon: Avoid doing laundry, cleaning windows, making preserves, painting.*

Nutrition

Food quality:
Fat

Cauliflower, artichoke, broccoli, sunflower seeds, flax seeds, nuts, rose hip, elder.

Weight gain: avoid indulging in rich foods. If overweight, eat smaller portions.

Supply nutrient materials to strengthen the body. Focus on foods that contain essential minerals and vitamins.

Stimulants and vitamins are more effective.

Pay attention to any particularly tempting foods today: Most likely the "wrong" things taste best.

High cholesterol: eat a low fat diet.

○ *Full Moon: A day of fasting.*

Positive affirmation:
"My heart is at peace."

Harvest Time
Ascending forces! Sap is rising, enhancing plant growth above ground, resulting in the most juicy fruits and vegetables.

gather strength rest, recover buildup
Waxing Moon

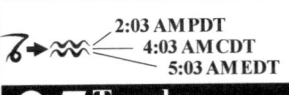

2:03 AM PDT
4:03 AM CDT
5:03 AM EDT

25 Tuesday

26 Wednesday
Women's Equality Day (US)

The Prophet's Birthday
No meat.

12:05 PM PDT
2:05 PM CDT
3:05 PM EDT

27 Thursday
Raksha Bandhan

○ **Full Moon** 9:20 PM PDT, 11:20 PM CDT, 12:20 AM EDT Friday
Solar Eclipse 9:14 PM PDT, 11:14 PM CDT, 12:14 AM EDT Friday

A U G U S T

The philosophers have only interpreted the world, in various ways: the point, however, is to change it.
Karl Marx

Color
Bright/ Dark Blue

Day
Air/Light

Element

Air   Aquarius

Success

Sensibility, intuition, and helpfulness.

Where possible, retreating is more favorable than dealing with business matters.

Dissolve restrictions, be patient and wait. Be aware that people can be more easily influenced.

Leisure

Your helpfulness will boost friendships.

Enjoy dancing or swimming, or watch a movie that will inspire your fantasies and imagination.

Retreat, relax, and recover.

Romance can be gentle and coziness will prevail.

If you plan outdoor excursions, be prepared for a shower here and there.

Health

Sensitive body parts:

Feet and Toes

All measures taken to flush out and detoxify the sensitive body parts are very effective.

Good for surgical operations except those on the sensitive body parts (see above), digestive organs, nerves, spleen, pancreas.
Scarring is less severe.

Teeth: Removal of tartar and amalgam. Best for fillings, crowns, and dentures!

Blood-purifying, detoxifying herbal infusions and teas.

Sensitive nervous system.

Drugs have a much stronger effect on your body. Monitor closely what you put into your body.

Lymphatic therapy.

Sluggishness or fatigue may occur in the transition into the next Zodiac sign of Aries.

Body Care

Aromas, scents:
Magnolia, Amaryllis, Clary Sage

Prepare home-made ointments and cosmetics.

Apply detoxing facial and body care.

Treatments of bumps and pimples on the skin, and exfoliating procedures.

Removing body hair.

Correction of the nail bed.

Massages that serve to relax, ease tension, and detoxify. Reflexology massage. Carry out with special care, people are more sensitive.

Removal of callused skin.

Treating obstinate athlete's foot, nail fungus, and warts.

Foot bath.

No haircuts, hair becomes shaggy and unmanageable.
Avoid washing your hair.

Garden/Nature

Plant part:

Leaf

Water plants.

Fertilize flowers.

Sow plants and vegetables that grow below ground, potatoes, leaf vegetables, and lettuce.
Dig over/plow to prepare soil for planting.
Trimming and cutting back plants.
Start a compost heap.

Mowing lawns.

Pest control. Weeding.

Harvested produce should be consumed as soon as possible.

Gather herbs for foot complaints.

Housework

Housework is dealt with much more successfully, efficiently, and effortlessly.

Problem stains are removed readily.

Best for doing laundry! Reduce on laundry detergent, support the environment.

Dry cleaning.

Clean and store seasonal clothing.

Thoroughly clean wooden and parquet floors, metals, china etc.

Cleaning, polishing, and waterproofing shoes.

Combating mold.

Ventilate rooms briefly and rapidly.

Avoid painting.

Preserving and storing should be avoided.

Nutrition

Food quality:

Carbohydrate

Lettuce, spinach, lamb's lettuce, Endive, parsley, leek, cabbage (Brussels sprouts, kale, Chinese cabbage), all leafy herbs, asparagus, mushrooms, cress, Swiss chard, rhubarb.

Weight associated with overeating is less likely. If underweight, eat larger portions.

Cleansing and detox diets. Fruit and juice days.

Flush out poisons. Treatment for drug abuse.

Caffeine, alcohol, drugs, certain foods, and stimulants have a much stronger effect.

A man should never be ashamed to own that he has been in the wrong, which is but saying in other words that he is wiser today than he was yesterday.
Alexander Pope

Color
Blueish White

Day

Wetness

Element

Pisces   **Water**

7:39 PM PDT
9:39 PM CDT   ⟶ ♓ ➝ ♈
10:39 PM EDT

28 Friday

No meat. Cutting and filing toenails and fingernails.

29 Saturday

A U G U S T

Harvest Time
Ascending forces! Sap is rising, enhancing plant growth above ground, resulting in the most juicy fruits and vegetables.

detox remove be active
Waning Moon

Success

Things get going and the way straight ahead seems the best.

People feel energetic, courageous, assertive, and at times anxious.

Good time for meetings and sales talks but impatience and selfishness do not favor teamwork.

Leisure

An enterprising spirit and spontaneity move people to enjoy outings, sports, competitions, cultural events, and travels.

Romance can be very passionate.

Good days for outings, even with cloudy skies the air still feels somewhat warm. Drying effect, get plenty to drink.

Health

Sensitive body parts:
Head, Brain, Eyes

All measures taken to flush out and detoxify the sensitive body parts are very effective.

Good for surgery, except on the sensitive body parts (see above), digestive organs, nerves, spleen, and pancreas.

Scarring is less severe.

Teeth: Removal of tartar and amalgam. Best for fillings, crowns, and dentures! Avoiding treatment of periodontitis and gums.

Blood-purifying, detoxifying herbal infusions and teas.

Sensitive sense organs.

If you suffer from migraines drink plenty of water, and avoid coffee, chocolate, and sugar.

Body Care

Aromas, scents:
Cloves, Peppermint, Thyme

Prepare home-made ointments and cosmetics.

Apply detoxing facial and body care.

Treatments of bumps and pimples on the skin, and exfoliating procedures.

Removing body hair.

Correction of the nail bed.

Massages that serve to relax, ease tension, and detoxify.

Reflexology massage.

Removal of callused skin.

Treating obstinate athlete's foot, nail fungus, and warts.

Eye compresses to relieve strained eyes.

Any kind of hair care.

Garden/Nature

Plant part:
Fruit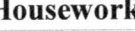

Sowing plants and vegetables that grow below ground.

Sowing and planting anything that is supposed to grow fast. Sowing and planting fruit and tomatoes.

Dig over/plow the soil to prepare for planting.

Spreading manure. Fertilizing grains, vegetables, and fruit.

Weeding. Pest control.

Pruning of fruit trees and bushes.

Harvesting and storing grains, vegetables, potatoes, fruits, and tomatoes.

Start a compost heap.

Gather herbs (roots) for eye complaints and headaches.

Day off on 8/30.

Housework

Housework is dealt with much more successfully, efficiently, and effortlessly.

Problem stains are removed readily.

Best for doing laundry!

Dry cleaning.

Clean and store seasonal clothing.

Thoroughly clean wooden and parquet floors, metals, china, etc.

Cleaning windows and glass.

Cleaning, polishing, and waterproofing shoes.

Combating mold.

Ventilate rooms sufficiently. Air beds.

Suitable for making cheese.

Preserving and freezing fruit and vegetables.

Baking bread, cakes, and cookies (use more leavening agent).

Painting.

Nutrition

Food quality:
Protein

Beans, peas, corn, tomatoes, pumpkin, lentils, soybeans, cucumber, eggplant, zucchini, berries, fruit, chili, bell pepper, figs, avocado, melon, olives.

Weight associated with overeating is less likely. If underweight, eat larger portions.

Cleansing and detox diets. Fruit and juice days.

Flush out poisons. Treatment for drug abuse.

Drink plenty of water.

The trouble about man is twofold. He cannot learn truths which are too complicated; he forgets truths which are too simple.
Rebecca West

Aries   Fire

Color — **Indigo Blue**

Day — **Warm**

Element

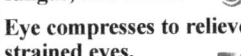

30 Sunday

31 Monday

Positive affirmation:
"My heart is at peace."

Harvest Time
Ascending forces! Sap is rising, enhancing plant growth above ground, resulting in the most juicy fruits and vegetables.

detox
remove
be active
Waning Moon

Success

Realism and material security are important. Persistence comes easy, thoughts and reactions are slower.

Assess financial areas.

Conservative tendencies may make people want to stay away from risk taking.

Leisure

Relax at a picnic/feast. Enjoy culinary pleasures and hobbies.

The earth feels cold to the touch, so take slightly warmer clothes.

Health

Sensitive body parts:
Head and Neck

All measures taken to flush out and detoxify the sensitive body parts are very effective.

Good for surgery, except on the sensitive body parts (see above), digestive organs, nerves, spleen, and pancreas. Scarring is less severe.

Teeth: Removal of tartar and amalgam. Best for fillings, crowns, and dentures! Avoiding treatment of periodontitis and gums.

Blood-purifying, detoxifying herbal infusions and teas.

Sensitive blood circulation.

Organs of speech, jaws, teeth, tonsils, thyroid gland, neck, and vocal chords get easily affected. Keep neck warm. On cold days ears should be protected. Sensitivity to noise.

High blood pressure: Avoid salty foods.

Massages, lymphatic therapy, and chiropractic treatment to release blockages.

Body Care

Aromas, scents: Geranium, Jasmine, Rose

Prepare home-made ointments and cosmetics.

Apply detoxing facial and body care.

Treatments of bumps and pimples on the skin, and exfoliating procedures.

Removing body hair.

Correction of the nail bed.

Massages that serve to relax, ease tension, and detoxify.

Reflexology massage.

Removal of callused skin.

Treating obstinate athlete's foot, nail fungus, and warts.

Garden/Nature

Plant part:
Root

Sow plants and vegetables that grow below ground.

Everything grows slowly and lasts well.

Dig over to prepare soil.

Trimming/cutting back plants. Weeding. Mulching.

Start a compost heap.

Combat vermin found in the soil.

Spread fertilizer and liquid manure.

Fertilize flowers with poorly formed roots.

Harvested produce is well suited for storage. Harvesting root vegetables.

Gather herbs (roots) for sinus issues, sore throat, and ear complaints.

Housework

Housework is dealt with much more successfully, efficiently, and effortlessly.

Problem stains are removed readily.

Best for doing laundry! Reduce on laundry detergent, support the environment.

Dry cleaning.

Clean and store seasonal clothing.

Thoroughly clean wooden and parquet floors, metals, china etc.

Cleaning, polishing, and waterproofing shoes.

Combating mold.

Air rooms only briefly.

Painting.

Preserving root vegetables.

Nutrition

Food quality:
Salt

Garlic, carrots, red beets, reddish, rutabaga, sugar beet, celery, potatoes, onions, kohlrabi.

Weight associated with overeating is less likely. If underweight, eat larger portions.

Cleansing and detox diets. Fruit and juice days.

Flush out poisons. Treatment for drug abuse.

Avoid large quantities of salty foods like bacon, ham, salted herring, fatty cheese, and the like.

When I pine at misfortune and call it evil, or am jealous and disappointed, then I know that there is awake in me again the eternal fool.
Sri Aurobindo

Color
Bright Blue

Day

Cool

Element

Taurus   **Earth**

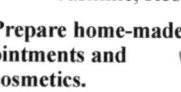

♈ → ♉ ← 1:02 AM PDT
3:02 AM CDT
4:02 AM EDT

1 Tuesday

2 Wednesday

No meat.

S E P T E M B E R

Positive affirmation:
"My heart is at peace."

Harvest Time
Ascending forces! Sap is rising, enhancing plant growth above ground, resulting in the most juicy fruits and vegetables.

detox remove be active
Waning Moon

Success

Open mindedness and curiosity. A changeable and hectic time.

Good time for talking, negotiating, networking, and exchanging ideas as well as for meetings of a nonbinding nature, conferences, and studies.

Leisure

Good time for family gatherings, parties, and short trips.

People enjoy stimulating their minds with reading and studying. Attending theater performances is a preferred enjoyment. Enhance friendships.

Stretching exercises.

Be prepared for sudden changes in weather or climate.

Health

Sensitive body parts:
Shoulders, Arms, Hands, Lungs

All measures taken to flush out and detoxify the sensitive body parts are very effective.

Good for surgery, except on the sensitive body parts (see above), digestive organs, nerves, spleen, pancreas. Scarring is less severe.

Teeth: Removal of tartar and amalgam. Best for fillings, crowns, and dentures! Avoid having any teeth pulled.

Blood-purifying, detoxifying herbal infusions and teas. Sensitive glandular system. Make sure you are dressed warm enough in cool weather.

Exercises for shoulders. Breathing exercises. Sensitivity to light, bring your sunglasses along. Massages, lymphatic therapy, and chiropractic treatment to release blockages.

Body Care

Aromas, scents: Lavender, Lemon Balm, Magnolia, Verbena

Prepare home-made ointments and cosmetics.

Apply detoxing facial and body care.

Treatments of bumps and pimples on the skin, and exfoliating procedures.

Removing body hair.

Correction of the nail bed.

Massages that serve to relax, ease tension, and detoxify.

Reflexology massage.

Removal of callused skin.

Treating obstinate athlete's foot, nail fungus, and warts.

Garden/Nature

Plant part:
Flower

Sow plants and vegetables that grow below ground.

Trimming and cutting back plants.

Start a compost heap.

Weeding. Pest control.

Fertilize flowers that no longer bloom.

Avoid watering plants.

Changes in weather are more likely.

Gather herbs (roots) for tensions in the shoulder and lung complaints.

Housework

Housework is dealt with much more successfully, efficiently, and effortlessly.

Problem stains are removed readily.

Best for doing laundry! Reduce on laundry detergent, support the environment.

Dry cleaning.

Clean and store seasonal clothing.

Thoroughly clean wooden and parquet floors, metals, china etc.

Cleaning windows and glass.

Cleaning, polishing, and waterproofing shoes.

Combating mold.

Ventilate rooms thoroughly.

Baking bread, cakes, and cookies (add more leavening agent).

Making preserves.

Painting.

Nutrition

Food quality:
Fat

Cauliflower, artichoke, broccoli, sunflower seeds, flax seeds, nuts, rose hip, elder.

Weight associated with overeating is less likely. If underweight, eat larger portions.

Cleansing and detox diets. Fruit and juice days.

Flush out poisons. Treatment for drug abuse.

Pay attention to any particularly tempting foods today: Most likely the "wrong" things taste best.

High cholesterol: eat a low fat diet.

The saddest aspect of life right now is that science gathers knowledge faster than society gathers wisdom.
Isaac Asimov

Color

Light Blue

Day

Air/Light

Element

Gemini   **Air**

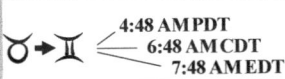
☿ → ♊ ← 4:48 AM PDT
6:48 AM CDT
7:48 AM EDT

3 Thursday

4 Friday
Krishna Janmashtami

☾ **Half Moon.** No meat. Cutting and and filing toenails and fingernails.

S E P T E M B E R

Positive affirmation:
"My heart is at peace."

Turning Point
Transition of ascending to descending forces. Both forces are at work and neutralize each other.

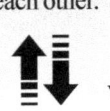
detox
remove
be active
Waning Moon

Success

Feelings, sensitivity, and cooperativeness. Many are overly sensitive, so beware of treading on someone's toes.

Be cautious if you are easily influenced.

During negotiations make use of the cognitive ability of your senses.

Leisure

Relax within your close family.

Retreat to your safe haven and enjoy your fantasy while reading or listening to music. The inner world becomes more colorful than the outer.

Romance can be gentle. Deep feelings will prevail.

If you plan outdoor excursions, be prepared for a shower here and there.

Health

Sensitive body parts:
Chest, Lungs, Liver, Stomach, Gall Bladder

All measures taken to flush out and detoxify the sensitive body parts are very effective.

Good for surgical operations except those on the sensitive body parts (see above), digestive organs, nerves, spleen, pancreas. Scarring is less severe.

Teeth: Removal of tartar and amalgam. Best for fillings, crowns, and dentures!

Blood-purifying, detoxifying herbal infusions and teas.

Sensitive nervous system.

Be cautious with alcohol since the liver is very sensitive.

Stomach could play up and cause gas and heartburn.

Rheumatism: Don't air bedding outside, damp will remain in the bedding.

Lymphatic therapy.

Body Care

Aromas, scents:
Lilac, Lilies of the Valley, Lilies, Violets

Prepare home-made ointments and cosmetics.

Apply detoxing facial and body care.

Treatments of bumps and pimples on the skin, and exfoliating procedures.

Removing body hair.

Correction of the nail bed.

Massages that serve to relax, ease tension, and detoxify.

Reflexology massage.

Removal of callused skin.

Treating obstinate athlete's foot, nail fungus, and warts.

No haircuts, hair becomes shaggy and unmanageable. Avoid washing your hair.

Garden/Nature

Plant part:
Leaf

Water plants.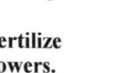

Fertilize flowers.

Sow plants and vegetables that grow below ground, leaf vegetables, and lettuce.

Dig over/plow to prepare soil for planting.

Trimming and cutting back plants. Transplanting. Weeding.

Combating pests above ground.

Start a compost heap.

Mowing lawns.

Gather herbs (roots) for bronchitis, stomach, liver, and gall bladder complaints.

Unfavorable for harvesting, storing, and preserving.

Housework

Housework is dealt with much more successfully, efficiently, and effortlessly.

Problem stains are removed readily.

Best for doing laundry! Reduce on laundry detergent, support the environment.

Dry cleaning.

Thoroughly clean wooden and parquet floors, metals, china etc.

Cleaning, polishing, and waterproofing shoes.

Combating mold.

Ventilate rooms briefly and rapidly.

Avoid painting.

Nutrition

Food quality:
Carbohydrate

Lettuce, spinach, lamb's lettuce, Endive, parsley, leek, cabbage (Brussels sprouts, kale, Chinese cabbage), all leafy herbs, asparagus, mushrooms, cress, Swiss chard, rhubarb.

Weight associated with overeating is less likely. If underweight, eat larger portions.

Moodiness may make you want to eat more than is healthy. If overweight avoid carbohydrates.

Cleansing and detox diets. Fruit and juice days.

Flush out poisons. Treatment for drug abuse.

If you get stomach troubles easily, avoid heavy meals.

Never miss a good chance to shut up.
Will Rogers

Ⅱ ➔ ♋ ← 7:32 AM PDT
9:32 AM CDT
10:32 AM EDT

Color
Green

Day

Wetness

Element

Cancer **Water**

5 Saturday

6 Sunday

Planting Time
Descending forces! Sap is drawn downward, enhancing root formation. Best days for sowing, planting, and transplanting.

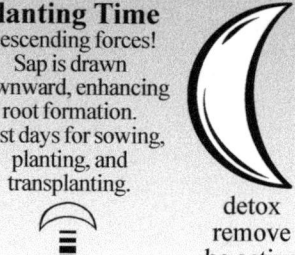

detox
remove
be active

Waning Moon

SEPTEMBER

Success

Determination reigns, and risks are taken more often. Master your tasks with more self-confidence and creativity.

Limits appear to be more easily surmountable.

Auspicious day for sales, advertising, and publicity.

Leisure

Zest for life is in the air. People want to have a fun time, enjoy parties, musical events, movies, etc.

Possessive feelings can harm a relationship. Romance can be very passionate.

Outings: even with cloudy skies the air still feels somewhat warm. Drying effect, get plenty to drink.

Danger of sudden storms, not only in the sky.

Health

Sensitive body parts:
Heart, Back, Diaphragm, Circulation, Arteries

All measures taken to flush out and detoxify the sensitive body parts are very effective.

Good for surgery, except on the sensitive body parts (see above), digestive organs, nerves, spleen, pancreas. Scarring is less severe.

Teeth: Removal of tartar and amalgam. Best for fillings, crowns, and dentures!

Blood-purifying, detoxifying herbal infusions and teas.

Sensitive sense organs.

Back and heart problems are more likely to occur.

Avoid overstraining of the heart and circulation with unusual physical activities.

Expect sleepless nights.

Body Care

Aromas, scents:
Hibiscus,
Oleander, Rose

Prepare home-made ointments and cosmetics.

Apply detoxing facial and body care.

Treatments of bumps and pimples on the skin, and exfoliating procedures.

Removing body hair.

Correction of the nail bed.

Massages that serve to relax, ease tension, and detoxify.

Reflexology massage.

Removal of callused skin.

Treating obstinate athlete's foot, nail fungus, and warts.

Good days for haircuts, hair becomes stronger. But be aware that if you get a perm, curls will become quite frizzy. Baby's first haircut.

Garden/Nature

Plant part:
Fruit

Sowing plants and vegetables that grow below ground.

Sowing and planting fruit. Also sow and plant vegetables that are highly perishable. Plant trees and bushes. Sow lawns.

Dig over/plow to prepare soil for planting.

Trimming and cutting back plants. Pruning of fruit trees and bushes.

Transplanting.

Not suitable for fertilizing.

Weeding. Pest Control.

Harvested produce should be consumed as soon as possible.

Gather herbs (roots) for heart and circulation complaints.

Start compost heap.

Housework

Housework is dealt with much more successfully, efficiently, and effortlessly.

Problem stains are removed readily.

Best for doing laundry!

Dry cleaning.

Thoroughly clean wooden and parquet floors, metals, china, etc.

Cleaning windows and glass.

Cleaning, polishing, and waterproofing shoes.

Combating mold.

Ventilate rooms sufficiently. Air beds.

Suitable for making cheese.

Preserving and freezing fruit and vegetables.

Baking bread, cakes, and cookies (use more leavening agent).

Avoid painting.

Nutrition

Food quality:
Protein

Beans, peas, corn, tomatoes, pumpkin, lentils, soybeans, cucumber, eggplant, zucchini, berries, fruit, chili, bell pepper, figs, avocado, melon, olives.

Weight associated with overeating is less likely. If underweight, eat larger portions.

Cleansing and detox diets. Fruit and juice days.

Flush out poisons. Treatment for drug abuse.

He who knows all the answers has not been asked all the questions.
Confucius

Leo

Color: **Green**

Day: **Warm**

Element: **Fire**

9:51 AM PDT
11:51 AM CDT
12:51 PM EDT
♋ → ♌

12:36 PM PDT
2:36 PM CDT
3:36 PM EDT
♌ → ♍

7 Monday Labor Day

8 Tuesday

9 Wednesday
No meat.

SEPTEMBER

Positive affirmation:
"My heart is at peace."

Planting Time
Descending forces! Sap is drawn downward, enhancing root formation. Best days for sowing, planting, and transplanting.

detox
remove
be active

Waning Moon

Success

Good time for details, organization, routine, concentration, and duty.

Take care of financial and administrative tasks.

Prepare for future success now with realistic and critical assessment.

● *New Moon: Confirm your resolutions. Finalize new decisions. Drop bad habits.*

Leisure

Enjoy a nature walk.

Good time for health regimes. Improve your health with stretching exercises and yoga.

The earth feels cold to the touch, so take slightly warmer clothes.

Health

Sensitive body parts:
Digestive Organs, Nerves, Spleen, Pancreas

All measures taken to flush out and detoxify the sensitive body parts are very effective.

Scarring is less severe.

Teeth: Removal of tartar and amalgam. Best for fillings, crowns, and dentures! Avoiding treatment of periodontitis and gums.

Blood-purifying, detoxifying herbal infusions and teas.

Sensitive blood circulation.

For a sensitive digestive system, a wholesome diet is recommended.

Dress slightly warmer.

High blood pressure: Avoid salty foods.

Massages, lymphatic therapy, and chiropractic treatment to release blockages.

● *New Moon: Avoid any surgery if possible.*

Body Care

Aromas, scents:
Lavender, Spruce Needles, Sage, Meadow Flowers

Prepare home-made ointments and cosmetics.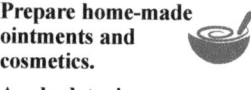

Apply detoxing facial and body care.

Treatments of bumps and pimples on the skin, and exfoliating procedures.

Removing body hair.

Correction of the nail bed.

Massages that serve to relax, ease tension, and detoxify.

Reflexology massage.

Removal of callused skin.

Treating obstinate athlete's foot, nail fungus, and warts.

Best for haircuts because it retains its shape longer. Perms turn out best.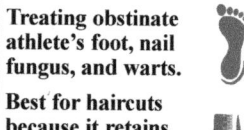

Garden/Nature

Plant part:
Root

Best for sowing and planting, except lettuce.

Plant trees which are supposed to grow very tall. Plant hedges and bushes that are meant to grow very fast.

Planting and re-potting balcony and indoor plants.

Dig over/plow to prepare soil for planting.

Trimming and cutting back plants. Planting cuttings.

Spread fertilizer and manure. Fertilize flowers with poorly formed roots.

Start a compost heap.

Transplanting. Mulching.

Weeding. Pest control (vermin in the soil).

Avoid harvesting and storing.

Gather herbs (roots) for digestive organs, pancreas, and nervous complaints.

● *New Moon: Change of weather is likely. Care for sickly plants.*

Housework

Housework is dealt with much more successfully, efficiently, and effortlessly.

Problem stains are removed readily.

Best for doing laundry! Reduce on laundry detergent, support the environment.

Dry cleaning.

Thoroughly clean wooden and parquet floors, metals, china etc.

Cleaning, polishing, and waterproofing shoes.

Combating mold.

Air rooms only briefly.

Painting.

Making pickles, preserves, and cheese yields suboptimal results and should be avoided.

Nutrition

Food quality:
Salt

Garlic, carrots, red beets, reddish, rutabaga, sugar beet, celery, potatoes, onions, kohlrabi.

Weight associated with overeating is less likely. If underweight, eat larger portions.

Cleansing and detox diets. Fruit and juice days.

Flush out poisons. Treatment for drug abuse.

Avoid large quantities of salty foods like bacon, ham, salted herring, fatty cheese, and the like. Avoid heavy and greasy foods.

● *New Moon: A day of fasting.*

Successful people are always looking for opportunities to help others. Unsuccessfull people are always asking, "What's in it for me?"
Brian Tracy

Color
Yellow

Day
Cool

Element
♍ **Earth**

Virgo

10 Thursday

● New Moon 8:28 PM PDT
10:28 PM CDT, 11:28 PM EDT

SEPTEMBER

Positive affirmation:
"My heart is at peace."

Planting Time
Descending forces!
Sap is drawn downward, enhancing root formation.
Best days for sowing, planting, and transplanting.

detox
remove
be active
Waning Moon

Success

Good time for details, organization, routine, concentration, and duty.

Take care of financial and administrative tasks.

Prepare for future success now with realistic and critical assessment.

Leisure

Enjoy a nature walk.

Good time for health regimes. Improve your health with stretching exercises and yoga.

The earth feels cold to the touch, so take slightly warmer clothes.

Health

Sensitive body parts:

Digestive Organs, Nerves, Spleen, Pancreas

All measures taken to supply nutrient materials and strengthen the sensitive body parts are very effective.

Healing ointments are easily absorbed.

Sensitive blood circulation.

For a sensitive digestive system, a wholesome diet is recommended.

Dress slightly warmer.

High blood pressure: Avoid salty foods.

Massages, lymphatic therapy, and chiropractic treatment to release blockages.

Body Care

Aromas, scents: Lavender, Spruce Needles, Sage, Meadow Flowers

Treatments with firming and moisturizing creams are more effective.

Massages that serve to regenerate, and strengthen, perhaps aided with beneficial massage oils.

Correcting and cutting ingrown nails.

Best for haircuts because it retains its shape longer. Perms turn out best. Hair dyes applied now, will look more vibrant.

Garden/Nature

Plant part:

Root

Best for sowing and planting, except lettuce.

Plant trees which are supposed to grow very tall. Plant hedges and bushes that are meant to grow very fast.

Sowing lawns.

Planting and re-potting balcony and indoor plants.

Transplanting.

Trimming and cutting back plants.

Planting cuttings.

Start a compost heap.

Avoid harvesting and storing.

Gather herbs (roots) for digestive organs, pancreas, and nervous complaints.

Housework

Light housework only.

Air rooms only briefly.

Making pickles, preserves, and cheese yields suboptimal results and should be avoided.

Nutrition

Food quality:

Salt

Garlic, carrots, red beets, reddish, rutabaga, sugar beet, celery, potatoes, onions, kohlrabi.

Weight gain: avoid indulging in rich foods. If overweight, eat smaller portions.

Supply nutrient materials to strengthen the body. Focus on foods that contain essential minerals and vitamins.

Stimulants and vitamins are more effective.

Avoid large quantities of salty foods like bacon, ham, salted herring, fatty cheese, and the like. Avoid heavy and greasy foods.

Positive affirmation:
"My mind is still."

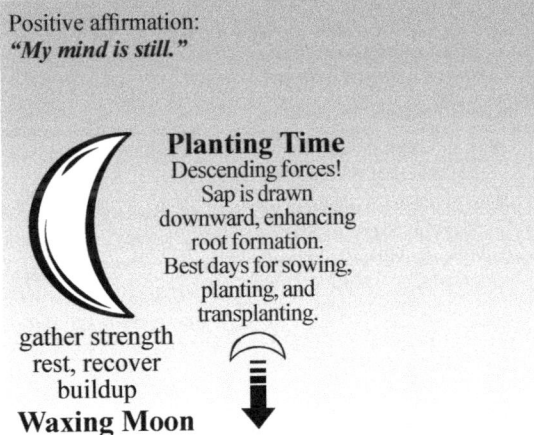

Planting Time
Descending forces!
Sap is drawn downward, enhancing root formation.
Best days for sowing, planting, and transplanting.

gather strength
rest, recover
buildup
Waxing Moon

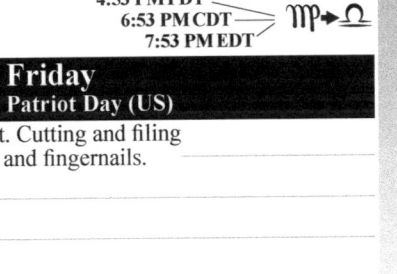

4:53 PM PDT
6:53 PM CDT
7:53 PM EDT
℘ → ♎

11 **Friday**
Patriot Day (US)

No meat. Cutting and filing toenails and fingernails.

S E P T E M B E R

In the case of good books, the point is not to see how many of them you can get through, but rather how many can get through to you.
Mortimer J. Adler

Color
Yellow

Day
Cool

Element
Earth

Virgo

Success

The artistic instinct rules, but so, too, does indecisiveness. The forces swing back and forth until equilibrium is achieved.

It's easy to reach compromises with tactful sensitivity.

A sense of judgment will support legal matters.

Leisure

Pursuit for harmony and cooperativeness supports good times in romance, friendship, and partnership.

Enjoy cultural events. Relax and get pampered with a spa treatment.

Romance can be passionate yet sensitive.

Health

Sensitive body parts:

Hips, Kidneys, Bladder

All measures taken to supply nutrient materials and strengthen the sensitive body parts are very effective.

Healing ointments are easily absorbed.

Sensitive glandular system.

Take special care to keep the area of bladder and kidneys warm.

Apply special exercises for the hip region.

Avoid having any teeth pulled.

Sensitivity to light, bring your sunglasses along.

Body Care

Aromas, scents: Roses, Violets, Daffodils

Treatments with firming and moisturizing creams are more effective.

Massages that serve to regenerate, and strengthen, perhaps aided with beneficial massage oils.

Correcting and cutting ingrown nails.

Hair dyes applied now, will look more vibrant.

Garden/Nature

Plant part:

Flower

Sow plants and vegetables that grow and flourish above ground, specially flowers, and medicinal herbs.

Transplanting.

Trimming and cutting back plants.

Avoid watering plants.

Start a compost heap.

Harvested produce should be consumed as soon as possible.

Gather herbs for kidneys, gall bladder, and hip complaints.

Day off on 9/12.

Housework

Light housework only.

Ventilate rooms thoroughly.

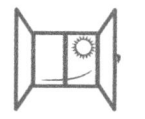

Baking cakes and cookies. Dough rises faster. (Except on New Moon)

Nutrition

Food quality:

Fat

Cauliflower, artichoke, broccoli, sunflower seeds, flax seeds, nuts, rose hip, elder.

Weight gain: avoid indulging in rich foods. If overweight, eat smaller portions.

Supply nutrient materials to strengthen the body. Focus on foods that contain essential minerals and vitamins.

Stimulants and vitamins are more effective.

Pay attention to any particularly tempting foods today: Most likely the "wrong" things taste best.

High cholesterol: eat a low fat diet.

Positive affirmation:
"My mind is still."

Planting Time
Descending forces! Sap is drawn downward, enhancing root formation. Best days for sowing, planting, and transplanting.

gather strength rest, recover buildup
Waxing Moon

12 Saturday
Rosh Hashanah

13 Sunday
National Grandparents Day (US)

The price good men pay for indifference to public affairs is to be ruled by evil men.
Plato

Color
Orange

Day
Air/Light

Element
Air

Libra

S E P T E M B E R

Success

Critical and superstitious behavior emerges, especially pertaining to money.

A penetrating power will strengthen your capacity to act.

An increased perception opens our interest for the essentials and helps to discover hidden potentials.

Leisure

Relax within your close family, with meditation, and relaxation exercises.

A longing to feel safe will be nurtured if you focus on habits and rituals. An increased sensitivity will help to enjoy every moment.

Romance can be very passionate.

If you plan outdoor excursions, be prepared for a shower here and there.

Health

Sensitive body parts:

Sex organs, Ureter

All measures taken to supply nutrient materials and strengthen the sensitive body parts are very effective.

Healing ointments are easily absorbed. Applying herbal ointments to the shoulders for rheumatic gout and alike.

Sensitive nervous system.

Female disorders: As a preventative measure apply hip baths using yarrow.

Pregnancy: Avoid any exertion, miscarriages are more likely.

Keep region of the pelvis, kidneys, and feet warm to prevent infection of the bladder and kidneys.

Lymphatic therapy.

Body Care

Aromas, scents:
Anemone, Cornflower
Oregano, Thuja

Treatments with firming and moisturizing creams are more effective.

Massages that serve to regenerate, and strengthen, perhaps aided with beneficial massage oils.

Correcting and cutting ingrown nails.

Hair dyes applied now, will look more vibrant.

Garden/Nature

Plant part:

Leaf

Watering all indoor and outdoor plants.

Sow plants, herbs, and vegetables that grow and flourish above ground, leaf vegetables (no lettuce).

Sowing, planting, harvesting, and drying every kind of medicinal herbs.

Transplanting.

Trimming and cutting back plants.
Combating slugs and snails.
Mowing lawns.

Start a compost heap.

Avoid pruning fruit trees and bushes. Avoid cutting down any trees.

Harvested produce should be consumed as soon as possible.

Housework

Light housework only.

Ventilate rooms briefly and rapidly. Don't air mattresses.

Any dirt and spots are easily removed in the laundry.

Avoid painting, as paint will take very long to dry.

Nutrition

Food quality:

Carbohydrate

Lettuce, spinach, lamb's lettuce, Endive, parsley, leek, cabbage (Brussels sprouts, kale, Chinese cabbage), all leafy herbs, asparagus, mushrooms, cress, Swiss chard, rhubarb.

Weight gain: avoid indulging in rich foods. If overweight, eat smaller portions and avoid carbohydrates.

Supply nutrient materials to strengthen the body. Focus on foods that contain essential minerals and vitamins. Stimulants and vitamins are more effective.

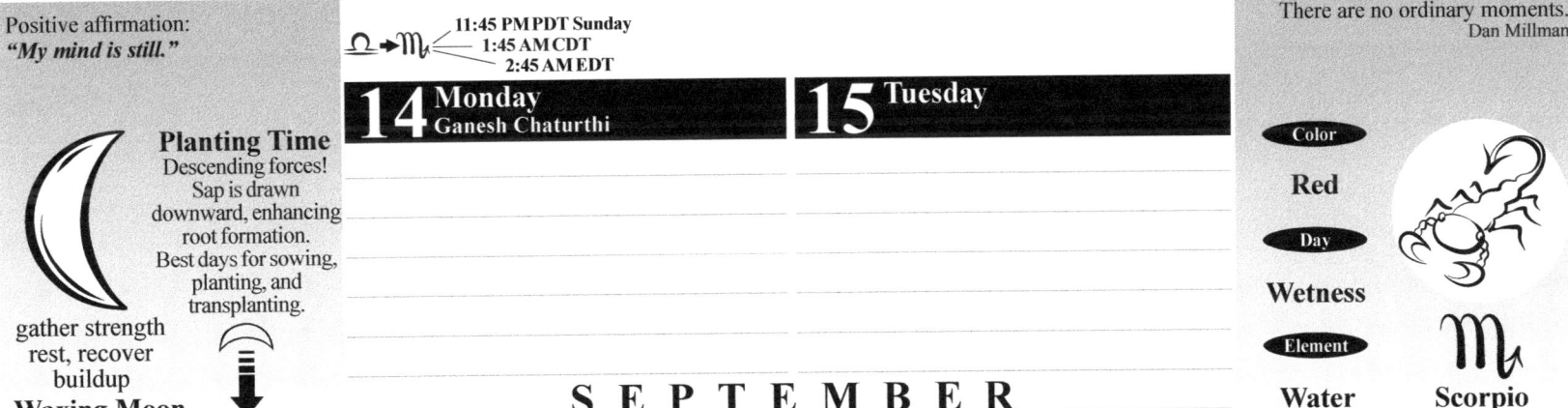

Positive affirmation:
"My mind is still."

Planting Time
Descending forces!
Sap is drawn downward, enhancing root formation. Best days for sowing, planting, and transplanting.

gather strength rest, recover buildup
Waxing Moon

11:45 PM PDT Sunday
1:45 AM CDT
2:45 AM EDT

14 Monday
Ganesh Chaturthi

15 Tuesday

SEPTEMBER

There are no ordinary moments.
Dan Millman

Color
Red

Day
Wetness

Element
Water

Scorpio

Success

Inquisitiveness and exuberant inspiration lead to new horizons. Insight and love for truth reign.

Bringing together is more important than splitting asunder.

Expansive forces will assist in legal matters, discussions, and debates.

Leisure

Expansion feels great, and travel, short trips, and outings are most welcome. A competitive spirit excites any sports event.

Talk things out when necessary.

Romance can be very passionate.

Good days for outings; even with cloudy skies the air still feels somewhat warm. Drying effect, get plenty to drink.

Health

Sensitive body parts:

Thighs and Veins

All measures taken to supply nutrient materials and strengthen the sensitive body parts are very effective.

Healing ointments are easily absorbed.

Sensitive sense organs.

Pains often arise in the sciatic nerve, veins, the small of the back, and thighs.

Avoid overstraining the body with unusual physical activities.

Body Care

Aromas, scents: Calendula (Marigold), Geranium, Rosemary

Treatments with firming and moisturizing creams are more effective.

Massages that serve to regenerate, and strengthen, perhaps aided with beneficial massage oils.

Correcting and cutting ingrown nails.

Hair dyes applied now, will look more vibrant.

Garden/Nature

Plant part:

Fruit

Sow plants and vegetables that grow and flourish above ground.

Sowing and planting fruit and vegetables that grow tall, and tomatoes, but no lettuce.

Transplanting.

Grafting onto fruit trees.

Cultivating grains, particularly corn.

Gather herbs for vein diseases.

Housework

Light housework only.

Ventilate sufficiently.

Freezing fruit and vegetables.

Baking bread, cakes, and cookies. Dough rises faster. (Except on New Moon)

Suitable for making cheese.

Making preserves.

Nutrition

Food quality:

Protein

Beans, peas, corn, tomatoes, pumpkin, lentils, soybeans, cucumber, eggplant, zucchini, berries, fruit, chili, bell pepper, figs, avocado, melon, olives.

Weight gain: avoid indulging in rich foods. If overweight, eat smaller portions.

Supply nutrient materials to strengthen the body. Focus on foods that contain essential minerals and vitamins.

Stimulants and vitamins are more effective.

Positive affirmation:
"My mind is still."

Turning Point

Transition of descending to ascending forces. Both forces are at work and neutralize each other.

gather strength
rest, recover
buildup
Waxing Moon

9:42 AM PDT
♏ ➤ ♐ ← 11:42 AM CDT
12:42 PM EDT

16 Wednesday
No meat.

17 Thursday

9:56 PM PDT
11:56 PM CDT ♐ ➤ ♑
Saturday 12:56 AM EDT

18 Friday
☾ **Half Moon.** No meat. Cutting and filing toenails and fingernails.

Books are mirrors: you only see in them what you already have inside you.
Carlos Ruiz Zafón

Color
Orange/ Yellow

Day
Warm

Element
Fire **Sagittarius**

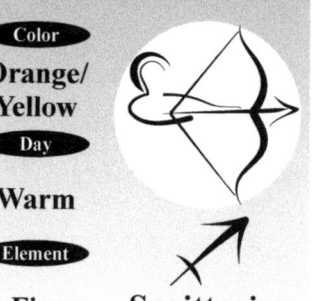

S E P T E M B E R

Success

Career and business are in the foreground now and thinking becomes clear and serious, but somewhat inflexible.

Perseverance and reasoning assist in financial matters, planning, and contracts.

The values of tradition, authority, and discipline impact our endeavors.

Leisure

Money is not likely to be wasted in a shopping spree.

Many are drawn to enjoy cultural events.

The earth feels cold to the touch, so take slightly warmer clothes.

Health

Sensitive body parts:
Knees, Joints, Bones, Skin

All measures taken to supply nutrient materials and strengthen the sensitive body parts are very effective.

Healing ointments are easily absorbed.

Sensitive blood circulation.

Avoid overstraining bones and knees, and apply gentle stretching exercises only.

Problems with meniscus: Don't overstrain.

Dress slightly warmer.

High blood pressure: Avoid salty foods.

Massages, lymphatic therapy, and chiropractic treatment to release blockages.

Body Care

Aromas, scents:
Cedar, Juniper

Treatments with firming and moisturizing creams are more effective.

Massages that serve to regenerate, and strengthen, perhaps aided with beneficial massage oils.

Correcting and cutting ingrown nails.

Every kind of skin care is beneficial.

Cutting and filing toenails and fingernails will make the nails grow stronger over time.

Hair dyes applied now, will look more vibrant.

Garden/Nature

Plant part:
Root

Sow plants, herbs, and vegetables that grow and flourish above ground.

Transplanting.

Harvest produce is suitable for storage. Harvest root vegetables.

Gather herbs for bone, joint, and skin diseases.

Housework

Light housework only.

Air rooms only briefly.

Preserving root vegetables.

Avoid dry cleaning, as the fabric may develop unwanted glossy blotches.

Nutrition

Food quality:
Salt

Garlic, carrots, red beets, reddish, rutabaga, sugar beet, celery, potatoes, onions, kohlrabi.

Weight gain: avoid indulging in rich foods. If overweight, eat smaller portions.

Supply nutrient materials to strengthen the body. Focus on foods that contain essential minerals and vitamins.

Stimulants and vitamins are more effective.

Avoid large quantities of salty foods like bacon, ham, salted herring, fatty cheese, and the like. Avoid heavy and greasy foods.

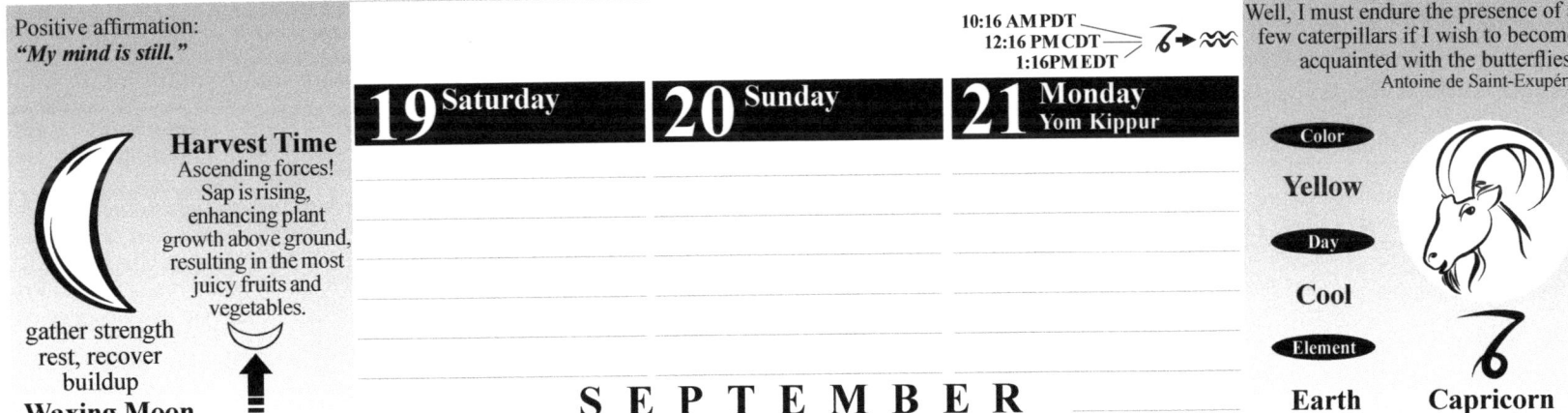

Positive affirmation:
"My mind is still."

Harvest Time
Ascending forces! Sap is rising, enhancing plant growth above ground, resulting in the most juicy fruits and vegetables.

gather strength
rest, recover
buildup
Waxing Moon

| 19 Saturday | 20 Sunday | 21 Monday Yom Kippur |

10:16 AM PDT
12:16 PM CDT
1:16 PM EDT

Well, I must endure the presence of a few caterpillars if I wish to become acquainted with the butterflies.
Antoine de Saint-Exupéry

Color
Yellow

Day
Cool

Element
Earth

Capricorn

S E P T E M B E R

Success

Inspiration, optimism, and impatience. Rational thinking, creativity and imagination spark new ideas and inspire planning for the future.

Shying away from routine tasks people will feel more drawn to anything new.

Instead of gridlocked structures choose new possibilities.

Leisure

Inspiration and optimism will boost friendship, social gatherings, and parties.

Express your creativity and imagination. Dwell in dreams and utopian ideas. It is easier now to perceive intuitive thoughts.

Health

Sensitive body parts:

Lower Legs, Veins

All measures taken to supply nutrient materials and strengthen the sensitive body parts are very effective.

Healing ointments are easily absorbed.

Sensitive glandular system.

Avoid inflammation of the veins. Apply ointments to lower legs, and rest legs in a raised position.

Varicose veins: Avoid long periods of standing.

While exercising go easy on the ankles.

Sensitivity to light, so bring your sunglasses along.

Body Care

Aromas, scents:
Cyclamen, Peach, Wild Roses

Treatments with firming and moisturizing creams are more effective.

Massages that serve to regenerate, and strengthen, perhaps aided with beneficial massage oils.

Correcting and cutting ingrown nails.

Hair dyes applied now, will look more vibrant.

Garden/Nature

Plant part:

Flower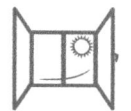

Avoid watering plants.

Harvested produce is well suitable for storage.

Gather herbs for vein diseases.

Housework

Light housework only.

Ventilate rooms thoroughly.

Baking cakes and cookies. Dough rises faster. (Except on New Moon)

Making preserves.

Nutrition

Food quality:

Fat

Cauliflower, artichoke, broccoli, sunflower seeds, flax seeds, nuts, rose hip, elder.

Weight gain: avoid indulging in rich foods. If overweight, eat smaller portions.

Supply nutrient materials to strengthen the body. Focus on foods that contain essential minerals and vitamins.

Stimulants and vitamins are more effective.

Pay attention to any particularly tempting foods today: Most likely the "wrong" things taste best.

High cholesterol: eat a low fat diet.

Positive affirmation:
"My mind is still."

Harvest Time
Ascending forces!
Sap is rising, enhancing plant growth above ground, resulting in the most juicy fruits and vegetables.

gather strength
rest, recover
buildup
Waxing Moon

22 Tuesday
Fall Equinox

23 Wednesday

No meat.

8:25 PM PDT
10:25 PM CDT
11:25 PM EDT

The inner fire is the most important thing mankind possesses.
Edith Södergra

Color
Bright/ Dark Blue

Day
Air/Light

Element
Air

Aquarius

S E P T E M B E R

Success

Sensibility, intuition, and helpfulness.

Where possible, retreating is more favorable than dealing with business matters.

Dissolve restrictions, be patient and wait. Be aware that people can be more easily influenced.

Leisure

Your helpfulness will boost friendships.

Enjoy dancing or swimming, or watch a movie that will inspire your fantasies and imagination.

Retreat, relax, and recover.

Romance can be gentle and coziness will prevail.

If you plan outdoor excursions, be prepared for a shower here and there.

Health

Sensitive body parts:

Feet and Toes

All measures taken to supply nutrient materials and strengthen the sensitive body parts are very effective.

Healing ointments are easily absorbed.

Sensitive nervous system.

Drugs have a much stronger effect on your body. Monitor closely what you put into your body.

Lymphatic therapy.

Sluggishness or fatigue may occur in the transition into the next Zodiac sign of Aries.

Body Care

Aromas, scents:
Magnolia, Amaryllis, Clary Sage

Treatments with firming and moisturizing creams are more effective.

Massages that serve to regenerate, and strengthen, perhaps aided with beneficial massage oils. Reflexology massage. Carry out with special care, people are more sensitive.

Correcting and cutting ingrown nails.

Foot bath.

No haircuts, hair becomes shaggy and unmanageable. Avoid washing your hair. Dandruff could develop.

Garden/Nature

Plant part:

Leaf

Watering all indoor and outdoor plants.

Sow plants, herbs, and vegetables that grow and flourish above ground, and leaf vegetables.

Transplanting.

Mowing lawns.

Avoid pruning fruit trees and bushes.

Harvested produce should be consumed as soon as possible.

Gather herbs for foot complaints.

Housework

Light housework only.

Ventilate rooms briefly and rapidly. Don't air mattresses.

Any dirt and spots are easily removed in the laundry.

Avoid painting, as paint will take very long to dry.

Preserving and storing should be avoided.

Nutrition

Food quality:

Carbohydrate

Lettuce, spinach, lamb's lettuce, Endive, parsley, leek, cabbage (Brussels sprouts, kale, Chinese cabbage), all leafy herbs, asparagus, mushrooms, cress, Swiss chard, rhubarb.

Weight gain: avoid indulging in rich foods. If overweight, eat smaller portions and avoid carbohydrates.

Supply nutrient materials to strengthen the body. Focus on foods that contain essential minerals and vitamins.

Caffeine, alcohol, drugs, certain foods, and stimulants have a much stronger effect.

Positive affirmation:
"My mind is still."

Harvest Time
Ascending forces! Sap is rising, enhancing plant growth above ground, resulting in the most juicy fruits and vegetables.

gather strength
rest, recover
buildup
Waxing Moon

24 Thursday

25 Friday

No meat. Cutting and filing toenails and fingernails.

S E P T E M B E R

The menu is not the meal.
Alan Wilson Watts

Color
Blueish White

Day
Wetness

Element
Water

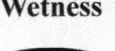

Pisces

Success

Things get going and the way straight ahead seems the best.

People feel energetic, courageous, assertive, and at times anxious.

Good time for meetings and sales talks but impatience and selfishness do not favor teamwork.

Leisure

An enterprising spirit and spontaneity move people to enjoy outings, sports, competitions, cultural events, and travels.

Romance can be very passionate.

Good days for outings, even with cloudy skies the air still feels somewhat warm. Drying effect, get plenty to drink.

Health

Sensitive body parts:

Head, Brain, Eyes

All measures taken to flush out and detoxify the sensitive body parts are very effective.

Scarring is less severe.

Teeth: Removal of tartar and amalgam. Best for fillings, crowns, and dentures! Avoiding treatment of periodontitis and gums.

Blood-purifying, detoxifying herbal infusions and teas.

Sensitive sense organs.

If you suffer from migraines drink plenty of water, and avoid coffee, chocolate, and sugar.

○ *Full Moon: Avoid any surgery and vaccination if possible.*

Body Care

Aromas, scents: Cloves, Peppermint, Thyme

Prepare home-made ointments and cosmetics.

Apply detoxing facial and body care.

Treatments of bumps and pimples on the skin, and exfoliating procedures.

Removing body hair.

Correction of the nail bed.

Massages that serve to relax, ease tension, and detoxify.

Reflexology massage.

Removal of callused skin.

Treating obstinate athlete's foot, nail fungus, and warts.

Eye compresses to relieve strained eyes.

Any kind of hair care.

Garden/Nature

Plant part:

Fruit

Sowing plants and vegetables that grow below ground.

Sowing and planting anything that is supposed to grow fast. Sowing and planting fruit and tomatoes.

Dig over/plow the soil to prepare for planting.

Spreading manure. Fertilizing grains, vegetables, and fruit.

Weeding. Pest control.

Pruning of fruit trees and bushes.

Harvesting and storing grains, vegetables, potatoes, fruits, and tomatoes.

Start a compost heap.

Gather herbs (roots) for eye complaints and headaches.

Day off on 9/26.

○ *Full Moon: Weather and climate changes. Herbs are most powerful.*

Housework

Housework is dealt with much more successfully, efficiently, and effortlessly.

Problem stains are removed readily.

Dry cleaning.

Clean and store seasonal clothing.

Thoroughly clean wooden and parquet floors, metals, china, etc.

Cleaning, polishing, and waterproofing shoes.

Combating mold.

Ventilate rooms sufficiently. Air beds.

Suitable for making cheese.

Freezing fruit and vegetables.

Baking bread, cakes, and cookies (use more leavening agent).

○ *Full Moon: Avoid doing laundry, cleaning windows, making preserves, painting.*

Nutrition

Food quality:

Protein

Beans, peas, corn, tomatoes, pumpkin, lentils, soybeans, cucumber, eggplant, zucchini, berries, fruit, chili, bell pepper, figs, avocado, melon, olives.

Weight associated with overeating is less likely. If underweight, eat larger portions.

Cleansing and detox diets. Fruit and juice days.

Flush out poisons. Treatment for drug abuse.

Drink plenty of water.

○ *Full Moon: A day of fasting.*

Inspiration is a slender river of brightness leaping from a vast and eternal knowledge, it exceeds reason more perfectly than reason exceeds the knowledge of the senses.
Sri Aurobindo

Color

Indigo Blue

Day

Warm

Element

Aries **Fire**

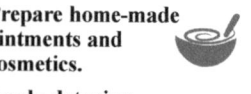

H→Y ← 3:24 AM PDT
5:24 AM CDT
6:24 AM EDT

26 Saturday
Shukkot

○ Full Moon 9:50 AM PDT, 11:50 AM CDT, 12:50 PM EDT

27 Sunday

Harvest Time
Ascending forces! Sap is rising, enhancing plant growth above ground, resulting in the most juicy fruits and vegetables.

detox
remove
be active

Waning Moon

S E P T E M B E R

Success

Realism and material security are important. Persistence comes easy, thoughts and reactions are slower.

Assess financial areas.

Conservative tendencies may make people want to stay away from risk taking.

Leisure

Relax at a picnic/feast. Enjoy culinary pleasures and hobbies.

The earth feels cold to the touch, so take slightly warmer clothes.

Health

Sensitive body parts:

Head and Neck

All measures taken to flush out and detoxify the sensitive body parts are very effective.

Good for surgery, except on the sensitive body parts (see above), hips, kidneys, and bladder.

Scarring is less severe.

Teeth: Removal of tartar and amalgam. Best for fillings, crowns, and dentures!

Avoiding treatment of periodontitis and gums.

Blood-purifying, detoxifying herbal infusions and teas.

Sensitive blood circulation.

Organs of speech, jaws, teeth, tonsils, thyroid gland, neck, and vocal chords get easily affected. Keep neck warm. On cold days ears should be protected. Sensitivity to noise.

High blood pressure: Avoid salty foods.

Massages, lymphatic therapy, and chiropractic treatment to release blockages.

Body Care

Aromas, scents: Geranium, Jasmine, Rose

Prepare home-made ointments and cosmetics.

Apply detoxing facial and body care.

Treatments of bumps and pimples on the skin, and exfoliating procedures.

Removing body hair.

Correction of the nail bed.

Massages that serve to relax, ease tension, and detoxify.

Reflexology massage.

Removal of callused skin.

Treating obstinate athlete's foot, nail fungus, and warts.

Garden/Nature

Plant part:

Root

Sow plants and vegetables that grow below ground.

Everything grows slowly and lasts well.

Dig over to prepare soil.

Trimming/cutting back plants. Weeding. Mulching.

Start a compost heap.

Combat vermin found in the soil.

Spread fertilizer and liquid manure.

Fertilize flowers with poorly formed roots.

Harvested produce is well suited for storage. Harvesting root vegetables.

Gather herbs (roots) for sinus issues, sore throat, and ear complaints.

Housework

Housework is dealt with much more successfully, efficiently, and effortlessly.

Problem stains are removed readily.

Best for doing laundry! Reduce on laundry detergent, support the environment.

Dry cleaning.

Clean and store seasonal clothing.

Thoroughly clean wooden and parquet floors, metals, china etc.

Cleaning, polishing, and waterproofing shoes.

Combating mold.

Air rooms only briefly.

Painting.

Preserving root vegetables.

Nutrition

Food quality:

Salt

Garlic, carrots, red beets, reddish, rutabaga, sugar beet, celery, potatoes, onions, kohlrabi.

Weight associated with overeating is less likely. If underweight, eat larger portions.

Cleansing and detox diets. Fruit and juice days.

Flush out poisons. Treatment for drug abuse.

Avoid large quantities of salty foods like bacon, ham, salted herring, fatty cheese, and the like.

Life is pleasant. Death is peaceful. It's the transition that's troublesome.
Isaac Asimov

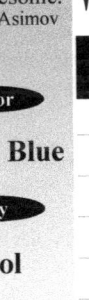

Taurus

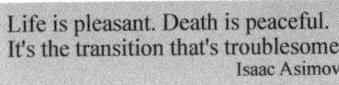
Color

Bright Blue

Day

Cool

Element

Earth

♈ → ♉   7:41 AM PDT
9:41 AM CDT
10:41 AM EDT

10:27 AM PDT
12:27 PM CDT   ♉ → ♊
1:27 PM EDT

28 Monday

29 Tuesday

30 Wednesday

No meat.

S E P T E M B E R

Harvest Time
Ascending forces! Sap is rising, enhancing plant growth above ground, resulting in the most juicy fruits and vegetables.

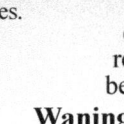

detox
remove
be active

Waning Moon

Success

Open mindedness and curiosity. A changeable and hectic time.

Good time for talking, negotiating, networking, and exchanging ideas as well as for meetings of a nonbinding nature, conferences, and studies.

Leisure

Good time for family gatherings, parties, and short trips.

People enjoy stimulating their minds with reading and studying. Attending theater performances is a preferred enjoyment. Enhance friendships.

Stretching exercises.

Be prepared for sudden changes in weather or climate.

Health

Sensitive body parts:
Shoulders, Arms, Hands, Lungs

All measures taken to flush out and detoxify the sensitive body parts are very effective.

Good for surgery, except on the sensitive body parts (see above), hips, kidneys, and bladder.
Scarring is less severe.

Teeth: Removal of tartar and amalgam. Best for fillings, crowns, and dentures! Avoid having any teeth pulled.

Blood-purifying, detoxifying herbal infusions and teas.

Sensitive glandular system.

Make sure you are dressed warm enough in cool weather.

Exercises for shoulders. Breathing exercises.

Sensitivity to light, bring your sunglasses along.

Massages, lymphatic therapy, and chiropractic treatment to release blockages.

Body Care

Aromas, scents:
Lavender, Lemon Balm, Magnolia, Verbena

Prepare home-made ointments and cosmetics.

Apply detoxing facial and body care.

Treatments of bumps and pimples on the skin, and exfoliating procedures.

Removing body hair.

Correction of the nail bed.

Massages that serve to relax, ease tension, and detoxify.

Reflexology massage.

Removal of callused skin.

Treating obstinate athlete's foot, nail fungus, and warts.

Garden/Nature

Plant part:
Flower

Sow plants and vegetables that grow below ground.

Trimming and cutting back plants.

Start a compost heap.

Weeding. Pest control.

Fertilize flowers that no longer bloom.

Avoid watering plants.

Changes in weather are more likely.

Gather herbs (roots) for tensions in the shoulder and lung complaints.

Housework

Housework is dealt with much more successfully, efficiently, and effortlessly.

Problem stains are removed readily.

Best for doing laundry! Reduce on laundry detergent, support the environment.

Dry cleaning.

Clean and store seasonal clothing.

Thoroughly clean wooden and parquet floors, metals, china etc.

Cleaning windows and glass.

Cleaning, polishing, and waterproofing shoes.

Combating mold.

Ventilate rooms thoroughly.

Baking bread, cakes, and cookies (add more leavening agent).

Making preserves.

Painting.

Nutrition

Food quality:
Fat

Cauliflower, artichoke, broccoli, sunflower seeds, flax seeds, nuts, rose hip, elder.

Weight associated with overeating is less likely. If underweight, eat larger portions.

Cleansing and detox diets. Fruit and juice days.

Flush out poisons. Treatment for drug abuse.

Pay attention to any particularly tempting foods today: Most likely the "wrong" things taste best.

High cholesterol: eat a low fat diet.

Count your age by friends, not years.
Count your life by smiles, not tears.
John Lennon

Color
Light Blue

Day
Air/Light

Element

Gemini   **Air**

12:55 PM PDT
2:55 PM CDT
3:55 PM EDT
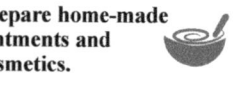 ♊ → ♋

1 Thursday Dussehra	**2** Friday
	No meat. Cutting and filing toenails and fingernails.

Turning Point
Transition of ascending to descending forces. Both forces are at work and neutralize each other.

detox
remove
be active
Waning Moon

O C T O B E R

Success

Feelings, sensitivity, and cooperativeness. Many are overly sensitive, so beware of treading on someone's toes.

Be cautious if you are easily influenced.

During negotiations make use of the cognitive ability of your senses.

Leisure

Relax within your close family.

Retreat to your safe haven and enjoy your fantasy while reading or listening to music. The inner world becomes more colorful than the outer.

Romance can be gentle. Deep feelings will prevail.

If you plan outdoor excursions, be prepared for a shower here and there.

Health

Sensitive body parts:
Chest, Lungs, Liver, Stomach, Gall Bladder

All measures taken to flush out and detoxify the sensitive body parts are very effective.

Good for surgical operations except those on the sensitive body parts (see above), hips, kidneys, and bladder. Scarring is less severe.

Teeth: Removal of tartar and amalgam. Best for fillings, crowns, and dentures!

Blood-purifying, detoxifying herbal infusions and teas.

Sensitive nervous system.

Be cautious with alcohol since the liver is very sensitive.

Stomach could play up and cause gas and heartburn.

Rheumatism: Don't air bedding outside, damp will remain in the bedding.

Lymphatic therapy.

Body Care

Aromas, scents:
Lilac, Lilies of the Valley, Lilies, Violets

Prepare home-made ointments and cosmetics.

Apply detoxing facial and body care.

Treatments of bumps and pimples on the skin, and exfoliating procedures.

Removing body hair.

Correction of the nail bed.

Massages that serve to relax, ease tension, and detoxify.

Reflexology massage.

Removal of callused skin.

Treating obstinate athlete's foot, nail fungus, and warts.

No haircuts, hair becomes shaggy and unmanageable. Avoid washing your hair.

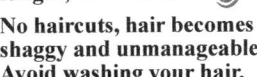

Garden/Nature

Plant part:
Leaf

Water plants.

Fertilize flowers.

Sow plants and vegetables that grow below ground, leaf vegetables, and lettuce.

Dig over/plow to prepare soil for planting.

Trimming and cutting back plants. Transplanting. Weeding.

Combating pests above ground.

Start a compost heap.

Mowing lawns.

Gather herbs (roots) for bronchitis, stomach, liver, and gall bladder complaints.

Unfavorable for harvesting, storing, and preserving.

Housework

Housework is dealt with much more successfully, efficiently, and effortlessly.

Problem stains are removed readily.

Best for doing laundry! Reduce on laundry detergent, support the environment.

Dry cleaning.

Thoroughly clean wooden and parquet floors, metals, china etc.

Cleaning, polishing, and waterproofing shoes.

Combating mold.

Ventilate rooms briefly and rapidly.

Avoid painting.

Nutrition

Food quality:
Carbohydrate

Lettuce, spinach, lamb's lettuce, Endive, parsley, leek, cabbage (Brussels sprouts, kale, Chinese cabbage), all leafy herbs, asparagus, mushrooms, cress, Swiss chard, rhubarb.

Weight associated with overeating is less likely. If underweight, eat larger portions.

Moodiness may make you want to eat more than is healthy. If overweight avoid carbohydrates.

Cleansing and detox diets. Fruit and juice days.

Flush out poisons. Treatment for drug abuse.

If you get stomach troubles easily, avoid heavy meals.

It is better to remain silent at the risk of being thought a fool, than to talk and remove all doubt of it.
Maurice Switzer

Color — **Green**

Day — **Wetness**

Element —

Cancer   **Water**

3:55 PM PDT
5:55 PM CDT
6:55 PM EDT

3 Saturday
Shemini Atzeret

☾ Half Moon.

4 Sunday Feast of St. Francis, Simchat Torah

Planting Time
Descending forces! Sap is drawn downward, enhancing root formation. Best days for sowing, planting, and transplanting.

detox
remove
be active

Waning Moon

OCTOBER

Success

Determination reigns, and risks are taken more often. Master your tasks with more self-confidence and creativity.

Limits appear to be more easily surmountable.

Auspicious day for sales, advertising, and publicity.

Leisure

Zest for life is in the air. People want to have a fun time, enjoy parties, musical events, movies, etc.

Possessive feelings can harm a relationship. Romance can be very passionate.

Outings: even with cloudy skies the air still feels somewhat warm. Drying effect, get plenty to drink.

Danger of sudden storms, not only in the sky.

Health

Sensitive body parts:
Heart, Back, Diaphragm, Circulation, Arteries

All measures taken to flush out and detoxify the sensitive body parts are very effective.

Good for surgery, except on the sensitive body parts (see above), hips, kidneys, and bladder. Scarring is less severe.

Teeth: Removal of tartar and amalgam. Best for fillings, crowns, and dentures!

Blood-purifying, detoxifying herbal infusions and teas.

Sensitive sense organs.

Back and heart problems are more likely to occur.

Avoid overstraining of the heart and circulation with unusual physical activities.

Expect sleepless nights.

Body Care

Aromas, scents:
Hibiscus, Oleander, Rose

Prepare home-made ointments and cosmetics.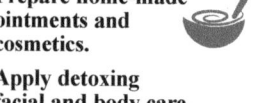

Apply detoxing facial and body care.

Treatments of bumps and pimples on the skin, and exfoliating procedures.

Removing body hair.

Correction of the nail bed.

Massages that serve to relax, ease tension, and detoxify.

Reflexology massage.

Removal of callused skin.

Treating obstinate athlete's foot, nail fungus, and warts.

Good days for haircuts, hair becomes stronger. But be aware that if you get a perm, curls will become quite frizzy. Baby's first haircut.

Garden/Nature

Plant part:
Fruit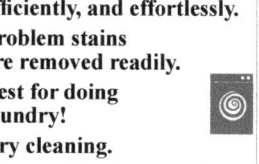

Sowing plants and vegetables that grow below ground.

Sowing and planting fruit. Also sow and plant vegetables that are highly perishable. Plant trees and bushes. Sow lawns.

Dig over/plow to prepare soil for planting.

Trimming and cutting back plants. Pruning of fruit trees and bushes.

Transplanting.

Not suitable for fertilizing.

Weeding. Pest Control.

Harvested produce should be consumed as soon as possible.

Gather herbs (roots) for heart and circulation complaints.

Start compost heap.

Housework

Housework is dealt with much more successfully, efficiently, and effortlessly.

Problem stains are removed readily.

Best for doing laundry!

Dry cleaning.

Thoroughly clean wooden and parquet floors, metals, china, etc.

Cleaning windows and glass.

Cleaning, polishing, and waterproofing shoes.

Combating mold.

Ventilate rooms sufficiently. Air beds.

Suitable for making cheese.

Preserving and freezing fruit and vegetables.

Baking bread, cakes, and cookies (use more leavening agent).

Avoid painting.

Nutrition

Food quality:
Protein

Beans, peas, corn, tomatoes, pumpkin, lentils, soybeans, cucumber, eggplant, zucchini, berries, fruit, chili, bell pepper, figs, avocado, melon, olives.

Weight associated with overeating is less likely. If underweight, eat larger portions.

Cleansing and detox diets. Fruit and juice days.

Flush out poisons. Treatment for drug abuse.

The desire to reach for the stars is ambitious. The desire to reach hearts is wise.
Maya Angelou

Color — **Green**
Day — **Warm**
Element — **Fire**

Leo

5 Monday

7:54 PM PDT
9:54 PM CDT
10:54 PM EDT
♌ ➡ ♍

6 Tuesday

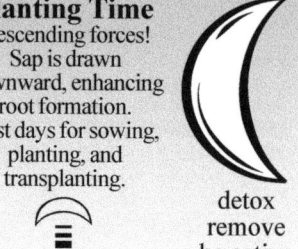

Planting Time
Descending forces! Sap is drawn downward, enhancing root formation. Best days for sowing, planting, and transplanting.

detox
remove
be active

Waning Moon

O C T O B E R

Success

Good time for details, organization, routine, concentration, and duty.

Take care of financial and administrative tasks.

Prepare for future success now with realistic and critical assessment.

Leisure

Enjoy a nature walk.

Good time for health regimes. Improve your health with stretching exercises and yoga.

The earth feels cold to the touch, so take slightly warmer clothes.

Health

Sensitive body parts:
Digestive Organs, Nerves, Spleen, Pancreas

All measures taken to flush out and detoxify the sensitive body parts are very effective.

Good for surgery, except on the sensitive body parts (see above), hips, kidneys, and bladder.
Scarring is less severe.
Teeth: Removal of tartar and amalgam. Best for fillings, crowns, and dentures!
Avoiding treatment of periodontitis and gums.
Blood-purifying, detoxifying herbal infusions and teas.
Sensitive blood circulation.

For a sensitive digestive system, a wholesome diet is recommended.

Dress slightly warmer.

High blood pressure: Avoid salty foods.

Massages, lymphatic therapy, and chiropractic treatment to release blockages.

Body Care

Aromas, scents:
Lavender, Spruce Needles, Sage, Meadow Flowers

Prepare home-made ointments and cosmetics.

Apply detoxing facial and body care.

Treatments of bumps and pimples on the skin, and exfoliating procedures.

Removing body hair.

Correction of the nail bed.

Massages that serve to relax, ease tension, and detoxify.

Reflexology massage.

Removal of callused skin.

Treating obstinate athlete's foot, nail fungus, and warts.

Best for haircuts because it retains its shape longer.
Perms turn out best.

Garden/Nature

Plant part:
Root

Best for sowing and planting, except lettuce.
Plant trees which are supposed to grow very tall.
Plant hedges and bushes that are meant to grow very fast.
Planting and re-potting balcony and indoor plants.
Dig over/plow to prepare soil for planting.
Trimming and cutting back plants. Planting cuttings.
Spread fertilizer and manure. Fertilize flowers with poorly formed roots.
Start a compost heap.
Transplanting. Mulching.
Weeding. Pest control (vermin in the soil).
Avoid harvesting and storing.
Gather herbs (roots) for digestive organs, pancreas, and nervous complaints.

Housework

Housework is dealt with much more successfully, efficiently, and effortlessly.
Problem stains are removed readily.

Best for doing laundry! Reduce on laundry detergent, support the environment.

Dry cleaning.

Thoroughly clean wooden and parquet floors, metals, china etc.

Cleaning, polishing, and waterproofing shoes.

Combating mold.

Air rooms only briefly.

Painting.

Making pickles, preserves, and cheese yields suboptimal results and should be avoided.

Nutrition

Food quality:
Salt

Garlic, carrots, red beets, reddish, rutabaga, sugar beet, celery, potatoes, onions, kohlrabi.

Weight associated with overeating is less likely. If underweight, eat larger portions.

Cleansing and detox diets. Fruit and juice days.

Flush out poisons. Treatment for drug abuse.

Avoid large quantities of salty foods like bacon, ham, salted herring, fatty cheese, and the like. Avoid heavy and greasy foods.

The public have an insatiable curiosity to know everything, except what is worth knowing.
Oscar Wilde

Color — Yellow

Day — Cool

Element — Earth

Virgo

7 Wednesday
No meat.

8 Thursday

O C T O B E R

Planting Time
Descending forces! Sap is drawn downward, enhancing root formation. Best days for sowing, planting, and transplanting.

detox
remove
be active

Waning Moon

Success

The artistic instinct rules, but so, too, does indecisiveness. The forces swing back and forth until equilibrium is achieved.

It's easy to reach compromises with tactful sensitivity.

A sense of judgment will support legal matters.

Leisure

Pursuit for harmony and cooperativeness supports good times in romance, friendship, and partnership.

Enjoy cultural events. Relax and get pampered with a spa treatment.

Romance can be passionate yet sensitive.

Health

Sensitive body parts:

Hips, Kidneys, Bladder

All measures taken to flush out and detoxify the sensitive body parts are very effective.

Good for surgery, except on the sensitive body parts (see above).
Scarring is less severe.

Teeth: Removal of tartar and amalgam. Best for fillings, crowns, and dentures! Avoid treatment of periodontitis and gums, avoid pulling teeth.

Blood-purifying, detoxifying herbal infusions and teas.

Sensitive glandular system.

Take special care to keep the area of the bladder and kidneys warm.

Apply special exercises for the hip region.

Sensitivity to light, so bring your sunglasses along.

Body Care

Aromas, scents: Roses, Violets, Daffodils

Prepare home-made ointments and cosmetics.

Apply detoxing facial and body care.

Treatments of bumps and pimples on the skin, and exfoliating procedures.

Removing body hair.

Correction of the nail bed.

Massages that serve to relax, ease tension, and detoxify.

Reflexology massage.

Removal of callused skin.

Treating obstinate athlete's foot, nail fungus, and warts.

Garden/Nature

Plant part:

Flower

Sow plants and vegetables that grow below ground.

Dig over/plow to prepare soil for planting.

Trimming and cutting back plants.

Start a compost heap.

Weeding. Pest control.

Fertilize flowers that no longer bloom.

Transplanting.

Avoid watering plants.

Harvested produce should be consumed as soon as possible.

Gather herbs (roots) for kidneys, gall bladder and hip complaints.

Day off on 10/9.

Housework

Housework is dealt with much more successfully, efficiently, and effortlessly.

Problem stains are removed readily.

Best for doing laundry! Reduce on laundry detergent, support the environment.

Dry cleaning.

Clean and store seasonal clothing.

Thoroughly clean wooden and parquet floors, metals, china etc.

Cleaning windows and glass.

Cleaning, polishing, and waterproofing shoes.

Combating mold.

Ventilate rooms thoroughly.

Baking bread, cakes, and cookies (add more leavening agent).

Making preserves.

Painting.

Nutrition

Food quality:

Fat

Cauliflower, artichoke, broccoli, sunflower seeds, flax seeds, nuts, rose hip, elder.

Weight associated with overeating is less likely. If underweight, eat larger portions.

Cleansing and detox diets. Fruit and juice days.

Flush out poisons. Treatment for drug abuse.

Pay attention to any particularly tempting foods today: Most likely the "wrong" things taste best.

High cholesterol: eat a low fat diet.

I knew my mind to be conquered when it admired the beauty of the hideous, yet felt perfectly why other men shrank back or hated.
Sri Aurobindo

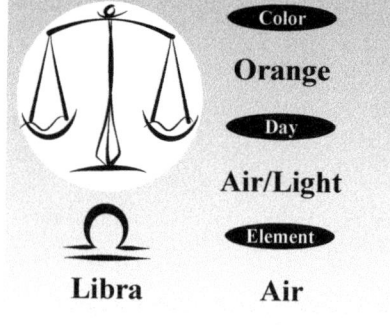

Color
Orange

Day

Air/Light

Element

Libra   Air

♏ → ♎
1:12 AM PDT
3:12 AM CDT
4:12 AM EDT

9 Friday

No meat. Cutting and filing toenails and fingernails.

O C T O B E R

Planting Time
Descending forces! Sap is drawn downward, enhancing root formation. Best days for sowing, planting, and transplanting.

detox remove be active

Waning Moon

Success

The artistic instinct rules, but so, too, does indecisiveness. The forces swing back and forth until equilibrium is achieved.

It's easy to reach compromises with tactful sensitivity.

A sense of judgment will support legal matters.

● *New Moon: Confirm your resolutions. Finalize new decisions. Drop bad habits.*

Leisure

Pursuit for harmony and cooperativeness supports good times in romance, friendship, and partnership.

Enjoy cultural events. Relax and get pampered with a spa treatment.

Romance can be passionate yet sensitive.

Health

Sensitive body parts:

Hips, Kidneys, Bladder

All measures taken to supply nutrient materials and strengthen the sensitive body parts are very effective.

Healing ointments are easily absorbed.

Sensitive glandular system.

Take special care to keep the area of bladder and kidneys warm.

Apply special exercises for the hip region.

Avoid having any teeth pulled.

Sensitivity to light, bring your sunglasses along.

● *New Moon: Avoid any surgery if possible.*

Body Care

Aromas, scents: Roses, Violets, Daffodils

Treatments with firming and moisturizing creams are more effective.

Massages that serve to regenerate, and strengthen, perhaps aided with beneficial massage oils.

Correcting and cutting ingrown nails.

Hair dyes applied now, will look more vibrant.

Garden/Nature

Plant part:

Flower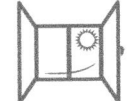

Sow plants and vegetables that grow and flourish above ground, specially flowers, and medicinal herbs.

Transplanting.

Trimming and cutting back plants.

Avoid watering plants.

Start a compost heap.

Harvested produce should be consumed as soon as possible.

Gather herbs for kidneys, gall bladder, and hip complaints.

● *New Moon: Change of weather is likely. Care for sickly plants.*

Housework

Light housework only.

Ventilate rooms thoroughly.

Baking cakes and cookies. Dough rises faster. (Except on New Moon)

Nutrition

Food quality:

Fat

Cauliflower, artichoke, broccoli, sunflower seeds, flax seeds, nuts, rose hip, elder.

Weight gain: avoid indulging in rich foods. If overweight, eat smaller portions.

Supply nutrient materials to strengthen the body. Focus on foods that contain essential minerals and vitamins.

Stimulants and vitamins are more effective.

Pay attention to any particularly tempting foods today: Most likely the "wrong" things taste best.

High cholesterol: eat a low fat diet.

● *New Moon: A day of fasting.*

Positive affirmation:
"I remember my innermost being."

Planting Time
Descending forces!
Sap is drawn downward, enhancing root formation.
Best days for sowing, planting, and transplanting.

gather strength rest, recover buildup
Waxing Moon

10 Saturday

● New Moon 8:51 AM PDT, 10:51 AM CDT, 11:51 AM EDT

O C T O B E R

It is an ironic habit of human beings to run faster when they have lost their way.
Rollo May

Color
Orange

Day
Air/Light

Element
Air

Libra

Success

Critical and superstitious behavior emerges, especially pertaining to money.

A penetrating power will strengthen your capacity to act.

An increased perception opens our interest for the essentials and helps to discover hidden potentials.

Leisure

Relax within your close family, with meditation, and relaxation exercises.

A longing to feel safe will be nurtured if you focus on habits and rituals. An increased sensitivity will help to enjoy every moment.

Romance can be very passionate.

If you plan outdoor excursions, be prepared for a shower here and there.

Health

Sensitive body parts:

Sex organs, Ureter

All measures taken to supply nutrient materials and strengthen the sensitive body parts are very effective.

Healing ointments are easily absorbed. Applying herbal ointments to the shoulders for rheumatic gout and alike.

Sensitive nervous system.

Female disorders: As a preventative measure apply hip baths using yarrow.

Pregnancy: Avoid any exertion, miscarriages are more likely.

Keep region of the pelvis, kidneys, and feet warm to prevent infection of the bladder and kidneys.

Lymphatic therapy.

Body Care

Aromas, scents:
Anemone, Cornflower
Oregano, Thuja

Treatments with firming and moisturizing creams are more effective.

Massages that serve to regenerate, and strengthen, perhaps aided with beneficial massage oils.

Correcting and cutting ingrown nails.

Hair dyes applied now, will look more vibrant.

Garden/Nature

Plant part:

Leaf

Watering all indoor and outdoor plants.

Sow plants, herbs, and vegetables that grow and flourish above ground, leaf vegetables (no lettuce).

Sowing, planting, harvesting, and drying every kind of medicinal herbs.

Transplanting.

Trimming and cutting back plants.
Combating slugs and snails.
Mowing lawns.

Start a compost heap.

Avoid pruning fruit trees and bushes. Avoid cutting down any trees.

Harvested produce should be consumed as soon as possible.

Housework

Light housework only.

Ventilate rooms briefly and rapidly. Don't air mattresses.

Any dirt and spots are easily removed in the laundry.

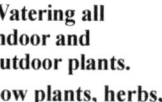

Avoid painting, as paint will take very long to dry.

Nutrition

Food quality:

Carbohydrate

Lettuce, spinach, lamb's lettuce, Endive, parsley, leek, cabbage (Brussels sprouts, kale, Chinese cabbage), all leafy herbs, asparagus, mushrooms, cress, Swiss chard, rhubarb.

Weight gain: avoid indulging in rich foods. If overweight, eat smaller portions and avoid carbohydrates.

Supply nutrient materials to strengthen the body. Focus on foods that contain essential minerals and vitamins. Stimulants and vitamins are more effective.

Positive affirmation:
"I remember my innermost being."

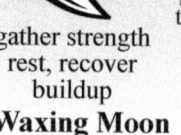

Planting Time
Descending forces!
Sap is drawn downward, enhancing root formation.
Best days for sowing, planting, and transplanting.

gather strength
rest, recover
buildup
Waxing Moon

♎→♏	8:22 AM PDT
	10:22 AM CDT
	11:22 AM EDT

11 Sunday Navratri

12 Monday Thanksgiving (CAN)

6:01 PM PDT
8:01 PM CDT ♏→♐
9:01 PM EDT

13 Tuesday Indigenous People Day (US)

Our ability to adapt is amazing. Our ability to change isn't quite as spectacular.
Lisa Lutz

Color
Red

Day

Wetness

Element ♏

Water   **Scorpio**

O C T O B E R

Success

Inquisitiveness and exuberant inspiration lead to new horizons. Insight and love for truth reign.

Bringing together is more important than splitting asunder.

Expansive forces will assist in legal matters, discussions, and debates.

Leisure

Expansion feels great, and travel, short trips, and outings are most welcome. A competitive spirit excites any sports event.

Talk things out when necessary.

Romance can be very passionate.

Good days for outings; even with cloudy skies the air still feels somewhat warm. Drying effect, get plenty to drink.

Health

Sensitive body parts:

Thighs and Veins

All measures taken to supply nutrient materials and strengthen the sensitive body parts are very effective.

Healing ointments are easily absorbed.

Sensitive sense organs.

Pains often arise in the sciatic nerve, veins, the small of the back, and thighs.

Avoid overstraining the body with unusual physical activities.

Body Care

Aromas, scents:
Calendula (Marigold), Geranium, Rosemary

Treatments with firming and moisturizing creams are more effective.

Massages that serve to regenerate, and strengthen, perhaps aided with beneficial massage oils.

Correcting and cutting ingrown nails.

Hair dyes applied now, will look more vibrant.

Garden/Nature

Plant part:

Fruit

Sow plants and vegetables that grow and flourish above ground.

Sowing and planting fruit and vegetables that grow tall, and tomatoes, but no lettuce.

Transplanting.

Grafting onto fruit trees.

Cultivating grains, particularly corn.

Gather herbs for vein diseases.

Housework

Light housework only.

Ventilate sufficiently.

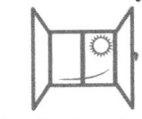

Freezing fruit and vegetables.

Baking bread, cakes, and cookies. Dough rises faster. (Except on New Moon)

Suitable for making cheese.

Making preserves.

Nutrition

Food quality:

Protein

Beans, peas, corn, tomatoes, pumpkin, lentils, soybeans, cucumber, eggplant, zucchini, berries, fruit, chili, bell pepper, figs, avocado, melon, olives.

Weight gain: avoid indulging in rich foods. If overweight, eat smaller portions.

Supply nutrient materials to strengthen the body. Focus on foods that contain essential minerals and vitamins.

Stimulants and vitamins are more effective.

Positive affirmation:
"I remember my innermost being."

Turning Point

Transition of descending to ascending forces. Both forces are at work and neutralize each other.

gather strength rest, recover buildup

Waxing Moon

14 Wednesday

No meat.

15 Thursday

Pity is sometimes a good substitute for love; but it is always no more than a substitute.
Sri Aurobindo

Color

Orange/ Yellow

Day

Warm

Element

Fire

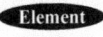

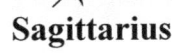

Sagittarius

O C T O B E R

Success

Career and business are in the foreground now and thinking becomes clear and serious, but somewhat inflexible.

Perseverance and reasoning assist in financial matters, planning, and contracts.

The values of tradition, authority, and discipline impact our endeavors.

Leisure

Money is not likely to be wasted in a shopping spree.

Many are drawn to enjoy cultural events.

The earth feels cold to the touch, so take slightly warmer clothes.

Health

Sensitive body parts:

Knees, Joints, Bones, Skin

All measures taken to supply nutrient materials and strengthen the sensitive body parts are very effective.

Healing ointments are easily absorbed.

Sensitive blood circulation.

Avoid overstraining bones and knees, and apply gentle stretching exercises only.

Problems with meniscus: Don't overstrain.

Dress slightly warmer.

High blood pressure: Avoid salty foods.

Massages, lymphatic therapy, and chiropractic treatment to release blockages.

Body Care

Aromas, scents:

Cedar, Juniper

Treatments with firming and moisturizing creams are more effective.

Massages that serve to regenerate, and strengthen, perhaps aided with beneficial massage oils.

Correcting and cutting ingrown nails.

Every kind of skin care is beneficial.

Cutting and filing toenails and fingernails will make the nails grow stronger over time.

Hair dyes applied now, will look more vibrant.

Garden/Nature

Plant part:

Root

Sow plants, herbs, and vegetables that grow and flourish above ground.

Transplanting.

Harvest produce is suitable for storage. Harvest root vegetables.

Gather herbs for bone, joint, and skin diseases.

Housework

Light housework only.

Air rooms only briefly.

Preserving root vegetables.

Avoid dry cleaning, as the fabric may develop unwanted glossy blotches.

Nutrition

Food quality:

Salt

Garlic, carrots, red beets, reddish, rutabaga, sugar beet, celery, potatoes, onions, kohlrabi.

Weight gain: avoid indulging in rich foods. If overweight, eat smaller portions.

Supply nutrient materials to strengthen the body. Focus on foods that contain essential minerals and vitamins.

Stimulants and vitamins are more effective.

Avoid large quantities of salty foods like bacon, ham, salted herring, fatty cheese, and the like. Avoid heavy and greasy foods.

Positive affirmation:
"I remember my innermost being."

Harvest Time
Ascending forces! Sap is rising, enhancing plant growth above ground, resulting in the most juicy fruits and vegetables.

gather strength rest, recover buildup
Waxing Moon

↗ ➙ ♑ 5:58 AM PDT
7:58 AM CDT
8:58 PM EDT

16 Friday
No meat. Cutting and filing toenails and fingernails.

17 Saturday

6:41 PM PDT ♑ ➙ ♒
8:41 PM CDT
9:41 PM EDT

18 Sunday
☾ Half Moon.

Man is always prey to his truths. Once he has admitted them, he cannot free himself from them.
Albert Camus

Color
Yellow

Day
Cool

Element
Earth

♑ **Capricorn**

O C T O B E R

Success

Inspiration, optimism, and impatience. Rational thinking, creativity and imagination spark new ideas and inspire planning for the future.

Shying away from routine tasks people will feel more drawn to anything new.

Instead of gridlocked structures choose new possibilities.

Leisure

Inspiration and optimism will boost friendship, social gatherings, and parties.

Express your creativity and imagination. Dwell in dreams and utopian ideas. It is easier now to perceive intuitive thoughts.

Health

Sensitive body parts:

Lower Legs, Veins

All measures taken to supply nutrient materials and strengthen the sensitive body parts are very effective.

Healing ointments are easily absorbed.

Sensitive glandular system.

Avoid inflammation of the veins. Apply ointments to lower legs, and rest legs in a raised position.

Varicose veins: Avoid long periods of standing.

While exercising go easy on the ankles.

Sensitivity to light, so bring your sunglasses along.

Body Care

Aromas, scents:
Cyclamen, Peach, Wild Roses

Treatments with firming and moisturizing creams are more effective.

Massages that serve to regenerate, and strengthen, perhaps aided with beneficial massage oils.

Correcting and cutting ingrown nails.

Hair dyes applied now, will look more vibrant.

Garden/Nature

Plant part:

Flower

Avoid watering plants.

Harvested produce is well suitable for storage.

Gather herbs for vein diseases.

Housework

Light housework only.

Ventilate rooms thoroughly.

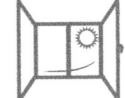

Baking cakes and cookies. Dough rises faster. (Except on New Moon)

Making preserves.

Nutrition

Food quality:

Fat

Cauliflower, artichoke, broccoli, sunflower seeds, flax seeds, nuts, rose hip, elder.

Weight gain: avoid indulging in rich foods. If overweight, eat smaller portions.

Supply nutrient materials to strengthen the body. Focus on foods that contain essential minerals and vitamins.

Stimulants and vitamins are more effective.

Pay attention to any particularly tempting foods today: Most likely the "wrong" things taste best.

High cholesterol: eat a low fat diet.

Positive affirmation:
"I remember my innermost being."

Harvest Time
Ascending forces! Sap is rising, enhancing plant growth above ground, resulting in the most juicy fruits and vegetables.

gather strength rest, recover buildup
Waxing Moon

19 Monday

20 Tuesday
Dussehra

O C T O B E R

Man reading should be man intensely alive. The book should be a ball of light in one's hand.
Ezra Pound

Color
Bright/ Dark Blue

Day
Air/Light

Element

Air   **Aquarius**

Success

Sensibility, intuition, and helpfulness.

Where possible, retreating is more favorable than dealing with business matters.

Dissolve restrictions, be patient and wait. Be aware that people can be more easily influenced.

Leisure

Your helpfulness will boost friendships.

Enjoy dancing or swimming, or watch a movie that will inspire your fantasies and imagination.

Retreat, relax, and recover.

Romance can be gentle and coziness will prevail.

If you plan outdoor excursions, be prepared for a shower here and there.

Health

Sensitive body parts:

Feet and Toes

All measures taken to supply nutrient materials and strengthen the sensitive body parts are very effective.

Healing ointments are easily absorbed.

Sensitive nervous system.

Drugs have a much stronger effect on your body. Monitor closely what you put into your body.

Lymphatic therapy.

Sluggishness or fatigue may occur in the transition into the next Zodiac sign of Aries.

Body Care

Aromas, scents: Magnolia, Amaryllis, Clary Sage

Treatments with firming and moisturizing creams are more effective.

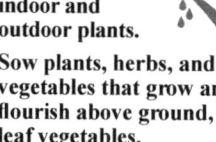

Massages that serve to regenerate, and strengthen, perhaps aided with beneficial massage oils. Reflexology massage. Carry out with special care, people are more sensitive.

Correcting and cutting ingrown nails.

Foot bath.

No haircuts, hair becomes shaggy and unmanageable. Avoid washing your hair. Dandruff could develop.

Garden/Nature

Plant part:

Leaf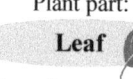

Watering all indoor and outdoor plants.

Sow plants, herbs, and vegetables that grow and flourish above ground, and leaf vegetables.

Transplanting.

Mowing lawns.

Avoid pruning fruit trees and bushes.

Harvested produce should be consumed as soon as possible.

Gather herbs for foot complaints.

Housework

Light housework only.

Ventilate rooms briefly and rapidly. Don't air mattresses.

Any dirt and spots are easily removed in the laundry.

Avoid painting, as paint will take very long to dry.

Preserving and storing should be avoided.

Nutrition

Food quality:

Carbohydrate

Lettuce, spinach, lamb's lettuce, Endive, parsley, leek, cabbage (Brussels sprouts, kale, Chinese cabbage), all leafy herbs, asparagus, mushrooms, cress, Swiss chard, rhubarb.

Weight gain: avoid indulging in rich foods. If overweight, eat smaller portions and avoid carbohydrates.

Supply nutrient materials to strengthen the body. Focus on foods that contain essential minerals and vitamins.

Caffeine, alcohol, drugs, certain foods, and stimulants have a much stronger effect.

Positive affirmation:
"I remember my innermost being."

Harvest Time
Ascending forces!
Sap is rising,
enhancing plant
growth above ground,
resulting in the most
juicy fruits and
vegetables.

gather strength
rest, recover
buildup
Waxing Moon

≈≈→)(5:36 AM PST
7:36 AM CST
8:36 AM EST

12:55 PM PST
2:55 PM CST)(→Υ
3:55 PM EST

21 Wednesday
No meat.

22 Thursday

23 Friday
No meat. Cutting and filing toenails and fingernails.

Like all magnificent things, it's very simple.
Natalie Babbitt

Color
Blueish White

Day
Wetness

Element
Water

Pisces

O C T O B E R

Success

Things get going and the way straight ahead seems the best.

People feel energetic, courageous, assertive, and at times anxious.

Good time for meetings and sales talks but impatience and selfishness do not favor teamwork.

Leisure

An enterprising spirit and spontaneity move people to enjoy outings, sports, competitions, cultural events, and travels.

Romance can be very passionate.

Good days for outings, even with cloudy skies the air still feels somewhat warm. Drying effect, get plenty to drink.

Health

Sensitive body parts:

Head, Brain, Eyes

All measures taken to supply nutrient materials and strengthen the sensitive body parts are very effective.

Healing ointments are easily absorbed.

Sensitive sense organs.

If you suffer from migraines drink plenty of water, and avoid coffee, chocolate, and sugar.

○ *Full Moon: Avoid any surgery and vaccination if possible.*

Body Care

Aromas, scents:
Cloves, Peppermint, Thyme

Treatments with firming and moisturizing creams are more effective.

Massages that serve to regenerate, and strengthen, perhaps aided with beneficial massage oils.

Correcting and cutting ingrown nails.

Eye compresses for strained eyes.

Any kind of hair care. Hair dyes applied now, will look more vibrant.

Garden/Nature

Plant part:

Fruit

Sow plants and vegetables that grow and flourish above ground, especially fruit and tomatoes.

Sowing and planting anything that is supposed to grow fast and for immediate use.

Grafting onto fruit trees.

Cultivating grains.

Transplanting.

Harvesting and storing grains, vegetables, potatoes, fruit, and tomatoes.

Gather herbs for eye complaints and headaches.

Day off on 10/24.

○ *Full Moon: Weather and climate changes. Herbs are most powerful.*

Housework

Light housework only.

Ventilate sufficiently.

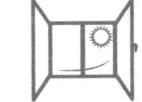

Preserving fruit.

Freezing fruit and vegetables.

Baking bread, cakes, and cookies. Dough rises faster. (Except on New Moon)

Suitable for making cheese.

○ *Full Moon: Avoid doing laundry, cleaning windows, making preserves, painting.*

Nutrition

Food quality:

Protein

Beans, peas, corn, tomatoes, pumpkin, lentils, soybeans, cucumber, eggplant, zucchini, berries, fruit, chili, bell pepper, figs, avocado, melon, olives.

Weight gain: avoid indulging in rich foods. If overweight, eat smaller portions.

Supply nutrient materials to strengthen the body. Focus on foods that contain essential minerals and vitamins.

Stimulants and vitamins are more effective.

Drink plenty of water.

○ *Full Moon: A day of fasting.*

Positive affirmation:
"I remember my innermost being."

Harvest Time
Ascending forces! Sap is rising, enhancing plant growth above ground, resulting in the most juicy fruits and vegetables.

gather strength rest, recover buildup

Waxing Moon

24 Saturday

4:36 PM PDT
6:36 PM CDT
7:36 PM EDT ♈→♉

25 Sunday

○ **Full Moon** 9:13 PM PDT, 11:13 PM CDT, 12:13 AM EDT Monday

O C T O B E R

Love is that condition in which the happiness of another person is essential to your own.
Robert A. Heinlein

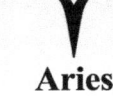

Color
Indigo Blue

Day
Warm

Element
Fire

Aries

Success

Realism and material security are important. Persistence comes easy, thoughts and reactions are slower.

Assess financial areas.

Conservative tendencies may make people want to stay away from risk taking.

Leisure

Relax at a picnic/feast. Enjoy culinary pleasures and hobbies.

The earth feels cold to the touch, so take slightly warmer clothes.

Health

Sensitive body parts:

Head and Neck

All measures taken to flush out and detoxify the sensitive body parts are very effective.

Good for surgery, except on the sensitive body parts (see above), sex organs, ureter. Scarring is less severe.

Teeth: Removal of tartar and amalgam. Best for fillings, crowns, and dentures! Avoiding treatment of periodontitis and gums.

Blood-purifying, detoxifying herbal infusions and teas. Sensitive blood circulation.

Organs of speech, jaws, teeth, tonsils, thyroid gland, neck, and vocal chords get easily affected. Keep neck warm. On cold days ears should be protected. Sensitivity to noise.

High blood pressure: Avoid salty foods.

Massages, lymphatic therapy, and chiropractic treatment to release blockages.

Body Care

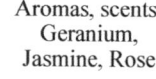

Aromas, scents: Geranium, Jasmine, Rose

Prepare home-made ointments and cosmetics.

Apply detoxing facial and body care.

Treatments of bumps and pimples on the skin, and exfoliating procedures.

Removing body hair.

Correction of the nail bed.

Massages that serve to relax, ease tension, and detoxify.

Reflexology massage.

Removal of callused skin.

Treating obstinate athlete's foot, nail fungus, and warts.

Garden/Nature

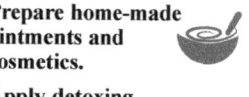

Plant part:

Root

Sow plants and vegetables that grow below ground.

Everything grows slowly and lasts well.

Dig over to prepare soil.

Trimming/cutting back plants. Weeding. Mulching.

Start a compost heap.

Combat vermin found in the soil.

Spread fertilizer and liquid manure.

Fertilize flowers with poorly formed roots.

Harvested produce is well suited for storage. Harvesting root vegetables.

Gather herbs (roots) for sinus issues, sore throat, and ear complaints.

Housework

Housework is dealt with much more successfully, efficiently, and effortlessly.

Problem stains are removed readily.

Best for doing laundry! Reduce on laundry detergent, support the environment.

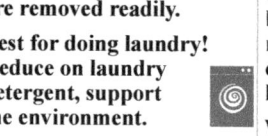

Dry cleaning.

Clean and store seasonal clothing.

Thoroughly clean wooden and parquet floors, metals, china etc.

Cleaning, polishing, and waterproofing shoes.

Combating mold.

Air rooms only briefly.

Painting.

Preserving root vegetables.

Nutrition

Food quality:

Salt

Garlic, carrots, red beets, reddish, rutabaga, sugar beet, celery, potatoes, onions, kohlrabi.

Weight associated with overeating is less likely. If underweight, eat larger portions.

Cleansing and detox diets. Fruit and juice days.

Flush out poisons. Treatment for drug abuse.

Avoid large quantities of salty foods like bacon, ham, salted herring, fatty cheese, and the like.

Ah coffee. The sweet balm by which we shall accomplish today's tasks.
Holly Black

Bright Blue — Color

Cool — Day

Element

Taurus   **Earth**

26 Monday

6:03 PM PDT
8:03 PM CDT → ♉ → ♊
9:03 PM EDT

27 Tuesday

Harvest Time
Ascending forces! Sap is rising, enhancing plant growth above ground, resulting in the most juicy fruits and vegetables.

detox
remove
be active

Waning Moon

O C T O B E R

Success

Open mindedness and curiosity. A changeable and hectic time.

Good time for talking, negotiating, networking, and exchanging ideas as well as for meetings of a nonbinding nature, conferences, and studies.

Leisure

Good time for family gatherings, parties, and short trips.

People enjoy stimulating their minds with reading and studying. Attending theater performances is a preferred enjoyment. Enhance friendships.

Stretching exercises.

Be prepared for sudden changes in weather or climate.

Health

Sensitive body parts:
Shoulders, Arms, Hands, Lungs

All measures taken to flush out and detoxify the sensitive body parts are very effective.

Good for surgery, except on the sensitive body parts (see above), sex organs, and ureter.
Scarring is less severe.
Teeth: Removal of tartar and amalgam. Best for fillings, crowns, and dentures! Avoid having any teeth pulled.
Blood-purifying, detoxifying herbal infusions and teas.
Sensitive glandular system.
Make sure you are dressed warm enough in cool weather.
Exercises for shoulders. Breathing exercises.
Sensitivity to light, bring your sunglasses along.
Massages, lymphatic therapy, and chiropractic treatment to release blockages.

Body Care

Aromas, scents:
Lavender, Lemon Balm, Magnolia, Verbena

Prepare home-made ointments and cosmetics.

Apply detoxing facial and body care.

Treatments of bumps and pimples on the skin, and exfoliating procedures.

Removing body hair.

Correction of the nail bed.

Massages that serve to relax, ease tension, and detoxify.

Reflexology massage.

Removal of callused skin.

Treating obstinate athlete's foot, nail fungus, and warts.

Garden/Nature

Plant part:
Flower 🌸

Sow plants and vegetables that grow below ground.

Trimming and cutting back plants.

Start a compost heap.

Weeding. Pest control.

Fertilize flowers that no longer bloom.

Avoid watering plants.

Changes in weather are more likely.

Gather herbs (roots) for tensions in the shoulder and lung complaints.

Housework

Housework is dealt with much more successfully, efficiently, and effortlessly.

Problem stains are removed readily.

Best for doing laundry! Reduce on laundry detergent, support the environment.

Dry cleaning.

Clean and store seasonal clothing.

Thoroughly clean wooden and parquet floors, metals, china etc.

Cleaning windows and glass.

Cleaning, polishing, and waterproofing shoes.

Combating mold.

Ventilate rooms thoroughly.

Baking bread, cakes, and cookies (add more leavening agent).

Making preserves.

Painting.

Nutrition

Food quality:
Fat

Cauliflower, artichoke, broccoli, sunflower seeds, flax seeds, nuts, rose hip, elder.

Weight associated with overeating is less likely. If underweight, eat larger portions.

Cleansing and detox diets. Fruit and juice days.

Flush out poisons. Treatment for drug abuse.

Pay attention to any particularly tempting foods today: Most likely the "wrong" things taste best.

High cholesterol: eat a low fat diet.

The secret of life, though, is to fall seven times and to get up eight times.
Paulo Coelho

Gemini

Color — **Light Blue**

Day — **Air/Light**

Element — **Air**

28 Wednesday
No meat.

7:07 PM PDT
9:07 PM CDT ⟶ ♊ ➜ ♋
10:07 PM EDT

29 Thursday

O C T O B E R

Positive affirmation:
"I remember my innermost being."

Turning Point
Transition of ascending to descending forces. Both forces are at work and neutralize each other.

detox
remove
be active
Waning Moon

Success

Feelings, sensitivity, and cooperativeness. Many are overly sensitive, so beware of treading on someone's toes.

Be cautious if you are easily influenced.

During negotiations make use of the cognitive ability of your senses.

Leisure

Relax within your close family.

Retreat to your safe haven and enjoy your fantasy while reading or listening to music. The inner world becomes more colorful than the outer.

Romance can be gentle. Deep feelings will prevail.

If you plan outdoor excursions, be prepared for a shower here and there.

Health

Sensitive body parts:
Chest, Lungs, Liver, Stomach, Gall Bladder

All measures taken to flush out and detoxify the sensitive body parts are very effective.

Good for surgical operations except those on the sensitive body parts (see above), sex organs, and ureter. Scarring is less severe.

Teeth: Removal of tartar and amalgam. Best for fillings, crowns, and dentures!

Blood-purifying, detoxifying herbal infusions and teas.

Sensitive nervous system.

Be cautious with alcohol since the liver is very sensitive.

Stomach could play up and cause gas and heartburn.

Rheumatism: Don't air bedding outside, damp will remain in the bedding.

Lymphatic therapy.

Body Care

Aromas, scents:
Lilac, Lilies of the Valley, Lilies, Violets

Prepare home-made ointments and cosmetics.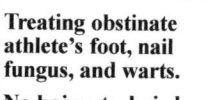

Apply detoxing facial and body care.

Treatments of bumps and pimples on the skin, and exfoliating procedures.

Removing body hair.

Correction of the nail bed.

Massages that serve to relax, ease tension, and detoxify.

Reflexology massage.

Removal of callused skin.

Treating obstinate athlete's foot, nail fungus, and warts.

No haircuts, hair becomes shaggy and unmanageable. Avoid washing your hair.

Garden/Nature

Plant part:
Leaf

Water plants.

Fertilize flowers.

Sow plants and vegetables that grow below ground, leaf vegetables, and lettuce.

Dig over/plow to prepare soil for planting.

Trimming and cutting back plants. Transplanting. Weeding.

Combating pests above ground.

Start a compost heap.

Mowing lawns.

Gather herbs (roots) for bronchitis, stomach, liver, and gall bladder complaints.

Unfavorable for harvesting, storing, and preserving.

Housework

Housework is dealt with much more successfully, efficiently, and effortlessly.

Problem stains are removed readily.

Best for doing laundry! Reduce on laundry detergent, support the environment.

Dry cleaning.

Thoroughly clean wooden and parquet floors, metals, china etc.

Cleaning, polishing, and waterproofing shoes.

Combating mold.

Ventilate rooms briefly and rapidly.

Avoid painting.

Nutrition

Food quality:
Carbohydrate

Lettuce, spinach, lamb's lettuce, Endive, parsley, leek, cabbage (Brussels sprouts, kale, Chinese cabbage), all leafy herbs, asparagus, mushrooms, cress, Swiss chard, rhubarb.

Weight associated with overeating is less likely. If underweight, eat larger portions.

Moodiness may make you want to eat more than is healthy. If overweight avoid carbohydrates.

Cleansing and detox diets. Fruit and juice days.

Flush out poisons. Treatment for drug abuse.

If you get stomach troubles easily, avoid heavy meals.

Any fool can know. The point is to understand.
Albert Einstein

9:19 PM PDT
11:19 PM CDT
Sunday 12:19 AM EDT

30 Friday
No meat. Cutting and filing toenails and fingernails.

31 Saturday
Halloween

Planting Time
Descending forces! Sap is drawn downward, enhancing root formation. Best days for sowing, planting, and transplanting.

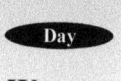

Cancer   **Water**

Color — **Green**
Day — **Wetness**
Element —

O C T O B E R

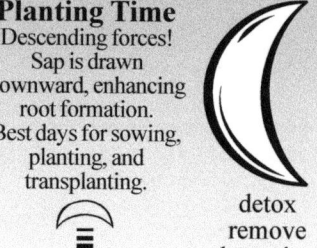
detox
remove
be active
Waning Moon

Success

Determination reigns, and risks are taken more often. Master your tasks with more self-confidence and creativity.

Limits appear to be more easily surmountable.

Auspicious day for sales, advertising, and publicity.

Leisure

Zest for life is in the air. People want to have a fun time, enjoy parties, musical events, movies, etc.

Possessive feelings can harm a relationship. Romance can be very passionate.

Outings: even with cloudy skies the air still feels somewhat warm. Drying effect, get plenty to drink.

Danger of sudden storms, not only in the sky.

Health

Sensitive body parts:
Heart, Back, Diaphragm, Circulation, Arteries

All measures taken to flush out and detoxify the sensitive body parts are very effective.

Good for surgery, except on the sensitive body parts (see above), sex organs, and ureter.
Scarring is less severe.

Teeth: Removal of tartar and amalgam. Best for fillings, crowns, and dentures!

Blood-purifying, detoxifying herbal infusions and teas.

Sensitive sense organs.

Back and heart problems are more likely to occur.

Avoid overstraining of the heart and circulation with unusual physical activities.

Expect sleepless nights.

Body Care

Aromas, scents:
Hibiscus, Oleander, Rose

Prepare home-made ointments and cosmetics.

Apply detoxing facial and body care.

Treatments of bumps and pimples on the skin, and exfoliating procedures.

Removing body hair.

Correction of the nail bed.

Massages that serve to relax, ease tension, and detoxify.

Reflexology massage.

Removal of callused skin.

Treating obstinate athlete's foot, nail fungus, and warts.

Good days for haircuts, hair becomes stronger. But be aware that if you get a perm, curls will become quite frizzy. Baby's first haircut.

Garden/Nature

Plant part:
Fruit

Sowing plants and vegetables that grow below ground.

Sowing and planting fruit. Also sow and plant vegetables that are highly perishable. Plant trees and bushes. Sow lawns.

Dig over/plow to prepare soil for planting.

Trimming and cutting back plants. Pruning of fruit trees and bushes.

Transplanting.

Not suitable for fertilizing.

Weeding. Pest Control.

Harvested produce should be consumed as soon as possible.

Gather herbs (roots) for heart and circulation complaints.

Start compost heap.

Housework

Housework is dealt with much more successfully, efficiently, and effortlessly.

Problem stains are removed readily.

Best for doing laundry!

Dry cleaning.

Thoroughly clean wooden and parquet floors, metals, china, etc.

Cleaning windows and glass.

Cleaning, polishing, and waterproofing shoes.

Combating mold.

Ventilate rooms sufficiently. Air beds.

Suitable for making cheese.

Preserving and freezing fruit and vegetables.

Baking bread, cakes, and cookies (use more leavening agent).

Avoid painting.

Nutrition

Food quality:
Protein

Beans, peas, corn, tomatoes, pumpkin, lentils, soybeans, cucumber, eggplant, zucchini, berries, fruit, chili, bell pepper, figs, avocado, melon, olives.

Weight associated with overeating is less likely. If underweight, eat larger portions.

Cleansing and detox diets. Fruit and juice days.

Flush out poisons. Treatment for drug abuse.

If God assigns to me a place in hell, I do not know why I should aspire for heaven. He knows best what is for my welfare.
Sri Aurobindo

Color — **Green**

Day — **Warm**

Element

Leo   **Fire**

1 Sunday All Saint's Day, Daylight Saving Time ends.

◖ Half Moon.

2 Monday All Souls Day

Planting Time
Descending forces! Sap is drawn downward, enhancing root formation. Best days for sowing, planting, and transplanting.

detox remove be active

Waning Moon

N O V E M B E R

Success

Good time for details, organization, routine, concentration, and duty.

Take care of financial and administrative tasks.

Prepare for future success now with realistic and critical assessment.

Leisure

Enjoy a nature walk.

Good time for health regimes. Improve your health with stretching exercises and yoga.

The earth feels cold to the touch, so take slightly warmer clothes.

Health

Sensitive body parts:
Digestive Organs, Nerves, Spleen, Pancreas

All measures taken to flush out and detoxify the sensitive body parts are very effective.

Good for surgery, except on the sensitive body parts (see above), sex organs, ureter. Scarring is less severe.

Teeth: Removal of tartar and amalgam. Best for fillings, crowns, and dentures! Avoiding treatment of periodontitis and gums.

Blood-purifying, detoxifying herbal infusions and teas.

Sensitive blood circulation.

For a sensitive digestive system, a wholesome diet is recommended.

Dress slightly warmer.

High blood pressure: Avoid salty foods.

Massages, lymphatic therapy, and chiropractic treatment to release blockages.

Body Care

Aromas, scents:
Lavender, Spruce Needles, Sage, Meadow Flowers

Prepare home-made ointments and cosmetics.

Apply detoxing facial and body care.

Treatments of bumps and pimples on the skin, and exfoliating procedures.

Removing body hair.

Correction of the nail bed.

Massages that serve to relax, ease tension, and detoxify.

Reflexology massage.

Removal of callused skin.

Treating obstinate athlete's foot, nail fungus, and warts.

Best for haircuts because it retains its shape longer. Perms turn out best.

Garden/Nature

Plant part: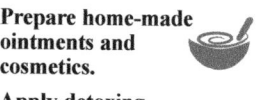
Root

Best for sowing and planting, except lettuce.

Plant trees which are supposed to grow very tall. Plant hedges and bushes that are meant to grow very fast.

Planting and re-potting balcony and indoor plants.

Dig over/plow to prepare soil for planting.

Trimming and cutting back plants. Planting cuttings.

Spread fertilizer and manure. Fertilize flowers with poorly formed roots.

Start a compost heap.

Transplanting. Mulching.

Weeding. Pest control (vermin in the soil).

Avoid harvesting and storing.

Gather herbs (roots) for digestive organs, pancreas, and nervous complaints.

Housework

Housework is dealt with much more successfully, efficiently, and effortlessly.

Problem stains are removed readily.

Best for doing laundry! Reduce on laundry detergent, support the environment.

Dry cleaning.

Thoroughly clean wooden and parquet floors, metals, china etc.

Cleaning, polishing, and waterproofing shoes.

Combating mold.

Air rooms only briefly.

Painting.

Making pickles, preserves, and cheese yields suboptimal results and should be avoided.

Nutrition

Food quality:
Salt

Garlic, carrots, red beets, reddish, rutabaga, sugar beet, celery, potatoes, onions, kohlrabi.

Weight associated with overeating is less likely. If underweight, eat larger portions.

Cleansing and detox diets. Fruit and juice days.

Flush out poisons. Treatment for drug abuse.

Avoid large quantities of salty foods like bacon, ham, salted herring, fatty cheese, and the like. Avoid heavy and greasy foods.

We must live together as brothers or perish together as fools.
Martin Luther King Jr.

♌ → ♍ ← 12:29 AM PST
2:29 AM CST
3:29 AM EST

Color
Yellow

Day

Cool

Element

♍ Virgo   Earth

3 Tuesday

4 Wednesday

No meat.

Planting Time
Descending forces! Sap is drawn downward, enhancing root formation. Best days for sowing, planting, and transplanting.

detox
remove
be active
Waning Moon

N O V E M B E R

Success

The artistic instinct rules, but so, too, does indecisiveness. The forces swing back and forth until equilibrium is achieved.

It's easy to reach compromises with tactful sensitivity.

A sense of judgment will support legal matters.

Leisure

Pursuit for harmony and cooperativeness supports good times in romance, friendship, and partnership.

Enjoy cultural events. Relax and get pampered with a spa treatment.

Romance can be passionate yet sensitive.

Health

Sensitive body parts:

Hips, Kidneys, Bladder

All measures taken to flush out and detoxify the sensitive body parts are very effective.

Good for surgery, except on the sensitive body parts (see above), sex organs, and ureter. Scarring is less severe.

Teeth: Removal of tartar and amalgam. Best for fillings, crowns, and dentures! Avoid treatment of periodontitis and gums, avoid pulling teeth.

Blood-purifying, detoxifying herbal infusions and teas.

Sensitive glandular system.

Take special care to keep the area of the bladder and kidneys warm.

Apply special exercises for the hip region.

Sensitivity to light, so bring your sunglasses along.

Body Care

Aromas, scents: Roses, Violets, Daffodils

Prepare home-made ointments and cosmetics.

Apply detoxing facial and body care.

Treatments of bumps and pimples on the skin, and exfoliating procedures.

Removing body hair.

Correction of the nail bed.

Massages that serve to relax, ease tension, and detoxify.

Reflexology massage.

Removal of callused skin.

Treating obstinate athlete's foot, nail fungus, and warts.

Garden/Nature

Plant part:

Flower

Sow plants and vegetables that grow below ground.

Dig over/plow to prepare soil for planting.

Trimming and cutting back plants.

Start a compost heap.

Weeding. Pest control.

Fertilize flowers that no longer bloom.

Transplanting.

Avoid watering plants.

Harvested produce should be consumed as soon as possible.

Gather herbs (roots) for kidneys, gall bladder and hip complaints.

Day off on 11/5.

Housework

Housework is dealt with much more successfully, efficiently, and effortlessly.

Problem stains are removed readily.

Best for doing laundry! Reduce on laundry detergent, support the environment.

Dry cleaning.

Clean and store seasonal clothing.

Thoroughly clean wooden and parquet floors, metals, china etc.

Cleaning windows and glass.

Cleaning, polishing, and waterproofing shoes.

Combating mold.

Ventilate rooms thoroughly.

Baking bread, cakes, and cookies (add more leavening agent).

Making preserves.

Painting.

Nutrition

Food quality:

Fat

Cauliflower, artichoke, broccoli, sunflower seeds, flax seeds, nuts, rose hip, elder.

Weight associated with overeating is less likely. If underweight, eat larger portions.

Cleansing and detox diets. Fruit and juice days.

Flush out poisons. Treatment for drug abuse.

Pay attention to any particularly tempting foods today: Most likely the "wrong" things taste best.

High cholesterol: eat a low fat diet.

The journey is what brings us happiness not the destination.
Dan Millman

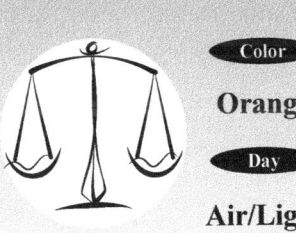

Color — Orange

Day — Air/Light

Element

Libra — Air

♍→♎ 6:39 AM PST / 8:39 AM CST / 9:39 AM EST

2:41 PM PST / 4:41 PM CST / 5:41 PM EST ♎→♏

5 Thursday

6 Friday — No meat. Cutting and filing toenails and fingernails.

7 Saturday

N O V E M B E R

Planting Time
Descending forces! Sap is drawn downward, enhancing root formation. Best days for sowing, planting, and transplanting.

detox remove be active

Waning Moon

Success

Critical and superstitious behavior emerges, especially pertaining to money.

A penetrating power will strengthen your capacity to act.

An increased perception opens our interest for the essentials and helps to discover hidden potentials.

Leisure

Relax within your close family, with meditation, and relaxation exercises.

A longing to feel safe will be nurtured if you focus on habits and rituals. An increased sensitivity will help to enjoy every moment.

Romance can be very passionate.

If you plan outdoor excursions, be prepared for a shower here and there.

Health

Sensitive body parts:

Sex organs, Ureter

All measures taken to flush out and detoxify the sensitive body parts are very effective.

Good for surgical operations except those on the sensitive body parts (see above). Scarring is less severe.

Teeth: Removal of tartar and amalgam. Best for fillings, crowns, and dentures!

Blood-purifying, detoxifying herbal infusions and teas.

Sensitive nervous system.

Female disorders: As a preventative measure apply hip baths using yarrow.

Pregnancy: Avoid any exertion, miscarriages are more likely.

Keep region of the pelvis, kidneys, and feet warm to prevent infection of the bladder and kidneys.

Lymphatic therapy.

Body Care

Aromas, scents:
Anemone, Cornflower
Oregano, Thuja

Prepare home-made ointments and cosmetics.

Apply detoxing facial and body care.

Treatments of bumps and pimples on the skin, and exfoliating procedures.

Removing body hair.

Correction of the nail bed.

Massages that serve to relax, ease tension, and detoxify.

Reflexology massage.

Removal of callused skin.

Treating obstinate athlete's foot, nail fungus, and warts.

Garden/Nature

Plant part:

Leaf

Water plants.

Fertilize flowers and meadows, no vegetables.

Sow plants and vegetables that grow below ground, leaf vegetables, and lettuce.

Sowing, planting, harvesting, and drying every kind of medicinal herbs.

Dig over/plow to prepare soil for planting.

Trimming and cutting back plants. Transplanting. Weeding. Pest control. Start a compost heap.

Mowing lawns.

Harvested produce should be consumed as soon as possible.

Avoid cutting down trees, danger of bark beetles.

Housework

Housework is dealt with much more successfully, efficiently, and effortlessly.

Problem stains are removed readily.

Best for doing laundry! Reduce on laundry detergent, support the environment.

Dry cleaning.

Thoroughly clean wooden and parquet floors, metals, china etc.

Cleaning, polishing, and waterproofing shoes.

Combating mold.

Ventilate rooms briefly and rapidly.

Avoid painting.

Nutrition

Food quality:

Carbohydrate

Lettuce, spinach, lamb's lettuce, Endive, parsley, leek, cabbage (Brussels sprouts, kale, Chinese cabbage), all leafy herbs, asparagus, mushrooms, cress, Swiss chard, rhubarb.

Weight associated with overeating is less likely. If underweight, eat larger portions.

Cleansing and detox diets. Fruit and juice days.

Flush out poisons. Treatment for drug abuse.

The small wisdom is like water in a glass: clear, transparent, pure. The great wisdom is like the water in the sea: dark, mysterious, impenetrable.
Rabindranath Tagore

Color

Red

Day

Wetness

Element

Water

Scorpio

8 Sunday
Diwali

Planting Time
Descending forces!
Sap is drawn downward, enhancing root formation.
Best days for sowing, planting, and transplanting.

detox
remove
be active

Waning Moon

NOVEMBER

Success

Critical and superstitious behavior emerges, especially pertaining to money.

A penetrating power will strengthen your capacity to act.

An increased perception opens our interest for the essentials and helps to discover hidden potentials.

● *New Moon: Confirm your resolutions. Finalize new decisions. Drop bad habits.*

Leisure

Relax within your close family, with meditation, and relaxation exercises.

A longing to feel safe will be nurtured if you focus on habits and rituals. An increased sensitivity will help to enjoy every moment.

Romance can be very passionate.

If you plan outdoor excursions, be prepared for a shower here and there.

Health

Sensitive body parts:

Sex organs, Ureter

All measures taken to supply nutrient materials and strengthen the sensitive body parts are very effective.

Healing ointments are easily absorbed. Applying herbal ointments to the shoulders for rheumatic gout and alike.

Sensitive nervous system.

Female disorders: As a preventative measure apply hip baths using yarrow.

Pregnancy: Avoid any exertion, miscarriages are more likely.

Keep region of the pelvis, kidneys, and feet warm to prevent infection of the bladder and kidneys.

Lymphatic therapy.

● *New Moon: Avoid any surgery if possible.*

Body Care

Aromas, scents:
Anemone, Cornflower
Oregano, Thuja

Treatments with firming and moisturizing creams are more effective.

Massages that serve to regenerate, and strengthen, perhaps aided with beneficial massage oils.

Correcting and cutting ingrown nails.

Hair dyes applied now, will look more vibrant.

Garden/Nature

Plant part:

Leaf

Watering all indoor and outdoor plants.

Sow plants, herbs, and vegetables that grow and flourish above ground, leaf vegetables (no lettuce).

Sowing, planting, harvesting, and drying every kind of medicinal herbs.

Transplanting.

Trimming and cutting back plants.
Combating slugs and snails.
Mowing lawns.

Start a compost heap.

Avoid pruning fruit trees and bushes. Avoid cutting down any trees.

Harvested produce should be consumed as soon as possible.

● *New Moon: Change of weather is likely. Care for sickly plants.*

Housework

Light housework only.

Ventilate rooms briefly and rapidly. Don't air mattresses.

Any dirt and spots are easily removed in the laundry.

Avoid painting, as paint will take very long to dry.

Nutrition

Food quality:

Carbohydrate

Lettuce, spinach, lamb's lettuce, Endive, parsley, leek, cabbage (Brussels sprouts, kale, Chinese cabbage), all leafy herbs, asparagus, mushrooms, cress, Swiss chard, rhubarb.

Weight gain: avoid indulging in rich foods. If overweight, eat smaller portions and avoid carbohydrates.

Supply nutrient materials to strengthen the body. Focus on foods that contain essential minerals and vitamins. Stimulants and vitamins are more effective.

● *New Moon: A day of fasting.*

Positive affirmation:
"I forgive others and myself."

Planting Time
Descending forces!
Sap is drawn downward, enhancing root formation.
Best days for sowing, planting, and transplanting.

No meat.

gather strength rest, recover buildup
Waxing Moon

9 Monday

● **New Moon** 12:03 AM PST, 2:03 AM CST, 3:03 AM EST

N O V E M B E R

You cannot protect yourself from sadness without protecting yourself from happiness.
Jonathan Safran Foer

 Color

Red

 Day

Wetness

 Element

Water

♏ Scorpio

Success

Inquisitiveness and exuberant inspiration lead to new horizons. Insight and love for truth reign.

Bringing together is more important than splitting asunder.

Expansive forces will assist in legal matters, discussions, and debates.

Leisure

Expansion feels great, and travel, short trips, and outings are most welcome. A competitive spirit excites any sports event.

Talk things out when necessary.

Romance can be very passionate.

Good days for outings; even with cloudy skies the air still feels somewhat warm. Drying effect, get plenty to drink.

Health

Sensitive body parts:

Thighs and Veins

All measures taken to supply nutrient materials and strengthen the sensitive body parts are very effective.

Healing ointments are easily absorbed.

Sensitive sense organs.

Pains often arise in the sciatic nerve, veins, the small of the back, and thighs.

Avoid overstraining the body with unusual physical activities.

Body Care

Aromas, scents: Calendula (Marigold), Geranium, Rosemary

Treatments with firming and moisturizing creams are more effective.

Massages that serve to regenerate, and strengthen, perhaps aided with beneficial massage oils.

Correcting and cutting ingrown nails.

Hair dyes applied now, will look more vibrant.

Garden/Nature

Plant part:

Fruit

Sow plants and vegetables that grow and flourish above ground.

Sowing and planting fruit and vegetables that grow tall, and tomatoes, but no lettuce.

Transplanting.

Grafting onto fruit trees.

Cultivating grains, particularly corn.

Gather herbs for vein diseases.

Housework

Light housework only.

Ventilate sufficiently.

Freezing fruit and vegetables.

Baking bread, cakes, and cookies. Dough rises faster. (Except on New Moon)

Suitable for making cheese.

Making preserves.

Nutrition

Food quality:

Protein

Beans, peas, corn, tomatoes, pumpkin, lentils, soybeans, cucumber, eggplant, zucchini, berries, fruit, chili, bell pepper, figs, avocado, melon, olives.

Weight gain: avoid indulging in rich foods. If overweight, eat smaller portions.

Supply nutrient materials to strengthen the body. Focus on foods that contain essential minerals and vitamins.

Stimulants and vitamins are more effective.

Positive affirmation:
"I forgive others and myself."

Turning Point

Transition of descending to ascending forces. Both forces are at work and neutralize each other.

gather strength rest, recover buildup

Waxing Moon

♏ ➜ ♐ 12:37 AM PST / 2:37 AM CST / 3:37 AM EST

10 Tuesday

11 Wednesday
Veterans Day (US)
Remembrance Day (CAN)
No meat.

12:28 PM PST / 2:28 PM CST / 3:28 PM EST ♐ ➜ ♑

12 Thursday

Care not for time and success. Act out thy part, whether it be to fail or to prosper.
Sri Aurobindo

Color
Orange/ Yellow

Day
Warm

Element
Fire

Sagittarius

N O V E M B E R

Success

Career and business are in the foreground now and thinking becomes clear and serious, but somewhat inflexible.

Perseverance and reasoning assist in financial matters, planning, and contracts.

The values of tradition, authority, and discipline impact our endeavors.

Leisure

Money is not likely to be wasted in a shopping spree.

Many are drawn to enjoy cultural events.

The earth feels cold to the touch, so take slightly warmer clothes.

Health

Sensitive body parts:

Knees, Joints, Bones, Skin

All measures taken to supply nutrient materials and strengthen the sensitive body parts are very effective.

Healing ointments are easily absorbed.

Sensitive blood circulation.

Avoid overstraining bones and knees, and apply gentle stretching exercises only.

Problems with meniscus: Don't overstrain.

Dress slightly warmer.

High blood pressure: Avoid salty foods.

Massages, lymphatic therapy, and chiropractic treatment to release blockages.

Body Care

Aromas, scents:

Cedar, Juniper

Treatments with firming and moisturizing creams are more effective.

Massages that serve to regenerate, and strengthen, perhaps aided with beneficial massage oils.

Correcting and cutting ingrown nails.

Every kind of skin care is beneficial.

Cutting and filing toenails and fingernails will make the nails grow stronger over time.

Hair dyes applied now, will look more vibrant.

Garden/Nature

Plant part:

Root

Sow plants, herbs, and vegetables that grow and flourish above ground.

Transplanting.

Harvest produce is suitable for storage. Harvest root vegetables.

Gather herbs for bone, joint, and skin diseases.

Housework

Light housework only.

Air rooms only briefly.

Preserving root vegetables.

Avoid dry cleaning, as the fabric may develop unwanted glossy blotches.

Nutrition

Food quality:

Salt

Garlic, carrots, red beets, reddish, rutabaga, sugar beet, celery, potatoes, onions, kohlrabi.

Weight gain: avoid indulging in rich foods. If overweight, eat smaller portions.

Supply nutrient materials to strengthen the body. Focus on foods that contain essential minerals and vitamins.

Stimulants and vitamins are more effective.

Avoid large quantities of salty foods like bacon, ham, salted herring, fatty cheese, and the like. Avoid heavy and greasy foods.

Positive affirmation:
"I forgive others and myself."

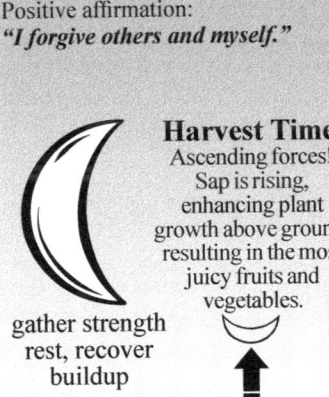

Harvest Time
Ascending forces! Sap is rising, enhancing plant growth above ground, resulting in the most juicy fruits and vegetables.

gather strength
rest, recover
buildup
Waxing Moon

13 Friday

No meat. Cutting and filing toenails and fingernails.

14 Saturday

N O V E M B E R

The trouble is you can shut your eyes but you can't shut your mind.
Terry Pratchett

Color

Yellow

Day

Cool

Element

Earth

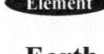

Capricorn

Success

Inspiration, optimism, and impatience. Rational thinking, creativity and imagination spark new ideas and inspire planning for the future.

Shying away from routine tasks people will feel more drawn to anything new.

Instead of gridlocked structures choose new possibilities.

Leisure

Inspiration and optimism will boost friendship, social gatherings, and parties.

Express your creativity and imagination. Dwell in dreams and utopian ideas. It is easier now to perceive intuitive thoughts.

Health

Sensitive body parts:
Lower Legs, Veins

All measures taken to supply nutrient materials and strengthen the sensitive body parts are very effective.

Healing ointments are easily absorbed.

Sensitive glandular system.

Avoid inflammation of the veins. Apply ointments to lower legs, and rest legs in a raised position.

Varicose veins: Avoid long periods of standing.

While exercising go easy on the ankles.

Sensitivity to light, so bring your sunglasses along.

Body Care

Aromas, scents: Cyclamen, Peach, Wild Roses

Treatments with firming and moisturizing creams are more effective.

Massages that serve to regenerate, and strengthen, perhaps aided with beneficial massage oils.

Correcting and cutting ingrown nails.

Hair dyes applied now, will look more vibrant.

Garden/Nature

Plant part:
Flower

Avoid watering plants.

Harvested produce is well suitable for storage.

Gather herbs for vein diseases.

Housework

Light housework only.

Ventilate rooms thoroughly.

Baking cakes and cookies. Dough rises faster. (Except on New Moon)

Making preserves.

Nutrition

Food quality:
Fat

Cauliflower, artichoke, broccoli, sunflower seeds, flax seeds, nuts, rose hip, elder.

Weight gain: avoid indulging in rich foods. If overweight, eat smaller portions.

Supply nutrient materials to strengthen the body. Focus on foods that contain essential minerals and vitamins.

Stimulants and vitamins are more effective.

Pay attention to any particularly tempting foods today: Most likely the "wrong" things taste best.

High cholesterol: eat a low fat diet.

Positive affirmation:
"I forgive others and myself."

Harvest Time
Ascending forces! Sap is rising, enhancing plant growth above ground, resulting in the most juicy fruits and vegetables.

gather strength rest, recover buildup
Waxing Moon

1:25 AM PST
3:25 AM CST
4:25 AM EST

15 Sunday

16 Monday

1:21 PM PST
3:21 PM CST
4:31 PM EST

17 Tuesday

☾ Half Moon.

Don't waste your time with explanations: people only hear what they want to hear.
Paulo Coelho

Color
Bright/ Dark Blue

Day
Air/Light

Element
Air   **Aquarius**

NOVEMBER

Success

Sensibility, intuition, and helpfulness.

Where possible, retreating is more favorable than dealing with business matters.

Dissolve restrictions, be patient and wait. Be aware that people can be more easily influenced.

Leisure

Your helpfulness will boost friendships.

Enjoy dancing or swimming, or watch a movie that will inspire your fantasies and imagination.

Retreat, relax, and recover.

Romance can be gentle and coziness will prevail.

If you plan outdoor excursions, be prepared for a shower here and there.

Health

Sensitive body parts:

Feet and Toes

All measures taken to supply nutrient materials and strengthen the sensitive body parts are very effective.

Healing ointments are easily absorbed.

Sensitive nervous system.

Drugs have a much stronger effect on your body. Monitor closely what you put into your body.

Lymphatic therapy.

Sluggishness or fatigue may occur in the transition into the next Zodiac sign of Aries.

Body Care

Aromas, scents: Magnolia, Amaryllis, Clary Sage

Treatments with firming and moisturizing creams are more effective.

Massages that serve to regenerate, and strengthen, perhaps aided with beneficial massage oils. Reflexology massage. Carry out with special care, people are more sensitive.

Correcting and cutting ingrown nails.

Foot bath.

No haircuts, hair becomes shaggy and unmanageable. Avoid washing your hair. Dandruff could develop.

Garden/Nature

Plant part:

Leaf

Watering all indoor and outdoor plants.

Sow plants, herbs, and vegetables that grow and flourish above ground, and leaf vegetables.

Transplanting.

Mowing lawns.

Avoid pruning fruit trees and bushes.

Harvested produce should be consumed as soon as possible.

Gather herbs for foot complaints.

Housework

Light housework only.

Ventilate rooms briefly and rapidly. Don't air mattresses.

Any dirt and spots are easily removed in the laundry.

Avoid painting, as paint will take very long to dry.

Preserving and storing should be avoided.

Nutrition

Food quality:

Carbohydrate

Lettuce, spinach, lamb's lettuce, Endive, parsley, leek, cabbage (Brussels sprouts, kale, Chinese cabbage), all leafy herbs, asparagus, mushrooms, cress, Swiss chard, rhubarb.

Weight gain: avoid indulging in rich foods. If overweight, eat smaller portions and avoid carbohydrates.

Supply nutrient materials to strengthen the body. Focus on foods that contain essential minerals and vitamins.

Caffeine, alcohol, drugs, certain foods, and stimulants have a much stronger effect.

Positive affirmation:
"I forgive others and myself."

Harvest Time
Ascending forces! Sap is rising, enhancing plant growth above ground, resulting in the most juicy fruits and vegetables.

gather strength rest, recover buildup
Waxing Moon

9:53 PM PST
11:53 PM CST
Friday 12:53 AM EST
)(→ Y

18 Wednesday
No meat.

19 Thursday

It is therefore senseless to think of complaining since nothing foreign has decided what we feel, what we live, or what we are.
Jean-Paul Sartre

 Color
Blueish White

 Day
Wetness

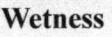 Element
Water

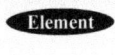

Pisces

N O V E M B E R

Success

Things get going and the way straight ahead seems the best.

People feel energetic, courageous, assertive, and at times anxious.

Good time for meetings and sales talks but impatience and selfishness do not favor teamwork.

Leisure

An enterprising spirit and spontaneity move people to enjoy outings, sports, competitions, cultural events, and travels.

Romance can be very passionate.

Good days for outings, even with cloudy skies the air still feels somewhat warm. Drying effect, get plenty to drink.

Health

Sensitive body parts:

Head, Brain, Eyes

All measures taken to supply nutrient materials and strengthen the sensitive body parts are very effective.

Healing ointments are easily absorbed.

Sensitive sense organs.

If you suffer from migraines drink plenty of water, and avoid coffee, chocolate, and sugar.

Body Care

Aromas, scents: Cloves, Peppermint, Thyme

Treatments with firming and moisturizing creams are more effective.

Massages that serve to regenerate, and strengthen, perhaps aided with beneficial massage oils.

Correcting and cutting ingrown nails.

Eye compresses for strained eyes.

Any kind of hair care. Hair dyes applied now, will look more vibrant.

Garden/Nature

Plant part:

Fruit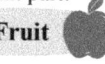

Sow plants and vegetables that grow and flourish above ground, especially fruit and tomatoes.

Sowing and planting anything that is supposed to grow fast and for immediate use.

Grafting onto fruit trees.

Cultivating grains.

Transplanting.

Harvesting and storing grains, vegetables, potatoes, fruit, and tomatoes.

Gather herbs for eye complaints and headaches.

Day off on 11/20.

Housework

Light housework only.

Ventilate sufficiently.

Preserving fruit.

Freezing fruit and vegetables.

Baking bread, cakes, and cookies. Dough rises faster. (Except on New Moon)

Suitable for making cheese.

Nutrition

Food quality:

Protein

Beans, peas, corn, tomatoes, pumpkin, lentils, soybeans, cucumber, eggplant, zucchini, berries, fruit, chili, bell pepper, figs, avocado, melon, olives.

Weight gain: avoid indulging in rich foods. If overweight, eat smaller portions.

Supply nutrient materials to strengthen the body. Focus on foods that contain essential minerals and vitamins.

Stimulants and vitamins are more effective.

Drink plenty of water.

Positive affirmation:
"I forgive others and myself."

Harvest Time
Ascending forces! Sap is rising, enhancing plant growth above ground, resulting in the most juicy fruits and vegetables.

gather strength rest, recover buildup

Waxing Moon

20 Friday

No meat. Cutting and filing toenails and fingernails.

21 Saturday

It's so hard to forget pain, but it's even harder to remember sweetness. We have no scar to show for happiness. We learn so little from peace.
Chuck Palahniuk

Color
Indigo Blue

Day
Warm

Element
Fire

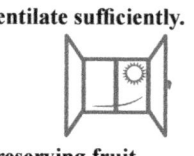

Aries

NOVEMBER

Success

Realism and material security are important. Persistence comes easy, thoughts and reactions are slower.

Assess financial areas.

Conservative tendencies may make people want to stay away from risk taking.

Leisure

Relax at a picnic/feast. Enjoy culinary pleasures and hobbies.

The earth feels cold to the touch, so take slightly warmer clothes.

Health

Sensitive body parts:

Head and Neck

All measures taken to supply nutrient materials and strengthen the sensitive body parts are very effective.

Healing ointments are easily absorbed.

Sensitive blood circulation.

Organs of speech, jaws, teeth, tonsils, thyroid gland, neck, and vocal chords get easily affected. Keep neck warm. On cold days ears should be protected. Sensitivity to noise.

High blood pressure: Avoid salty foods.

Massages, lymphatic therapy, and chiropractic treatment to release blockages.

Body Care

Aromas, scents: Geranium, Jasmine, Rose

Treatments with firming and moisturizing creams are more effective.

Massages that serve to regenerate, and strengthen, perhaps aided with beneficial massage oils.

Correcting and cutting ingrown nails.

Hair dyes applied now, will look more vibrant.

Garden/Nature

Plant part:

Root

Sow plants, herbs, and vegetables that grow and flourish above ground.

Sowing and planting trees, bushes, hedges, and root vegetables. Everything grows slowly and lasts well.

Transplanting.

Harvesting and storing root vegetables. Harvested produce is well suited for storage.

Gather herbs for sinus issues, sore throat, and ear complaints.

Housework

Light housework only.

Air rooms only briefly.

Preserving root vegetables.

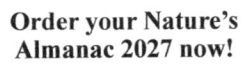

Nutrition

Food quality:

Salt

Garlic, carrots, red beets, reddish, rutabaga, sugar beet, celery, potatoes, onions, kohlrabi.

Weight gain: avoid indulging in rich foods. If overweight, eat smaller portions.

Supply nutrient materials to strengthen the body. Focus on foods that contain essential minerals and vitamins.

Stimulants and vitamins are more effective.

Avoid large quantities of salty foods like bacon, ham, salted herring, fatty cheese, and the like.

Positive affirmation:
"I forgive others and myself."

Harvest Time
Ascending forces! Sap is rising, enhancing plant growth above ground, resulting in the most juicy fruits and vegetables.

gather strength rest, recover buildup

Waxing Moon

♈ → ♉   2:11 AM PST
4:11 AM CST
5:11 AM EST

22 Sunday

23 Monday

N O V E M B E R

Piglet noticed that even though he had a very small heart, it could hold a rather large amount of Gratitude.
Alan Alexander Milne

 Color

Bright Blue

 Day

Cool

 Element

Earth   **Taurus**

Success

Open mindedness and curiosity. A changeable and hectic time.

Good time for talking, negotiating, networking, and exchanging ideas as well as for meetings of a nonbinding nature, conferences, and studies.

Leisure

Good time for family gatherings, parties, and short trips.

People enjoy stimulating their minds with reading and studying. Attending theater performances is a preferred enjoyment. Enhance friendships.

Stretching exercises.

Be prepared for sudden changes in weather or climate.

Health

Sensitive body parts:
Shoulders, Arms, Hands, Lungs

All measures taken to flush out and detoxify the sensitive body parts are very effective.
Scarring is less severe.
Teeth: Removal of tartar and amalgam. Best for fillings, crowns, and dentures! Avoid having any teeth pulled.
Blood-purifying, detoxifying herbal infusions and teas.
Sensitive glandular system.
Make sure you are dressed warm enough in cool weather.
Exercises for shoulders. Breathing exercises.
Sensitivity to light, bring your sunglasses along.
Massages, lymphatic therapy, and chiropractic treatment to release blockages.
○ **_Full Moon:_** _Avoid any surgery and vaccination if possible._

Body Care

Aromas, scents:
Lavender, Lemon Balm, Magnolia, Verbena

Prepare home-made ointments and cosmetics.

Apply detoxing facial and body care.

Treatments of bumps and pimples on the skin, and exfoliating procedures.

Removing body hair.

Correction of the nail bed.

Massages that serve to relax, ease tension, and detoxify.

Reflexology massage.

Removal of callused skin.

Treating obstinate athlete's foot, nail fungus, and warts.

Garden/Nature

Plant part:
Flower

Sow plants and vegetables that grow below ground.

Trimming and cutting back plants.

Start a compost heap.

Weeding. Pest control.

Fertilize flowers that no longer bloom.

Avoid watering plants.

Changes in weather are more likely.

Gather herbs (roots) for tensions in the shoulder and lung complaints.

○ **_Full Moon:_** _Weather and climate changes. Herbs are most powerful._

Housework

Housework is dealt with much more successfully, efficiently, and effortlessly.

Problem stains are removed readily.

Dry cleaning.

Clean and store seasonal clothing.

Thoroughly clean wooden and parquet floors, metals, china etc.

Cleaning, polishing, and waterproofing shoes.

Combating mold.

Ventilate rooms thoroughly.

Baking bread, cakes, and cookies (add more leavening agent).

○ **_Full Moon:_** _Avoid doing laundry, cleaning windows, making preserves, painting._

Nutrition

Food quality:
Fat

Cauliflower, artichoke, broccoli, sunflower seeds, flax seeds, nuts, rose hip, elder.

Weight associated with overeating is less likely. If underweight, eat larger portions.

Cleansing and detox diets. Fruit and juice days.

Flush out poisons. Treatment for drug abuse.

Pay attention to any particularly tempting foods today: Most likely the "wrong" things taste best.

High cholesterol: eat a low fat diet.

○ **_Full Moon:_** _A day of fasting._

If you're reading this... Congratulations, you're alive. If that's not something to smile about, then I don't know what is.
Chad Sugg

Color
Light Blue

Day
Air/Light

Element

Gemini   **Air**

○ **Turning Point**
Transition of ascending to descending forces. Both forces are at work and neutralize each other.

Positive affirmation:
"I forgive others and myself."

detox
remove
be active
Waning Moon

☿ → ♊ ← 3:11 AM PST
5:11 AM CST
6:11 AM EST

24 Tuesday
○ **Full Moon** 6:55 AM PST, 8:55 AM CST, 9:55 AM EST

25 Wednesday
No meat.

N O V E M B E R

Success

Feelings, sensitivity, and cooperativeness. Many are overly sensitive, so beware of treading on someone's toes.

Be cautious if you are easily influenced.

During negotiations make use of the cognitive ability of your senses.

Leisure

Relax within your close family.

Retreat to your safe haven and enjoy your fantasy while reading or listening to music. The inner world becomes more colorful than the outer.

Romance can be gentle. Deep feelings will prevail.

If you plan outdoor excursions, be prepared for a shower here and there.

Health

Sensitive body parts:
Chest, Lungs, Liver, Stomach, Gall Bladder

All measures taken to flush out and detoxify the sensitive body parts are very effective.

Good for surgical operations except those on the sensitive body parts (see above), thighs, and veins.
Scarring is less severe.

Teeth: Removal of tartar and amalgam. Best for fillings, crowns, and dentures!

Blood-purifying, detoxifying herbal infusions and teas.

Sensitive nervous system.

Be cautious with alcohol since the liver is very sensitive.

Stomach could play up and cause gas and heartburn.

Rheumatism: Don't air bedding outside, damp will remain in the bedding.

Lymphatic therapy.

Body Care

Aromas, scents:
Lilac, Lilies of the Valley, Lilies, Violets

Prepare home-made ointments and cosmetics.

Apply detoxing facial and body care.

Treatments of bumps and pimples on the skin, and exfoliating procedures.

Removing body hair.

Correction of the nail bed.

Massages that serve to relax, ease tension, and detoxify.

Reflexology massage.

Removal of callused skin.

Treating obstinate athlete's foot, nail fungus, and warts.

No haircuts, hair becomes shaggy and unmanageable.
Avoid washing your hair.

Garden/Nature

Plant part:
Leaf

Water plants.

Fertilize flowers.

Sow plants and vegetables that grow below ground, leaf vegetables, and lettuce.

Dig over/plow to prepare soil for planting.

Trimming and cutting back plants. Transplanting. Weeding.

Combating pests above ground.

Start a compost heap.

Mowing lawns.

Gather herbs (roots) for bronchitis, stomach, liver, and gall bladder complaints.

Unfavorable for harvesting, storing, and preserving.

Housework

Housework is dealt with much more successfully, efficiently, and effortlessly.

Problem stains are removed readily.

Best for doing laundry! Reduce on laundry detergent, support the environment.

Dry cleaning.

Thoroughly clean wooden and parquet floors, metals, china etc.

Cleaning, polishing, and waterproofing shoes.

Combating mold.

Ventilate rooms briefly and rapidly.

Avoid painting.

Nutrition

Food quality:
Carbohydrate

Lettuce, spinach, lamb's lettuce, Endive, parsley, leek, cabbage (Brussels sprouts, kale, Chinese cabbage), all leafy herbs, asparagus, mushrooms, cress, Swiss chard, rhubarb.

Weight associated with overeating is less likely. If underweight, eat larger portions.

Moodiness may make you want to eat more than is healthy. If overweight avoid carbohydrates.

Cleansing and detox diets. Fruit and juice days.

Flush out poisons. Treatment for drug abuse.

If you get stomach troubles easily, avoid heavy meals.

Cancer

- Color
Green
- Day
Wetness
- Element

Water

2:52 AM PST
4:52 AM CST
5:52 AM EST

26 Thursday
Thanksgiving (US)

27 Friday
No meat. Cutting and filing toenails and fingernails.

Positive affirmation:
"I forgive others and myself."

Planting Time
Descending forces! Sap is drawn downward, enhancing root formation. Best days for sowing, planting, and transplanting.

detox
remove
be active
Waning Moon

N O V E M B E R

Success

Determination reigns, and risks are taken more often. Master your tasks with more self-confidence and creativity.

Limits appear to be more easily surmountable.

Auspicious day for sales, advertising, and publicity.

Leisure

Zest for life is in the air. People want to have a fun time, enjoy parties, musical events, movies, etc.

Possessive feelings can harm a relationship. Romance can be very passionate.

Outings: even with cloudy skies the air still feels somewhat warm. Drying effect, get plenty to drink.

Danger of sudden storms, not only in the sky.

Health

Sensitive body parts:
Heart, Back, Diaphragm, Circulation, Arteries

All measures taken to flush out and detoxify the sensitive body parts are very effective.

Good for surgery, except on the sensitive body parts (see above), thighs, and veins.

Scarring is less severe.

Teeth: Removal of tartar and amalgam. Best for fillings, crowns, and dentures!

Blood-purifying, detoxifying herbal infusions and teas.

Sensitive sense organs.

Back and heart problems are more likely to occur.

Avoid overstraining of the heart and circulation with unusual physical activities.

Expect sleepless nights.

Body Care

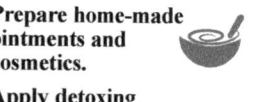

Aromas, scents:
Hibiscus, Oleander, Rose

Prepare home-made ointments and cosmetics.

Apply detoxing facial and body care.

Treatments of bumps and pimples on the skin, and exfoliating procedures.

Removing body hair.

Correction of the nail bed.

Massages that serve to relax, ease tension, and detoxify.

Reflexology massage.

Removal of callused skin.

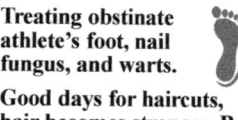

Treating obstinate athlete's foot, nail fungus, and warts.

Good days for haircuts, hair becomes stronger. But be aware that if you get a perm, curls will become quite frizzy. Baby's first haircut.

Garden/Nature

Plant part:
Fruit

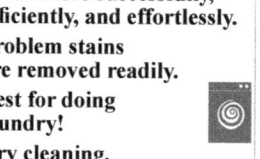

Sowing plants and vegetables that grow below ground.

Sowing and planting fruit. Also sow and plant vegetables that are highly perishable. Plant trees and bushes. Sow lawns.

Dig over/plow to prepare soil for planting.

Trimming and cutting back plants. Pruning of fruit trees and bushes.

Transplanting.

Not suitable for fertilizing.

Weeding. Pest Control.

Harvested produce should be consumed as soon as possible.

Gather herbs (roots) for heart and circulation complaints.

Start compost heap.

Housework

Housework is dealt with much more successfully, efficiently, and effortlessly.

Problem stains are removed readily.

Best for doing laundry!

Dry cleaning.

Thoroughly clean wooden and parquet floors, metals, china, etc.

Cleaning windows and glass.

Cleaning, polishing, and waterproofing shoes.

Combating mold.

Ventilate rooms sufficiently. Air beds.

Suitable for making cheese.

Preserving and freezing fruit and vegetables.

Baking bread, cakes, and cookies (use more leavening agent).

Avoid painting.

Nutrition

Food quality:
Protein

Beans, peas, corn, tomatoes, pumpkin, lentils, soybeans, cucumber, eggplant, zucchini, berries, fruit, chili, bell pepper, figs, avocado, melon, olives.

Weight associated with overeating is less likely. If underweight, eat larger portions.

Cleansing and detox diets. Fruit and juice days.

Flush out poisons. Treatment for drug abuse.

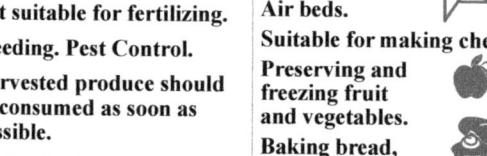

You yourself, as much as anybody in the entire universe, deserve your love and affection.
Gautama Buddha

Color: **Green**
Day: **Warm**
Element: **Fire**

Leo

♋→♌ 3:22 AM PST
5:22 AM CST
6:22 AM EST

28 Saturday

29 Sunday
1. Advent

Positive affirmation:
"I forgive others and myself."

Planting Time
Descending forces! Sap is drawn downward, enhancing root formation. Best days for sowing, planting, and transplanting.

detox
remove
be active
Waning Moon

N O V E M B E R

Success

Good time for details, organization, routine, concentration, and duty.

Take care of financial and administrative tasks.

Prepare for future success now with realistic and critical assessment.

Leisure

Enjoy a nature walk.

Good time for health regimes. Improve your health with stretching exercises and yoga.

The earth feels cold to the touch, so take slightly warmer clothes.

Health

Sensitive body parts:
Digestive Organs, Nerves, Spleen, Pancreas

All measures taken to flush out and detoxify the sensitive body parts are very effective.

Good for surgery, except on the sensitive body parts (see above), thighs, and veins. Scarring is less severe.

Teeth: Removal of tartar and amalgam. Best for fillings, crowns, and dentures! Avoiding treatment of periodontitis and gums.

Blood-purifying, detoxifying herbal infusions and teas.

Sensitive blood circulation.

For a sensitive digestive system, a wholesome diet is recommended.

Dress slightly warmer.

High blood pressure: Avoid salty foods.

Massages, lymphatic therapy, and chiropractic treatment to release blockages.

Body Care

Aromas, scents:
Lavender, Spruce Needles, Sage, Meadow Flowers

Prepare home-made ointments and cosmetics.

Apply detoxing facial and body care.

Treatments of bumps and pimples on the skin, and exfoliating procedures.

Removing body hair.

Correction of the nail bed.

Massages that serve to relax, ease tension, and detoxify.

Reflexology massage.

Removal of callused skin.

Treating obstinate athlete's foot, nail fungus, and warts.

Best for haircuts because it retains its shape longer. Perms turn out best.

Garden/Nature

Plant part:
Root

Best for sowing and planting, except lettuce.

Plant trees which are supposed to grow very tall. Plant hedges and bushes that are meant to grow very fast.

Planting and re-potting balcony and indoor plants.

Dig over/plow to prepare soil for planting.

Trimming and cutting back plants. Planting cuttings.

Spread fertilizer and manure. Fertilize flowers with poorly formed roots.

Start a compost heap.

Transplanting. Mulching.

Weeding. Pest control (vermin in the soil).

Avoid harvesting and storing.

Gather herbs (roots) for digestive organs, pancreas, and nervous complaints.

Housework

Housework is dealt with much more successfully, efficiently, and effortlessly.
Problem stains are removed readily.

Best for doing laundry! Reduce on laundry detergent, support the environment.

Dry cleaning.

Thoroughly clean wooden and parquet floors, metals, china etc.

Cleaning, polishing, and waterproofing shoes.

Combating mold.

Air rooms only briefly.

Painting.

Making pickles, preserves, and cheese yields suboptimal results and should be avoided.

Nutrition

Food quality:
Salt

Garlic, carrots, red beets, reddish, rutabaga, sugar beet, celery, potatoes, onions, kohlrabi.

Weight associated with overeating is less likely. If underweight, eat larger portions.

Cleansing and detox diets. Fruit and juice days.

Flush out poisons. Treatment for drug abuse.

Avoid large quantities of salty foods like bacon, ham, salted herring, fatty cheese, and the like. Avoid heavy and greasy foods.

I am ignorant of absolute truth. But I am humble before my ignorance and therein lies my honor and my reward.
Kahlil Gibran

Color
Yellow

Day
Cool

Element
Earth

♍ **Virgo**

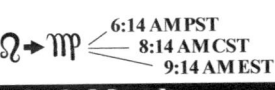

♌→♍ 6:14 AM PST / 8:14 AM CST / 9:14 AM EST

12:05 PM PST / 2:05 PM CST / 3:05 PM EST ♍→♎

30 Monday

1 Tuesday
☽ Half Moon.

2 Wednesday
No meat.

NOVEMBER/DECEMBER

Positive affirmation:
"I forgive others and myself."

Planting Time
Descending forces! Sap is drawn downward, enhancing root formation. Best days for sowing, planting, and transplanting.

detox
remove
be active

Waning Moon

Success

The artistic instinct rules, but so, too, does indecisiveness. The forces swing back and forth until equilibrium is achieved.

It's easy to reach compromises with tactful sensitivity.

A sense of judgment will support legal matters.

Leisure

Pursuit for harmony and cooperativeness supports good times in romance, friendship, and partnership.

Enjoy cultural events. Relax and get pampered with a spa treatment.

Romance can be passionate yet sensitive.

Health

Sensitive body parts:

Hips, Kidneys, Bladder

All measures taken to flush out and detoxify the sensitive body parts are very effective.

Good for surgery, except on the sensitive body parts (see above), thighs, and veins. Scarring is less severe.

Teeth: Removal of tartar and amalgam. Best for fillings, crowns, and dentures! Avoid treatment of periodontitis and gums, avoid pulling teeth.

Blood-purifying, detoxifying herbal infusions and teas.

Sensitive glandular system.

Take special care to keep the area of the bladder and kidneys warm.

Apply special exercises for the hip region.

Sensitivity to light, so bring your sunglasses along.

Body Care

Aromas, scents: Roses, Violets, Daffodils

Prepare home-made ointments and cosmetics.

Apply detoxing facial and body care.

Treatments of bumps and pimples on the skin, and exfoliating procedures.

Removing body hair.

Correction of the nail bed.

Massages that serve to relax, ease tension, and detoxify.

Reflexology massage.

Removal of callused skin.

Treating obstinate athlete's foot, nail fungus, and warts.

Garden/Nature

Plant part:

Flower

Sow plants and vegetables that grow below ground.

Dig over/plow to prepare soil for planting.

Trimming and cutting back plants.

Start a compost heap.

Weeding. Pest control.

Fertilize flowers that no longer bloom.

Transplanting.

Avoid watering plants.

Harvested produce should be consumed as soon as possible.

Gather herbs (roots) for kidneys, gall bladder and hip complaints.

Day off on 12/3.

Housework

Housework is dealt with much more successfully, efficiently, and effortlessly.

Problem stains are removed readily.

Best for doing laundry! Reduce on laundry detergent, support the environment.

Dry cleaning.

Clean and store seasonal clothing.

Thoroughly clean wooden and parquet floors, metals, china etc.

Cleaning windows and glass.

Cleaning, polishing, and waterproofing shoes.

Combating mold.

Ventilate rooms thoroughly.

Baking bread, cakes, and cookies (add more leavening agent).

Making preserves.

Painting.

Nutrition

Food quality:

Fat

Cauliflower, artichoke, broccoli, sunflower seeds, flax seeds, nuts, rose hip, elder.

Weight associated with overeating is less likely. If underweight, eat larger portions.

Cleansing and detox diets. Fruit and juice days.

Flush out poisons. Treatment for drug abuse.

Pay attention to any particularly tempting foods today: Most likely the "wrong" things taste best.

High cholesterol: eat a low fat diet.

As if you could kill time without induring eternity.
Henry David Thoreau

Color
Orange

Day
Air/Light

Element

Libra   **Air**

8:36 PM PST
10:36 PM CST
11:36 PM EST

$\Omega \rightarrow m$

3 Thursday

4 Friday

No meat. Cutting and filing toenails and fingernails.

Positive affirmation:
"I forgive others and myself."

Planting Time
Descending forces! Sap is drawn downward, enhancing root formation. Best days for sowing, planting, and transplanting.

detox
remove
be active

Waning Moon

D E C E M B E R

Success

Critical and superstitious behavior emerges, especially pertaining to money.

A penetrating power will strengthen your capacity to act.

An increased perception opens our interest for the essentials and helps to discover hidden potentials.

Leisure

Relax within your close family, with meditation, and relaxation exercises.

A longing to feel safe will be nurtured if you focus on habits and rituals. An increased sensitivity will help to enjoy every moment.

Romance can be very passionate.

If you plan outdoor excursions, be prepared for a shower here and there.

Health

Sensitive body parts:

Sex organs, Ureter

All measures taken to flush out and detoxify the sensitive body parts are very effective.

Good for surgical operations except those on the sensitive body parts (see above), thighs, and veins. Scarring is less severe.

Teeth: Removal of tartar and amalgam. Best for fillings, crowns, and dentures!

Blood-purifying, detoxifying herbal infusions and teas.

Sensitive nervous system.

Female disorders: As a preventative measure apply hip baths using yarrow.

Pregnancy: Avoid any exertion, miscarriages are more likely.

Keep region of the pelvis, kidneys, and feet warm to prevent infection of the bladder and kidneys.

Lymphatic therapy.

Body Care

Aromas, scents:
Anemone, Cornflower
Oregano, Thuja

Prepare home-made ointments and cosmetics.

Apply detoxing facial and body care.

Treatments of bumps and pimples on the skin, and exfoliating procedures.

Removing body hair.

Correction of the nail bed.

Massages that serve to relax, ease tension, and detoxify.

Reflexology massage.

Removal of callused skin.

Treating obstinate athlete's foot, nail fungus, and warts.

Garden/Nature

Plant part:

Leaf

Water plants.

Fertilize flowers and meadows, no vegetables.

Sow plants and vegetables that grow below ground, leaf vegetables, and lettuce.

Sowing, planting, harvesting, and drying every kind of medicinal herbs.

Dig over/plow to prepare soil for planting.

Trimming and cutting back plants. Transplanting. Weeding. Pest control. Start a compost heap.

Mowing lawns.

Harvested produce should be consumed as soon as possible.

Avoid cutting down trees, danger of bark beetles.

Housework

Housework is dealt with much more successfully, efficiently, and effortlessly.

Problem stains are removed readily.

Best for doing laundry! Reduce on laundry detergent, support the environment.

Dry cleaning.

Thoroughly clean wooden and parquet floors, metals, china etc.

Cleaning, polishing, and waterproofing shoes.

Combating mold.

Ventilate rooms briefly and rapidly.

Avoid painting.

Nutrition

Food quality:

Carbohydrate

Lettuce, spinach, lamb's lettuce, Endive, parsley, leek, cabbage (Brussels sprouts, kale, Chinese cabbage), all leafy herbs, asparagus, mushrooms, cress, Swiss chard, rhubarb.

Weight associated with overeating is less likely. If underweight, eat larger portions.

Cleansing and detox diets. Fruit and juice days.

Flush out poisons. Treatment for drug abuse.

Expectations make people miserable, so whatever yours are, lower them. You'll definitely be happier.
Simone Elkeles

Scorpio

Color: **Red**

Day: **Wetness**

Element: **Water**

5 Saturday
Hannukah Starts

6 Sunday
2. Advent, St. Nicholas

Planting Time
Descending forces! Sap is drawn downward, enhancing root formation. Best days for sowing, planting, and transplanting.

detox
remove
be active

Waning Moon

DECEMBER

Success

Inquisitiveness and exuberant inspiration lead to new horizons. Insight and love for truth reign.

Bringing together is more important than splitting asunder.

Expansive forces will assist in legal matters, discussions, and debates.

● *New Moon: Confirm your resolutions. Finalize new decisions. Drop bad habits.*

Leisure

Expansion feels great, and travel, short trips, and outings are most welcome. A competitive spirit excites any sports event.

Talk things out when necessary.

Romance can be very passionate.

Good days for outings; even with cloudy skies the air still feels somewhat warm. Drying effect, get plenty to drink.

Health

Sensitive body parts:

Thighs and Veins

All measures taken to flush out and detoxify the sensitive body parts are very effective.

Scarring is less severe.

Teeth: Removal of tartar and amalgam. Best for fillings, crowns, and dentures!

Blood-purifying, detoxifying herbal infusions and tea.

Sensitive sense organs.

Pains often arise in the sciatic nerve, veins, the small of the back, and thighs.

Avoid overstraining the body with unusual physical activities.

● *New Moon: Avoid any surgery if possible.*

Body Care

Aromas, scents: Calendula (Marigold), Geranium, Rosemary

Prepare home-made ointments and cosmetics.

Apply detoxing facial and body care.

Treatments of bumps and pimples on the skin, and exfoliating procedures.

Removing body hair.

Correction of the nail bed.

Massages that serve to relax, ease tension, and detoxify.

Reflexology massage.

Removal of callused skin.

Treating obstinate athlete's foot, nail fungus, and warts.

Garden/Nature

Plant part:

Fruit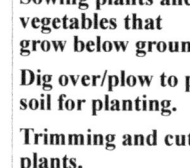

Sowing plants and vegetables that grow below ground.

Dig over/plow to prepare soil for planting.

Trimming and cutting back plants.
Pruning of fruit trees and bushes.

Cultivating grains, particularly corn.

Fertilize grains, vegetables, and fruit.

Combating pests above ground.
Weeding.

Gather herbs (roots) for vein diseases.

Avoid hoeing and harrowing.

Start a compost heap.

● *New Moon: Change of weather is likely. Care for sickly plants.*

Housework

Housework is dealt with much more successfully, efficiently, and effortlessly.

Problem stains are removed readily.

Best for doing laundry!

Dry cleaning.

Thoroughly clean wooden and parquet floors, metals, china, etc.

Cleaning windows and glass.

Cleaning, polishing, and waterproofing shoes.

Combating mold.

Ventilate rooms sufficiently.
Air beds.

Suitable for making cheese.

Preserving and freezing fruit and vegetables.

Baking bread, cakes, and cookies (use more leavening agent).

Painting.

Nutrition

Food quality:

Protein

Beans, peas, corn, tomatoes, pumpkin, lentils, soybeans, cucumber, eggplant, zucchini, berries, fruit, chili, bell pepper, figs, avocado, melon, olives.

Weight associated with overeating is less likely. If underweight, eat larger portions.

Cleansing and detox diets. Fruit and juice days.

Flush out poisons. Treatment for drug abuse.

● *New Moon: A day of fasting.*

The act of taking the first step is what separates the winners from the losers.
Brian Tracy

Sagittarius

Color
Orange/Yellow

Day
Warm

Element
Fire

♏ → ♐ 7:08 AM PST
9:08 AM CST
10:08 AM EST

7 Monday Pearl Harbor Remembrance Day (US)

8 Tuesday Feast of Immaculate Conception
● New Moon 4:53 PM PST, 6:53 PM CST, 7:53 AM EST

Positive affirmation:
"I forgive others and myself."

Turning Point
Transition of descending to ascending forces. Both forces are at work and neutralize each other.

detox
remove
be active
Waning Moon

D E C E M B E R

Success

Inquisitiveness and exuberant inspiration lead to new horizons. Insight and love for truth reign.

Bringing together is more important than splitting asunder.

Expansive forces will assist in legal matters, discussions, and debates.

Leisure

Expansion feels great, and travel, short trips, and outings are most welcome. A competitive spirit excites any sports event.

Talk things out when necessary.

Romance can be very passionate.

Good days for outings; even with cloudy skies the air still feels somewhat warm. Drying effect, get plenty to drink.

Health

Sensitive body parts:

Thighs and Veins

All measures taken to supply nutrient materials and strengthen the sensitive body parts are very effective.

Healing ointments are easily absorbed.

Sensitive sense organs.

Pains often arise in the sciatic nerve, veins, the small of the back, and thighs.

Avoid overstraining the body with unusual physical activities.

Body Care

Aromas, scents: Calendula (Marigold), Geranium, Rosemary

Treatments with firming and moisturizing creams are more effective.

Massages that serve to regenerate, and strengthen, perhaps aided with beneficial massage oils.

Correcting and cutting ingrown nails.

Hair dyes applied now, will look more vibrant.

Garden/Nature

Plant part:

Fruit

Sow plants and vegetables that grow and flourish above ground.

Sowing and planting fruit and vegetables that grow tall, and tomatoes, but no lettuce.

Transplanting.

Grafting onto fruit trees.

Cultivating grains, particularly corn.

Gather herbs for vein diseases.

Housework

Light housework only.

Ventilate sufficiently.

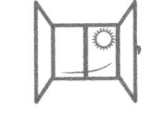

Freezing fruit and vegetables.

Baking bread, cakes, and cookies. Dough rises faster. (Except on New Moon)

Suitable for making cheese.

Making preserves.

Nutrition

Food quality:

Protein

Beans, peas, corn, tomatoes, pumpkin, lentils, soybeans, cucumber, eggplant, zucchini, berries, fruit, chili, bell pepper, figs, avocado, melon, olives.

Weight gain: avoid indulging in rich foods. If overweight, eat smaller portions.

Supply nutrient materials to strengthen the body. Focus on foods that contain essential minerals and vitamins.

Stimulants and vitamins are more effective.

Positive affirmation:
"Gratitude is my guide."

Turning Point

Transition of descending to ascending forces. Both forces are at work and neutralize each other.

gather strength
rest, recover
buildup
Waxing Moon

7:10 PM PST
9:10 PM CST
10:10 PM EST

9 Wednesday

No meat.

D E C E M B E R

When you come to the edge of all that you know, you must believe one of two things: either there will be ground to stand on, or you will be given wings to fly.
O.R. Melling

Color
Orange/ Yellow

Day
Warm

Element

Fire   **Sagittarius**

Success

Career and business are in the foreground now and thinking becomes clear and serious, but somewhat inflexible.

Perseverance and reasoning assist in financial matters, planning, and contracts.

The values of tradition, authority, and discipline impact our endeavors.

Leisure

Money is not likely to be wasted in a shopping spree.

Many are drawn to enjoy cultural events.

The earth feels cold to the touch, so take slightly warmer clothes.

Health

Sensitive body parts:

Knees, Joints, Bones, Skin

All measures taken to supply nutrient materials and strengthen the sensitive body parts are very effective.

Healing ointments are easily absorbed.

Sensitive blood circulation.

Avoid overstraining bones and knees, and apply gentle stretching exercises only.

Problems with meniscus: Don't overstrain.

Dress slightly warmer.

High blood pressure: Avoid salty foods.

Massages, lymphatic therapy, and chiropractic treatment to release blockages.

Body Care

Aromas, scents:

Cedar, Juniper

Treatments with firming and moisturizing creams are more effective.

Massages that serve to regenerate, and strengthen, perhaps aided with beneficial massage oils.

Correcting and cutting ingrown nails.

Every kind of skin care is beneficial.

Cutting and filing toenails and fingernails will make the nails grow stronger over time.

Hair dyes applied now, will look more vibrant.

Garden/Nature

Plant part:

Root

Sow plants, herbs, and vegetables that grow and flourish above ground.

Transplanting.

Harvest produce is suitable for storage. Harvest root vegetables.

Gather herbs for bone, joint, and skin diseases.

Housework

Light housework only.

Air rooms only briefly.

Preserving root vegetables.

Avoid dry cleaning, as the fabric may develop unwanted glossy blotches.

Nutrition

Food quality:

Salt

Garlic, carrots, red beets, reddish, rutabaga, sugar beet, celery, potatoes, onions, kohlrabi.

Weight gain: avoid indulging in rich foods. If overweight, eat smaller portions.

Supply nutrient materials to strengthen the body. Focus on foods that contain essential minerals and vitamins.

Stimulants and vitamins are more effective.

Avoid large quantities of salty foods like bacon, ham, salted herring, fatty cheese, and the like. Avoid heavy and greasy foods.

Positive affirmation:
"Gratitude is my guide."

Harvest Time
Ascending forces!
Sap is rising, enhancing plant growth above ground, resulting in the most juicy fruits and vegetables.

gather strength
rest, recover
buildup
Waxing Moon

10 Thursday

11 Friday

No meat. Cutting and filing toenails and fingernails.

Know thyself?
If I knew myself, I'd run away.
Johann Wolfgang von Goethe

Color
Yellow

Day
Cool

Element
Earth

Capricorn

D E C E M B E R

Success

Inspiration, optimism, and impatience. Rational thinking, creativity and imagination spark new ideas and inspire planning for the future.

Shying away from routine tasks people will feel more drawn to anything new.

Instead of gridlocked structures choose new possibilities.

Leisure

Inspiration and optimism will boost friendship, social gatherings, and parties.

Express your creativity and imagination. Dwell in dreams and utopian ideas. It is easier now to perceive intuitive thoughts.

Health

Sensitive body parts:
Lower Legs, Veins

All measures taken to supply nutrient materials and strengthen the sensitive body parts are very effective.

Healing ointments are easily absorbed.

Sensitive glandular system.

Avoid inflammation of the veins. Apply ointments to lower legs, and rest legs in a raised position.

Varicose veins: Avoid long periods of standing.

While exercising go easy on the ankles.

Sensitivity to light, so bring your sunglasses along.

Body Care

Aromas, scents: Cyclamen, Peach, Wild Roses

Treatments with firming and moisturizing creams are more effective.

Massages that serve to regenerate, and strengthen, perhaps aided with beneficial massage oils.

Correcting and cutting ingrown nails.

Hair dyes applied now, will look more vibrant.

Garden/Nature

Plant part:
Flower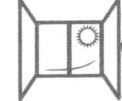

Avoid watering plants.

Harvested produce is well suitable for storage.

Gather herbs for vein diseases.

Housework

Light housework only.

Ventilate rooms thoroughly.

Baking cakes and cookies. Dough rises faster. (Except on New Moon)

Making preserves.

Nutrition

Food quality:
Fat

Cauliflower, artichoke, broccoli, sunflower seeds, flax seeds, nuts, rose hip, elder.

Weight gain: avoid indulging in rich foods. If overweight, eat smaller portions.

Supply nutrient materials to strengthen the body. Focus on foods that contain essential minerals and vitamins.

Stimulants and vitamins are more effective.

Pay attention to any particularly tempting foods today: Most likely the "wrong" things taste best.

High cholesterol: eat a low fat diet.

Positive affirmation:
"Gratitude is my guide."

Harvest Time
Ascending forces! Sap is rising, enhancing plant growth above ground, resulting in the most juicy fruits and vegetables.

gather strength rest, recover buildup
Waxing Moon

8:07 AM PST
10:07 AM CST
11:07 AM EST

12 Saturday
Hannukah Final Day

13 Sunday
3. Advent

8:37 PM PST
10:37 PM CST
11:37 PM EST

14 Monday

D E C E M B E R

There is music you never hear unless you play it yourself.
Marty Rubin

Color
Bright/ Dark Blue

Day
Air/Light

Element

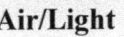

Air   Aquarius

Success

Sensibility, intuition, and helpfulness.

Where possible, retreating is more favorable than dealing with business matters.

Dissolve restrictions, be patient and wait. Be aware that people can be more easily influenced.

Leisure

Your helpfulness will boost friendships.

Enjoy dancing or swimming, or watch a movie that will inspire your fantasies and imagination.

Retreat, relax, and recover.

Romance can be gentle and coziness will prevail.

If you plan outdoor excursions, be prepared for a shower here and there.

Health

Sensitive body parts:

Feet and Toes

All measures taken to supply nutrient materials and strengthen the sensitive body parts are very effective.

Healing ointments are easily absorbed.

Sensitive nervous system.

Drugs have a much stronger effect on your body. Monitor closely what you put into your body.

Lymphatic therapy.

Sluggishness or fatigue may occur in the transition into the next Zodiac sign of Aries.

Body Care

Aromas, scents: Magnolia, Amaryllis, Clary Sage

Treatments with firming and moisturizing creams are more effective.

Massages that serve to regenerate, and strengthen, perhaps aided with beneficial massage oils. Reflexology massage. Carry out with special care, people are more sensitive.

Correcting and cutting ingrown nails.

Foot bath.

No haircuts, hair becomes shaggy and unmanageable. Avoid washing your hair. Dandruff could develop.

Garden/Nature

Plant part:

Leaf

Watering all indoor and outdoor plants.

Sow plants, herbs, and vegetables that grow and flourish above ground, and leaf vegetables.

Transplanting.

Mowing lawns.

Avoid pruning fruit trees and bushes.

Harvested produce should be consumed as soon as possible.

Gather herbs for foot complaints.

Discover more about the lunar cycle and it's effects in the reference book "Nature's Daily Guide". ISBN 978-0-9854637-8-6

Housework

Light housework only.

Ventilate rooms briefly and rapidly. Don't air mattresses.

Any dirt and spots are easily removed in the laundry.

Avoid painting, as paint will take very long to dry.

Preserving and storing should be avoided.

Nutrition

Food quality:

Carbohydrate

Lettuce, spinach, lamb's lettuce, Endive, parsley, leek, cabbage (Brussels sprouts, kale, Chinese cabbage), all leafy herbs, asparagus, mushrooms, cress, Swiss chard, rhubarb.

Weight gain: avoid indulging in rich foods. If overweight, eat smaller portions and avoid carbohydrates.

Supply nutrient materials to strengthen the body. Focus on foods that contain essential minerals and vitamins.

Caffeine, alcohol, drugs, certain foods, and stimulants have a much stronger effect.

Positive affirmation:
"Gratitude is my guide."

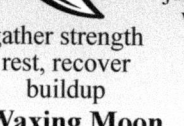

Harvest Time
Ascending forces! Sap is rising, enhancing plant growth above ground, resulting in the most juicy fruits and vegetables.

gather strength rest, recover buildup
Waxing Moon

15 Tuesday

16 Wednesday

☾ **Half Moon.** No meat.

If you can't fight and you can't flee, flow.
Robert Elias

Color
Blueish White
Day
Wetness
Element
Water   **Pisces**

D E C E M B E R

Success

Things get going and the way straight ahead seems the best.

People feel energetic, courageous, assertive, and at times anxious.

Good time for meetings and sales talks but impatience and selfishness do not favor teamwork.

Leisure

An enterprising spirit and spontaneity move people to enjoy outings, sports, competitions, cultural events, and travels.

Romance can be very passionate.

Good days for outings, even with cloudy skies the air still feels somewhat warm. Drying effect, get plenty to drink.

Health

Sensitive body parts:
Head, Brain, Eyes

All measures taken to supply nutrient materials and strengthen the sensitive body parts are very effective.

Healing ointments are easily absorbed.

Sensitive sense organs.

If you suffer from migraines drink plenty of water, and avoid coffee, chocolate, and sugar.

Body Care

Aromas, scents:
Cloves, Peppermint, Thyme

Treatments with firming and moisturizing creams are more effective.

Massages that serve to regenerate, and strengthen, perhaps aided with beneficial massage oils.

Correcting and cutting ingrown nails.

Eye compresses for strained eyes.

Any kind of hair care. Hair dyes applied now, will look more vibrant.

Garden/Nature

Plant part:
Fruit

Sow plants and vegetables that grow and flourish above ground, especially fruit and tomatoes.

Sowing and planting anything that is supposed to grow fast and for immediate use.

Grafting onto fruit trees.

Cultivating grains.

Transplanting.

Harvesting and storing grains, vegetables, potatoes, fruit, and tomatoes.

Gather herbs for eye complaints and headaches.

Day off on 12/17.

Housework

Light housework only.

Ventilate sufficiently.

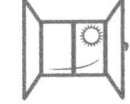

Preserving fruit.

Freezing fruit and vegetables.

Baking bread, cakes, and cookies. Dough rises faster. (Except on New Moon)

Suitable for making cheese.

Nutrition

Food quality:
Protein

Beans, peas, corn, tomatoes, pumpkin, lentils, soybeans, cucumber, eggplant, zucchini, berries, fruit, chili, bell pepper, figs, avocado, melon, olives.

Weight gain: avoid indulging in rich foods. If overweight, eat smaller portions.

Supply nutrient materials to strengthen the body. Focus on foods that contain essential minerals and vitamins.

Stimulants and vitamins are more effective.

Drink plenty of water.

Harvest Time
Ascending forces! Sap is rising, enhancing plant growth above ground, resulting in the most juicy fruits and vegetables.

gather strength rest, recover buildup
Waxing Moon

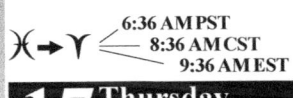

6:36 AM PST
8:36 AM CST
9:36 AM EST

12:31 PM PST
2:31 PM CST
3:31 PM EST

17 Thursday

18 Friday

No meat. Cutting and filing toenails and fingernails.

19 Saturday

D E C E M B E R

Color
Indigo Blue

Day
Warm

Element
Fire

Aries

Success

Realism and material security are important. Persistence comes easy, thoughts and reactions are slower.

Assess financial areas.

Conservative tendencies may make people want to stay away from risk taking.

Leisure

Relax at a picnic/feast. Enjoy culinary pleasures and hobbies.

The earth feels cold to the touch, so take slightly warmer clothes.

Health

Sensitive body parts:

Head and Neck

All measures taken to supply nutrient materials and strengthen the sensitive body parts are very effective.

Healing ointments are easily absorbed.

Sensitive blood circulation.

Organs of speech, jaws, teeth, tonsils, thyroid gland, neck, and vocal chords get easily affected. Keep neck warm. On cold days ears should be protected. Sensitivity to noise.

High blood pressure: Avoid salty foods.

Massages, lymphatic therapy, and chiropractic treatment to release blockages.

Body Care

Aromas, scents: Geranium, Jasmine, Rose

Treatments with firming and moisturizing creams are more effective.

Massages that serve to regenerate, and strengthen, perhaps aided with beneficial massage oils.

Correcting and cutting ingrown nails.

Hair dyes applied now, will look more vibrant.

Garden/Nature

Plant part:

Root

Sow plants, herbs, and vegetables that grow and flourish above ground.

Sowing and planting trees, bushes, hedges, and root vegetables. Everything grows slowly and lasts well.

Transplanting.

Harvesting and storing root vegetables. Harvested produce is well suited for storage.

Gather herbs for sinus issues, sore throat, and ear complaints.

Housework

Light housework only.

Air rooms only briefly.

Preserving root vegetables.

Nutrition

Food quality:

Salt

Garlic, carrots, red beets, reddish, rutabaga, sugar beet, celery, potatoes, onions, kohlrabi.

Weight gain: avoid indulging in rich foods. If overweight, eat smaller portions.

Supply nutrient materials to strengthen the body. Focus on foods that contain essential minerals and vitamins.

Stimulants and vitamins are more effective.

Avoid large quantities of salty foods like bacon, ham, salted herring, fatty cheese, and the like.

Positive affirmation:
"Gratitude is my guide."

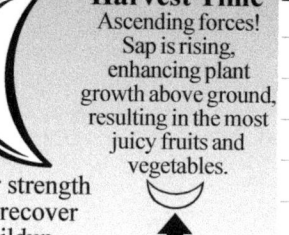

Harvest Time
Ascending forces! Sap is rising, enhancing plant growth above ground, resulting in the most juicy fruits and vegetables.

gather strength rest, recover buildup
Waxing Moon

20 Sunday
4. Advent, Asarah B'Tevet

21 Monday
Winter Solstice

2:28 PM PST
4:28 PM CST
5:28 PM EST
♉ → ♊

When you feel someone else's pain and joy as powerfully as if it were your own, then you know you really loved them.
Ann Brashares

Color
Bright Blue

Day
Cool

Element
Earth

Taurus

D E C E M B E R

Success

Open mindedness and curiosity. A changeable and hectic time.

Good time for talking, negotiating, networking, and exchanging ideas as well as for meetings of a nonbinding nature, conferences, and studies.

Leisure

Good time for family gatherings, parties, and short trips.

People enjoy stimulating their minds with reading and studying. Attending theater performances is a preferred enjoyment. Enhance friendships.

Stretching exercises.

Be prepared for sudden changes in weather or climate.

Health

Sensitive body parts:

Shoulders, Arms, Hands, Lungs

All measures taken to supply nutrient materials and strengthen the sensitive body parts are very effective.

Healing ointments are easily absorbed. Applying herbal ointments to the shoulders for rheumatic gout and alike.

Sensitive glandular system.

Make sure you are dressed warm enough in cool weather.

Exercises for shoulders. Breathing exercises.

Avoid having any teeth pulled.

Sensitivity to light, bring your sunglasses along.

Massages, lymphatic therapy, and chiropractic treatment to release blockages.

○ *Full Moon: Avoid any surgery and vaccination if possible.*

Body Care

Aromas, scents: Lavender, Lemon Balm, Magnolia, Verbena

Treatments with firming and moisturizing creams are more effective.

Massages that serve to regenerate, and strengthen, perhaps aided with beneficial massage oils.

Correcting and cutting ingrown nails.

Hair dyes applied now, will look more vibrant.

Garden/Nature

Plant part:

Flower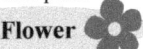

Sow plants, herbs, and vegetables that grow and flourish above ground.

Sowing and planting any creeping or climbing plants, flowers, and medicinal herbs.

Transplanting.

Avoid watering plants.

Gather herbs for tensions in the shoulder and lung complaints.

Changes in weather are more likely.

○ *Full Moon: Weather and climate changes. Herbs are most powerful.*

Housework

Light housework only.

Ventilate rooms thoroughly.

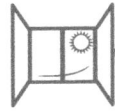

Making preserves.

Baking cakes and cookies. Dough rises faster. (Except on New Moon)

○ *Full Moon: Avoid doing laundry, cleaning windows, making preserves, painting.*

Nutrition

Food quality:

Fat

Cauliflower, artichoke, broccoli, sunflower seeds, flax seeds, nuts, rose hip, elder.

Weight gain: avoid indulging in rich foods. If overweight, eat smaller portions.

Supply nutrient materials to strengthen the body. Focus on foods that contain essential minerals and vitamins.

Stimulants and vitamins are more effective.

Pay attention to any particularly tempting foods today: Most likely the "wrong" things taste best.

High cholesterol: eat a low fat diet.

○ *Full Moon: A day of fasting.*

Positive affirmation:
"Gratitude is my guide."

Turning Point

Transition of ascending to descending forces. Both forces are at work and neutralize each other.

gather strength rest, recover buildup

Waxing Moon

2:00 PM PST
4:00 PM CST
5:00 PM EST
♊ → ♋

22 Tuesday

23 Wednesday

○ **Full Moon** 5:29 PM PST, 7:29 PM CST, 8:29 PM EST
No meat

D E C E M B E R

You can cut all the flowers but you cannot keep Spring from coming.
Pablo Neruda

Light Blue

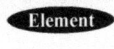
Air/Light

Element

Air

Gemini

Success

Feelings, sensitivity, and cooperativeness. Many are overly sensitive, so beware of treading on someone's toes.

Be cautious if you are easily influenced.

During negotiations make use of the cognitive ability of your senses.

Leisure

Relax within your close family.

Retreat to your safe haven and enjoy your fantasy while reading or listening to music. The inner world becomes more colorful than the outer.

Romance can be gentle. Deep feelings will prevail.

If you plan outdoor excursions, be prepared for a shower here and there.

Health

Sensitive body parts:
Chest, Lungs, Liver, Stomach, Gall Bladder

All measures taken to flush out and detoxify the sensitive body parts are very effective.

Good for surgical operations except those on the sensitive body parts (see above), knees, bones, joints, and skin. Scarring is less severe.

Teeth: Removal of tartar and amalgam. Best for fillings, crowns, and dentures!

Blood-purifying, detoxifying herbal infusions and teas.

Sensitive nervous system.

Be cautious with alcohol since the liver is very sensitive.

Stomach could play up and cause gas and heartburn.

Rheumatism: Don't air bedding outside, damp will remain in the bedding.

Lymphatic therapy.

Body Care

Aromas, scents:
Lilac, Lilies of the Valley, Lilies, Violets

Prepare home-made ointments and cosmetics.

Apply detoxing facial and body care.

Treatments of bumps and pimples on the skin, and exfoliating procedures.

Removing body hair.

Correction of the nail bed.

Massages that serve to relax, ease tension, and detoxify.

Reflexology massage.

Removal of callused skin.

Treating obstinate athlete's foot, nail fungus, and warts.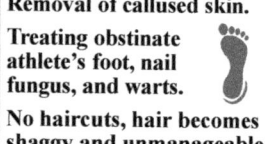

No haircuts, hair becomes shaggy and unmanageable. Avoid washing your hair.

Garden/Nature

Plant part:
Leaf

Water plants.

Fertilize flowers.

Sow plants and vegetables that grow below ground, leaf vegetables, and lettuce.

Dig over/plow to prepare soil for planting.

Trimming and cutting back plants. Transplanting. Weeding.

Combating pests above ground.

Start a compost heap.

Mowing lawns.

Gather herbs (roots) for bronchitis, stomach, liver, and gall bladder complaints.

Unfavorable for harvesting, storing, and preserving.

Housework

Housework is dealt with much more successfully, efficiently, and effortlessly.

Problem stains are removed readily.

Best for doing laundry! Reduce on laundry detergent, support the environment.

Dry cleaning.

Thoroughly clean wooden and parquet floors, metals, china etc.

Cleaning, polishing, and waterproofing shoes.

Combating mold.

Ventilate rooms briefly and rapidly.

Avoid painting.

Nutrition

Food quality:
Carbohydrate

Lettuce, spinach, lamb's lettuce, Endive, parsley, leek, cabbage (Brussels sprouts, kale, Chinese cabbage), all leafy herbs, asparagus, mushrooms, cress, Swiss chard, rhubarb.

Weight associated with overeating is less likely. If underweight, eat larger portions.

Moodiness may make you want to eat more than is healthy. If overweight avoid carbohydrates.

Cleansing and detox diets. Fruit and juice days.

Flush out poisons. Treatment for drug abuse.

If you get stomach troubles easily, avoid heavy meals.

We must be willing to let go of the life we planned so as to have the life that is waiting for us.
Joseph Campbell

Color — Green
Day — Wetness
Element — Water

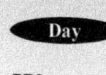

Cancer   **Water**

24 Thursday
Christmas Eve

1:13 PM PST
3:13 PM CST
4:13 PM EST

25 Friday
Christmas Day
No meat. Cutting and filing toenails and fingernails.

Planting Time
Descending forces! Sap is drawn downward, enhancing root formation. Best days for sowing, planting, and transplanting.

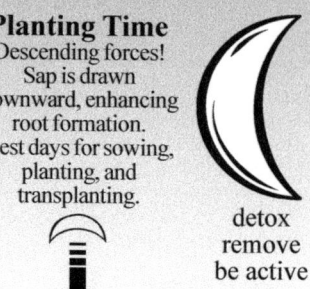

detox remove be active
Waning Moon

D E C E M B E R

Success

Determination reigns, and risks are taken more often. Master your tasks with more self-confidence and creativity.

Limits appear to be more easily surmountable.

Auspicious day for sales, advertising, and publicity.

Leisure

Zest for life is in the air. People want to have a fun time, enjoy parties, musical events, movies, etc.

Possessive feelings can harm a relationship. Romance can be very passionate.

Outings: even with cloudy skies the air still feels somewhat warm. Drying effect, get plenty to drink.

Danger of sudden storms, not only in the sky.

Health

Sensitive body parts:
Heart, Back, Diaphragm, Circulation, Arteries

All measures taken to flush out and detoxify the sensitive body parts are very effective.

Good for surgery, except on the sensitive body parts (see above), knees, bones, joints, and skin.
Scarring is less severe.

Teeth: Removal of tartar and amalgam. Best for fillings, crowns, and dentures!

Blood-purifying, detoxifying herbal infusions and teas.

Sensitive sense organs.

Back and heart problems are more likely to occur.

Avoid overstraining of the heart and circulation with unusual physical activities.

Expect sleepless nights.

Body Care

Aromas, scents:
Hibiscus,
Oleander, Rose

Prepare home-made ointments and cosmetics.

Apply detoxing facial and body care.

Treatments of bumps and pimples on the skin, and exfoliating procedures.

Removing body hair.

Correction of the nail bed.

Massages that serve to relax, ease tension, and detoxify.

Reflexology massage.

Removal of callused skin.

Treating obstinate athlete's foot, nail fungus, and warts.

Good days for haircuts, hair becomes stronger. But be aware that if you get a perm, curls will become quite frizzy. Baby's first haircut.

Garden/Nature

Plant part:
Fruit

Sowing plants and vegetables that grow below ground.

Sowing and planting fruit. Also sow and plant vegetables that are highly perishable. Plant trees and bushes. Sow lawns.

Dig over/plow to prepare soil for planting.

Trimming and cutting back plants. Pruning of fruit trees and bushes.

Transplanting.

Not suitable for fertilizing.

Weeding. Pest Control.

Harvested produce should be consumed as soon as possible.

Gather herbs (roots) for heart and circulation complaints.

Start compost heap.

Housework

Housework is dealt with much more successfully, efficiently, and effortlessly.

Problem stains are removed readily.

Best for doing laundry!

Dry cleaning.

Thoroughly clean wooden and parquet floors, metals, china, etc.

Cleaning windows and glass.

Cleaning, polishing, and waterproofing shoes.

Combating mold.

Ventilate rooms sufficiently.
Air beds.

Suitable for making cheese.

Preserving and freezing fruit and vegetables.

Baking bread, cakes, and cookies (use more leavening agent).

Avoid painting.

Nutrition

Food quality:
Protein

Beans, peas, corn, tomatoes, pumpkin, lentils, soybeans, cucumber, eggplant, zucchini, berries, fruit, chili, bell pepper, figs, avocado, melon, olives.

Weight associated with overeating is less likely. If underweight, eat larger portions.

Cleansing and detox diets. Fruit and juice days.

Flush out poisons. Treatment for drug abuse.

The mouth is made for communication, and nothing is more articulate than a kiss.
Jarod Kintz

Color

Green

Day

Warm

Element

Leo   **Fire**

2:14 PM PST
4:14 PM CST
5:14 PM EST

♌ → ♍

26 Saturday
Kwanzaa starts, Boxing Day (CAN)

27 Sunday

D E C E M B E R

Planting Time
Descending forces! Sap is drawn downward, enhancing root formation.
Best days for sowing, planting, and transplanting.

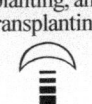

detox
remove
be active

Waning Moon

Success

Good time for details, organization, routine, concentration, and duty.

Take care of financial and administrative tasks.

Prepare for future success now with realistic and critical assessment.

Leisure

Enjoy a nature walk.

Good time for health regimes. Improve your health with stretching exercises and yoga.

The earth feels cold to the touch, so take slightly warmer clothes.

Health

Sensitive body parts:
Digestive Organs, Nerves, Spleen, Pancreas

All measures taken to flush out and detoxify the sensitive body parts are very effective.

Good for surgery, except on the sensitive body parts (see above), knees, bones, joints, and skin.
Scarring is less severe.
Teeth: Removal of tartar and amalgam. Best for fillings, crowns, and dentures!
Avoiding treatment of periodontitis and gums.
Blood-purifying, detoxifying herbal infusions and teas.
Sensitive blood circulation.
For a sensitive digestive system, a wholesome diet is recommended.
Dress slightly warmer.
High blood pressure:
Avoid salty foods.
Massages, lymphatic therapy, and chiropractic treatment to release blockages.

Body Care

Aromas, scents:
Lavender, Spruce Needles, Sage, Meadow Flowers

Prepare home-made ointments and cosmetics.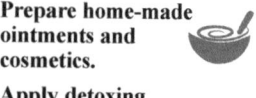

Apply detoxing facial and body care.

Treatments of bumps and pimples on the skin, and exfoliating procedures.

Removing body hair.

Correction of the nail bed.

Massages that serve to relax, ease tension, and detoxify.

Reflexology massage.

Removal of callused skin.

Treating obstinate athlete's foot, nail fungus, and warts.

Best for haircuts because it retains its shape longer.
Perms turn out best.

Garden/Nature

Plant part:
Root

Best for sowing and planting, except lettuce.
Plant trees which are supposed to grow very tall.
Plant hedges and bushes that are meant to grow very fast.
Planting and re-potting balcony and indoor plants.
Dig over/plow to prepare soil for planting.
Trimming and cutting back plants. Planting cuttings.
Spread fertilizer and manure. Fertilize flowers with poorly formed roots.
Start a compost heap.
Transplanting. Mulching.
Weeding. Pest control (vermin in the soil).
Avoid harvesting and storing.
Gather herbs (roots) for digestive organs, pancreas, and nervous complaints.

Housework

Housework is dealt with much more successfully, efficiently, and effortlessly.

Problem stains are removed readily.

Best for doing laundry! Reduce on laundry detergent, support the environment.

Dry cleaning.

Thoroughly clean wooden and parquet floors, metals, china etc.

Cleaning, polishing, and waterproofing shoes.

Combating mold.

Air rooms only briefly.

Painting.

Making pickles, preserves, and cheese yields suboptimal results and should be avoided.

Nutrition

Food quality:
Salt

Garlic, carrots, red beets, reddish, rutabaga, sugar beet, celery, potatoes, onions, kohlrabi.

Weight associated with overeating is less likely. If underweight, eat larger portions.

Cleansing and detox diets. Fruit and juice days.

Flush out poisons. Treatment for drug abuse.

Avoid large quantities of salty foods like bacon, ham, salted herring, fatty cheese, and the like. Avoid heavy and greasy foods.

I don't understand people who say they need more "Me Time." What other time is there? Do these people spend part of their day in someone else's body?
Jarod Kintz

Color
Yellow

Day
Cool

Element
Earth

Virgo

6:28 PM PST
8:28 PM CST
9:28 PM EST

♍ → ♎

28 Monday

29 Tuesday

Planting Time
Descending forces!
Sap is drawn downward, enhancing root formation.
Best days for sowing, planting, and transplanting.

detox
remove
be active
Waning Moon

D E C E M B E R

Success

The artistic instinct rules, but so, too, does indecisiveness. The forces swing back and forth until equilibrium is achieved.

It's easy to reach compromises with tactful sensitivity.

A sense of judgment will support legal matters.

Leisure

Pursuit for harmony and cooperativeness supports good times in romance, friendship, and partnership.

Enjoy cultural events. Relax and get pampered with a spa treatment.

Romance can be passionate yet sensitive.

Health

Sensitive body parts:
Hips, Kidneys, Bladder

All measures taken to flush out and detoxify the sensitive body parts are very effective.

Good for surgery, except on the sensitive body parts (see above), knees, bones, joints, and skin. Scarring is less severe.

Teeth: Removal of tartar and amalgam. Best for fillings, crowns, and dentures! Avoid treatment of periodontitis and gums, avoid pulling teeth.

Blood-purifying, detoxifying herbal infusions and teas.

Sensitive glandular system.

Take special care to keep the area of the bladder and kidneys warm.

Apply special exercises for the hip region.

Sensitivity to light, so bring your sunglasses along.

Body Care

Aromas, scents:
Roses, Violets, Daffodils

Prepare home-made ointments and cosmetics.

Apply detoxing facial and body care.

Treatments of bumps and pimples on the skin, and exfoliating procedures.

Removing body hair.

Correction of the nail bed.

Massages that serve to relax, ease tension, and detoxify.

Reflexology massage.

Removal of callused skin.

Treating obstinate athlete's foot, nail fungus, and warts.

Garden/Nature

Plant part:
Flower

Sow plants and vegetables that grow below ground.

Dig over/plow to prepare soil for planting.

Trimming and cutting back plants.

Start a compost heap.

Weeding. Pest control.

Fertilize flowers that no longer bloom.

Transplanting.

Avoid watering plants.

Harvested produce should be consumed as soon as possible.

Gather herbs (roots) for kidneys, gall bladder and hip complaints.

Day off on 12/30.

Housework

Housework is dealt with much more successfully, efficiently, and effortlessly.

Problem stains are removed readily.

Best for doing laundry! Reduce on laundry detergent, support the environment.

Dry cleaning.

Clean and store seasonal clothing.

Thoroughly clean wooden and parquet floors, metals, china etc.

Cleaning windows and glass.

Cleaning, polishing, and waterproofing shoes.

Combating mold.

Ventilate rooms thoroughly.

Baking bread, cakes, and cookies (add more leavening agent).

Making preserves.

Painting.

Nutrition

Food quality:
Fat

Cauliflower, artichoke, broccoli, sunflower seeds, flax seeds, nuts, rose hip, elder.

Weight associated with overeating is less likely. If underweight, eat larger portions.

Cleansing and detox diets. Fruit and juice days.

Flush out poisons. Treatment for drug abuse.

Pay attention to any particularly tempting foods today: Most likely the "wrong" things taste best.

High cholesterol: eat a low fat diet.

There is a wisdom of the head, and... there is a wisdom of the heart.
Charles Dickens

Color

Orange

Day

Air/Light

Element

Libra   **Air**

30 Wednesday
☾ **Half Moon.** No meat.

31 Thursday
New Year's Eve

Planting Time
Descending forces! Sap is drawn downward, enhancing root formation. Best days for sowing, planting, and transplanting.

detox
remove
be active

Waning Moon

D E C E M B E R

www.ingramcontent.com/pod-product-compliance
Lightning Source LLC
Chambersburg PA
CBHW041512120626
46551CB00018B/2395